The Western Métis

The Western Métis:
Profile of a People

Edited by
Patrick C. Douaud

———
2007

Canadian Plains Research Center
University of Regina
Regina, Saskatchewan S4S 0A2
Canada
Tel: (306) 585-4758/Fax: (306) 585-4699
e-mail: canadian.plains@uregina.ca
http://www.cprc.uregina.ca

Library and Archives Canada Cataloguing in Publication
The western Métis : profile of a people / edited by Patrick C. Douaud.

(Canadian plains studies, ISSN 0317-6290 ; 54)
Essays orginally published in Prairie forum between 1978–2004.
Includes bibliographical references and index.
ISBN 978-0-88977-199-4

1. Métis—Prairie Provinces--History. 2. Prairie Provinces—History. 3. Northwest Territories—Politics and government—1870–1905. I. Douaud, Patrick C., 1949–II. University of Regina. Canadian Plains Research Center. III. Series.

FC109.W48 2007   971.2004'97   C2007-905386-6

Cover design: Donna Grant, Regina
Cover image: "Métis Jigging," courtesy, Sherry Farrell Racette (*The Flower Beadwork People*) and the Gabriel Dumont Institute Archives
Index prepared by Patricia Furdek (www.userfriendlyindexes.com)
Printed and bound in Canada

Publisher's Note:
We acknowledge the financial support of the Government of Canada through the Book Publishing Industry Development Program (BPDIP) for our publishing activities. We also acknowledge the support of the Canada Council for the Arts for our publishing program.

Contents

1. Genesis

Patrick C. Douaud

> *Closely associated with the history of the western regions in all the phases of their development, ... [the Métis population] forms the link between present and past, and serves as tradition in a country where events are soon absorbed into the movement of modern life and leave no memory.* (Giraud 1945: 1250; my translation)

The Concept of Métis

The word *Métis* comes from Low Latin *mixticium* through Middle French *mestis*, "racially mixed"; one of its earliest occurrences goes back to the end of the 12th century, when Girard de Roussillon mentioned "ces mestis Franceis, demi Borgoings" ("those French 'Métis', half-Burgundians"). The word is related to Spanish *Mestizo*, meaning a person of mixed ancestry. Both genetic and cultural halfbreeds exist throughout the colonized world; yet the Canadian Métis, with perhaps the Cape Coloured and the Haitians, are unique in that they were able to "successfully assert political and legal rights, for a period at least, against the national government" (Daniels 1979a: 7). Those Métis, who gave Canada her only semblance of an Indian war with the 1885 Riel Rebellion (now generally called "Resistance"), were the result of unions between French *voyageurs*, *coureurs de bois*, or traders with Indian or Halfbreed women: "These first 'half-breeds' were literally that, probably the offspring of Frenchmen from Champlain's company, which established Quebec in 1608, and of Indian women among the Huron and Algonquin tribes" (Howard 1974: 39). Later, "families became very important for many voyageurs who worked for long periods in the trade and especially for those who decided not to leave the Northwest, settling down with their families in the interior and forming the foundations of Métis communities" (Podruchny

2006: 267). The Cree especially were instrumental in these unions: they were first identified by the French as *Kristinaux* in the 17th century, and were trading with them at Lake Nipigon by 1684 (Dickason 1980: 32).

Price notes that

> Differences between the Europeans who arrived in the New World played an important role in determining the nature of Indian-European relations. For example, the French, Spanish and Portuguese were more tolerant than northern Europeans of intermarriage with the Natives. Thus, since early historical times there have been significant populations of Spanish-Indian 'Mestizos' and French-Indian 'Métis,' but few British-Indian 'Halfbreeds,' considering the size of the British population in North America. (Price 1978: 82)

Even though this argument should not be overstated, at the beginning of the colonial period the French do seem to have conciliated the Indians to a greater extent than did the British: the former were interested in trade, whereas the latter were land-hungry. Moreover, "women were not brought out from France, which gave an added incentive for friendly attitudes" (Eccles 1972: 11). This mixing of the French with the Indians really began in the 16th century about the Gulf of St. Lawrence amid cod-fishing and fur-trading activities. It was quickly intensified by the policies of the Catholic government in French Canada, which made any Indian who embraced Catholicism a French subject, "with all the rights and privileges appertaining, including the right to settle in France whenever they wished" (Eccles 1972: 39). Although few, if any, availed of them, such overtures were conducive to potentially harmonious relationships between the two ethnic groups. Soon the French halfbreeds were the most numerous, and the French word *Métis* has come to designate all persons of mixed European and Indian ancestry in Canada.

The Métis as a distinctive ethnic group are now largely a western phenomenon, but they were born out of a long period of interaction between Indians and Whites in the St. Lawrence and Upper Great Lakes regions. Trading communities were also found on the periphery of the Great Lakes, as far south as Cahokia, Illinois (Peterson 1978: 45), and most of their inhabitants were of mixed race. However, the aggressive colonization of the American Middle-West in the first half of the 19th century forced those half-breeds to take refuge among Indian tribes or in the Red River area of Manitoba, or more rarely to merge with American Whites. The Métis—mostly Indian and French Canadian, but Highland Scot, English and Yankee as well—survived as a separate group mainly north of the international border. Trading in what are now the Prairie provinces, they "spent a large part of their lives in the northwest, living among the Indian nations, marrying Indian girls, more Indian than French in their way of life and their values" (Eccles 1972: 146). Assumption of the broker role necessitated a continuous cycle of intermarriage which allowed the Métis to function "not only as human carriers linking Indians and Europeans, but as buffers behind which the ethnic boundaries of antagonistic cultures remained relatively secure" (Peterson 1978: 55). Many of them were involved in buffalo hunting, an activity which supplied the provisions essential to the boreal forest fur trade—along which, indeed, "there is no section of the route that does not have a Métis presence" (Marchildon and Robinson 2002: 28). They were to be found where the frontier then was, and thus provided Canada with the genuine facilitators of western expansion that the United States always lacked; it is possible indeed that "without their help the process would have been much bloodier than it was" (Howard 1974: 40).

The Métis are traditionally portrayed as a marginal society with a distinctive culture characterized by a blend of Indian "reticence" (Preston 1976) and Gallic *joie de vivre*—or, to use Giraud's (1945: 874ff) stereotype, by a temperament reserved first, then congenial and impulsive. All these rough facets of the Métis' personality made them a colourful people with their own privileged place in Canadian folklore, where they are identified "as much by their blue pantaloons, capote and fiddle, as by their leggings, red finger-woven sash, moccasins, hair feathers and tattoos" (Peterson 1978: 53).

Whereas the term *Métis* formerly characterized "less a racial category than an incipient ethnic group, entry into which could be acquired through marriage and self-designation, as well as birth" (Peterson 1978: 46), today it is also an administrative and, since the 1982 Canadian Constitution Act, a legal definition. A Métis is now a person with any degree of Indian blood who is not registered on a reserve. As such, the term *Métis* covers about one million people in Canada, as compared to some 250,000 registered Indians. It covers "many non-Status Indians [who] live in Métis colonies on land to which they have no title, and which is not reserved under the Indian Act" (Manuel and Posluns 1974: 243).

The Métis "Race"

Canada's contemporary Métis are genetic and cultural halfbreeds of Amerindian and White ancestry. Physically, they exhibit a continuum of phenotypes ranging from the features generally associated with American Mongoloid groups, to those considered characteristic of Caucasoid groups.

Culturally, they share an ambivalent status owing to their marginal legal position halfway between the registered Indians and the dominant White society. Some Métis leaders (e.g., Daniels 1979a) have claimed that the future of their people lies in an integration of the normally conflicting Indian and White lifestyles; according to them, the Métis are best equipped for such symbiosis because they were born from the contact. This comparatively recent revival of hybrid ethnicity has been accompanied by references to the Métis' colourful history of canoe expeditions and buffalo hunting; and from countless apocryphal anecdotes there emerges the figure of what can be called the "ideal Métis." This ideal human type was supposedly endowed with physical attributes superior to those of the mean parental populations, as well as with great personal vitality and buoyancy (see, e.g., such culture heroes as James McKay, Jerry Potts, or Gabriel Dumont). These characteristics can be considered representative of the controversial phenomenon of hybrid vigour, or heterosis.

On the one hand, it seems well established that exogamy brings about an increase in overall body size (Damon 1965), perhaps because exogamous individuals are more heterozygous, and heterozygotes are believed to be more adaptable, their genetic configuration allowing them to exploit their environment more efficiently. On the other hand, heterosis in animal crosses is "usually manifested to its fullest extent by the first filial generation" (Trevor 1953: 26), and in the human case of Mongoloid/Caucasoid miscegenation there is generally Mongoloid dominance after the first few generations (Olivier 1964). It must be also noted that the breakdown of genetic isolates leading to heterosis may be accompanied in some cases by negative changes in physiological responses, such as the onset of increased systolic blood pressure with age (Kirk 1981: 146).

It seems reasonable to assume that the mean body development of a first generation hybrid group, when expressed through anthropometric measurements, will be significantly superior to the parental average (Hiernaux and Heintz 1967); but this increased development is likely to fluctuate in the following generations according to such intervening factors as selective mating and differential death rates. Bearing this restriction in mind, it appears that "the hybrid series in general have a greater degree of non-European than of European ancestry" (Trevor 1953: 31), and that heterosis in Mongoloid/Caucasoid miscegenation is marked by an apparent enlargement of the head, characterized by a greater cephalic index and an increase in trunk size. In the past century, however, these positive features have been somewhat tempered by a widespread breakdown in health, owing to the usual anomic repercussions of an unsatisfactory state of acculturation.

Giraud (1945: 1266) had already made the point:

> Venereal diseases often ravage these constitutions already debilitated by alcohol and malnutrition, exposed through insufficient clothing to the effects of the cold, vulnerable to tuberculosis. (My translation)

To this list we can now add diabetes, whose incidence is even higher in people of Aboriginal ancestry than among the mainstream population.

Isolated Métis communities where research has been conducted (see, e.g., Douaud 1985, Bakker 1997) have often shown a high level of endogamy since the end of the 19th century, and exhibit a wide range of variation in terms of skin pigmentation and eye colour. Hair form and body size, however, are held remarkably constant: the hair is black and straight, and the build generally mesomorph with pyknic tendency (especially in males). Also—and this fact has been commented upon by many earlier observers (e.g., De Trémaudan 1979 [1935]: 33, 47)—the Métis are often above Euro-Canadian average in stature, especially as regards the French Canadians, who were the most involved in Indian-White miscegenation. It is also common for Caucasoid-dominant Métis to have children exhibiting strong recessive Mongoloid phenotypic traits. Of course, some of these characteristics would apply equally well to numerous contemporary Canadian Indians, very few of whom are genetically pure Aboriginals (Card et al. 1963: 187).

These overall physical characteristics, coupled with the cultural vitality and adaptability typical of traditional Métis communities, point indeed to the existence of a phenomenon akin to heterosis. However, Métis ethnicity is no longer based on shared physical characteristics, which in any case are felt to have lost some of their uniformity. Instead, it is subordinated to a *perception* of ethnicity brought about by a flexible definition of community boundaries and by an idealization of the past; as Bakker (1997: 62) has noted, "even the most acculturated of the Métis, those living in big cities, usually socialize with members of their group alone." A community is rarely bounded by fences and signposts: much more often it is shaped by the overlap of adjacent cultural continua of social organization, language, dress, diet, etc; and its boundaries are integrated as a series of cues, "built into the psychoneural systems of its human components and systematized by the activities of each individual" (Thompson 1967: 73). These elusive cues may well be the real binding agent in contemporary hybrid ethnicity: here heterosis, in so far as it has an objective reality, only serves the idealization of a symbol of past glory. Being a Métis nowadays seems to be largely a matter of perception; or, as Brown (1985: 204) remarked,

The full story of *métissage* (racial mixing) as a sociocultural and political phenomenon in northern North America involves the study and understanding of a wide range of individual and group experiences—both those that led to *la nation métisse* and those in which *métissage* was a potentiality denied, unrecognized, or left unfulfilled, perhaps to be discovered some generations later.

The Métis Nation

The Métis people are often called "the offspring of the Canadian fur trade." As the European fur traders in the east needed wives, they simply chose them from the Indian tribes whose territories overlapped the trade—mainly Cree and Ojibwa, both being close relatives within the Woodlands culture of Algonquian-speaking Aboriginals. From the 17th century on, as the fur trade expanded westward, the Métis proliferated in Rupert's Land:

> The French colonies of the West, so largely of mixed blood, had begun, and the *coureur de bois*, restless and lawless, was to give way to the *voyageur*, an *engagé* (indentured worker) who toiled at the paddle and the portage but did not winter with the Indians or collect furs. (Morton 1969: 96)

Voyageurs represented "a time of possibilities, when the pattern of colonization was not inevitable or inexorable" (Podruchny 2006: 308). The Métis came to embody these possibilities: at the same time as they were instrumental in the fur trade and the concomitant geographic explorations, they became semi-settled and some even farmed part of the year; their homes, grouped around the European trading posts, formed the basis for the Métis settlements which would later radiate in the organized buffalo hunt.

In 1811 Lord Selkirk obtained from the Hudson's Bay Company a grant enabling him to settle a number of evictees from the Scottish land clearances on an area of land by the Assiniboine and Red rivers, which became known as District of Assiniboia. In 1814 the governor of Assiniboia attempted to forbid the buffalo hunt and to limit the pemmican trade—the very essence of Métis economic and cultural life—in the hope of boosting the White settlers' economy. Led by Cuthbert Grant, the Métis resisted; there followed a period of harassment between the two factions, neither side realizing that they were pawns in the game played by the North West Company and the Hudson's Bay Company over fur trade monopoly. The White settlers were finally driven away by the Métis after the battle of Seven Oaks (1816); however, the conflict went on between the two Companies until their eventual merger in

1821. The latter operation encouraged the emergence of new Anglo settlements on the Red River, so that "the French Canadians were now cut off from the vast spaces of the west which they had always regarded as their country, where their language was the lingua franca" (Eccles 1972: 248). Also, a number of Métis who until then had had regular employment with either Company were forced to settle or else to move farther west.

The Red River Settlement thus comprised a semi-nomadic population (Métis, Hudson Bay English, and Indians) and a White contingent of sedentary farmers (Kildonan Scots, French Canadians, and others). The Métis were distinctly predominant (Foster 1972: 96), and their activities typically included buffalo hunting and employment in the fur trade, as well as gardening. The task of educating them was shared by the Roman Catholic Church and the Protestant Church, the former assuming a preponderant role because of its association with the more numerous francophone Métis. After the Treaty of Paris (1763), religion had become increasingly important to French Canadians as a social and spiritual solace, all the more so as they found themselves further alienated from the culture of France's *Ancien Régime* by the Revolution and the Napoleonic Empire (Eccles 1972: 247). The soothing role of the Church was reinforced by the failure of the *Patriotes* rebellion in the Montreal region in 1837, and very soon French Catholicism began to spread to the remotest areas of the west. Thus it is that the cohesion of isolated Métis communities was largely maintained by Oblate priests and lay brothers, as well as Grey Nuns, of French, Breton, Belgian, or Quebecois origin. The association of the Canadian Métis with the Church began early, and it is no exaggeration to say with Sealey and Kirkness (1974: 43) that "the Church and its teachings touched every aspect of Métis life."

While the Roman Catholic Church had established its first mission in the Red River colony in 1818 (the first settlers of Lord Selkirk were Catholics), the Protestant Church arrived there in 1820. Apart from their commitment to keeping in check the moral standards of their flocks, the two Churches were strong advocates of farming and related activities. Also the Catholic Church, mostly French-speaking, urged the Métis to preserve their French language in the same way as it later urged the Irish to revive the Gaelic tongue: the ecclesiastic authorities knew well that linguistic/cultural separateness tends to strengthen internal social and spiritual bonds. The English Métis were thus allowed to merge into White society to a far greater extent than the French ones, all the more so because of the traditional Protestant concern for spreading literacy.

Recognized as a "majority group and, therefore, socially acceptable" (Sealey and Lussier 1975: 47) due to their essential role in the still little-civilized life of Assiniboia, the Métis throve and expanded, becoming the masters of the plains south of Fort Garry (now Winnipeg) thanks to their buffalo-hunting skills. Around 1850 the total population of the Red River settlement was 5,000, three quarters of whom were halfbreeds. Métis buffalo hunting was an adaptive strategy for the whole settlement, as environmental and technological conditions for agriculture were less than favourable: the hunters thus supplied not only the Hudson's Bay Company, but also the river-lot farmers (Sprenger 1972). This was also the time when the Métis were able to beat an army of several hundred Sioux warriors at the battle of Grand Coteau in 1851, and to trade officially with the United States after breaking the Hudson's Bay Company's trade monopoly in Rupert's Land in 1849.

At the same time, their culture was becoming more European under the Church's influence—except in the case of the Métis "winterers," i.e., those free traders who were operating as far west as "Whoop-up Country" (southern Alberta and Saskatchewan, and Montana) and were thus dependent on no one (Sharp 1973: 38). The progress of civilization in the West was felt more strongly from 1857 onwards, as more White settlers arrived, steamboats appeared on the Red River (supplanting the overland transportation system by cart), and the buffalo herds dwindled rapidly. However, it was difficult for the Métis to understand that their prosperity was built on precarious frontier conditions, and would therefore be doomed when the prevalent system of opportunities vanished. This inevitable change was precipitated by the taking over by Canada of the administration of the Northwest from the Hudson's Bay Company in 1869—a momentous transfer that marked the end of two centuries of Company rule in non-civilized Canada.

The Métis, whose interests clashed with those of the alien Canadian government in remote Ottawa, went through a period of insurrections, first in Manitoba (1870), then in what is now Saskatchewan (1885). As Manuel and Posluns (1974: 22) remark, "it was not even armed resistance, so much as an effort to set up a government to meet the needs that Ottawa so consistently ignored." Governmental ruthlessness, driven by the rise of nationalism and capitalism, expressed itself in the same fashion all over the New World, associated as it was with the push westwards and the building of transcontinental railways. In Argentina, for example,

> The railway from Rosario to Córdoba, the Central Argentino, stipulated the gift of one league on either side of the track to the capitalists. The Central Argentino thus expelled the settlers on its entire stretch, and then formed subsidiary companies that sold those lands in large lots to

various individuals. [...] it was a common occurrence in high-risk countries such as Argentina, and it was also done in the United States and in India, because there was a desperate need to unite regions which until then had been separated. (Luna 1993: 114–15; my translation)

Following the Métis defeat at Batoche in 1885, their leader Louis Riel, both an astute politician and an unstable millenarian prophet (see Stanley 1963, Flanagan 1979 and Siggins 1994 for three complementary descriptions of Riel's personality), was executed. This was the end of a small-scale, unspectacular war whose consequences, however, would be far-reaching:

> The North-West Field Force and its Alberta counterpart suffered precious little in terms of dead and wounded, but few armies have gained so much for so small a sacrifice. The destruction of the Métis republic confirmed for once and all the transfer of power in western Canada from the Hudson's Bay Company to Ottawa. [...] the Métis movement was finished. (Vandervort 2006: 227)

The Métis Nation now dead, its members were considered traitors whose rebellious activities had "frightened away many land-seekers and discouraged western investors" (Sharp 1973: 315). The Métis proceeded to intensify a dispersion which had begun in 1870 when a number of them, dissastisfied with the outcome of their first insurrection and harassed by the White settlers' hostility, migrated farther west, or south to the United States (especially North Dakota and Montana, where their descendants are still living). Furthermore, small isolated groups had been leaving Manitoba regularly since the 1820s for distant regions in what are now Saskatchewan and Alberta. However, ties between the Red River and remote communities remained for some time, in the face of economic exploitation:

> It was almost a hundred years in 1884 that the Hudson's Bay Company had been facing competition on the part of the Lac La Biche people, who openly practiced a 'free' fur trade in spite of the Company's interdiction. Challenging the Company's monopoly and refusing to accept a ridiculous price for furs that were worth a lot of money, the Métis used to go to the Red River to sell them. (Le Treste 1997: 100, note 1; my translation)

Thus it is that at the end of the 19th century the Western Métis found themselves without land or status, rejected by the Whites, kept off the Indian reserves, and deprived of their economic and cultural basis: the gregariousness of the large organized buffalo hunt, with its emphasis on disciplined self-sufficiency and cooperation. They had become an ambulatory, rather than migratory, people.

Entry Into the Modern World

Some Métis integrated into White society while others became incorporated into the Indian reserve system, but these were marginal cases: as a rule, the Métis after 1885 were a semi-nomadic destitute people, and life for them was of the moment. Whole families wandered from job to job, trapping, hunting and fishing the comparatively depleted areas they covered. They turned fringe dwellers who, gathering outside White communities in shanty towns, or along roads and railways, were then known as the "road allowance people"; this label quickly became associated with the traditional image of a beaten people, connoting alcoholism, fights, prostitution, jail sentences, etc.—not unlike the social stigma attached to the European Gypsies or the Irish Travellers living in shanty-towns (Fraser 1992; Douaud and Cronin 1992). This state of affairs lasted until well after World War II, when Campbell (1973: 1–2) notes: "The Halfbreed families who squatted on the road allowance have moved to nearby towns where welfare handouts and booze are handier, or else deeper into the bush as an escape from reality."

Those Métis who had been living in isolated rural communities since before the 1885 Resistance led a secluded existence far away from the political and economic turmoils, converted to part-time farming and protected by the Catholic Church, whose influence on many Canadian Aboriginal people had been constant since the 17th century (De Trémaudan 1979: 66; Leacock 1981: 43–62). As for those who had integrated early into the mainstream of Canadian society, they were especially contemptuous of their less acculturated relatives. The Indians had been granted treaties and lived on reserves where, however unsatisfactory the conditions may have been, they could at least retain their identity and tribal cohesion. The ordinary Métis had none of this—they were definitely outside the general path of "progress," yet they were not marginal enough to be put aside under special status: as a result, "the mental set of the Métis was one of hopelessness, and a feeling that failure would be their lot no matter what efforts were expended" (Sealey and Lussier 1975: 144–45); or, as Giraud put it earlier, "squashed between two economies and two societies, they are in a sense looked upon as white trash (Pauvres Blancs)" (1945: 1258, my translation). However, in spite or because of this lack of outside support, the Métis maintained the collective vitality that characterized their short-lived Nation on the Red River; they depended on nobody except the Church, and thus could retain a semblance of freedom, even though it had been dearly acquired. It is possible to differentiate them into four categories, from more modern to more traditional:

(i) those integrated Métis who had settled definitively and had successfully adapted to Euro-Canadian culture; they had either crossed the colour line or become *historical Métis*, i.e., people proud of their past grandeur but resentful of the "degeneration" characterizing the other modern Métis;

(ii) those living on the fringe of White settlements: the "road allowance people" described in Campbell (1973), wandering from job to job and destitute;

(iii) those living on the fringe of Indian reserves: a common phenomenon, aptly illustrated by Dion (1979: 159), then a schoolteacher on Kehiwin's Reserve in 1903: "At the Indian agent's first visit to our little schoolhouse he noted that it was bursting at the seams and I had to confess that a number of children came from Métis parents who were staying in the vicinity. The agent immediately ordered the removal of all halfbreeds from the reserve";

(iv) those living in small isolated communities, with an economy based on fishing, trapping and hunting: this group best preserved the traditional Métis identity and was to provide most of the Métis leaders who arose after World War II.

The reason why the great majority of the Métis did not readily integrate into White society is simple: like so many people of Aboriginal descent, they "were asked to work within an economic structure they poorly understood, with obligations and responsibilities to be assumed that their previous lifestyle inhibited" (Sealey and Lussier 1975: 136). As *voyageurs* and meat suppliers, the Métis could only last as long as the frontier lasted: then, their economy would have to be based on more settled activities such as agriculture and commercial fishing. The White man's attempts at forcing them into such a transition generally failed for three reasons: a) the Métis were expected to adapt quickly to the new lifestyle; b) White speculators often manipulated those holding land scrips into selling them for a pittance—in 1901, a Fort Chipewyan Métis even sold his scrip to finance his wedding! (Scollon and Scollon 1979: 40); and c) seldom did the White authorities show much understanding or provide thorough aid (as in the case of the Indians, farming implements and seeds were often of inferior grade, or lacking altogether). For example, such an experimental transition failed at St. Paul-des-

Métis (Alberta) at the turn of the century: the newly created Métis farming colony was unable to expand its land exploitation and produce a surplus; also, its members became easily discouraged if they did not see immediate results, and were all too inclined to abandon the project. This is exactly what happened—following which White farmers took over the land (see Drouin 1968 for further details). It became evident that the Métis, if they could be efficient gardeners or "bush farmers," were at any rate unable or unwilling to adapt to the large-scale dominant agricultural system; moreover, they traditionally preferred stock to crop farming (De Trémaudan 1979: 385).

The fate of the Canadian Métis thus resembles more that of the American Indians than of the Canadian Indians: the land they lived on was taken, and they were forcibly driven west until eventually they were allowed to open some settlements there. Like the Métis, the American Indians were allotted land (through the Dawes Act of 1887) which they often sold for a pittance as they were not ready to farm, did not know how to transact operations, and were not honestly encouraged to learn about either (Deloria 1969: 46–47). Governmental attitudes towards all people of aboriginal ancestry, on the other hand, were remarkably similar in both countries: one is thus forced to extend to the Métis Dawson's (2002: 11) assertion that often "the decisions made by these officials were for the benefit of the government rather than of the First Nations farmers and ranchers whom they were supposed to be representing."

During the Great Depression the Métis were worse off than ever. However, as frequently happens in the direst situations, it was then that the first modern Métis political leaders began to emerge in Saskatchewan and in Alberta, and these strove to improve the condition of their people. For a long time, Canadian Métis were not defined legally by the federal government: only provincial governments dealt with them qua Métis. In this respect, the Prairie provinces alone concerned themselves with this minority group: Saskatchewan provided its Métis with education and employment assistance; Manitoba gave Métis and Indians priority for trapping licences, and purveyed Métis communities with special schools geared to the needs of their culture (Rivard and Parker 1975: 1–49). In Alberta, Métis colonies were established under the Métis Betterment Act of 1938, and a Métis Trust Fund was created to receive royalties for the resources taken from Métis land. Dion (1979: 185) writes:

> These Métis settlements are not Indian reserves. The administration differs in that the Métis settlements are under a rehabilitation plan aimed at bringing the Métis back to their former independent status and to protect them until such a

time when they will be able to handle their own business to advantage.

This time has come and the quest for land continues, although the White administration is slow to relax its paternalistic protection. Métis educator Bev Cardinal has stated, "My Elders [...] say that the only people who truly own the land are the generations yet unborn" (Cardinal 2002: 76). If this is true, time is on the Métis' side.

After World War II and the subsequent opening of the common social attitude towards cultural minorities, the "Métis problem" gained more recognition and local organizations were created. Also, the National Indian Council was founded in 1961, to split in 1968 into the National Indian Brotherhood and the Canadian Métis Society—the latter including enfranchised Indians. The Native Council of Canada was born in 1971 with the aim of achieving full Native (mixed and "full" blood) participation in the life of modern Canadian society. Here is a significant excerpt from the Council's Declaration of Rights (Daniels 1979b):

> We the Métis and non-Status Indians, descendants of the 'original people' of this country, declare: That Métis nationalism is Canadian nationalism. We embody the true spirit of Canada and we are the source of Canadian identity.
>
> (...)
>
> That we have the right to preserve our identity and to flourish as a distinct people with a rich cultural heritage.
>
> (...)
>
> That we are a people with a right to special status in Confederation.

This Declaration asserts the old Métis claim that they are the true Canadians: both Indians and Whites are immigrants with only a difference in time between their respective arrivals—whereas the Métis represent a genuinely indigenous hybrid race. As such they see themselves as a frame of reference in which Canada might find her long-sought identity, thereby transcending the petty factionalism and latent racism that are an integral part of her ethnic mosaic. The Métis are exposed to both Indian and White traditions: given the opportunity, they could "have the best of both cultures," as Albertan Métis Elder Adrian "Pete" Hope was fond of saying. The mention at the time of a "right to special status in Confederation" raised perhaps the thorniest issue in a society then officially opposed to special status of any kind—a position made clear by the Trudeau government's 1969

White Paper, which purported to promote integration but was unanimously rejected by Aboriginal organizations (Titley 1979). Yet, fully granting the Métis claim would perhaps simply amount to the recognition of what Manuel and Posluns (1974) termed the "Fourth World," representing the world of indigenous minorities and a concept which has since been slowly accepted. Some Métis leaders consider their people best equipped for a symbiosis of the Fourth World and the dominant society, as they were biologically and culturally born from such a contact. This claim to special status rests on the belief that the colonizing process which bestowed guilt upon the Whites and despair upon the Indians gave *substance* to the Métis.

The Métis drew their originality from the fusion of two cultures that formerly were non-static and interacting. Now that one of them has become more static—or in certain cases, anomic—under the repression of the other, it might appear that the way to internal harmony lies in the creation of a new type of dynamism in the less urbanized areas of Canada. This is the goal to which a number of Métis leaders have been devoting themselves since the 1960s, their prime objective being the cementing of Métis unity. This task has been comparatively easy, as a clear sense of distinct political identity has prevailed among them since the days of the Métis Nation. This is quite unlike the Aboriginal situation, where the various tribes found unity in their common Indian-ness only well into the 20th century and began to develop a pan-Indian identity when they realized it gave Aboriginal groups some survival advantage.

Unlike the Aboriginals, too, the Métis have been "forgotten": because in a post-industrial society which still has some difficulty comprehending social or ideological overlaps and which instinctively imposes clear-cut characteristic labels on all its members, no one knows exactly on which side the Métis are. For some they are europeanized Indians, for others indianized Whites; from the very beginning, "members of two mutually exclusive groups, they were rebuffed by both" (Howard 1974: 42). So far the label *Métis* has hardly been synonymous with political success, yet it is on the basis of their former Nation that the people concerned want to be "remembered" and recognized as a distinct cultural group, regardless of superficial physical or behavioural variation among them. One of the means leading to this end is of course land ownership. The Métis living outside settlements have wanted to possess some land in order to be safe from exploiters taking over their government-leased lands; those who live in settlements have viewed with trepidation the depletion of natural resources closing in on them, and the expansion of industrialization; many now consider that the future of the settlements lies in the development of small industries which will render welfare allowances unnecessary.

Métis unity can be strengthened by a concept of unity that transcends the principle of ethnic distinctiveness and absorbs the various aboriginal peoples who share common difficulties in the face of White society and development. One such attempt was the creation in 1972 of the National Indian Movement of Canada, which purported to unite Status Indians, enfranchised Indians, Métis and Inuit. The common political action of all these peoples may well contribute to shaping the future of White society too, and enable it to achieve finally what should be the goal of its enormous technological effort: a comprehensive cultural equipoise. Métis architect Douglas Cardinal shared this vision when he wrote: "The measure of a man is seen through the prosperous life that surrounds him, not the inanimate objects he has forcibly acquired" (Cardinal and Melnyk 1977: 55).

The Land Problem

One of the best-known—one could say hackneyed—differences between Aboriginal and White worldviews is that Aboriginals think they belong to the land, whereas Whites consider the land belongs to them: "many fundamental Indian values are not only incompatible with those of American culture, but work directly in opposition to the principles on which the modern competitive capitalistic order is based" (Ablon 1964: 297). Much of the failure which characterizes Aboriginal-White arrangements or agreements can be accounted for on the basis of this difference. The situation is even more complicated in the case of the Métis because they exhibit a dual pattern of attitudes that White society deems irreconcilable:

> (i) on the one hand the Métis traditionally share with Indians a lack of interest for hoarding material wealth, and are therefore viewed as Indians by the Whites. Campbell (1973: 27) typifies this cultural incompatibility very neatly through a Saskatchewan Métis' view of White settlers just after World War II: "These people rarely raised their voices, and never shared with each other, borrowing or buying instead. They didn't understand us, just shook their heads and thanked God they were different."

> (ii) on the other hand the Métis also differ from the Indians by their spontaneous exuberance and lack of social restraint. Campbell again (1973: 25): "There was never much love lost between Indians and Halfbreeds. They were completely different from us—quiet when we were noisy, dignified even at dances and go-togethers."

Even though these differences should not be exaggerated and have probably been somewhat levelled by the flow of time, it is clear from such observations that the Métis have always had their own distinct values. Métis leader Harry Daniels capitalized on this fact when he warned: "If the Métis are to found effective organizations, these should have their roots in past traditions" (Daniels 1979a: 27). These past traditions emphasized distinctiveness from both Indians and Whites, and based survival on action and resistance—a line of conduct that can indeed be readily taken up by any repressed minorities wishing to assert themselves. The Métis reaction in the middle of the 20th century was timely: "At present they are re-emerging as an ethnic group, with only informal—not legal—recognition by the federal government," noted Frideres (1974: 3). More concerned than the federal government, the three Prairie provinces (Manitoba, Saskatchewan and Alberta, which include the majority of the Canadian Métis) have launched helping programs carried out with various degrees of determination. The Métis settlements of Alberta are a case in point:

> For many years the Métis in the 2 000 square miles of Métis land would be forced to eke out a living through agriculture, trapping, hunting and fishing. The discovery and exploitation of natural gas and oil deposits in the Métis settlements in recent decades promised better days but instead resulted in over $30 million in oil and gas bypassing the Métis Trust Fund on its way to the Alberta Heritage Trust, the petro-dollar account of the provincial government. (Daniels 1979a: 81)

As in the case of the First Nations, provincial efforts to control oil and gas resources, hence economic and political power, have triggered off endless law suits concerning land claims, as the Métis have considered it a breach of trust that underground resources are not allocated to them in the same way as surface resources. It is the same old story:

> To this day, the authorities, the public, and even the people affected, think in terms of 'Indian and Métis' problems, or of injustices done to 'Natives.' They posit solutions with ethnic boundaries in mind, not realising that they are buying into a racist perspective. (St-Onge 2004: 96)

How could it ever come to this? Such is the question that this book is trying to answer.

About this Book

There follows a collection of articles concerning the Western Métis, published in *Prairie Forum* over a quarter of a century between 1978 and 2004—with the only exception of David McCrady's recent (2007) piece on three heretofore unpublished letters of Louis Riel. These articles have been chosen for the breadth and scope of the investigations upon which they are based, and for the reflections they will arouse in anyone interested in Western Canadian history and politics.

The first one, "The Métis: the People and the Term," by John Foster (1978), clears up some of the confusion surrounding the meanings of the terms "Métis," "Halfbreed," and "Iroquois" in their historical contexts by distinguishing two trading systems, the St. Lawrence-Great Lakes and the Hudson Bay systems, each endowed with its particular fur trade tradition. The second article, by Ruth Swan and Edward Jerome (2004), is titled "Indigenous Knowledge, Literacy and Research on Métissage and Métis Origins on the Saskatchewan River: The Case of the Jerome Family"; it makes use of Métis genealogies to trace early French penetration into the Saskatchewan River area and identifies one François Jérôme as among La Vérendrye's original companions in the middle of the 18th century and one of the ancestors of the Red River buffalo-hunting Métis. The third essay, Arthur Ray's "The Northern Great Plains: Pantry of the Northwestern Fur Trade, 1774–1885," written in 1984, highlights the economic importance of the Métis in the transient Aboriginal/White culture of the central part of the North American continent at a crucial time in its history. It is followed by "The Twatt Family, 1780–1840: Amerindian, Ethnic Category, or Ethnic Group Identity?," authored by Paul Thistle (1997) and which examines early problems of identity among mixed-descent people, focusing this time on the lower Saskatchewan River region, on the margins of the Great Plains.

The fifth article of this collection, "Wintering, the Outsider Adult Male and the Ethnogenesis of the Western Plains Métis," by John Foster (1994), traces the origins of the latter group to the practices of wintering in the late 18th century and the transformation of the *engagé* into a freeman. It is followed by Thomas Flanagan's "The Market for Métis Lands in Manitoba: An Exploratory Study" (1991), which disputes the claim that the Métis of Assiniboia were dispossessed by the government and argues that they made every effort to adapt to and exploit a market which, contrary to common belief, they actually understood. On the heels of which article we naturally had to place its rebuttal: "Dispossession vs. Accommodation in Plaintiff vs. Defendant Accounts of Métis Dispersal from Manitoba, 1870–1881," by D.N. Sprague (1991), a major proponent of the dispossession thesis. The controversy had begun with "Métis Land Claims at St. Laurent: Old Arguments and New Evidence," an article written earlier (1987) by Thomas Flanagan, which discussed the interpretation of the relations between Ottawa and the Métis on the eve of the 1885 rebellion, and which is included here. And for good measure we have included "Thomas Scott and the Daughter of Time," by J.M. Bumsted (1998), a provoking reassessment of the character of a man whose innate villainy had never before been seriously challenged.

The tenth article, Manfred Mossmann's "The Charismatic Pattern: Canada's Riel Rebellion of 1885 as a Millenarian Protest Movement" (1985), puts the events of 1885 into a global context and reinterprets them as a prophet-inspired movement similar to others that took place in India, Burma, New Zealand and Brazil. There follows "Louis Riel and Sitting Bull's Sioux: Three Lost Letters," by David McCrady (2007). These three unpublished letters were addressed by the Métis leader to Lieutenant Colonel Henry Moore Black, commanding officer at Fort Assiniboine, in March 1880. They throw an unusual light on the American side of Riel's life, at a time when he very much identified with the Montana Métis and was trying to protect their interests by encouraging the Sioux to surrender to American authorities, thereby ridding the shrinking local hunting grounds of unwanted interlopers. The part that Riel played later in the Resistance was therefore supposed to be a mere interlude in a life otherwise focused on the United States. He intended to be back there by September of 1884 and, as McCrady remarks, "there is no reason not to believe him."

The twelfth essay of this collection, written by Walter Hildebrandt in 1985, naturally concerns "The Battle of Batoche": the events leading up to it, the military strategy of the Métis, and various details and episodes which influenced the outcome of this pivotal battle, including the *Northcote* incident and the presence of a Gatling gun. The last essay, "Another Father of Confederation?," by Allen Ronaghan (1999), argues that Louis Riel should be put squarely at the forefront of those who created Canada, thereby illustrating the polarization which has always characterized the exchange of educated opinions concerning Riel. As Charlotte Gray (2004: 405) remarks,

> Prime Minister Sir John A. Macdonald couldn't wait to get rid of him, regardless of the cost to Anglo-French relations:
>
> "He shall hang though every dog in Quebec bark in his favour," he is said to have snapped.
>
> More recently, Riel has been touted as a prototype defender of First Nations people within an increasingly racist society

and as an early advocate of western interests against a rapacious central Canada. In the 1960s, he morphed into a sort of Prairies Che Guevara, fighting for the simple life against a capitalist onslaught from the east.

The reader will thus have in handy format a broad panorama of the Western Métis as treated over a quarter of a century in the pages of *Prairie Forum*: their genesis and identity, their population movements and inter-breeding patterns, their historical importance and military prowess, and finally their political successes and failures.

2.   The Métis: the People and the Term (1978)

John E. Foster

*From "Iroquois" to "English Halfbreeds," the Canadian Métis
have been notoriously difficult to categorize. One step towards
clarification consists in distinguishing two fur trade traditions:
the St. Lawrence-Great Lakes and the Hudson Bay systems. A second step consists in understanding that historically the names
given the Métis first characterized a way of life, and then took on
socially or racially prejudiced overtones.*

In the Canadian West much confusion surrounds the use of the term
"Métis." While scholars and laymen alike agree that the term refers to persons of mixed Indian and Euro-Canadian ancestry, it is difficult to obtain a
more precise definition. "Métis" can refer to individuals and communities
who derive some of their cultural practices from non-Indian native communities whose origins lie in the pre-1870 West. In other instances, the term is
used to refer to individuals whose circumstances of birth suggest "Métis" as
preferable to the frequently pejorative term, "Halfbreed." On occasion, the
term also encompasses non-status Indians. Thus, in one circumstance, the
term conveys a sense of cultural identity and, in another, a quasi-legal status. Perhaps the most useful view of the term today is as a label identifying
a segment of western society which, in addition to recognizing an ancestry
of mixed Indian and Euro-Canadian origins, seeks to realize various interests through particular political goals and actions. It is possible that such
Métis political activity will lead to a Métis cultural cohesiveness not now
evident.[1] Even without such a development, significant questions emerge as
to the cultural links between the 19th-century Métis and those to whom the
term refers today. In essence such questions are problems in historical
understanding.

Confusion in the use of the term "Métis" is not new; it existed prior to 1870. There would appear to be agreement on what might be termed the classical image of the Métis as conveyed in some of Paul Kane's paintings[2] and Alexander Ross's writings.[3] The French-speaking, Roman Catholic, non-Indian native buffalo hunters of the Red River Settlement emerged distinct from the socio-cultural mosaic of the period and the region. As these people constituted Louis Riel's following (a principal reason for Canadian interest in their history), there seems to be some justification for labelling them as a distinct entity. Yet, problems in terminology emerge after a short perusal of the literature. What of the other non-Indian native peoples of the pre-1870 West who did not fit the "classical" image of the Métis? After the 1840s, what of the English-speaking, Protestant, buffalo hunters of Portage la Prairie, Prince Albert and Fort Victoria east of Fort Edmonton?[4] Did not their mixed Indian and Euro-Canadian ancestry as well as their way of life qualify them as Métis in spite of their predilection for the English tongue and Protestant Churchmen? And what of others? The French and Saulteaux speaking, Roman Catholic voyageur-farmers in Red River and their neighbours, the English-speaking, Protestant farmer-tripmen and occasional merchants— could they be considered "Métis"?[5] The French and Cree-speaking, Roman Catholic, buffalo hunters of the North Saskatchewan river valley would appear to fit the "classical" image of the Métis with ease.[6] But, what of their neighbours to the north in the valleys of the Peace and Athabasca Rivers, the Cree-speaking, Roman Catholic, "Iroquois" trapper-hunters?[7] Many of their descendants would demand halfbreed scrip rather than treaty status at the Treaty Eight signings in 1899.[8] Were these people Indians, Métis or...? In attempting to answer these questions writers have chosen a variety of terms to describe people of mixed ancestry who were not considered to be Indians.

Most writers dealing with the pre-1870 West accept the existence of two recognizable entities of mixed ancestry. The Métis, occasionally styled the *Bois Brulés* or *Chicot*,[9] provoke little debate although it is not always clear to whom the term applies. It is the "British" and "Protestant" segment as opposed to the "French" and "Catholic" part of the mixed-blood population which appears to provide most of the difficulties. The term "Halfbreed" is used in a similar way to the term "Métis," capitalized and uncapitalized.[10] But, it is apparent that the term can apply to both collectivities as well. Scots Halfbreeds, English Métis and Métis *écossais* are other favourites. More recent additions have included "Country-born" and "Rupert'slander."[11] The confusion surrounding some of the terms suggests that some writers have an inadequate understanding of the times and regions in which some of the terms flourished and to whom they applied.

Reflecting their own cultural antecedents and the traditions of interpretation in their discipline, historians studying the pre-1870 West have tended to emphasize a metropolitan perspective in viewing the passage of events. Whether it is Paris or London, Montreal or, near the end of the period, Toronto, the extension of metropolitan influence and control for purposes of resource exploitation is viewed empathetically.[12] The interests of the populations of these centres and more frequently the interests of their agents in the hinterland are central to the historian's narrative. The primary sources themselves heighten the sense of the predominance of metropolitan interests because these documents were the creations of the agents of metropolitan centres. While amenable to analysis from a hinterland perspective, most of the documents lend themselves more readily to an analysis of processes central to metropolitan concerns. The value of this approach is evident in the sophisticated and sensitive analysis of the actions of men and institutions whose cultural ties lay with the distant homeland.[13] Too frequently these same subjects can suffer from superficial analysis and dehumanizing assessment in other disciplinary approaches. Yet in historical analysis the narrative too often shifts its focus when the interests of the metropolis no longer hold sway. To obtain an acceptable historical understanding of the pre-1870 West, historians must attempt to perceive hinterland happenings in terms of a hinterland perspective as well as the traditional metropolitan perspective. One without the other is inadequate.

A basic premise in elaborating a hinterland perspective for the pre-1870 West is that the importance of the fur trade lay as much in the changing ways of life of the participants as it did in the commercial and political processes by which the metropolis extended and elaborated its interests in the hinterland. From a hinterland perspective, the appearance of agents from the different metropolitan centres introduced not only new material goods but new social elements into Western society. In adapting their ways to new realities, the newcomers and their goods stimulated Indian responses whose particular nature was determined by their cultural antecedents and fur trade roles such as Home Guard-provisioners, middleman-traders and trappers.[14] Over time, the particular nature of influences emanating from specific metropolitan centres left distinctive cultural legacies. As these legacies were incorporated in the various ways of life of the participants in each of the two trading systems, they created two distinct fur trade traditions.

For French mercantilists in the early modern period, commerce was a key means of enhancing the interests of the French state.[15] Thus, the Government of Louis XIV saw the fur trading system of the St. Lawrence-Great Lakes region as a tool of imperial expansion rather than a reason for it. Fur trade alliances with Indian bands were the means of extending French influence into the interior of the North American continent and denying its resources to European rivals. Diplomacy and the military as much as the market-place furnished the skills necessary for survival in the St. Lawrence trading system.[16] After the Conquest, the British, as evidenced in Pontiac's uprising in 1763, abandoned French practices at their peril. The emergence of a hostile United States of America to the south of the Great Lakes in the closing decades of the 18th century emphasized, in the mind of British colonial authorities, the necessity of adopting the French practice of establishing politico-military alliances with Indian bands.[17] Such alliances depended upon the exchange of furs for European goods. The success of French practice, which rested as much on the social ties of kinship as it did on political and economic interests,[18] led the Highland Scots, who succeeded to the control of the St. Lawrence fur trade system at Montreal, to think more in terms of elaboration rather than replacement when adapting their traditions to the legacy of *Canadien* ways.[19] In this trading system, of course, both the Indian and the Euro-Canadian faced the continuing challenge of adapting traditions to changing realities. The coherence of the process evolved what can be termed a St. Lawrence fur trade tradition. Central to this tradition and of crucial importance to both Indians and Euro-Canadians was the "Indian trader."

With the destruction of Huronia at the hands of the Iroquois in 1649–50, the French on the St. Lawrence had to exercise increasing control over the conduct of the fur trade if their alliance system was to survive. To this end the *coureur de bois* emerged.[20] Reflecting the military, diplomatic and merchant-adventuring skills of their heritage they established, through marriages and adoptions, the necessary bonds of kinship with Indian bands. Political and commercial activity depended upon such social ties. In time, with specialization and sophistication, the *coureur de bois* gave way to the voyageur on one hand and the commandant-trader on the other.[21] Critical to the French tradition was the practice of carrying trade goods to the Indian trappers and returning with furs.[22] Expeditions from major forts established outposts, and from them parties visited bands in their hunting and trapping grounds. Frequently ties of kinship linked the commandants of major forts, the bourgeois heading the outpost, and the trader who led the *en dérouine* party.[23] For both Euro-Canadians and Indians this latter figure, a kinsman playing a mediational or broker role, was crucial to maintaining the fur trade alliance. In time, most of these brokers were of mixed Indian and Euro-Canadian ancestry.

Jacqueline Peterson, in a timely article, describes a most interesting family survival strategy resting upon "middleman" control of trading activity in the Great Lakes region.[24] A newly arrived trader would undertake a short term "country marriage" with a woman of a prominent family in an Indian band to establish the kinship basis necessary for trading activity. Afterwards, possibly after other country marriages, a more permanent marriage with a *Canadien* woman of mixed Indian and *Canadien* ancestry or simply *Canadien* ancestry would be established. This wife would raise not only her own children but frequently the children of her husband by his "country wives." Later, some sons would follow in their father's footsteps and contract alliances with Indian women before undertaking more permanent marriages. Their sisters as well fulfilled a similar role, marrying potential competitors to facilitate "understandings." Several families appear to have survived the disruption of the Conquest by forming marriage alliances with incoming British traders.[25] These traders in turn quickly came to appreciate the advantage that such family ties conveyed in the hectic competition of the fur trade. The broker skills of a brother-in-law of mixed ancestry, leading an *en dérouine* party, were as crucial as British manufactures in achieving a successful trade.

With the founding of the Hudson's Bay Company in 1670, a second fur trading system came into existence. The Company's first half-century dictated a strategy termed the "coast-side factory system."[26] This policy was criticized as the "sleep by the frozen sea."[27] The Company did not abandon this policy and move into the interior in strength until the latter quarter of the 18th century. As a result, trade with the Indians of the interior was controlled by Cree and Assiniboine middlemen.[28] These trading chiefs filled the broker role for the interior Indians in the Hudson Bay trading system. For the Home Guard Cree bands living in the environs of the coastal factories, however, the goodwill of the post commander was crucial to their interests.[29] He was styled "Ukimow" or "patriarch," a position of pre-eminence in their world. In the trading post among the British-born he occupied the highest social position, received the greatest material benefits, and exercised the most power. To the Home Guard Cree, British-born servants and officers in the trading post, he was the "Indian Trader" in the Hudson Bay tradition.

In each of the fur trade traditions the inhabitants made the basic socio-cultural distinction between Indians and Europeans. The distinction was not one of race; rather, it emphasized ways of life. This is most apparent in the manner in which the inhabitants classified children of mixed European and Indian ancestry.[30] In both fur trade traditions the child was associated with the mother and classified socio-culturally with her way of life. If the mother remained with the Indian band the child was an "Indian." In the Hudson Bay tradition the term "Native" could be used as well, referring, it would appear, to an "Indian" who had a real or fictive kinship tie with personnel in the trading post. If the mother and child resided in the trading post for an extended period the child was "*Canadien*" or "*Scots*" (Euro-Canadian) in the St. Lawrence tradition, and "English" in the posts of the Hudson's Bay Company.[31]

A circumstance recorded in the York Factory Journals and Account Books in the early 1760s demonstrates how the historical actors viewed themselves and their fellows in the Bay traditions. Two native youths, Robert and Thomas Inksetter, sons of tailor Robert Inksetter who served at the Bottom of the Bay and York Factory from the early 1720s through to the late 1740s, enlisted as servants in the Company's service on five-year contracts.[32] In the parlance of the Fort and the surrounding bands they had become English. After two years, the young men requested permission to have wives live with them in the fort.[33] Their request was refused on the grounds that, among the English, only the commanding officer enjoyed this privilege.[34] With their Indian heritage allowing them an additional option to those enjoyed by British-born servants, the brothers broke their contracts and left the Fort.[35] They undoubtedly lived with bands who continued to trade with the Company and were known by name, but their English names did not survive their departure. As far as the Company's records are concerned, Thomas and Robert Inksetter did not exist after 1761.[36] They had ceased being "English" and had become "Indian" or "Native" again.

It was in the St. Lawrence fur trade tradition that a term first emerged distinguishing a socio-cultural entity of mixed Indian and Euro-Canadian ancestry from either the Indian or Euro-Canadian in the West. By the second decade of the 19th century the term "Métis" or the English equivalent "Halfbreed" identified the newly emerged collectivity.[37] It would appear that neither term, at least initially, was meant to be complimentary. "Halfbreed" apparently could suggest a child of a morganatic liaison or marriage, while "Métis" could suggest "mongrel" rather than "mixed" as is frequently suggested.[38] Such terminology, however, did not necessarily indicate low social status for those to whom it applied. Rather, it seems plausible to suggest that such terms initially reflected the resentment of Euro-Canadians who found themselves dependent upon such individuals or more likely unable to effect marriage alliances which would tie such individuals to their interests. It would appear that the derogatory term was soon flaunted in the faces of those who used it by those to whom it referred. "Métis" was the term by which some families of mixed ancestry in the St. Lawrence tradition came to identify themselves.

In the region of the Red and Assiniboine River valleys in the first two decades of the 19th century, a second element, probably related to the first, became associated with the term "Métis." These were the provisioning bands of mixed ancestry who hunted buffalo in the region, and through "recognized hunters"[39] supplied pemmican and dried meat to the traders. After 1810, as the North West Company entered the closing decade of fur trade competition challenged by a revitalized and modernizing Hudson's Bay Company, kinsmen as traders to Indian bands or recognized hunters on the plains were critical to any hope of success. It was natural that North West Company officers would encourage these people, the "Métis," to see themselves as the "New Nation" whose interests were threatened by the arrival of the Selkirk settlers and the policies of the Hudson's Bay Company.[40] The events of the decade, focussing on the Battle of Seven Oaks, June 16, 1815, did not bring success to the North West Company but they caused the Métis to emerge as a self-conscious entity with a sense of a particular past and a particular destiny.

In the decade following the end of the fur trade competition in 1820, numerous families of mixed Indian and Euro-Canadian ancestry in the St. Lawrence tradition journeyed to Red River to join the Métis. As a result, differences amongst the Métis appeared. The pre-eminent elements were the plains hunters and the old trading families. Others functioned as fishermen on the lakes to the north. Still others enlisted as voyageurs on the York boats of the Hudson's Bay Company and on private freighters.[41] In later years some Métis families, including the Riels, took concerted action to emphasize their French and Roman Catholic orientation in contrast to the lifestyles of their neighbours.[42] As all these elements considered themselves "Métis" in Red River and were considered to be a single collectivity by other communities, the term would appear to be applicable beyond the limits of the Settlement.

The non-Indian native peoples in the St. Lawrence fur trade tradition, hunting buffalo from settlements near the North Saskatchewan river valley, apparently created few problems in being described as Métis. Throughout the half-century before Confederation, individuals and families migrated from the region to Red River and a movement of individuals and families flowed in the opposite direction as well.[43] To the north in the valleys of the Peace and Athabasca rivers another distinctive people emerged in the St. Lawrence fur trade tradition. But were they Métis? A number certainly identified themselves as such and do so today.

In the late 1790s, finding the Indians of the Upper Saskatchewan and neighbouring river valleys harvesting furs according to their needs and not the needs of the traders, the North West Company brought into the interior as many as 200 Iroquois, Ottawa, Nipissing and Saulteaux trapper-voyageurs.[44] These eastern Indians, amongst whom the Iroquois predominated, had lifestyles that demanded more Euro-Canadian goods than did the Indians resident in the region. Accorded privileges of price, goods and social prestige similar to the trading families in the Great Lakes and Red River regions, the Iroquois radiated outward from Fort Edmonton. South of the Saskatchewan River many died in conflicts with members of the Blackfoot Confederacy. Others soon returned to the East. The remainder, joined by a few *Canadien* freemen, flourished to the north and west. In spite of the tension between them and the Cree and Beaver peoples, the Iroquois were outstandingly successful. Taking wives from amongst the Cree they established the kinship ties that made them effective traders as well as hunters and trappers. The special relationship which they had enjoyed with the North West Company was continued with the Hudson's Bay Company after 1820, although in a somewhat attenuated form.[45] At the end of the century a number of descendants of these families chose scrip rather than treaty as, in their minds, they were not Indians, but Halfbreeds[46] or Métis who derived many of their ways from the St. Lawrence fur trading tradition.

In the Hudson Bay tradition in the early years of the 19th century, a term distinguishing a third community, distinct from the "Indians" or "Natives" and the "English" did not arise. In contrast to the St. Lawrence tradition in which the term "Métis" and its English equivalent "Halfbreed" arose, people in the Bay tradition remained "Native" or "English." It is noteworthy that Peter Fidler, a Hudson's Bay Company officer, and one of the first individuals to use the term "Halfbreed" in referring to peoples in the St. Lawrence tradition, did not apply the term to individuals in the Hudson Bay tradition.[47] Fidler's own children were clearly "English," not "Native" and certainly not "Halfbreeds." After 1820 a number of Hudson Bay "English" (the *Anglais* of the Métis) moved to Red River to become river lot farmers, tripmen in the York boats and private merchants.[48] They were joined by Hudson Bay Native kinsmen who in some instances joined them as "English." Others were encouraged to join Peguis's band of Saulteaux at the Indian village below the Red River Settlement.[49] The appearance of officers with British wives in the 1830s created problems of terminology for the Hudson Bay "English."[50] By the end of the 1840s they no longer saw themselves as English, as evidenced in the strikingly belligerent manner in which a Hudson Bay English Anglican catechist referred to himself as "only Half-an-Englishman."[51] At the same time the term "Halfbreed" was taking on a definition separate from that of the Métis.

The Anglican missionaries who were involved with the Hudson Bay English used three terms to identify them. The term "half-caste" disappeared after Rev. John West's departure.[52] "Country-born," to distinguish them from the "Native-born," appeared as early as 1852.[53] However, "Halfbreed" was the most frequently encountered term in missionary writings.[54] This development was unfortunate as the term at the time was taking on racial and cultural connotations of a negative nature. The Hudson Bay English in Red River seem to have been as confused as their observers. Occasional references to "my Countrymen" demonstrate a sense of their distinctiveness from Indians and Métis.[55] When acting in concert with the Métis they used the term "Halfbreed" to refer to their collective interest.[56] Yet as mentioned previously, this choice may have indeed been rather unfortunate.

Governor George Simpson of the Hudson's Bay Company's North American operations initially followed the Hudson Bay tradition in the use of the term "Native" to designate individuals of mixed ancestry.[57] Quite quickly he switched to the use of "Halfbreed," the term originating in the St. Lawrence tradition.[58] It is readily apparent that Simpson associated the term with individuals of mixed ancestry whose habits of life were at odds with his enthusiasm for "modernism" with its emphasis on efficiency of process, whether commercial or administrative. Simpson could recall Hudson Bay English families such as the Cooks and the Birds, whose concerns with privileges derived from rank and kinship emphasized the particularism that was the principal barrier to efficient process in the fur trade in Rupert's Land.[59] The Hudson Bay "English" in his experience were the unprogressive opponents of modernism. To Simpson it was obvious that their unsteady habits were functions of their "Indian" ancestry. His "character" book demonstrates clearly that he was biased against individuals of mixed ancestry.[60] Nevertheless, Simpson was too able a modernist to allow his prejudice to interfere with his recognition of demonstrated merit. The career of Chief Factor William Sinclair, Junior, the descendant of an old Hudson Bay English family, is a case in point. It would appear that Simpson simply removed the individual from the category of his prejudice while still retaining his prejudice against "Halfbreeds." To Simpson, Chief Factor William Sinclair, Junior, was an effective officer, not a "Halfbreed."[61] Officers recently arrived from Great Britain shared Simpson's views on "Halfbreeds,"[62] whose traditionalist ways were seen as antagonistic to the effective and efficient operation of the fur trade. By mid-century it would appear that the term "Halfbreed" had come to encompass all persons of mixed ancestry from both fur trade traditions. Unfortunately, the concept was essentially negative.

The Hudson Bay English apparently never did successfully resolve their problem of creating a term around which they could identify their common interests. They saw themselves as distinct from the Métis.[63] Others viewed them as a socio-cultural element distinct from Métis. In these circumstances, scholars have faced a labelling problem. While a plethora of terms has been used to identify them for purposes of study, no single term has gained wide acceptance. Perhaps in spite of its serious limitations "Red River Halfbreed" may yet emerge as the most useful term to identify this cultural entity.

The same problem does not emerge with the term "Métis." With a conceptual framework that equates a hinterland perspective with a metropolitan perspective, two distinct trading systems, each with its particular tradition, can be seen to emerge. In each tradition the person of mixed ancestry was socio-culturally identified with his way of life, not his biological heritage. Particular historical circumstances saw some individuals, who tended to be of mixed ancestry, emerge as distinct entities. In the Hudson Bay tradition these individuals emerged from Home Guard bands, not the middleman trading bands. In the St. Lawrence tradition it was the trader-broker role which some persons of mixed ancestry controlled. In the Bay tradition, historical circumstances confused the emergence of a clearly identifiable community label. In the St. Lawrence tradition historical circumstances singled out the traders and the provisioning hunters for recognition and exaltation. The events of the decade before the signing of the Deed Poll in 1821 provided the basis for the folk history of the "New Nation." Beyond the limits of the Red and Assiniboine river valleys, the term identified socio-cultural elements derived from the St. Lawrence tradition who functioned as trader-brokers and as provisioners. Thus the hunters of mixed ancestry in the North Saskatchewan river valley, many of whom were more familiar with Cree than French, were Métis as well. Similarly, the "Iroquois" of North Western Alberta were considered a Métis people. It was the trader-broker role and the provisioning role in the St. Lawrence tradition that called forth the existence of the Métis. These same roles would determine the nature of their culture. Elements of that culture survive among some Métis people today.

3. Indigenous Knowledge, Literacy and Research on Métissage and Métis Origins on the Saskatchewan River: The Case of the Jerome Family (2004)

Ruth Swan and Edward A. Jerome[1]

The difficulties of tracing the origins of a hybrid group where one expects only oral traditions can often be mitigated by researching written archives. The archives of the Jerome family extend over some 200 years: from the French middlemen of the Northwest and the Hudson's Bay Companies to the cultural brokers who in about three generations developed a separate identity as they moved from the Great Lakes to the Northwest to the Red River.

In order to trace the origins of the Red River Valley Métis, the authors used the genealogy of Edward A. Jerome, of Hallock, Minnesota, members of whose family have lived on their farm for over a century and have been in the Red River Valley since the late 1790s. Hallock is 20 miles from Pembina and the farm is located on the Two Rivers, a tributary of the Red River. The Jerome family can trace their paternal roots through the Canadian fur trade in Rupert's Land, although the ethnic designation of "Métis" has no legal status in the United States. Edward Jerome wanted to trace his ancestry, and various lines led him backwards to Jeromes who were the earliest ancestors from Quebec. Jerome discovered that he is a descendant of The Buffaloe, a Pembina Ojibwe hunter, and of his daughter who was the country wife of Alexander Henry the Younger; she was later baptized as "Magdeleine Saulteaux."[2] We researched these ancestors to determine at what point they arrived in Red River, but also to trace Métis family lines as far back in time as possible to determine their origins in New France as well as their Aboriginal connections. What we discovered is that Jerome's father's line had been "Métis" for nearly 200 years.

Stereotypes of Native people take various forms, but often subtly suggest that Aboriginal history is based on oral history rather than archival research. The implicit message is that Native history is difficult to document and unreliable, so oral history is not as valid as written history; many historians privilege the written text over oral sources and ignore the problems of unreliable texts. The other problem is that not all families possess an oral tradition. While an oral tradition might be possible in some families, it does not work in many cases where family and community history has been ignored. Cultural memory is often repressed in the face of racism, where people are made to feel ashamed of their Aboriginal background and are taught to forget about their Native ancestors while promoting immigrant (European or Canadian) relatives who are acceptable in the dominant society because they are "white." This is particularly true in cases like Métis history in the United States, where the Métis descendants of the fur trade are not even recognized as Aboriginal. If they do not have Indian status with a particular band, they are not "Indian"; yet they often experience racism in local communities, especially if they look different from other people who are the descendants of immigrants. How do they offset the shame engendered from the cruelty of racism?

Edward Jerome encountered this repression of Métis history when he asked his father, Edward Jerome, Sr., about his background: His father told him to "forget it because it will never do you any good." When interviewed by a local historian in the 1980s, Jerome Sr. was reluctant to talk.[3] Edward Jr. had been curious when his cousin Frank Jerome wrote to the Hudson's Bay Company Archives (HBCA) in London, UK, and found references in HBCA journals to Jeromes who were Cree interpreters along the North Saskatchewan River. Another cousin, Dorothy Jerome Kalka of Pembina, North Dakota, also researched family history in the Saint Boniface and Pembina Church records. Edward Jr. undertook genealogy research on various fronts and then in the 1980s and 1990s carried on the research into the HBCA in Winnipeg. Swan started to collaborate with him in 1991, and we have published several articles on ancestors from the Saskatchewan and Lake Superior areas, and produced Swan's doctoral dissertation: "The Crucible: Pembina and the Origins of the Red River Valley Métis."[4]

The intention of this article is to demonstrate that Métis genealogies can be followed up with archival research to produce historical family studies. This is an option for Aboriginal and Métis families where the oral tradition and stories have been lost or culturally repressed, or as a complement to existing oral histories. This methodolgy is also a challenge to the stereotype that Aboriginal history is only based on the oral tradition. Ethnohistorians using insights from anthropology and history have demonstrated that indigenous knowledge can also be based on the expertise gained from archival research. Jerome personally felt that it was important for him to document from written sources information about his ancestors; using his family insights into language and other cultural issues rounded out the picture. We feel this approach has been remarkably successful, partly because the Hudson's Bay Company in Winnipeg provides extensive documentation of the fur trade through documentary sources such as post journals, account books, district reports, correspondence and maps. This type of research can answer historical controversies about such questions as the origins of the Métis outside of the Red River Valley. Although this ethnic identity was first articulated during the Fur Trade War in 1815–16, we wanted to document how the Jerome family moved to Red River, from where, and when? Who were these Métis ancestors and who were in the formative generation of French Canadian voyageurs and Native women? Can they be named?

Edward Jerome identified François Jerome as the earliest voyageur from Quebec who was in the North West during the French regime and made the transition to the new fur trade in the British regime as a trader after 1763. There were several generations of Jeromes on the Saskatchewan River before they moved south in the 1820s. While it is difficult to identify exactly who was the first Métis in this family, our research showed that it is possible to trace the family and their movements through the generations and to show how they developed as voyageurs, traders, interpreters, buffalo hunters, and later as Red River Valley settlers.

French Canadian voyageurs did not always move directly from Quebec to the North West. As Jacqueline Peterson pointed out, communities of mixed ancestry people grew up in the Great Lakes region, especially at major trading centres like Detroit, Michilimackinac and La Baye (Green Bay, Wisconsin, on Lake Michigan).[5] As the Great Lakes trade was developing in the 1700s, fur traders from Quebec also penetrated the Western Plains, looking for the North West Passage to the Orient, and more specifically the *mer de l'ouest*. Indian reports suggested a large, inland body of water which French explorers hoped would lead them to a river running west to the Pacific Ocean and an easy sailing route to China.[6] The La Vérendrye men found that there was much confusion over the geography of the interior of North America.[7]

The family of Pierre Gaultier, Sieur de la Vérendrye, led and organized these early French explorations of the interior of North America, opening up the area west of Lake Superior, called the *pays d'en haut* (the upper country, or, in English, the North West).[8] The goals of the fur trade and exploration sometimes conflicted. The French government and colonial administrators in New France wanted to know the potential of the western side of the continent for economic development, but did not want the expense of subsidizing the expeditions. To finance their explorations, the colonial administrations of New France encouraged Pierre Gaultier, his sons and their *engagés* (voyageurs), to trade with the local Indians. The Sieur de la Vérendrye undertook the fur trade cautiously, but had the genius to establish a string of posts along the interior waterways which could provide food and support for his explorations because it was too far to return to Quebec each fall. He thus pioneered the system of wintering in the interior which made the Montreal-based fur trade possible. The posts they built included Kaministiquia at Thunder Bay, Fort St. Charles on Lake of the Woods in 1732, Fort Maurepas on the southern edge of Lake Winnipeg in 1734, Fort Rouge at the Forks of the Red and Assiniboine in 1737, and Fort La Reine on the Assiniboine near present-day Portage la Prairie in 1738. After the father Pierre retired in 1742, his sons continued his work by establishing Fort Bourbon on Cedar Lake, at the entrance to the Saskatchewan River west of Lake Winnipeg, and Fort St. Louis (Fort à la Corne), near the forks of the Saskatchewan River, several years before the fall of New France (1763). As Gerald Friesen noted:

> This chain of posts was designed not only to control the highways of the fur trade and to protect the most effective route to the Rockies and the western sea, but also to cut directly across the flow of furs to the English on the shores of Hudson Bay. Thus, the competitions between French and English intensified once again. As was the case at the close of the preceding century, the French won the lion's share of the trade.[10]

As a result of these interior posts, the French were able to intercept Cree and Assiniboine middlemen before they took their furs to Hudson's Bay, and traded with them along the fringe of plains and parkland, so that the transportation of furs and goods was undertaken by the French rather than the Indians. Through loss of furs, the Hudson's Bay Company traders in their bayside posts realized that Canadian competition was cutting into their business, and they began sending young men westward with their Indians to gather intelligence about the competition and to recommend new methods of dealing with the Canadian "pedlars," as they called them.

The fur trade was a lucrative business, but it also became dangerous when the French allied themselves with the Cree, Ojibwe and Assiniboine against the Dakota/Sioux. The newcomers were drawn into traditional tribal alliances and Indian warfare, which often prevented the easy flow of goods. Eldest son Jean-Baptiste La Vérendrye lost his life along with Father Aulneau on June 8, 1734, at Lake of the Woods when the whole expedition was killed by the Sioux "as a penalty for having armed the Indians of his command against the Sioux in 1734."[11] The father had sent his son to live with the Cree to learn their language and customs, and the French explorers and traders continued this practice as good communication with their allies and customers was a priority.

To undertake these great journeys to the west, La Vérendrye recruited young men from Quebec who paddled the canoes for his expeditions and carried out the labouring jobs of the posts where they wintered. According to voyageur contracts in Quebec notarial records, François Jérôme, the son of a French militia officer by the same name, was one of these young men. His father's whole name was François Jérôme dit Latour dit Beaume, who had come from Brittany to Montreal in 1698 and married Marie-Angélique Dardennes in 1705 in Montreal.[12] They had 13 children, including two sets of twins; the eldest son, François Jr. was born in August 1706. After 1718, the family moved to the parish of St. Laurent on the island of Montreal.[13]

François Jr. first engaged for the West in 1727, his voyageur contract vaguely stipulating that he was engaged by M. De Villiers to make a trip to the *pays d'en haut*.[14] The exact destination was not named. On October 12, 1733, he married Marie-Denise Denoe *dite* Destaillis. His mother-in-law was Jeanne Adhémar, a sister of the Royal Notary. Her father was Antoine Adhémar de Saint-Martin, and his son, Jeanne's brother, succeeded him to the title; Jean-Baptiste Adhémar became Royal Notary in 1714, and he was François's uncle by marriage. The prestige of being married to the Royal Notary was passed down through several generations of Métis families in the North West, along the Saskatchewan and into Red River, as various descendants used the label "dit St. Martin" or "St. Matthe," corrupted in English as "Samart."[15]

François Jerome and Marie-Denise Denoe had eight children, baptized in Montreal between 1735 and 1746; the five boys and three girls were registered in the parish of Notre Dame de Montreal. Two died as infants. In the genealogy of Tanguay, however, there are no continuing descenants of this line, although there are listed descendants of some of François's brothers, Nicholas-Charles and Jean-Baptiste.[16] This is perhaps an indication that François's male descendants moved out of Montreal, most likely because of the fur trade.

François's career as a voyageur and later a trader continued from 1727 to 1757 (see Figure 1 for the geographical extent of his contracts). In the 1730s,

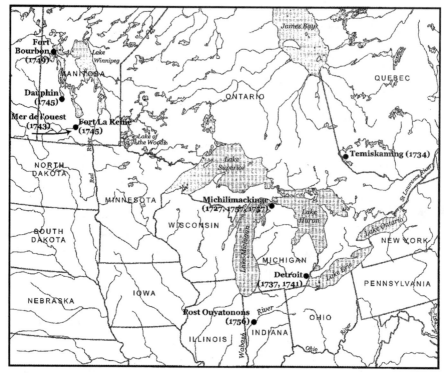

Figure 1. Fur trade voyageur contracts for François Jerome, 1700s.

Note: Modern provincial and state boundaries are included for reference. Source: Rapports de l'Archiviste du Québec. Cartography by Douglas Fast, University of Manitoba.

he was appointed to the French post at Detroit, south of Lake Huron.[17] The father, Pierre Gaultier, Sieur de la Vérendrye, had retired in 1742, but his sons were carrying on his exploration work.

In 1743, François Jérôme made a contract with the "Sieur de la Vérenderie" [sic] to go to the Sea of the West.[18] In 1745, François was hired by the Sieur Maugras to go to Forts La Reine and Dauphin in the same vicinity as the famous sons.[19] Fort La Reine was located on the Assiniboine River near Portage la Prairie, and Fort Dauphin was between Lake Manitoba and Lake Winnipegosis. In 1749, François Jérôme had a contract for Fort Maurepas[20] and Fort La Reine on the Assiniboine.[21] Both these forts had been established by the La Vérendrye family, as they were located on strategic waterways which connected with Manitoba Lakes that led to the northern reaches. In 1756, François Jérôme *dit* Latour contracted to the Sieur Louis Lamay Desfonds to Aposte Ouyatonons, the Wabash Post in the Illinois country southwest of Lake Michigan.[22] The following year, he must have made enough money to hire his own voyageurs and thus became a trader himself: "Sieur François Jérôme *dit* Latour" hired Joseph Beaumayer and Gabriel St. Michel to go to Michilimackinac.[23] This suggests that the latter French post on the Michigan shore between Lake Michigan and Lake Superior was now François's base of operations and that he may have stopped returning to Montreal each season.

If a trader wanted to penetrate the forested interior beyond Lake Superior, he had to establish a base in the Great Lakes and arrange to have the goods brought from Montreal; then when the furs came out, a Montreal crew would return with them. The voyageurs from Montreal were called *mangeurs de porc* (pork-eaters). The North West voyageurs in the interior were known as the winterers; although their diet at the posts consisted mainly of fish and meat, or pemmican, the canoe brigades ate Indian corn and wild rice traded from the Indians. The Canadian companies used the model of La Vérendrye to organize posts at regular intervals to stockpile food, as the voyageurs did not have time to hunt and fish on their long journeys. Men like François, who organized the trade and supervised the voyageurs, were called "wintering partners" and they had the support of Montreal merchants and financiers who organized the trade goods to go to the Great Lakes as well as the selling of the furs in Montreal and Europe. The pioneering efforts by the La Vérendrye family and the Great Lakes traders like François Jérôme *dit* Latour, who obviously learned a great deal when he worked for them, developed the extensive Montreal-based trade network which culminated in the North West Company, which spanned the continent to the Pacific and the Arctic Ocean by the 1790s. Obviously, when British partners became involved in the Canadian companies after 1763, they did not have the expertise and depended on the experience of their French traders and voyageurs to keep pushing north and west to the finest fur fields of the Athabaska. Generally, anglophone historians like A.S. Morton emphasized the British leadership of the NWC after 1763, and little is known of the French traders and voyageurs who continued to work for the Canadian concerns after the fall of New France.

The sons of Pierre de la Vérendrye continued with the fort-building north of the Assiniboine and west of Lake Winnipeg. Between 1741 and 1743, Pierre Gaultier de La Vérendrye (second son of Pierre Sr.) built Fort Dauphin, near Lake Winnipegosis, while other members of their group built Fort Bourbon to the northwest of Lake Winnipeg, and Fort Paskaya (The Pas) to the northwest of Cedar Lake.[24] François Jérôme may have been involved in the establishment of the posts west of Lake Winnipeg. Jérôme became associated with the La Vérendrye family in 1743 when he signed a contract to explore for the *mer de l'ouest*, and later in 1745 with the Sieur Maugras for Forts La Reine and Dauphin.

The Sieur Pierre Gamelin Maugras was the cousin by marriage of Louis-Joseph Gaultier de la Vérendrye, also known as Le Chevalier, Louis Joseph Gaultier (the fourth son of Pierre Gaultier de la Vérendrye and Marie-Anne Dandonneau),[25] so it appears that Jérôme was most closely associated with this member of the famous family. Le Chevalier had spent from the spring of 1742 to July 1743 exploring the plains south-east of Fort La Reine, looking for the "Sea of the West." According to his biographer, Antoine Champagne, he was accompanied by his brother, François Gaultier du Tremblay, two Frenchmen, and some Indian guides. Although François Jérôme was engaged to explore for the Sea of the West in 1743, it is not clear whether he accompanied the La Vérendrye brothers in 1742–43.[26] This trip greatly increased geographical knowledge of the central plains, and also proved there was no Sea of the West in that area: the large body of water described by the Indians was probably Lake Winnipeg.[27] Before he died, La Vérendrye Sr. decided to focus his explorations on the north and the Saskatchewan River.

The governor of New France, Charles de Beauharnois, had a master plan to extend French control of the west; but it suffered from the vagaries of French politics and the explorers had trouble getting the financial support they needed. Pierre Sr. had been replaced as commandant for the *poste de l'Ouest* in 1743 while his sons stayed in the west:

> In 1747 [Beauharnois] sent Pierre and the Chevalier [Louis Joseph] de la Vérendrye to carry on the trade of the Western Posts, doubtless hoping that the Court would relent, as indeed it did and reappoint the father [Pierre as commandant]. The sons spent the winter at the northerly posts facing the English. In the spring of 1749, the Chevalier ascended the River Saskatchewan [Paskoyac] probably from Fort Bourbon, to the confluence of the north and south branches "where [there] is the rendezvous every spring of the Crees of the Mountains, Prairies and Rivers to deliberate as to what they shall do—go and trade with the French or with the English." That year the French carried off the main part of the trade in small furs at the expense of York Fort.[28]

In the late 1740s the sons stayed in the west, while their father tried to raise more capital for their exploring projects and their men continued to pursue the fur trade and take furs away from the English on the bay.

Unfortunately, Pierre Sr. died in December 1749 in Montreal while his sons were recalled to Quebec for various military engagements.[29] It is generally assumed by historians that when the French officers were recalled to New France to defend it, everyone left and the French lost the colony in 1763[30]; little is known of the French traders who worked with the military and who were taking the furs away from the HBC.

When Jérôme went to Fort Bourbon in 1749, he was not a soldier like the La Vérendrye brothers but a voyageur and trader. In May 1749, the master of York Factory received a letter from François Jérôme, asking for a list of prices and proposing a little *commerce caché*, or private trade. The French trader also showed his wisdom based on experience in dealing with the Natives:

> As it came to our knowledge by the bearer of the said letter
> that you was ready to send one of your men in those parts,
> you may do it with all safety and fear nothing on our side.
> Leave the Indians quiet as we do. Although we have an offi-
> cer with us, If you have any money, Goods or otherwise, we
> might settle a little private trade. Send us word at what
> price you take Beaver...

He sent along his broken oboe with the Cree middlemen, asking that it be repaired by the blacksmith at the fort: "I send by the Bearer of the Letter a Hautbois to get mended and in so doing, you will do me a sensible pleasure. You will give it to the Bearer of the Letter, and I shall have the Honour to send you the payment next year or bring it myself."[31] Historian A.S. Morton noted that this was the "first evidence of the plaintive reed by the shores of a western lake."[32] John Newton, the master at York, dismisssed the French trader's proposal, but copied a translation of his letter in his journal; the original must have been in French.[33]

In the early 1750s, the HBC masters at York Factory were so concerned at the threat to their trade that they began sending young men back with the Cree traders to explore and gather information about the Canadian traders, the "pedlars." Anthony Henday left York Factory in June 1754 and travelled along both branches of the Saskatchewan, reporting on the vast buffalo herds and resources of the plains. He also learned that the Cree and Assiniboine were middlemen in the trade, gathering up the furs of the Blackfeet who did not want to make the long trip to Hudson's Bay.[34] Gerald Friesen described the problems that Henday encountered in getting the plains furs back to York:

> But when his party commenced the long journey toward
> York, their sixty newly built canoes heavy with the furs they

had gained in trade, they did not breeze past the French posts as Henday had hoped but rather stopped at each one for a little relaxation. At Fort la Corne,[35] for example, "the master gave the natives ten gallons of adulterated brandy and has traded from them above one thousand of the finest skins." The story was repeated at Fort Basquia, and when the flotilla reached Hudson Bay in later June, many of the best and lightest furs had been left behind with the French...[36]

In one version, Henday described the French trader he met at Basquea (The Pas):

> The Master invited me in to sup with him, and was very kind: He is dressed very Genteel, but the men wear nothing but thin drawers, and striped cotton shirts ruffled at the hands and breast. This House has been long a place of Trade belonging to the French, and named Basquea. It is 26 feet long; 12 feet wide; 9 feet high to the ridge ... and divided into three Apartments: One for Trading-goods, one for Furs, and the third they dwell in.[37]

Geographer A.J. Ray noted that the only reason the Cree and Assiniboine made the arduous trip to the Bay, according to Henday, was to get Brazil tobacco from the English traders.[38] Henday had complained in his journal: "It is surprizing to observe what an influence the French have over the Natives; I am certain he hath got above 1000 of the richest skins."[39]

Friesen also contends that the problems arising from French competition were not communicated to the London Committee, who only saw an "expurgated version of Henday's full journal, and his information was not acted on for another two decades."[40] Presumably he is referring to the establishment of the first HBC post in the interior, Cumberland House, established by Samuel Hearne in 1774.[41] The York masters continued to send out exploring expeditions which brought back information about the French pedlars in the 1760s and 1770s, involving people such as Joseph Smith, Joseph Waggoner, Isaac Batt, George Potts, Henry Pressick, William Pink and Matthew Cocking. A.S. Morton noted that nine voyages were made into the interior from 1754 to 1762.[42]

François Jérôme was obviously part of these early French trading operations along the Saskatchewan, and he gained valuable experience about the logistics of the trade without having to deal with the politics of the French court and colonial adminstration like the La Vérendrye family. The French traders saw an opportunity when the war in New France called their officers home, and they took advantage of the lack of colonial control to continue their Indian trade on the strategic Saskatchewan route. Encounters documented in the HBC journals by the inland British visitors suggest their continuing presence, although Canadian historians have largely ignored them. The fact that HBC men kept journals that have survived meant that explorers like Anthony Henday were extolled while the French traders were almost invisible.[43] Morton observed this contradiction more than most:

> The Frenchmen remaining at the posts were little more than voyageurs and clerks long in the trade. Among them, probably, were Louis Menard at Nipigon, the elusive François on the Saskatchewan, and perhaps a Blondeau at La Reine. One by one the posts were abandoned, no doubt for lack of goods. La Reine was still open in the winter of 1757–58, when Joseph Smith was on the Assiniboine. In the spring Fort Bourbon was burnt. It was not reoccupied. In 1757, La Corne's Fort St. Louis was closed; in 1759, Fort Paskoyac. That summer a Frenchman named Jean-Baptiste Larlee came down from this last post to York Fort to seek employment. He was sent off to England... He reported that ... Frenchmen were building where Henday had proposed that the Company should open a post (at Moose Lake). By 1760 all the French posts on the Saskatchewan were closed.[44]

It seems unlikely that all the French military posts closed by 1760, because some of the traders stayed in the west. When HBC man William Pink encountered the French pedlars in the spring of 1767, the Indians told him that the Canadian houses had been on the Saskatchewan for at least ten years, i.e. 1757, before the end of the French regime. François Jérôme had been sent to the Wabash River in Illinois country in 1756; but at that time the trade became free and he hired his own men at Michilimackinac in 1757 and returned to the Saskatchewan.[45] Morton reports a story from Fort Bourbon in 1757, when HBC trader Joseph Smith met the French master over a pot of brandy. The French leader questioned his guest about their involvement in the Seven Years War and whether the fur traders should allow military conflicts to interfere with the trade: "What if the King of England and the King of France are att [*sic*] war together, that is no reason why we should, so Lett us be friends."[46]

The Elusive "Franceway"

It was a long way back to Montreal and it was probably around this time that the French traders started using Michilimackinac and Grand Portage as rendezvous points[47] so that they could take their furs out in the spring and return with their Canadian goods before the cold weather in October.[48] After the Seven Years War ended, there was no official sanction for interior trading and no licenses granted until 1767.[49] After working west of Lake Superior since 1743, François Jérôme had acquired knowledge of local Indian customs and of the Cree language, which helped him pursue a successful trading career. By 1757, he was in charge of his own crews and continued his role as a wintering partner for another 20 years along the Saskatchewan.

There is some disagreement in the literature about when the first Canadian traders entered the North West after the end of the war because trade licenses were not issued until 1767. However, contemporary documents hint at an illegal trade before licenses were authorized. W.S. Wallace observed that the Moose Factory journals from James Bay reported that Indians had seen the Canadians since 1761.[50] A.S. Morton noted that Benjamin and Joseph Frobisher wrote to Governor Haldimand that the first trader from Michilimackinac to the interior was reported in 1765. He asked rhetorically:

> There were men, then, who snapped their fingers at the Regulations, and from 1765 slunk through into the North-West. Who were they? The historians must now put on the mantle of Sherlock Holmes, point out the delinquents, and track them to their lair.[51]

The use of his language suggests colonial dishonesty, rather than entrepreneurial competitiveness. W.S. Wallace identified "Franceway" (surname not mentioned) as the first master pedlar to reach the Saskatchewan in 1767. HBC explorer William Pink saw Franceway's buildings near The Pas in the spring; but the French were not there, possibly having already left for the Great Lakes rendezvous.[52]

In 1767, there was a license issued to François Le Blanc (printed as "Blancell"). In the fur trade returns for 1767 at Michilimackinac, Le Blancell was listed as being financed by Alexander Baxter of Montreal to take six canoes to Fort Daphne (Dauphin) and La Pierce (Portage La Prairie or Fort La Reine), valued at 2,400 livres. This was the largest consignment of goods that year; the next highest value was 1,106 livres to Louis Menard, financed by Forrest Oakes.[53] "That François Le Blanc was handling business (for himself or for others) in a large way is shown by the value of his cargo," muses Morton.[54] Le Blanc as a name then disappeared from the records, but genealogists suggested that this was a surname used by the Jerome family.[55]

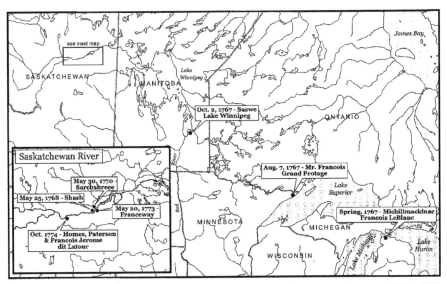

Figure 2. Reports of Mr. François, Saswe, Franceway and François Jerome, 1767–1774.
Cartography by Douglas Fast, University of Manitoba.

A number of the HBC traders sent inland encountered a man known to them as "Franceway" or by his Indian name, "Saswe," or a variant of it from 1767 to 1777. This figure has remained somewhat mysterious because no surname identified him, but circumstantial evidence suggests he was François Jérôme who had been at Fort Bourbon in 1749. Figure 2, tracing Franceway's movements between 1767 and 1774, suggests that François Le Blanc of Michilimackinac, Franceway and Saswe were the same person. For example, in August of the same summer, British explorers Captain James Tute and Jonathan Carver met "Mr. Francois" at Grand Portage when the Michilimackinac commander Robert Rogers sent along messages with the trader to the starving expedition.[56]

A month later, William Tomison had come inland for the HBC from Fort Severn on the Hudson Bay coast. He did not meet Franceway himself, but observed the Canadian traders on Lake Winnipeg who threatened British trade on September 3, 1767:

> Arrived at the great Lake [Lake Winnipeg] where I found many Indians, waiting for the arrival of the English and French pedlars. They informed me that there were two Houses at Misquagamaw [Red] River within 2 days padle across the Lake.[57]

This suggests the first documented penetration of Red River since La

Vérendrye, but it is possible that Canadian traders like Jerome, Charles Boyer and Forrest Oakes had used it before they were observed by the HBC. Tomison also commented on the variety of goods the Canadian traders were bringing into the interior:

> they take all kinds of furs, the natives were cloathed in french cloth, blankets, printed callicoes and other stuffs ready made-up and many other sorts of trading goods, their tobacco is white and made up in rolls and brinks, their guns are lightly made.[58]

He was "humiliated" to find that he could not prevent the Indians from selling their best furs to these Canadians.[59]

A month later, in October 1767, on Lake Winnipeg, Tomison met a French trader with ten Frenchmen and fourteen Indians in six large canoes on their way to The Pas, west of Lake Winnipeg, and identified the leader as "Saswe." This was two months after "Mr. François" left Tute and Carver at Grand Portage. Tomison complained that Saswe refused to talk "Indian" with him. Perhaps this is because the French trader chose not to give out information. Intelligence gathering on the opposition was an important rule for inland men: HBC inland traders were instructed to gather intelligence about the competition, and Saswe may have been reluctant to divulge his destination. Tomison learned through an interpreter that Saswe was financed by a Frenchman in Montreal and was not connected with the traders at Misquagamaw (Red) River. He described Saswe as follows:

> his dress was a ruffled shirt, a Blanket Jacket, a pair of long trousers without stockings or showes, his own hair with a hatt bound about with green binding, a poor-looking small man about 50 years of age, he seemed to have a great command over the men, he lay in the middle of the canoes with his wife and son, each of these canoes carie about 3 tons, his Indian conductor guide padled in a small canoe with his wife who was dresed [sic] very fine, when the wind favoured, they have a square sail which helps them greatly.[60]

Tomison's description provides details of the material culture of the French Canadian traders coming into the North West after 1763. François Jerome was born in 1706, so in 1767 he would have been 61; but a man doing this kind of hard travelling twice a year would have been in good physical shape, even if he was not paddling the canoe like a voyageur. The "poor-looking" comment suggests that he was not ostentatious, but dressed for practicality, like the Indians. Instead of Canadian shoes, he probably wore moccasins made by his Indian wife. The "blanket jacket" refers to the typical Canadian voyageur *capote* made from a blanket. The reference to the family suggests he had an Indian country wife (she was probably at least twenty years younger than him, since the son sounds like a child; if the son had been a teenager, he would have been paddling the canoe).

Saswe must have enjoyed the respect of his Indian companions as he commanded a large fleet of six canoes. Since he sat in the middle of the canoe with his family and was not paddling, he was in a higher social position than his men, suggesting that he was no longer a voyageur and had become a "bourgeois" or wintering partner. Since he had "great command over the men"—not a given in the social hierarchy of the fur trade—he must have had a gift for treating his men well and with respect, i.e., he was a good leader. After trading four bags of wild rice from Tomison's Indians, Saswe pushed on and did not stop at The Pas as he had told the HBC man, but continued to Pemmican Point on the Saskatchewan.

Although the HBC traders often underestimated their Canadian competition, Saswe was a successful trader who got along well with his French Canadian engagés as well as his Indian customers, to such an extent that the bayside managers realized that they were losing about a third of their furs every season to these newcomers. William Pink, another HBC trader inland from York, passed the Canadian houses in the spring of 1767, also trying to get information on the Canadian traders for his master, Ferdinand Jacobs. The following spring of 1768, on May 25, Pink passed the house where "Shash" had resided.[61] He was told that Shash was in partnershp with James Finley of Montreal, "the first British Pedlar of whom we have record on the Saskatchewan after the 'conquest.' He noted that the chiefest persons name is Shash, they are all French men that are heare upon the account that the English did not now the way."[62] The following year, on May 16, 1769, Pink observed:

> this day i came down to the plase whare the people of Quebeck ware staying as i went up heare i find the people belonging to this man ware not yet come up ... one English man with 12 Frenchmen with him, his name is James Finley from Montreal, he came up with three canewes.[63]

On Pink's fourth journey, on May 30, 1770, he noted that no Canadian canoes came up in the fall of 1769. He met a canoe with four Frenchmen who told him that "Sarchstreee" would be coming with four canoes; but that winter had come on too early and they had a good deal of goods taken, presumably by Indians. They had come from forts "at the Bottom of the Bay." Usually this term referred to the bottom of James Bay, but that was not on the Canadian route to the interior. Perhaps Pink misunderstood, and the French Canadians were referring to Traverse Bay at the bottom of Lake Winnipeg on the southeast side. The Canadian route through the Winnipeg River emptied into the lake at this point. Although there were no forts there in 1770 (the post farthest west of Lake Superior was at Rainy Lake), it was customary for the traders to meet the Indians (and vice versa) at the mouths of significant rivers, as Tomison had done.[64] It would take 20 years for the Canadians to realize that it would be a good idea to have a provisioning post at this site (Fort Bas de la Rivière Winipic and Fort Alexander) where they could supply the canoe brigades with pemmican for their long journeys to the Athabasca.[65]

To summarize the reports of this French trader, Figure 3 outlines his progress from the Great Lakes to the Saskatchewan. In the summer of 1767, François Le Blanc obtained the fur trade license at Michilimackinac. On August 7, 1767, Mr. François met Captain Tute and Jonathan Carver at Grand Portage, Lake Superior. On October 2, William Tomison met Saswe with six large canoes and fourteen Indians on Lake Winnipeg, claiming he was going to The Pas. On May 25, 1768, the following spring, on the Saskatchewan River, William Pink passed the house where Shash had resided and then visited the new post where he was partners with James Finley from Montreal. These reports apparently were about the same trader, a man well-known to the Indians along the Saskatchewan, who was the principal Canadian opponent of the HBC.

The third HBC trader who encountered the trader he called Franceway was Matthew Cocking, but before they actually met he received information about him from his Indian companions.[66] For example, on March 4, 1763, Cocking heard from a young hunter that "Franceway had sent some of his Men through the Country among the Natives to collect provisions…" Franceway knew the importance of collecting country produce before the long winter. Later, he would use the same deployment, called *en dérouine*, to send his men to the Indian camps to collect their furs without waiting for them to bring these furs into the posts. On March 17, 1773, Cocking observed that "several canoes are laying in places all the way down to the Pedlers principal settlement at the Grand Carrying Place." The Indians told Cocking that they were dissatisfied with Franceway's trading practices and threatened to take away his furs by force if he refused to comply with their demands. This may have been said only to impress the Englishman, because in fact the Indians liked the French traders and Franceway in particular.

On May 20, 1773, Cocking and his Indians arrived at Franceway's settlement and the trader greeted the Indians with a gift of four inches of tobacco.

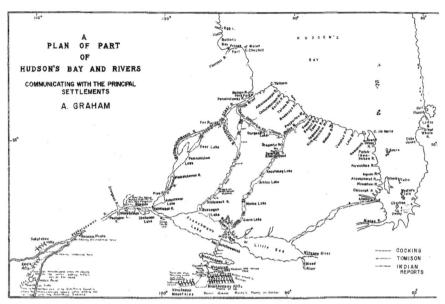

Figure 3. Saswaus House on Andrew Graham's map.
This map was prepared by R.I. Ruggles, from two original manuscripts (maps G.2/15 and G.2/17) in the HBCA, London. It was based on information received by HBC traders who were sent inland by Graham who remained at York Factory at the bay as well as Indian reports. Graham notes "Saswaus House" on the "Keskathcewan River" east of the fork in the Saskatchewan River. He notes: "Mr. Cocking disimbarked here." See John Warkentin and Richard Ruggles, *Historical Atlas of Manitoba*, Historical & Scientific Society of Manitoba, 1970: 94–95.

Cocking estimated that he had about 20 men with him. He described Franceway's trading post as follows:

> Franceway's dwelling is a long square Log house, half of it appropriated to the use of a kitchen and the other half used as a Trading and Bedroom with a loft above the whole length of the Building where he lays his Furrs. Also 3 small Log Houses, the Mens appartments, the whole enclosed with ten-foot stockades forming a square of about 20 yards. His canoes are 24 feet long measuring along the Gunwhale, 5 quarters broad and 22 inches deep.[67]

Cocking complained about the way the Indians gave away all their furs for a low price and a gift of "spiritous liquors." Cocking was surprised that the Indians who had previously complained about Franceway were on such good terms with him and were willing to trade away all their furs. On May 21 "The Natives all owned and complained at their hard Dealing of

Franceway and at the same time cannot account for their folly in expending their Furrs."

On May 22, 1773, Cocking accepted an invitation to dinner with Franceway and his country wife. The latter employed a translator, whom Cocking thought was an Irishman; but possibly it was Peter Pangman, whose New England accent might have been confused for an Irish one. Pangman later that summer travelled to York Factory to see if he could import his goods through Hudson Bay; but Cocking's superior, Ferdinand Jacobs, disabused him of that notion.[68] What really bothered Cocking was that François allowed the natives and engagés to come and go inside his house when they liked. "They never keep a watch in the night, his reason was that the men would not consent to any such order if given by him."[69] In the hierarchical nature of the Hudson's Bay Company, there were social distinctions between officers and "servants," their term for the labourers, and social distances between the officers, men and Indians. Since the HBC had not yet moved inland, they were not used to dealing with Indians in their own territory. Keeping a distance between traders and clients of whom Cocking was somewhat afraid was an issue for him. Cocking was critical of Franceway's methods of dealing with the Indians, but this was more a reflection of his own prejudices than an objective assessment of the French trader's success. A.S. Morton saw through the pretence:

> Cocking, with no goods, no rum, and but little tobacco, a stranger, with a great gulf—an English gulf—between him and the Indians, was helpless before this Indianized Frenchman.[70]

It was precisely the French traders' ability to live like "Indianized Frenchmen" that made them successful traders in the interior. As Thomas Hutchins at Albany Post pointed out in 1776:

> The Canadians have great influence over the natives by adopting all their customs and making them companions. They drink, sing, conjure, scold with them like one of themselves and the Indians are never kept out of their houses whether drunk or sober, night or day.[71]

British traders like Hutchins and Cocking found the Canadians' egalitarian attitudes disturbing to their accepted ideas of the British class structure. Readers should therefore be cautious about accepting literally the judgmental attitudes of traders like Cocking, for example, when he called Franceway "an ignorant old Frenchman." He also mocked Indian rituals that they used to ensure good hunting and regarded their medicine as superstitious. On October 30, 1772, he observed:

> Indians all employed looking after their Traps. The
> evenings are all spent in smoking and singing their God
> Songs, every Indian in his turn inviting the rest to smook
> and partake of a cold collation of Beries; this is done that
> they may be fortunate in trapping, live long, etc. Which
> they think has a great effect at the same time neglecting the
> only method of building many traps, most of them being
> very dilatory.[72]

Unlike Anthony Henday who enjoyed living with the Indians and made the
most of their hospitality, Cocking depended on them to guide him in a
foreign country, but at the same time acted judgmental and wrote
critically—not a good way to ensure strong trading relations.[73]

Franceway understood the nature of fur trade rituals, immediately giving Cocking's Indians some tobacco when they arrived at his camp. Some of
his Indian informants told Cocking that they had collected forty skins at the
buffalo pound and sent them to Franceway expecting a supply of ammunition and liquor in return. Cocking was at a disadvantage because he only
had Brazil tobacco, highly prized by the Indians, but few goods to trade.
"But I know Liquor is the chiefest inducement which I find the Natives
always go for to the Pedlers in the Winter."[74]

There were other references to Franceway/Saswe in the records of the fur
traders. Now the inland traders were not just from York, but from other bayside posts, such as William Tomison from Severn. Moses Norton, master at
Churchill, sent Joseph Hanson inland in 1773 to report on the invasion of
pedlars. A.S. Morton writes:

> Joseph Frobisher and François were on the Saskatchewan in
> the Frobisher-McGill—Blondeau interest... An old
> Canadian who had been upwards of 30 years among the
> Indians, had come in with three canoes equipped by one
> Solomon, a Jew from Montreal.[75]

Victor Lytwyn identified this French trader as François Jerome dit Latour,
and his financial backer as Ezekial Solomon.[76] A.J. Rae indicated that in 1774
William Holmes came into the Saskatchewan Country with Charles
Paterson and François Jerome dit Latour, with seven canoes on their way to
their post at Fort des Prairies (Fort à la Corne, Saskatchewan).[77] A.S. Morton
found references to these pedlars in Samuel Hearne's Cumberland House
Journal:

> A month after Hearne finished his log hut [at Cumberland
> House], the Pedlars came up the Saskatchewan on their

> way to their wintering grounds. The two Frobishers, Joseph and Thomas, and their partner, Charles Paterson, with Francois, in the company came... Their partner, Paterson, with François, was going up the Saskatchewan with 12 canoes and 60 men. These two, while in friendly association, were probably connected with different firms in Montreal—Paterson ... with the Frobisher-McGill partnership, and François with Finlay. François, as has been seen, had come inland the year before independently of Blondeau, but had entered into an arrangement and occupied what came to be called Isaac's House jointly with him... Thus, the Pedlars were on all the water-ways converging on Cumberland House.[78]

The fierce competition taught the pedlars that they were better off combining their interests and cooperating so that they could all profit while putting the HBC at a disadvantage.

In 1775, Alexander Henry travelled along the Saskatchewan with Paterson, Holmes and two Frenchmen (unnamed) which is odd because he was probably with the Canadians along the Saskatchewan. He did not mention Franceway, although the latter was still wintering in the area. Morton writes that

> There was a Frobisher post somewhere beyond Lake Winipegosis. A Master along with Isaac Batt was to winter at some place to be agreed upon with the Indians.[79]

After 1784, the references to Franceway were less frequent; and they stopped by 1777, when Cocking reported Franceway had left the country after killing an Indian.[80] He retired to Detroit, and his death date is unknown.[81]

To recapitulate, François Jérôme *dit* Latour, the son of the militia captain in New France, went to the Great Lakes and *pays d'en haut* in 1727. By 1743, he was assigned to the La Vérendrye party to explore for the *mer de l'Ouest*. In 1749, he was working at Fort Bourbon on Cedar Lake, on the strategic route linking York Factory with the interior, and the competition of these Canadians forced masters at York Factory to send men inland to gather information about the competition and persuade the Indians to maintain their custom of trading at the Bay. Several of these men, such as William Tomison, William Pink and Matthew Cocking, encountered a trader named Franceway, Saswe, Shash, or Shashree. His surname was never mentioned and the only French Canadian who had a fur trade license out of Michilimackinac at this time was François Le Blanc. Genealogist Cyprian

Tanguay suggested that the Jerome family used other surnames, such as Beaume/Beaune, "*dit* Latour," and Le Blanc. Both fur trade historians A.J. Ray and Victor Lytwyn argued that the famous Franceway, who was one of the earliest French Canadian traders up the North Saskatchewan and who had been in the country (according to Cocking) for thirty years, was François Jérôme *dit* Latour.

The other piece of the puzzle is that there were Jeromes mentioned in fur trade records as living on the Saskatchewan River, in the area around Fort Carlton, for three generations after François before they moved to the Red River Settlement in the 1820s.[82] Pierre Jerome/Gerome was an interpreter at Fort des Prairies on the Saskatchewan in 1799 and 1804.[83] Similarly, when Alexander Henry the Younger moved to Fort Vermilion in 1809, he hired "Jerome" as his Cree interpreter.[84] The fact that this man was working as a Cree interpreter suggests that either he had been living in the area for a long time or he had a Cree wife and children.

Pierre Jerome died at Carlton in 1821 and the officer in charge, John Peter Pruden, suggested that he had been "many years in the service of the NWC as Interpreter for the Crees and I should suppose he must be upwards of 80 years of age."[85] This would put his birth at about 1740.[86] At the same time there was at Fort Carlton a young Martin Jerome aged about 20 years old, but it appears that a Martin Jerome Sr. was between the generations of Pierre and Martin Jr. Martin Jr. listed his father as Martin Sr. on his marriage certificate; and his sister, Marie Louis Jerome, born in 1803, listed her father as Martin on her St. Boniface marriage record.

Henry's journal also suggests that the man he used as Cree interpreter was younger and more active. When he worked at Fort Vermilion in the winter of 1809–10, he worked *en dérouine* collecting furs from the Crees: for example, September 19, "Jerome returned from the Cree camp, where there are 20 tents"; February 13, "I sent Jerome off *en dérouine* to Mistanbois"; February 20, "Jerome and [La]Rocque cutting out pemmican bags"; May 21, "Jerome & the lads supply us with fish."[87] Jerome also appears on Henry's census of 1809 with no wife, but with four children. On the June 3, 1810, roster of families we find that in 17 tents for Henry's men, Jerome and LaPierre shared a tent with 2 men, 1 woman and 5 children.[88] These records suggest that Jerome had lost his wife and was raising the four children himself. However, only two of the four later showed up in Red River Settlement in the 1820s. Jerome's father was probably Martin Jerome Sr., who had no birth record in Quebec and was probably born along the Saskatchewan and lived there all his life.

In the North West Company Fort des Prairies Equipment Book of 1821,

Martin Jerome, age 19 (born around 1802) has an account, showing him to be a "Native of Fort des Prairie," i.e., born on the Saskatchewan; his good friend, Jean-Baptiste Letendre Jr., was also listed in the account book. Called "Samart Gerome," Martin did some work for the master at Carlton House in 1821–22. For example: December 17, "Sent off Wm. Gibson and 2 half Breed young men with the packet for Dog Rump Creek"; January 30, "Samart Gerome and Battoshes Son [Letendre] arrived from Dog Rump Creek House, but brought no letters from Edmonton House"; June 5, "Mr. Monro, Samart Gerome, Beauchamps and Gausawap arrived with horses from Edmonton, 15 of which belonged to the Company [HBC] and 6 to private individuals."[89] Chief Factor Colin Robertson at Norway House requested Pruden to have guides ready for his trip from Carlton to Edmonton in 1822, and suggested that "Jerome and the White Eagle's son are supposed to be the best guides."[90]

In the early 1820s, Martin Jerome Jr. became a freeman and moved to Red River Settlement with the Letendre family after the death of Pierre Jerome. He married Jean-Baptiste's sister Angelique and is listed in many of the subsequent censuses.[91] This migration to Red River by the Jerome and Letendre families paralleled the general movement of freemen and their families to the settlement, where they could raise their families close to schools and churches.[92] These young men were thus typical of Cuthbert Grant's Métis cavalry: multilingual with French and Cree as their main languages, expert buffalo hunters, and plains traders with no ties to Quebec.

It is not possible to determine the exact relationship of François, Pierre, Martin Sr. and Martin Jerome Jr. (Samart Jerome). It appears that Pierre was born in Quebec, and Martin Sr. and Jr. on the Saskatchewan. Their mothers must have been Indian or mixed-blood, but their identity is unknown. The fate of François's Indian wife and child is also unknown. It seems likely that Pierre was the nephew of François Jérôme dit Latour, the son of the latter's brother Pierre, born in 1718. A Pierre Jerome was married in Quebec in 1740; it is possible that he had a son Pierre a year or so later, which would be the right age for the man who was Cree interpreter at Fort Carlton and died at the approximate age of 80 in 1821.[93] The difference in ages suggests that Pierre was Martin Jr.'s grandfather, and that Martin Sr. died between Henry's departure (1812) and the consolidation of the fur trade companies in 1821. It is not unreasonable to suggest that there were three generations of Jeromes on the Saskatchewan after François, and that they must have had some connection with him.[94]

John Foster speculated that it was freemen of the 1770s and later, like François and Pierre, who married native women and gave birth to the young people who became the New Nation, the Métis of the Red River Valley. He argued that going *en dérouine* to the Indian camps, marrying Native women, but still being outsiders led to the development of this separate identity.[95] The only example he used was that of the Dumont family, whose descendant Gabriel became famous in the 1885 confrontation with the Canadian government.[96] This was the first step in an inter-generational process of ethnogenesis. Language was also a good indicator of new ethnic identity. It probably took several decades for the in-group language of Michif (French nouns and Cree syntax) to develop in the buffalo hunters' camps, but I think that Foster would have agreed that this probably happened outside of Red River before 1815.

The Jerome family are thus a useful prototype of Métis ethnogenesis; by the third generation of French Canadian descendants living as Cree interpreters, they evolved a separate identity from the parent groups. They became the great horsemen and buffalo hunters, fluent in Cree and using Indian technology to survive on the plains and parkland. They were economically and psychologically independent, giving rise to the name by which they called themselves: *gens libres* or Freemen. They could support their families and hunt communally, sharing with their friends and relatives, while at the same time participating in the capitalist system of profit by trading their surplus dried meat and fat for pemmican to the fur trade companies, who were dependent on them for country produce to supply the canoe brigades to the northern fur fields. Although Ray suggested that the Plains Cree and Assiniboine became the provisioners in the Plains fur trade in the 1790s because the pedlars were taking the furs, it may be that the sons of mixed ancestry who travelled with the Cree bands and spoke Michif took over this function to make a profit rather than for subsistence.[97]

Foster identified the first step in the process, but he was only partly right. It was young men like Martin Jerome Jr. and his friend Jean-Baptiste Letendre Jr. who developed the freemen culture and carved out their economic niche in the provisioning trade, separate from the Quebec traders and Plains Indians, which led to the development of the Métis. After the consolidation of 1821, when large numbers of these familes were no longer employed in the fur trade war, they moved to Red River, where they became the dominant group and claimed their birthright to the settlement of the North West.

4. The Northern Great Plains: Pantry of the Northwestern Fur Trade, 1774–1885 (1984)

Arthur J. Ray

Famous for their large-scale buffalo hunts and their ingenious Red River carts the Métis, indebted to their Indian lineage for their adaptation to local terrain and climate, played a crucial role in the provision of the fur trade. Taking advantage of the buffalo's repro- duction rates, which were sufficient to allow for a constant supply in spite of the inevitable wastage, Métis economy also came to rely on an involvement in the buffalo robe and hide trade.

The expansion of the fur trade into the Athabasca and Mackenzie River drainage basins in the late 18th century had major implications for the trading system that had already been established in the northern Great Plains. Operating a burgeoning network of posts posed serious logistical problems for the competing Hudson's Bay and North West companies. The boreal forests could not provide sufficient food to feed men stationed at the growing number of posts and those who manned the canoe and boat brigades plying the routes between them. European food was too costly to import in large quantities. Even more important, cargo space in canoes and York boats was limited. The proportion of that space devoted to provisions had to be kept to a minimum. Complicating this problem, the transportation season was too short to permit crews to hunt and fish along the way. For these reasons, food had to be obtained in the country and stockpiled at strategic locations along the transportation routes.

The European traders quickly realized that the parkland and prairie areas could serve as the pantry for the western fur trade. This region could produce large food surpluses and it was strategically located beside the main supply line of the northwestern fur trade (Figure 1). In order to collect

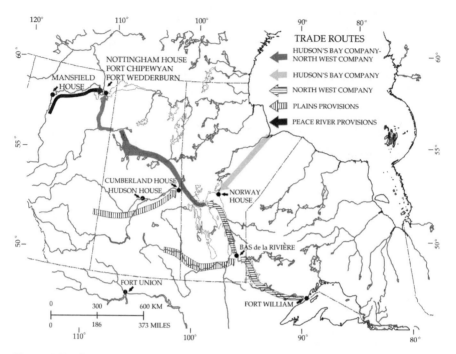

Figure 1. Trade routes.

plains provisions, the Hudson's Bay Company and the North West Company built posts along the North Saskatchewan as well as the Red and Assiniboine rivers between 1779 and 1821. The provisions obtained from the Saskatchewan area were forwarded to Cumberland Lake for use by the Athabasca-bound brigades of the two companies. In the southern Manitoba area, the North West Company sent its foodstuffs to Fort Bas de la Rivière on the lower Winnipeg River for use by its canoe brigades as they travelled between Cumberland Lake and the Rainy Lake-Fort William area. The Hudson's Bay Company forwarded its provisions from southern Manitoba to Norway House, at the head of Lake Winnipeg, where they were picked up by inland brigades travelling to and from York Factory. Even with these new logistical arrangements a large proportion of cargo space continued to be taken up with provisions (Table 1).

Indians were quick to appreciate the opportunities the new provision market offered to them. For instance, in 1779 the Hudson's Bay Company built Hudson House on the North Saskatchewan River to obtain provisions for Cumberland House. Within a year, the local Indians were burning the surrounding prairies in the autumn to prevent the buffalo (*Bison bison*) herds from approaching the post. By making it impossible for the traders to hunt

| Table 1. Proportion of North West Company Canoe Space Devoted to Provisions, 1814 ||
Destination from Fort William	% Provisions
Athabasca	34
Athabasca River	39
English River	38
Rat River	42
Upper Fort des Prairies	48
Lower Fort des Prairies	38
Upper Red River	25
Lower Red River	24
Fort Dauphin	28
Lake Winnipeg	37
Based on data in Williams S. Wallace, *Documents Relating to the North West Company* (Toronto: n.p., 1934), 277–79.	

buffalo themselves, the Indians hoped to increase the prices that they could demand for the provisions they brought to barter. This Native practice became commonplace in the parklands.[1]

The foodstuffs that the Indians supplied consisted almost entirely of dried buffalo meat (jerk meat), pounded (powdered) meat, grease and pemmican. The butchering and processing was done by Native women. Drying meat involved cutting it into long strips about 0.6 cm (0.25″) thick. The strips were then hung on wooden slats supported by tripods of sticks. It took two or three days for the meat to dry. The better quality dried meat was packed into bundles. The remainder was dried further over a hot fire until brittle. It was then laid out on a buffalo hide and pounded into a powder. This powdered meat was dumped into a kettle containing boiling fat or marrow. As it cooked the mixture turned into a paste. Crushed berries were often added at this time. While still boiling hot, the paste was poured into leather bags which were sealed as tightly as possible. The mixture was then allowed to cool until it was hard. This very nutritious food concentrate was known as pemmican.[2] It was highly stable and could be stored for long periods of time. For these reasons, pemmican was an ideal food for people on the move. It could be eaten right from the bag without any further preparation, roasted in its own fat, or boiled.[3]

The expanded market for buffalo meat products after 1780 had significant implications for the Native suppliers. For example, it is reasonable to suppose that the prehistoric demand for dried provisions by parkland/grassland groups was limited because these groups hunted buffalo to some extent at all seasons of the year. Therefore, a large portion of their food consumption would have consisted of fresh or previously frozen (in winter) meat.[4] Dried provisions were used in emergencies when herds were not present locally, when travelling, or when engaged in raiding expeditions. Pemmican was especially important in the latter circumstances since it did not have to be cooked. Being able to avoid using fires while on the warpath was an important consideration in the open grasslands, where smoke was visible for miles.

Besides domestic use, nomadic hunters probably also traded dried meat and pemmican with horticultural Indians who lived in the Missouri valley during the late prehistoric period.[5] In addition, some exchange undoubtedly took place when local food shortages were common in the forests. However, there is no reason to suppose that this trade was extensive.

In light of these considerations, it is clear that the fur trade provision market would have served to increase the importance of pemmican as an article of commerce. Whether or not this market stimulated the initial commercialization of the hunt is uncertain at this time because there is some archaeological evidence that suggests there may have been an increased output of dried provisions in the late prehistoric era.[6] On the basis of this evidence the archaeologist Thomas Kehoe has argued that the commercialization of the hunt began before European contact.[7] If Kehoe is correct, the development of a fur trade provision market may have simply served as a catalyst which accelerated a trend that had begun earlier. It is unclear why the process would have begun in the prehistoric/protohistoric periods. Possibly the incentive for increased pemmican production in the late precontact period was related to the increase in warfare that was associated with the northward spread of the horse. Acquisition of this animal may also have served to increase intertribal trade. Whatever the causes for the increased output may have been, it is clear that in the historic period the expanded output of provisions was aimed at serving a new external market.

While a changing economic climate provided the incentive, technological changes resulting from European contact made it easier for Native groups to expand their production of traditional meat products and to transport them. For instance, historical accounts of pemmican-making indicate that buffalo fat was melted in copper or brass kettles.[8] It is uncertain how fat would have been melted down on a large scale in prehistoric times given the relatively poor quality ceramics that Indians possessed (judged by modern technical standards) and the fact that plains Indians used the buffalo paunch extensively as a cooking container. Being limited to this domestic equipment meant that most foods had to be either stone-boiled or roasted over an open fire. Indeed, when writing about the Métis (descendants of Indians and

Europeans) buffalo hunts in the middle of the 19th century, Red River settler Alexander Ross noted that a great deal of meat, fat, and bone marrow was wasted because the Métis hunters lacked a sufficient number of kettles to process it.[9] Ross's observation is of particular interest given the fact that the Métis undoubtedly were better equipped with kettles than their Plains Indian cousins. Thus, although kettles would have offered the prospect of improved efficiency of meat processing, the limited quantity of kettles available as late as the middle of the 19th century was a factor that set limits on the amount of pemmican that groups could make from their kill. In other words, food wastage may have been partly a function of the per capita distribution of kettles. It may be that prehistoric pemmican production occurred only on a relatively small scale owing to technological constraints.

Hunting efficiency and transportation capability were affected by the introduction northward of horses from the southern plains where they had been brought by the Spaniards. By the early 1700s horses were found in the southern Alberta region, and by the 1740s they were being adopted by Indians in southern Manitoba. Horses altered summer hunting practices in that the animals enabled Indians, and later Métis, to "run" the herds. This involved having a group of men approach a herd as closely as possible before it took flight. Once the buffalo stampeded, the Indian hunters chased after them on their horses. Being faster than the fleeing buffalo (a buffalo was said to run at two-thirds the pace of a horse), a good buffalo pony enabled Indian hunters to ride up alongside of their prey and kill them at close range with arrows, lances or muskets. The chase usually continued until the horses were tired. As in the past, the Indian women and children followed, often on foot, to butcher the fallen prey. Although not without its hazards, this method of hunting was less risky and probably more efficient than the older walking surround or fire drive. Ross witnessed a Métis "buffalo run" that lasted two hours and yielded 137 animals. This is a kill rate of slightly more than 11 per minute. In terms of the 40 men involved, however, it is less impressive, giving each hunter an average of 3.5 animals.[10] Perhaps of greater importance, horses gave the plains hunters the potential of carrying larger loads at a faster pace than when dogs were the sole beasts of burden.[11] However, the potential was not fully realized because of limited availability. Many Indian groups in southern Manitoba and eastern Saskatchewan were "horse-poor." They did not have enough mounts for everyone. Therefore, the speed of these groups was limited to their slowest pedestrian members. In contrast, the Métis had a relative abundance of horses. They often travelled with riding horses, buffalo-running ponies (which were used solely for that purpose), cart horses and pack horses.

As the fur traders pushed into the Athabasca and Mackenzie River country, they quickly realized it was necessary to have an advance food supply base to augment meat products obtained in the prairie region. The mainline of the fur trade skirted the edge of the Canadian Shield, where many large lakes (Great Bear Lake, Great Slave Lake, Lake Athabasca, Lake Winnipegosis and Lake Winnipeg) teemed with fish. The fisheries developed on these lakes supported a number of trading posts. However, even though fish could be smoked, dried or, in the case of sturgeon, processed into pemmican, it did not become an important voyaging food.[12] It is unclear why. Perhaps it was related to food preferences. It is also likely that fish pemmican would have had a shorter "shelf life" than buffalo pemmican. The failure to exploit the great inland fisheries meant that alternative sources had to be developed. The Nor'Westers were the first to confront this problem and in the late 1870s they turned to the Beaver Indians living in the Peace River valley to supply them with the additional food. By the turn of the century the North West Company was relying on the Peace River area for all of its dried provisions in the region. This meat was sent from the Peace River valley to Fort Chipewyan where the Nor'Westers used it to outfit their canoes bound for Cumberland House from Peace River, Great Slave Lake, and Lake Athabasca.

In 1802 the Hudson's Bay Company moved into this area and built Nottingham House on Lake Athabasca, near Fort Chipewyan. It was hoped that the men at this post would be able to feed themselves on fish. Like the Nor'Westers, the Hudson's Bay Company men also realized that they would need to tap the Peace River country for more food. They launched this effort with the construction of Mansfield House on the Peace River in 1802. Realizing the strategic importance of the Peace River supply base and wanting to block the Hudson's Bay Company's push into Athabasca and Mackenzie river country, the Nor'Westers quickly moved to intimidate the Hudson's Bay Company on the Peace River. This venture was successful and the Hudson's Bay Company was forced to withdraw. Having failed to secure a supply base in the Peace River area, the Hudson's Bay Company also found it was necessary to close Nottingham House in 1809 and temporarily abandon the Athabasca country. They did not return again until 1815 when they built a new post, Fort Wedderburn, on Lake Athabasca. Once again the Hudson's Bay Company battled with the Nor'Westers for access to the provision trade of the Peace River country. This time they were successful and secured a toehold in the region by 1819.[13]

The battle for control of the provision trade at this time was not limited to the Peace River country. It erupted in the Red River area also. In 1812 the

Hudson's Bay Company established the Selkirk agricultural colony on the banks of the Red River. This posed a strategic threat to the North West Company since the colony lay astride its provision supply line in that quarter. The seriousness of the danger was manifest in the winter of 1814. The colony was seriously short of provisions. In an effort to deal with the problem Miles Macdonell, the autocratic colonial governor, issued his "Pemmican Proclamation" on January 8, 1814, forbidding the export from the area of any provisions that had been secured or grown there. All provisions were to be reserved for the colony's consumption.[14] Macdonell's action provoked the so-called "Pemmican War" in which the Nor'Westers, using the Métis as pawns, sought to destroy the colony.

The struggle for control of shares of the vital Plains provision trade continued in all quarters until the union of the two rival companies in 1821. Although this union temporarily reduced the overall labour force of the fur trade by as much as one-third, thereby temporarily diminishing the size of the provision market, this market rebounded a short while later. But after 1821 a new group emerged as one of the major suppliers—this group was comprised of French (the Métis) and English mixed-blood men. Most of these men were laid off by the Hudson's Bay Company in the early 1820s. Some simply quit. Previously most of them had been stationed at the parkland posts and had Native wives of Parkland Indian ancestry. The mixed-bloods congregated near the Red River colony and around the present town of Pembina, North Dakota, until they abandoned the latter location in 1823. These men and their families combined the older Indian ways with the newer ones of the settlers. They established small farms, but between sowing and harvest they hunted buffalo for dried provisions and hides. From late August until early November many of them left for the plains a second time to secure fresh meat and buffalo robes for the winter. Their hunts were like those of their Plains Indian relatives, but there were also some differences. One was in the mode of transportation that the mixed-bloods used. The Métis employed two-wheeled carts fashioned of local materials (wood, leather and sinew) instead of the travois. These were the famed Red River carts. They were pulled by one horse, or an ox, and carried some 900 pounds of cargo—nearly double that of the travois. The carts gave the mixed-bloods great mobility, enabling them to extend their foraging range as far westward as was necessary to pursue the buffalo herds. Further, Indians tended to follow the herds, hunting them at all seasons. Since the mixed-bloods, who lived in fixed settlements, worked for the Hudson's Bay Company on a seasonal basis, and farmed on a part-time basis they could not hunt all year round. Therefore, their buffalo hunting was confined largely to two hunts annually. These hunts were much like those organized by the Indians, except that Métis hunters skinned the slain buffalo and brought the carcasses back to camp rather than having their women and children follow in their wake. For both groups, the women did the butchering and meat processing.[15]

Recently it has been argued that the mixed economy of the Métis was better suited to the regional economic situation between 1821 and 1870 than was the way of life chosen by settlers who attempted farming on a full-time basis.[16] The farmers were frequently devastated by natural disasters. Colonial observer James Hargrave noted in 1870 that the Red River settlement had been completely flooded in 1808, 1826, 1852, and 1861, and had been plagued with locusts in 1818, 1819, 1857, 1858, and 1864 through 1868.[17] Besides these 13 major calamities in 60 years, droughts and early frosts were also a frequent problem. These recurring misfortunes kept the colony from producing a steady agricultural output sufficient to meet its own provision requirements. Poor storage and handling procedures frequently reduced the size of any surpluses produced.[18] Therefore, the developing colony remained partially dependent on the buffalo hunt to survive. This dependency extended the size of the provision market beyond that provided by the Hudson's Bay Company.

The Métis, as competitors of the Parkland Indians for the provision market, were most successful in southern Manitoba. One can assume that they satisfied nearly all of the colony's needs and a significant portion of the Hudson's Bay Company's requirements in that quarter. Posts situated along the middle and upper reaches of the Assiniboine River and North and South Saskatchewan Rivers and their tributaries supplemented the provisions that the mixed-bloods brought to Red River. Most of these western posts conducted the bulk of their provision trade with Indian groups. As in earlier years, these provisions were transported to Cumberland House and Norway House.

The dimensions of the provision market created by the fur trade can be pieced together by employing scattered bits of information that are available. For example, in the first decade of the 19th century the North West Company was obtaining an average of 12,600 lb. of pemmican from its Red River department and 27,000 to 45,0W lb. from the Saskatchewan area.[19] This gives an average annual total of between 39,600 and 57,600 lb. of pemmican for the North West Company from the prairie/ parkland area. Historical accounts provide somewhat contradictory statements about the amounts of fresh meat that were needed to produce a bag of pemmican. James Hargrave stated that the meat of one bull made a 100-lb. bag of pemmican, while Father G.A. Belcourt claimed it took two buffalo cows to produce a 90-lb.

bag of pemmican (one cow yielded 45 lb. of pemmican). But he added that experienced hunters reckoned it took eight to 10 cows' meat to fill one cart with pemmican (one cow = 90 to 112.5 lb. of pemmican).[20] There is a discrepancy in these figures of over 100%. Guillaume Charette, a Métis, observed that it took 4,000 cows to fill 500 carts with pemmican, or eight per cart.[21] This suggests that Belcourt's second figure is the more accurate estimate. Data obtained from the North West Company post of Fort Pembina reveal that the mean dressed weight of 35 bulls killed during the winter was 514 lb. while that of 112 cows was 402 lb.[22] In light of these various sets of figures, it would have taken approximately 350-440 lb. of fresh meat to produce 90–100 lb. of pemmican. This represents a weight loss of between 72% and 80% using cows and bulls. Using cows exclusively the range is 72–77.5%.

All historical sources agree that cow's meat was preferable for all types of consumption. F.G. Roe concluded that this preference was on the order of 10 to one.[23] More bulls would be taken only if there were not enough cows. Given the very strong historical preference for cows, and assuming a 75% weight loss in processing, it is possible to estimate the number of buffalo required to meet the pemmican demands of the fur trade as well as Métis and Indian subsistence requirements. For this reason, the estimates for slaughter will be expressed in "cow equivalents." On this basis it would have taken between 158,400 and 230,000 lb. of fresh meat to yield the quantity of pemmican the North West Company needed annually in the early 19th century. This represented roughly 400 to 575 buffalo cows. If we assume that the Hudson's Bay Company's requirements were the same during this period, the combined demand could have been met by killing fewer than 1,200 animals.

Table 2 gives the provision demand of the Hudson's Bay Company at 10-year intervals between 1830 and 1870. These figures have been translated into equivalents. These data reveal that the size of the company's pemmican and dried meat market increased over two and one-half times between 1840 and 1870. But the numbers of animals needed for slaughter remained relatively low, suggesting that the provision market accounted for only a small percentage of the total output of provisions in the northern plains region.

This conclusion is based on an estimation of the magnitude of the demand for buffalo meat products by the Red River Colony and the Native population. This estimation takes into account census figures for the colony, approximations of the Native population in the mid-19th century, scattered data dealing with food consumption at the beginning of that century, the ration rates employed by the Hudson's Bay Company, and transportation capabilities of the mixed-blood population. During the winter of 1807–08, 41

Table 2. Provision Demand of the Hudson's Bay Company				
Commodity	1840	1850	1860	1870
Pemmican (lb.)*	90,900	120,375	137,610	202,680
Dried Meat (lb.)**	20,000	16,600	11,000	9,000
Total	110,000	136,975	148,610	211,680
Price (sterling)/lb.****	£ s.d	£ s.d	£ s.d	£ s.d
Pemmican	3d	3d	4d	6d
Dried Meat	2d	2d	3d	4d
Inventory Value**** (sterling)				
Pemmican	£1,136 5s	£1,504 14s	£2,293 10s	£5,067
Dried Meat	£166 13s	£138 7s	£137 10s	£150
Total	£1,302 18s	£1,643 1s	£2,431	£5,217
Equivalent in Red River Cart Loads ***	122	152	165	315
Equivalent in fresh meat (lb.)	482,000	579,870	615,625	864,053
Equivalent number of buffalo cows	1,205	1,450	1,539	2,160

* Ray, Indians in the Fur Trade, 200–10.
** According to Belcourt, 1 cow = 67.50 lb. dried meat.
*** Cart load = 900 lb.
**** British Columbia Provincial Archives, Add MS, 220, "Standing Rules and Regulations, Northern Department, Rupert's Land, 1847–67."

men stationed at the North West Company post of Fort Pembina consumed 63,000 lb. of fresh buffalo meat over a 213-day period (September 1–March 31). This represents an average of 7.2 lb./man/day or about 5,360 calories. In addition, during the same period the men consumed three red deer (*Cervus elaphus*), five black bear (*Ursus americanus*), four beaver (*Castor canadensis*), three swans (*Cygnus* sp.), one white crane (*Grus americana*), 12 outards, 36 ducks, and 1,150 fish of various kinds.[24] This level of consumption was only slightly below the rations that the Hudson's Bay Company provided for its boat brigades. Company boatmen were given eight lb. of fresh meat per day, their wives four, and their children two. Allowances for employees and their families stationed at trading posts were one-half that of the brigades. A variety of other foods was consumed also. Applying the Hudson's Bay Company rates to the population censuses of Red River suggests that the buffalo meat consumption of the colony would have ranged between approximately 2,200,000 lb. and 4,400,000 lb./year in 1831, potentially rising to between 7,500,000 lb. and 15,000,000 lb./year in 1870.[25]

This simple prediction must be modified, however, to account for additional factors besides human population growth. The colony was making slow, if erratic, progress in its agricultural output. Also, transportation capacity did not expand sufficiently to carry the quantity of meat projected by the 1870 estimate. In 1870 Hargrave wrote that an average of 1,200 carts took part in the two annual hunts—roughly the same number as in the late 1840s despite the population increase. This indicates that the Métis hunters could have supplied a maximum of 1,080,000 lb. of pemmican (the equivalent of 4,320,000 lb. of fresh meat) from the August hunt and 1,080,000 lb. of fresh meat in the autumn if all of their cargo space was devoted to provision supplies. Of course, this was not the case given that they also carried hides and robes. Thus, the annual buffalo consumption by the Red River colony in 1870 would have had to be less than the equivalent of 5,400,000 lb. of fresh buffalo meat per year. This indicates a daily ration of meat of less than three pounds of fresh buffalo meat per adult male, or one-quarter less than the post allowance rate of the Hudson's Bay Company.

These calculations indicate that provision demands of the colony in 1831 would have generated a slaughter on the order of between 5,500 and 11,000 buffalo cows, while that of 1870 would have been under 13,500. This suggests that the maximum probable increase would have been less than two and one-half times between 1831 and 1870.

In 1856 Governor George Simpson of the Hudson's Bay Company calculated that the Plains Indians numbered just under 30,000.[26] Using this figure and applying the ration rates of the trading companies, the potential buffalo meat requirements of the Indians would have necessitated the slaughter of between 54,000 and almost 110,000 cows/year. In this case, the mean figure of about 82,000 is more likely, given that this number would closely approximate the size of slaughter that would be generated by a population of nearly 30,000 having a diet very similar to that of the men stationed at Fort Pembina in 1807–08.

As large as it appears, it should be pointed out that a projected kill rate of 82,000 animals per year is probably a conservative estimate bearing in mind that hunts were wasteful. During the summer season Indians sometimes slaughtered herds just to obtain the tongues and bosses for feasts. The rest of the carcass was left to spoil. Even without such profligate behaviour the hunt was wasteful by its very nature. The buffalo being a herd animal that was easily spooked to stampede, it was difficult for the Indians or Métis to kill only those that were needed. The most obvious example would be a cliff drive where it would have been impossible to control the number of animals that stampeded over a precipice. When running buffalo, hunters could not predict how many animals they could successfully skin and butcher. A number of problems could arise that would abbreviate the butchering.

These included raiding parties of hostile Native groups, rainstorms which rendered exposed meat useless, and nightfall. Predators, most notably wolves (*Canis lupus*), were effective scavengers after dark and took a heavy toll. According to one Métis hunter, besides these problems, the blinding dust of a run often made it impossible to carefully pick out the choice fat cows and many undesirable quarry were killed.[27] For all these reasons a significant allowance has to be made for wastage. Alexander Ross claimed that 2,500 animals were slain in one hunt by Métis, but the meat of only 750 buffalo was processed—scarcely one-third.[28] Given all of the factors that could influence the ability of a party to process the meat of its hunt, wastage rates would not have been constant. If we assume that Ross's experience represented extreme conditions, then presumably they ranged up to as much as 66%.

Taken together, it is clear that the combined food needs of the Hudson's Bay Company, the Red River Colony and the Indians would have necessitated a slaughter that amounted to the equivalent of just under 100,000 cows (2,160 + 13,500 + 82,000) per year. Considering wastage, a range of 100,000 to 300,000 is a possibility. Of this, just over 2% of the kill would have been generated by the fur trade.

Although a slaughter of this magnitude might appear to represent a serious threat to the survival of the wild buffalo herds, this apparently was not the case if Roe's estimation of the natural rate of increase of the species is correct. Based on data obtained from the captive animals in Wainwright Buffalo Park, Roe concluded the population increased 18%/year.[29] At that rate the combined provision hunt could have been sustained by a herd of between 555,555 (if 100,000 were killed) and 1,666,666 animals (if the slaughter equalled 300,000). Most calculations of the size of the northern herds exceed these figures by a wide margin. Therefore, it seems likely that other economic developments in the 19th century served to accelerate the slaughter beyond the level of a sustainable harvest and eventually destroyed this vital food resource. The first of these developments was the emergence of a strong market for robes. A few robes had been traded ever since the beginning of the fur trade in the area in the late 17th century. However, the volume of this traffic was limited since there were no sizeable markets in eastern North America or Europe. Also, these articles were bulky and heavy and, therefore, it was difficult to transport large quantities of them by canoe. But by the early 19th century the picture began to change. American traders pushed up the Missouri River and established Fort Union at the confluence of the Yellowstone and Missouri rivers. This post became an important hub of trade, drawing Indians from a large area including the prairies south of the Saskatchewan and Assiniboine rivers. Using bateaux and steamboats the American traders' transportation costs were substantially less than those of the Hudson's Bay Company which continued to depend heavily on the less efficient York boat and canoe. The Americans' cheaper transportation costs enabled them to cater to the growing market for buffalo robes in eastern North America. This market developed to the point where it triggered off a virtual flood of robes down the Missouri River toward St. Louis. It has been estimated that between 1815 and the early 1860s the trade of the Missouri River area fluctuated between 20,000 and 200,000 robes/year.[30] Probably 50% of this trade came from the Canadian prairies north of the upper Missouri.

In the early 1820s Governor George Simpson of the Hudson's Bay Company made a few exploratory efforts to see if the company could take part in this new market, either by making overland shipments to Montreal or by exporting robes via York Factory to London for reshipment from that city to New York. These initial efforts were failures.[31] Somewhat later the company became involved in the robe trade, but its share of the enterprise remained very small (Figure 2). The Company's annual trade never reached 20,000. The Métis also became involved, and in 1844 they began carting robes overland to the St. Paul area of Minnesota. Few data exist concerning the volume of traffic. However, in 1856 it amounted to more than 7,500 robes.[32] That year the Hudson's Bay Company traded almost 16,000 robes, suggesting that Métis trade comprised about 50% of that of the company's volume.

These sketchy data (in the case of the Métis) suggest that the combined robe trade of the Métis and the Hudson's Bay Company ranged between 10,000 and 40,000/year between 1840 and 1879. Added to the 10,000 to 100,000 robes that probably flowed southward from the Canadian prairies to the Missouri River posts, an annual winter slaughter of 20,000 to 140,000 animals is indicated.

The robe hunt must be considered in relation to the provision hunt to understand the combined impact that it had on the Native economy (Indian and Métis) and on the buffalo resource. Recall that the fur trade provision market consisted entirely of dried produce obtained from the summer hunts; therefore, no robes would have been taken as by-products of the 2,160 cows needed. Almost 11,000 of the 13,500 animals slaughtered for the colony's consumption were killed to produce dried meat products. Therefore, only about 2,500 (perhaps 7,500 if we allow for waste at the maximum rate) would have been killed for food during the robe season. There were about 6,000 Métis in Red River in 1870.[33] Allowing one robe for every man, woman and child per year for personal use, it is clear there would not

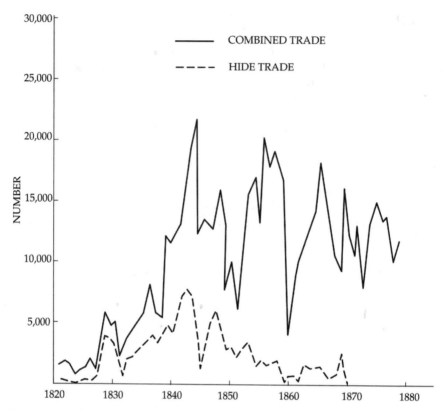

Figure 2. Hudson's Bay Company Northern Department hide and robe trade, 1821–1879.

have been any surplus left for trade. If, for the sake of discussion, we assume that the provision hunts of the Indians were spread out over the entire year, then 66% of the approximately 82,000 buffalo needed would have been slain at a time when robes could have been obtained as a by-product. This amounts to some 54,120 robes (perhaps 135,000 with a maximum wastage allowance). If we allocate two robes per Indian per year for clothing and bedding purposes (probably a conservative figure), it is necessary to sub-tract some 50,000 robes from the above figure to determine the number available for trading purposes. The result suggests that no by-product robes would have been available if Indian hunts were highly efficient and aimed primarily at meeting their food needs.

Adding together the median values of the estimated ranges of the volume of Canadian Indian robe trade to the Missouri River posts, the Hudson's Bay Company's robe trade, and the Métis traffic to Minnesota territory, it appears that the magnitude of the robe market for the region at mid-century was something on the order of 60,000 robes (40,000 + 13,000 + 6,000 = 59,000). This suggests that the development of the robe market could have had the effect of almost doubling the winter slaughter of buffalo (e.g., increasing it from just under some 56,600 to nearly 110,000). The problem is that we do not know if the Indians were able to take and process robes more efficiently than meat. If this was the case, then the robe trade may not have increased the Indians' winter kill at all if provision wastage was as high as 66%. If this was so, and all of the robes of the wasted animals were collected, then perhaps as many as 85,000 were available for trade. This seems unlikely, however, as robe processing, like meat preparation, was time-consuming although the rapid spoilage of the raw material was less critical.[34] Added to the summer hunt, conservatively estimated at just over 40,000 (27,060 + 2,160 + 11,000), the annual provision and robe slaughter probably ranged between 150,000 (assuming little wastage in the provision hunts), as much as 354,000 (if two-thirds of the provision kill were wasted and no robes were obtained from the carcasses). The latter scenario is unlikely.

The magnitude of the difference in the economic importance of the provision and robe markets is not easy to gauge since we have good data only for the Hudson's Bay Company markets and, as noted earlier, the company took part in only a fraction of the robe trade. As Table 2 shows, the dried meat and pemmican that the Hudson's Bay Company purchased was valued in Sterling at £1,302 18s. in 1840, increasing to £5,217. Considering the number of Métis and Indians involved in the trade, these are very small figures. In contrast, the Company bought between 4,000 and 22,000 robes/year during this period (Figure 2). In 1843, at the height of the company's trade, it valued prime robes at 5s. and common ones at 2s.6d. Using an average price of 2s.9d. (the returns did not specify the quantities of prime and common) the 1843 trade was worth about £3,025 or nearly two and one-half times more than the provision market. In 1870 prime robes fetched 10s. and common 5s. for an average price of 7s.6d. At these prices the approximately 11,500 robes bought by the company were worth about £4,312 10s. to the Indians and Métis. In other words, the Hudson's Bay Company's robe market was of roughly the same value as its provision market. Since the company's prices for provisions and robes had doubled between 1840 and 1870, the shift in relative value of the markets represented the growing volume of the provision trade (it almost doubled between 1840 and 1870), whereas the volume of the robe trade showed an irregular decline. Thus, for Indians and Métis who traded solely with the Hudson's Bay Company, it would appear that the provision trade was of increasing relative importance. However, few traded exclusively with the company. Given the very large market for robes in the United States until the 1870s, one can speculate that before 1870 most Indian and Métis hunters derived the bulk of their hunting income from selling robes.

In the 1870s technological developments in the tanning industry made it possible to process buffalo hides. This had the effect of creating an extremely large market. Attention very quickly shifted from robes to hides to take advantage of this new economic opportunity. The development of this new trade served to accelerate the buffalo slaughter for a number of reasons. Hides could be prepared more quickly than robes and required less skilled labour. This meant that Euro-Canadians could enter the field on a much larger scale than previously. The hide market was larger than that for robes, although the Hudson's Bay Company played a smaller role (Figure 2). Unlike the robe hunts, the kill was concentrated in a relatively short period. The dried provision needs of the Indians, Métis and the Hudson's Bay Company could have yielded something on the order of 40,560 hides. If the Indian and Métis population used two hides/year, probably a conservative number given the many uses hides served in their cultures, 60,000 hides would have been required for the Native population annually. In short, there was no surplus. Indeed, the need for hides likely led the Native population to slaughter more animals than their provision needs would have dictated, hence the "waste" noted earlier. If the estimates of food and hide needs are in the "ball park," one-third of the meat of the summer hunt could have been wasted as a result of the Native demand for hides which necessitated a higher slaughter rate. In any event, it is clear that the hide trade probably increased the Indian and Métis level of hunting much more sharply simply because there was virtually no surplus available as a by-product of provision hunting. Thus, the robe and hide trade greatly increased the attack on the herds, hastening the day when they would vanish forever.

The tell-tale effects of overkill were manifest as early as the 1820s. By that time buffalo ceased to frequent the Red River valley near the colony. In the late 1850s their appearance in the southern Manitoba area was becoming irregular and this caused Alexander Ross to comment that the combined attack on the herds, from the north by Canadian groups and from the south by Americans, was forcing the herds to retreat westward.[35] He foresaw the day when they would be totally destroyed. By the 1860s the buffalo were in sharp decline north of the Qu'Appelle and South Saskatchewan rivers. By the late 1870s, the herds were largely confined to southwestern Saskatchewan and southern Alberta areas.

In the early 1880s the buffalo had declined to the point where Native groups could no longer depend upon them for subsistence, much less produce a surplus of provisions, hides and robes for a commercial market. Thus, pemmican, once a staple of the fur trade, became very expensive (Table 2), rising from 3¢/pound in the 1830s to between 9.5 and 10¢/pound in the late 1870s. Also, the quality deteriorated. For these reasons, in 1880 the Hudson's Bay Company's chief factor at York Factory stated he was looking forward to the day when the company's dependence on this commodity would end entirely.[36] This came to pass a very short time later, and brought a great deal of hardship and suffering to the Indians and many of the Métis. Alternative game supplies could not meet their subsistence needs and provide them with a sufficient quantity of marketable products to maintain their former lifestyle. The blow was severe. In the 19th century these groups had become the most economically independent and powerful groups in the west. But their economy and society had a fatal flaw: it was based on the exploitation of a single renewable resource, at a rate that exceeded the level required for a sustained yield harvest. Thus the once-proud Grassland Indians and many Métis were reduced to poverty levels by the 1880s, and found themselves in a much worse socio-economic situation than their cousins in the wooded areas of the plains. The latter had never reached the same economic heights, but were spared reaching the same lows. The local provision market in the Peace River country led to the serious depletion of the wood buffalo population. But the market was organized very differently. Most of the meat was obtained by a relatively few Indians who were hired as post hunters. Therefore, income from this activity was not spread as broadly through the population. Also, since moose (*Alces alces*) was the preferred food animal for most of the local Indians, the assault on the buffalo in this area had very different implications for the Native inhabitants.[37] As this resource declined, the Woodland Indian bands were able to continue to support themselves by hunting, fishing and trapping. Meanwhile their grassland counterparts were reduced to subsisting on ground squirrels ("gophers") (*Spermophilus* sp.), and prairie dogs (*Cynomys ludovicianus*), and to relying increasingly on government assistance. The pantry of the prairie plains was bare and could never be stocked with natural surpluses again. There and then the era of the hunter yielded to that of the farmer and rancher.

5.   **The Twatt Family, 1780–1840: Amerindian, Ethnic Category, or Ethnic Group Identity? (1997)**

Paul C. Thistle

The northern Métis have often been neglected in favour of their Red River cousins. To redress this imbalance students of history need many focused, exploratory studies based on detailed archival research, permitting to identify the beginnings of mixed-descent groups in the old fur trade area. At the root of this pattern of mixed descent are interest groups which define a corporate identity and therefore shape the ethnic profile of future generations.

Introduction

The genesis of this study derives from some intriguing findings on the possible early development of a mixed-descent ethnic group in the Nipawin, Saskatchewan area which were not able to be used extensively in my earlier work on the history of initial cross-cultural contact and the resulting fur trade relations between Amerindian[1] people and Europeans in the lower Saskatchewan River region.[2] It was also stimulated by the early observation of Richard Slobodin that the distinctive cultures and histories of northern Métis groups have been (and we can say to a large degree continue to be) ignored in all of the scholarly attention paid to the Red River and more generally the Plains Métis groups.[3] In fact, one of the primary characteristics of the mixed-descent peoples in the Canadian West is the wide variety of social positions and settings, ecological and economic niches, as well as forms of self- and other-identifications which made these northern mixed-descent groups and their histories notably different from the Red River Métis.[4]

The major historical problem to be addressed here is: did a mixed-descent ethnic population develop as a separate self- and other-identified corporate group at this time and place and, if so, how was this process accomplished? This article is presented as a vehicle for testing some preliminary ideas and to identify some potential directions for further research. One particular mixed-descent group inhabiting the Nipawin, Saskatchewan area in the latter part of the 18th and the first half of the 19th centuries has been named in the Hudson's Bay Company (HBC) documents. This examination is a first step in a proposed full-scale study of the emergence of such populations along the lower Saskatchewan River. The current discussion is narrowly limited by the nature of the original research which focussed primarily on Amerindian-European trade relations in this region, as revealed in the HBC journal records from Cumberland House. I also acknowledge the criticism by Frank Tough that this earlier work relied too heavily on "impressionistic data" from the HBC journals, without reference to the statistical sources available in the accounts and census data for example.[5] This preliminary study remains open to this critique. However, it is recognized that, as discussed below, the research will have to be extended well beyond the Hudson's Bay Company Archives series of post journals.

The theoretical underpinnings of this study derive from some of the social scientific approaches to ethnicity. As a starting point, I take it as axiomatic that historical analysis can be broadened and strengthened a great deal by employing social science theory, methods, and data. In combination with historiographical considerations this approach is known as ethnohistory.[6] Such adjuncts are useful to historiography as long as the caution of R.A. Schermerhorn is kept in mind: that social theory developed within a modern social context cannot automatically be applied to explain historic situations which may lack the structural characteristics assumed for the validity of the theory.[7] Its true relevance must be tested on data such as those presented here and in the proposed study.

When looking at the history of the development of mixed-descent groups along the lower Saskatchewan River, the social science theories of ethnicity become useful to the analysis.[8] Several factors including geographic origin, common ancestry, kinship, endogamy, physical characteristics, culture, worldview, consciousness of kind, relations of the internal *Gemeinschaft* (or "primary group") type, separate institutions, ecological factors, and territoriality should be considered.[9] The reliance on the use of culture alone to define ethnic groups has been criticized,[10] and alternative discussions of ethnicity theory have focussed on the concept of boundaries (social, physical, psychological) which, although salient, in practice tend to be permeable and flexible—indeed "situational"—and may vary according to whether it is a self- and/or other-identified attribute.[11] Because ethnicity is such a slippery concept,[12] it is well also to consider Bruce G. Trigger's introduction of the

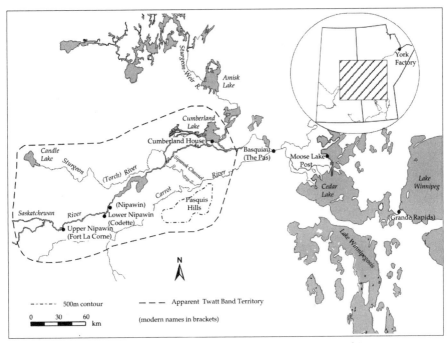

Figure 1. Map of study area showing location of names mentioned in text.

concept of "interest group" as the focus of analysis which examines common goals, behaviour, and, most importantly, common action demonstrated by a particular group.[13] This study will examine the available data using the markers of ethnicity identified in the social science literature, in order to help determine whether or not a functional self- and other-identified mixed-descent ethnic group evolved in the setting in question.

In this approach it is important to distinguish between what is referred to as an "ethnic category" (i.e. a grouping based solely on the perceptions of others) compared to a true "ethnic group" (i.e. a self-identified association of people who act as a corporate body).[14] People may be differentiated into a separate category by outsiders, but unless they identify themselves with and act in concert to pursue common interests, a true ethnic group can scarcely be said to exist. I take the "synthesist position" which holds that both self- and other-identification are necessary for the establishment of an ethnic group.[15] The discussion of whether a true mixed-descent ethnic group developed along the lower Saskatchewan River during this time period must await the full-scale study proposed. The focus here will be on only one particular mixed-descent family grouping and their characteristics.

Origins of Mixed-Descent Groups in the Region

Several factors—some of which are directly relevant to the case at hand—have been identified in the historical literature as being important in the development of self-aware corporate mixed-descent groups. The early scholarship of Marcel Giraud[16] pointed to the significance in this process of isolation from metropolitan influence and control, combined with the absence of European settlement.[17] The enduring impact of fur trade influences has also been identified as being central to the development of mixed-descent identity.[18] For example, Slobodin has indicated that, in the Mackenzie River district, the origins of the group he labels "Northern Métis" were bound up inherently with the fur trade frontier, in contrast to the "Red River Métis" group in the region who associated together more on the political and other factors related to their specific history in the Red River diaspora.[19] The observations of Hudson's Bay Company chroniclers James Isham and Andrew Graham had identified the existence of a new order of distinctive mixed-descent people in Rupert's Land by the 1740s and 1760s.[20] For example, differences in the physical appearance of mixed-descent individuals in comparison to Amerindians were being recognized in populations of the region by the mid- to late 1700s.[21] The factors of isolation from metropolitan influences, the relatively low proportion of Europeans in the "demographic ratio" which resulted in a lack of control by non-Natives over the social situation, and the entire context of the fur trade in the distant hinterland of Red River clearly apply to the following case.

Origins of the Twatt Band of Mixed Descent

The progenitor of the group of mixed descent which is the focus of this study was Hudson's Bay Company servant Magnus Twatt. He was born in 1751, a native of Orphir parish in the Orkney Islands.[22] Further research is required, but, if representative of his compatriots who by the end of the 18th century made up close to 80% of the HBC labour force, his background likely would have been subsistence farming in rather harsh, poverty-stricken conditions—a factor which made employment in the wilds of Rupert's Land relatively attractive to many Orcadians. Most of those entering the fur trade from this locale were from families with little land or influence occupying the lower ranks of Orkney society, until retirement from the fur trade with a sizeable fund of saved wages served to raise their status within their home community.[23] The Orcadians were also strongly influenced by Calvinism and some possessed a sound education.[24] Magnus Twatt had a level of schooling sufficient to enable him to pen some of the Cumberland House journals.

By 1771, Twatt had been taken on by the HBC as a general labourer to begin his service at York Factory.[25] In 1783 he was transferred to Severn post, returning to York Factory the following year. In 1785 his position was listed as "canoeman, " which would have meant that his duties began to take him inland into the study area. Between 1786 and 1791 he was carpenter and canoeman, becoming carpenter and steerman by 1792. In 1794, at his York inland posting, the titles canoe builder and occasional maritimer had been added. The year 1795 saw Magnus Twatt on a trip to England. He must have returned to Hudson Bay the following year (not in 1797 as the HBCA biographical reference maintains) as, at the end of September 1796, the Cumberland House journal showed that he was placed in charge of Cumberland House upon the departure of Peter Fidler.[26] Until 1800, Twatt was listed as a trader in his York inland posting.

The HBC records reveal that Magnus Twatt was highly regarded as an employee. Writing at Cumberland House in October 1793, Malcholm Ross described Twatt as a "trusty servant" who was worthy of much confidence and responsibility.[27] Evidently, he was also extremely "handy" for, on top of his titled duties as canoe builder, the post journal of January 1794 reported him to be working at the manufacture of sleds and snowshoes, articles for which the company was still largely dependent upon Amerindians.[28] Magnus Twatt also was designated as leader of many parties *en dérouine* which took him directly into Amerindian camps at a distance from the post with a supply of trade goods.[29] This would have placed him in close extended contact with Cree society, and would have helped to establish the close relations in evidence later. His name headed many of the Cumberland House journals between June 1791 and May 1795 as he was left in charge of the trade.

The first mention of Magnus Twatt's "family" to appear in the Cumberland House journals came on October 21, 1801 when his unnamed wife and sons arrived at the post, likely to sojourn with him during an illness which was described as the loss of power in the lower part of his body accompanied by delirium.[30] Even though Twatt remained ill, only one day later William Tomison entrusted him with leadership of an expedition to oppose the North West Company (NWC), which was establishing a post in the Carrot River area at the time.[31] In the past, Malcholm Ross had indicated that Twatt was remarkable for his dedication to his duties at Cumberland House. In spite of an injury from a fall in April 1794, Ross had noted, "his will to Work ... is such that I cannot Prevail on him to be at Rest a few days till he gets Better. but is Working now ... & he is hardly able to stand."[32] This is rather significant, as the vast majority of comments recorded in HBC journals regarding the attributes of workers were negative in character.[33] The

Cumberland House journal reported that Magnus Twatt died on October 23, 1801 while on the mission from Cumberland House to the Carrot River area.[34]

It is evident that Twatt had gained the respect not only of his supervisors but of Amerindians as well. One piece of evidence to support this contention arose in April 1779 when he took up the interests of some Amerindians who had been incarcerated near the Upper Hudson House post by NWC trader William Holmes in an attempt to force them to trade their furs with his concern. When Magnus Twatt protested this treatment, Holmes beat him "in a cruel manner."[35] Although such an interest may have been motivated more by loyalty to his employer than pure sympathy for the Amerindians involved, it would have served to place Twatt on the side of the aggrieved Amerindians, gained him some currency in their eyes, and may even indicate the operation of the kinship link to his wife's family. A review of the Hudson House records yet to be undertaken should help to clarify this question.

Further evidence of Twatt's relatively close relationship with Amerindians became apparent after his death when, on June 6, 1802, Tomison wrote to John Ballanden from Cumberland House that Twatt had been buried by the Amerindians at Carrot River: "the Indians had taken great pains in burying him, they also when in life did attempt to bring him to the House but he was too heavy for them to carry being a long distance from the water."[36] Such consideration would be consistent with a kin relationship to his wife's family and positive social connections developed over his time spent *en dérouine*.

Emergence of the Twatt Band of Mixed Descent

If we can assume that Magnus Twatt's two sons were at least in their teens when first mentioned directly as being involved in the trade by HBC Cumberland House journalists, their births would have occurred in the late 1780s. This timing would have coincided with Magnus Twatt's journeys inland from York Factory, beginning in 1785 when he was employed as a canoeman. Of course, company strictures against relations with Amerindian women were much less successfully imposed on HBC servants while they were away from the confines of York Factory.[37] Even lower-ranking company servants such as Twatt often were able to establish long-term and relatively stable relations with Amerindian women.[38]

After the death of Magnus Twatt, the first specific mention of his family being engaged in trading at Cumberland House was made by William Tomison in the journal entry of December 20, 1802.[39] This reference mentioned their arrival "for their father in law," bringing only ten made beaver,[40] which was his entire hunt since the previous August. From this we can see that the two young men continued to live with their mother's people and, as was commonly the case with the families of lower-ranking servants,[41] they were being accommodated within the Amerindian social setting, apparently associating themselves with their wives' father in the traditional Cree practice of "bride service" which was expected until the birth of a first child.[42] This was in marked contrast to other "boys" mentioned at that time in the Cumberland House journals who, as the offspring of HBC "gentlemen" such as I.P. Holmes, Alex Kennedy and George Sutherland, were obviously more closely integrated as part of the local society and labour force at Cumberland House then and previously.[43] The status of the father within the hierarchy of the HBC—increasingly in the 19th century two nearly exclusive categories of "gentleman" and "servant"—was a factor which has been identified as being crucial in determining the social placement of mixed-descent children.[44]

It seemed, therefore, that the Twatt boys had been enculturated into a Cree social milieu with what appeared to be limited direct influence from their father. With the present data at hand, it is not possible to determine how much contact Magnus would have had with his family while employed *en dérouine* away from Cumberland House. This may in fact have been substantial if his wife and family travelled with him while on his missions remote from the post. To paraphrase the lesson HBC seaman and explorer Samuel Hearne had learned several years earlier from his Amerindian mentor Matonabbee, "women were made for carrying," and success at almost any enterprise depended on their labour.[45] Traders such as Philip Tumor travelled long distances with women alone and reported that they were as useful as men on journeys.[46] Magnus Twatt himself wrote in August 1793 Cumberland House journal entries that women were sent with HBC servants to help carry provisions to the post[47] and HBC servants were often mentioned to be travelling with their families.[48] Thus, Twatt may have had more contact with and influence on his family than is immediately apparent from the journal records. Further research is required here.

In October 1806 the two Twatt boys were reported arriving at Cumberland House among a party of nine canoes in the company of Brassy and Chukoopan. "Old Brassy," who may have been the young men's father-in-law (or perhaps by this time their grandfather should children have been born serving to end bride service obligations in the meantime), was a leading Cree trader and supplier of country produce, whose territory extended to the north and west of Cumberland House. He was highly respected by Amerindians who, it was noted, brought presents to him from as far afield as Moose Lake.[49] The Twatts were reported to be in Brassy's party as it left the post on October 5, 1806 with a consignment of cargo from Cumberland House for "Ind" (inland or Indians?). Brassy's death on January 5, 1807 was noted in the post journal as follows: "he was the only old Indian belonging to this place—& much beloved by all the other Indians here—and according to custom the rest will do very little this winter.[50] It is not clear from the journals whether the young Twatts were still included among the five hunters who were said to be associated with Old Brassy at the time.

The Twatt boys, still named only as Magnus Twatt's sons, were next mentioned in association with a party of thirteen canoes under the leaders Belbird, One Eye, Jickoopan (almost certainly Chukoopan above), Cathead's son, Weenitisaway, and others who arrived at Cumberland House on May 26, 1807.[51] Belbird's territory was reported to be near the forks of the Saskatchewan River, some thirteen days' travel west from Cumberland House.[52] It may be that the Twatts were the grandsons (or perhaps sons-in-law) of Jickoopan (Chukoopan) rather than Brassy, since they were named immediately after the former in both the above cases. Further research in the account records should help to firmly establish the Twatt's family ties.

When the Cumberland House journals begin again after an unfortunate eleven-year gap between 1807 and 1818, Thomas Isbister reported the arrival of the Twatts with their mother, their wives and families on July 2, 1818 with 100 muskrat pelts "& are being noisy because we have no rum to give them."[53] As their mother had apparently remarried the year following Magnus Twatt's death, they may have associated themselves with her new husband's band or, as was typical of the highly flexible and dissoluble nature of Cree social organization, had begun a new co-residential group of their own. If included among the group of "Cumb^d House Indians" referred to subsequently, the Twatts may have traded their "old Iron works, such as hatchets, Chizels, Spears & Fils" at the nearby NWC post for the alcohol they were "very Clamorous for want of." The post journals were silent on the presence of the Twatts again until May 4, 1819 when they arrived with most of the other Cumberland House Cree "in order to partake of the general Spring Bouze."[54] In such cases, their general approach to the consumption of alcohol (which it should be acknowledged was derived from European practice[55]) and the overall fur trade economy was comparable to that pursued by the Amerindians in the region.[56]

By July 1819, we have been informed that the first names of Magnus Twatt's sons were "Mansack" and "Willock."[57] Named first in the journal entry (which tended to be indicative of a leadership role) among a group including Winter Child, Nesannecappoe, Ka Kee Ki Huggeemaco, Wethiny, and Long Legs, the Twatts and their wives arrived with a good deal of dried meat for the Cumberland House larder. "Mansag" (a variant spelling of Mansack) arrived in company with Big Frog and many others, again with dried provisions, on October 13 the same year.[58] In his Cumberland House report for 1819, Alex Kennedy named "Mansag Twatt" as "A good hunter who knows his value."[59] In concert with a significant number of Cree hunters, therefore, he was obviously participating in the fur trade economy in large part as a provisioner, which meant an intensification of hunting productivity rather than a complete conversion to a dedicated trapping lifestyle.[60]

The variation in spelling continued in an entry made on November 13, 1819 during a measles and whooping cough epidemic: "Mansae Twat a half Breed sent a request by the abovementioned Indians [reference is unclear] to Mr. Holmes to send some provisions for their relief. they are only one Days walk distant in the NW side of the lake in Sturgeon [modern Torch] River."[61] Notable in that the usual terminology applied to the Twatts to date had been "Indians," this is the first instance in which the Cumberland House journals distinguish them as "Half Breeds."[62] According to Jennifer Brown, the term itself was picked up from the NWC in the early 1800s, but was used by the HBC to refer simply to the objective facts of parentage, rather than in the sense of a distinctive sociocultural category as recognized by the NWC.[63] Nevertheless, the HBC traders must have found some real descriptive utility in this term in order to introduce it into their lexicon. The challenge of the proposed research will be to determine the meaning and context of its use in this region.

This terminology for the Twatts continued to be repeated on a sporadic basis such as in naming Willock in September 1829.[64] As became typical practice in HBC parlance,[65] however, the traders referred to the Twatts interchangeably by both terms—sometimes in the same reference—as did Thomas Isbister in this December 14, 1832 journal entry: "Twatt the Half Breed being very Solicitous all fall to purchase a Horse. rather than displease a good Indian I have Sold him one for 40 Skins 1/2 in fine furs."[66] It is clear, however, that the Cumberland House traders had specifically recognized the Twatts as being notable for their mixed descent by the end of the second decade of the 19th century. This is significant as the "other definition" which is one important marker for a true ethnic group.

In late September 1821, Mansack and Willock Twatt were being referred to as "Indians" by Cumberland House master Thomas Swain when they arrived with 350 pounds of dried meat.[67] At this time, their wintering territory was said to have been "some distance" away. From information in the

Cumberland House journals, they appeared to have been maintaining a migratory pattern—based on the seasonal fluctuations in the availability of food resources—similar to that of local Amerindians.[68] Their arrival at the post was variously reported as being from up the Saskatchewan River, Carrot River, Gun Worm River, Candle Lake, Shoal Lake, the Pasquia Hills, and from the Sturgeon [Torch] River areas. Anthropologists would classify this type of subsistence-settlement pattern as rather closer to the latter on the forager-collector continuum, meaning that their "logistical strategy" was based on the well-planned use of several types of resource locations and moving goods to consumers rather than continually shifting camps to game kills.[69] A study of their yearly cycle using the graphic approach suggested by historical geographer Frank Tough[70] could be employed profitably here to identify the seasonal round of the Twatts and compare it to that characteristic of Amerindians in the region. Prior to any formal study of this nature, it appears as if the yearly migratory cycles of the Twatts and local Cree bands were quite similar in nature at the time.

By 1825, however, the Twatts seemed to have established themselves more or less permanently around Nipawin. The locational data in the Cumberland House journals show that this appeared to have been particularly so for Willock by this date.[71] However, both Mansack and Willock also tended to winter at a common haunt in the Candle Lake district, a distance of about 100 kilometres to the northwest of Nipawin.[72] Nevertheless, references in the journals to either Mansack or Willock appearing from directions other than Nipawin essentially disappeared by 1827. If additional corroborating evidence can be found, these data may indicate the establishment of two other factors characteristic of an ethnic group: a centralized home base, and territoriality.

There is also evidence for the corporate nature of the Twatt's identity. As early as April 1826, the HBC journals were referring to "The Twatts Band."[73] For example, the corporate term "Mansack Twatts band" also was used to identify two young men who came to Cumberland House on March 25, 1838 to request that the group's furs be fetched from "Nepawan" by the HBC men.[74] The Twatt group, therefore, had clearly been specifically named as an identifiable corporate body by the HBC in the mid-1820s. According to sociologist Wsevlod Isajiw, such a perception by others is another crucial marker in the evolution of an ethnic group character.[75]

However, in terms of the perceptions of Amerindians about the Twatt's identity, on May 1, 1825 Kewaymettaway, a Sturgeon [Torch] River Cree, brought furs to Cumberland House, "Being the hunt of his *brother* [emphasis added] Willock also, Says that Mansack and his party are there also, Not having got their Credits prevents them from coming to the Fort till they have a trial amongst the rats."[76] This may indicate that Amerindians such as Kewaymettaway did not perceive the Twatts to be a separate and distinct social group, but rather had integrated them within the notion of affinal kinsmen. The Cree in this region considered and named parallel cousins as siblings.[77] Kewaymettaway, therefore, was likely Willock's parallel cousin, that is a son of Willock's mother's sister.

During the time of intense competition between the Hudson's Bay Company and the North West Company in this region prior to the union of the two companies in 1821, the Twatt brothers and the group of hunters associated with them had become the focus of a good deal of attention from both adversaries. The Twatts were employing the same strategies as Amerindians were in order to exploit the competitive situation successfully.[78] Cumberland House master I.P. Holmes reported the arrival of Long Legs, who was often mentioned as a provisioner for Cumberland House, and Willock Twatt with 313 muskrat skins on July 29, 1820 stating: "the latter Indian has for some time been trading with the NW[t] but has been induced again to join us, however this cannot be reckon'd any acquisition as both him and his brother Mansack will always be more expense to us than the value of their hunts will amount.[79] Of course, what was being reported here is that, as was common for Amerindian traders, Willock was following his own best interests, which did not necessarily coincide with those of the HBC. This rather rare negative view concerning the value of the HBC trade relationship with the Twatts was contradicted by Alex Kennedy's positive evaluation in his Cumberland House report of the previous year,[80] and this evaluation improved substantially in later years. Even so, the Twatts continued to exploit the trade situation vis-à-vis the HBC from this time until the end of the period under consideration. For example, even after monopoly conditions obtained after 1821, they were able to force the HBC to continue the earlier competitive practice of supplying them with trade goods directly in their camp rather than having to absorb the transportation costs themselves.[81]

In comparison to their Amerindian confreres, it is evident that the Twatts had developed some elements of a special relationship with the HBC at Cumberland House. For example, as Thomas Swain reported on 11 September 1820 when it was learned that they were ill, Willock Twatt and his wife were ordered to Cumberland House until they could recover.[82] Three days later it was noted that Twatt brought geese to the post, and so we can assume he was employed as a hunter for Cumberland House on occasion. Just as the Cumberland House traders depended on local Amerindians for crucial supplies of "country produce," meaning that many Amerindians adapted to the fur trade by intensifying traditional big-game hunting activities,[83] the Twatts also contributed a great deal to the Cumberland House larder. At the end of July 1825, Willock Twatt was reported to have arrived "from lower Nepowin"[84] with a good supply of "beat meat," "piece meat," grease, dressed moose, swans, and rats, part of which belonged to "three other Indians." This served to pay credits and trade for rum, tobacco, and ammunition.[85]

As the Twatts tended to be listed first among arrivals at the post, often in company with those such as the Flying Indian, Kewaymettaway, and others, it appeared as if they had become "leading Indians" in the eyes of the HBC in the 1820s. Mansack was reported to have visited the post in mid-October 1827 at the head of a group of ten Amerindians, with the hunts of five others accounting for a total of 10,758 muskrat pelts.[86] It also appeared as if they were similarly regarded by Amerindians. For example, in February 1827 James Leith wrote in the Cumberland House journal that the two Twatts had arrived at the post with nothing to support themselves, as they had used up all the provisions intended to supply a planned marten hunt in order to feed starving Amerindians from Lac la Ronge.[87] Such generosity was commonly expected from their leaders by Amerindians.[88] Indeed, by July 1837 Cumberland House clerk Charles Ross referred in a slip of the pen to "Magnus" (i.e. Mansack) Twatt as "Chief from the Nepiwans." In July 1839 John Lee Lewes named Mansack as "the principal of our upper Indians," referring to the Nipawin area.[89]

As early as 1824, the Twatt band clearly was being treated differently than Amerindians were, in that the former group received various special considerations from the traders at Cumberland House. For example, Chief Factor James Leith, after determining to reduce the amount of credit advanced to such consistent old Sturgeon (Torch) River Cree customers as Bucks Head and Methatoes, shortly thereafter greeted Mansack Twatt and advanced his credit along with six gallons of mixed rum "as encouragement."[90] When Mansack and his son-in-law arrived at the post in December 1825, the former was trusted with fifty skins in credit as the latter turned over his hunt to Mansack.[91] This trust was extended according to a report on September 27, 1826: "Mansack is to be answerable for the advances given to his Son in law and Brother and Willock to be answerable for his Son in law and Brother in law" to the tune of 130 skins and 110 skins respectively.[92] Credits continued to be advanced to the Twatts more readily than to Amerindians. In May 1827, when Amerindians were generally provided with only twenty skins in advance, Mansack and Willock were given fifty skins' credit each "as they are always sure in paying."[93] Indeed, Thomas

Isbister indicated in late August 1828 that the Twatts were regarded as the best trappers trading at Cumberland House, to the extent that they were given 100 skins each on credit on top of an additional 180-skin balance from the previous spring![94] On January 3, 1833, Isbister entrusted goods totalling 100 skins' worth of ammunition and tobacco to one of the Twatt brothers (unclear which), apparently for trading purposes, and stated: "he is an honest Indian & is responsible for the property he has in charge."[95] In March 1839 it was further reported that the Twatt band at "Neppowin" had "exerted themselves well this Year having up to this date doubled their hunts of last Year."[96] By the end of the period under consideration, therefore, the Mansack and Willock Twatt band was dearly held in high regard by Cumberland House traders, which in turn led to preferential treatment.

Mansack and Willock Twatt also came to be relied upon by the Cumberland House traders for intelligence and counsel which they trusted and acted upon. In August 1827, Thomas Isbister depended on Mansack Twatt to verify Amerindian claims that muskrats were plentiful in their territory before granting credits to them to support this hunt, at a time when the advances ranging from twenty to eighty skins' value were rarely being given out to Amerindians.[97] On July 7, 1839, John Lee Lewes went to the trouble of recording in the Cumberland House journal a rather lengthy response from Mansack Twatt regarding his views on the recently imposed prohibition on alcohol.[98] The opinions of no others were given such prominence by HBC journalists on this or any other such questions.

Discussion

For the present, the story of the mixed-descent Twatt family group will have to be interrupted due to the temporal limitation of my original research which was selected to coincide with 1840, the date when major new influences were introduced into the social setting along the lower Saskatchewan River in the person of Henry Budd—himself a mixed-descent Cree from Norway House—who became the first missionary to be established permanently in the region.[99] Budd commenced his Anglican mission at Cumberland House, moving it shortly thereafter to The Pas, and later spent several years at "Nepowewin"; thus, more useful documentation on the Twatt mixed-descent group can be expected to be found in this source. In concert with documents left by Roman Catholic missionaries who arrived on the lower Saskatchewan River shortly after Budd, research in mission records will provide an important additional perspective to help balance the HBC records relied on to date. Further documentation found in federal government records dealing with the study area became available beginning with the signings of the adhesion to Treaty Five and Treaty Six in 1876. The treaty-making process, the subsequent scrip commission activities, and the efforts of various individuals and families to move in and out of treaty will reveal a good deal about the ultimate disposition of the Twatt band of mixed descent. Another valuable source of information will be the genealogical work which is being carried out on the Twatt family by Alexander Deetz.[100] Of course, as mentioned at the outset, the financial and other records of the HBC which were not consulted during the original research should provide further information of significant value.

Beyond the work of Giraud and Slobodin on the distinctive natures of northern Métis groups, there are a number of factors which point to the logic and importance of a detailed study of the mixed-descent groups such as the Twatts along the lower Saskatchewan River. To begin, the ecological context of ethnicity will be rooted in the physiographic unity of the region, which is divided between the Saskatchewan River Lowlands Landscape Unit and, below the head of the Sipanok Channel, the Saskatchewan River Delta.[101] This boreal forest landscape and the river system itself provided a unifying "riverine" ecological base for the adaptation of the Twatts in a manner similar to that which played a role in the development of other northern mixed-descent groups.[102] Being the major east-west transportation corridor in these latitudes, the Saskatchewan River also carried along the length of its lower reaches both of the main outside influences: in Giraud's terms, the "Southern Nucleus" or the French speakers of the Campagnie du Nord and the North West Company, and the "Northern Nucleus" or the English speakers of the HBC. Thus, conditions for, and external influences on, nascent corporate groups were similar throughout the region.

Secondly, there existed a common pre-contact First Nations cultural base throughout this region in the form of the Late Woodlands Period archaeological tradition referred to as Selkirk. This archaeological culture is generally regarded to be pre-contact Cree.[103] Major Selkirk culture rendezvous sites have been found at regularly spaced locations from the forks of the Saskatchewan River all the way downstream to Grand Rapids, where the river flows into Lake Winnipeg.[104] With the exception of the Grand Rapids locale, where Rainy River culture predominated, all of these sites upriver evidence strong representation of Selkirk materials. These data demonstrate a common maternal cultural base for the development of mixed-descent groups in the study area. If confirmed by further testing, the archaeological hypothesis identifying distinctive Métis site characteristics proposed by David Burley[105] also may have significance in making a more decisive determination in this region.

In the early documentation referred to in this study, it is also clear that other mixed-descent groups emerged along the lower Saskatchewan River in locations apart from Nipawin. One in particular, known variously as "Basquiau," "Rivière du Pas," later "the Paw," or what is now The Pas, Manitoba, became an important base for groups of "freemen" and their families. As individuals who had left the service of the fur trade companies—French Canadians from the NWC and less commonly English speakers from the HBC—they established themselves as more or less independent actors in the homelands of their Amerindian wives' families.[106] Indeed, some 1,200 men (half in the Northern Department) were dropped from the HBC labour force after unification with the NWC in 1821.[107] A good deal of documentation—in some cases more extensive than that available on the Twatts—is available for the mixed-descent groups led by the freemen who had established themselves at The Pas during this period. These individuals included Joseph Constant, Tommie Humpherville, Baptiste Dejarlais, Jean Baptiste Gardipee, James Chaplette, Paul Laventure, Louis Versailles, Martin Lavalle, John Turner, and others. Except for the last named, the majority of these freeman-headed mixed-descent families at The Pas, referred to by the HBC as "halfbreed freemen,"[108] appear to have derived from Giraud's "Southern Nucleus" or French-Canadian paternal origins.

Apart from those amalgamations of freeman origin, there were also populations of mixed-descent who were associated much more closely with Cumberland House society than the sons of Magnus Twatt. These were the families belonging to a number of men engaged in continuous employment with the HBC. Among them were individuals such as John Ballendine, who was HBC post manager at Moose Lake beginning in 1829, as well as Cumberland House gentlemen George Sutherland, Thomas Isbister, George Flett, I.P. Holmes, and Alex Kennedy. For example, the Cumberland House journal of December 24, 1821 mentioned HBC servants McKay, Came(rere?), and Lajre(?) as returning to the post from The Pas: "The above three men are servants of the Company, but on account of their families (which would be a great burthen to us at the house) are allowed to provide for themselves during the Winter and are allowed the same price for their furs as the Indians."[109] In her seminal work *Strangers in Blood*, Jennifer Brown has indicated that such mixed-descent children became a significant demographic factor in Rupert's Land during this period.[110] The available documentation will have to be queried regarding the differences and similarities among these various mixed-descent categories, in order to determine the general patterns of ethnic identification and corporate action as distinct social groups—or otherwise.

Unfortunately, the present study cannot determine whether the Mansack and Willock Twatt band can be considered to be part of a separate functional mixed-descent ethnic group centred in this region, without recourse to the additional documentation referred to above, since the data brought to bear up to this point are suggestive, but not conclusive. The Twatts obviously were recognized by Cumberland House traders as identifiable "Half Breeds." They were explicitly regarded and clearly treated differently than their Amerindian confreres. By the mid-1820s they had firmly established a home base in the Nipawin area, apparently abandoning the seasonal migratory adaptation of Amerindians. The Twatt brothers were acknowledged as leaders of an identifiable group: they lived, travelled, and clearly acted in concert, and can thus be considered to be an "interest group" in Trigger's terms. If negative evidence has any value, the Twatts were never mentioned in the post's journals as being among the participants in the ceremonial feasting and dancing carried out on a regular basis by the Amerindians trading at Cumberland House. If positive confirmation can be found, this may indicate a cultural difference between the Twatts and the Amerindians of the region which would be further evidence of a potentially separate ethnicity.

On the other hand, Mansack and Willock Twatt appeared to have been raised by their mother as Amerindians away from the influences of Cumberland House society (although influence by their father is not out of the question) and, early on, were associated with Cree leaders such as Brassy and Chukoopan. They were classed as "brothers" by Kewaymettaway. Although in later years they may have served as jobbers for the HBC, until recourse is made to the Cumberland House account records it appears that their economic adaptation to the fur trade was identical to that of Amerindians at that time.[111] This is not to say that the Twatt brothers failed to identify themselves as a group distinct from Amerindians. However, there are no data currently available to me at this preliminary stage which indicate any particular ethnic boundary maintaining mechanisms at work in the case of the Twatts. Further research is required in order to make this determination.

What appears to be in evidence from the HBC journal records consulted to date is that the Twatt group constituted at least what anthropologists refer to as a "hunting (or task) group": in other words, a "local band" structured as a "sibling set" and operating in a manner similar to Amerindian co-residential groups found throughout subarctic Canada.[112] The question which cannot be answered at this stage of the research is whether or not the Twatts regarded themselves as a hunting group/local band which was ethnically distinct from their Cree relatives and hunting partners. Apparently, HBC traders placed them in what sociologists refer to as an "ethnic category." It remains to be determined by means of the research program identified above whether or not Mansack and Willock perceived themselves to be part of a functional corporate ethnic group characterized by mixed descent and interests which were distinctive from their Cree relatives and hunting partners. Despite the doubts of some scholars,[113] the possibility of such an identification and distinct set of mutual interests exists, especially given the presence of other groups at The Pas and elsewhere in the region who also potentially identified themselves as different from Amerindians. I feel that a full-scale study of the potential development of self-aware corporate mixed-descent groups along the lower Saskatchewan River would be fruitful and prove to be of significance to the history of this rather neglected region. It also would be a potentially worthwhile contribution to the general field of Métis historiography, which could counteract the problem recognized as "Red River myopia."

6. Wintering, the Outsider Adult Male and the Ethnogenesis of the Western Plains Métis (1994)

John E. Foster

For some fur trade employees, wintering provided an opportunity to engage in profitable manly activities. Ideally they would make trading contacts with Indian groups, forge marriage alliances, and enjoy the status and prestige accruing to freemen. Duly enculturated, their children would in time become cultural brokers in a local system of obligations serving the needs of both parental groups as well as their own Métis interests.

Over the past half-century the historical assessment of the 19th-century Plains Métis experience has altered from that of "losers" to that of "winners." The appearance of *les hivernants* (winterers) on the western Plains in the 1840s was, for Marcel Giraud, evidence that "primitivism" had won out over "civilization" in the lives of many of the Plains Métis.[1] More recently, for Gerhard Ens, the same evidence suggests a highly effective entrepreneurial response to an industrial market opportunity.[2] With the emergence of this scholarly reassessment historians have exhibited heightened interest in the fate of the Métis with the onset of settlement in the last decades of the 19th century. Métis primitivism is no longer an acceptable explanation for the marginalization of the Métis in this period. This same historical reassessment has heightened interest as well in the questions of what were, a century earlier, the circumstances and processes which gave rise to the Métis. As scholars have come to appreciate mixed Euro-Canadian and Indian ancestry as simply a biological fact, shared among many individuals who may choose to identify culturally as Indian,[3] Métis or Euro-Canadian, their interest has sharpened in terms of the circumstances and processes which constitute Métis ethnogenesis.[4] No longer are mixed ancestry and the social circumstances which gave rise to it sufficient explanation for the origins of the Métis on the western Plains.

The context for the processes and social relationships which gave rise to the Plains Métis was wintering as it was practiced by Montreal-based fur traders in the last quarter of the 18th century in *le pays sauvage* (Indian country).[5] The focal person was the *coureur de dérouine* (itinerant trader) or commis (clerk), the "outsider" from an Indian perspective, who led a trading party seeking to make contact with Indian hunters on their wintering grounds. The process of establishing this trade constituted the first step in the two-step process that gave rise to the Métis. During the first step three critical relationships were formed. The first was the country marriage of the outsider to a prominent woman of the Indian band. The second relationship involved the outsider in a kin relationship with the adult males of the Indian band. And the last relationship involved the *coureur de dérouine* in association with his fellow *engagés* (servants) as comrades and workmates. The shared experiences of these relationships gave expression to the Métis when the outsider with his country wife and family chose to live apart from both the trading post and the Indian band.

L'homme libre, the freeman, looms large in the process of Métis ethnogenesis. His historical importance in part lies in his social ties to indigenous Indian bands who came to consider this outsider as one of themselves. Rarely of British origin, the *Canadien* or "eastern Indian" freeman was a phenomenon of the Montreal-based fur trade and its *en dérouine* (itinerant peddling) system of trade. Usually he was an *engagé* who had established himself as a man of consequence among his fellows. Physical prowess counted for much, but not all; generosity and a penchant for an evocative song and an entertaining story were recognized as well. The man of consequence influenced others and affected the image of being less influenced by others. The man of consequence acted to become a "master" of his own affairs and circumstances. The logic of this ethos among the fur trade *engagés* led some to end their relationship with the trading post as *engagés* and become *les hommes libres*. This means of expressing their sense of consequence, by becoming free, was the beginning of the second stage in a two-step process which was intimately and critically involved in the emergence of the Plains Métis.

Particular behaviours distinguish the historical Plains Métis from indigenous Indians and from Euro-Canadians. The nature of these distinguishable behaviours in significant measure may well be "degree" rather than "kind." Further, such behaviours can be said to be central to the culture of these people. To explain their cultural origins it is useful to acknowledge the enculturation of children as a fundamental mechanism in the transmission of culture generationally. Thus the critical feature in explaining Métis ethnogenesis is not mixed ancestry; rather, it is the historical circumstances and processes which saw some children enculturated differently than those children associated with Indian bands or with the very few Euro-Canadian communities that could be said to exist in the presettlement West. Few would quarrel with the observation that children born to Indian mothers and enculturated in Indian bands did, and do, function culturally as Indians. In the closing decades of the 18th century on the western Plains there were only Indian mothers. Thus to have some children experience a different enculturation, to the extent that the historical actors themselves recognized them as culturally distinct from Indians, it is necessary to posit an enculturation circumstance for these children apart from indigenous Indian bands. The freeman, the outsider adult male, was a critical factor in creating these historical circumstances.

Two scholars in particular have offered insight in this area. Jacqueline Peterson, in her article "Prelude to Red River: A Social Portrait of the Great Lakes Métis," details an historical mechanism which would see some children enculturated in circumstances apart from an Indian band.[6] Her focus is the early 18th-century Great Lakes fur trade and the small party of traders dispatched *en dérouine* by a *bourgeois* (merchant) at a major trading post.[7] The trading party of perhaps four to six men, led by a *commis*, sought out Indian bands on their home territories. Frequently the basis for a commercial trade between the two was a sociopolitical tie linking the traders, particularly the commis, to the principal adult males of the band. The vehicle for such a relationship in most instances was the "country marriage" of the *commis* and a principal woman in the band. Peterson goes on to suggest that should the *commis* enjoy success, emerging in time as a *bourgeois* and contracting a more enduring marriage from his own social circle, he could still gather some of the children of his previous country marriages to be raised in his own home circumstances. Peterson's article argues that sufficient experiences of this nature over two or three generations contributed significantly to the rise of the Great Lakes Métis. In terms of the western Plains, the immediate question arising from Peterson's article is whether a similar process can be identified which would have some children enculturated, as were some children of the *commis*, in circumstances distinct from Indian bands.

Jennifer Brown, in her book *Strangers in Blood*, offers the concept of patrifocality to explain why most children in the families of fur trade officers and their Native wives in the 19th century did not emerge as Métis.[8] Brown argues that the dominant position of fur trade officers in their families allowed them to influence the enculturation of their children to the extent that they did not become Métis. An implication for readers of Brown's book is whether matrifocality rather than patrifocality would explain the appearance of the Métis. Were the Métis the cultural product of children enculturated apart from the band in a family in which the wife and mother was the dominant factor in their enculturation? In part Brown returned to this discussion in a later article, "Woman as Centre and Symbol in the Emergence of Métis Communities."[9]

The historical record argues persuasively for the significance of the outsider male in the historical processes that gave rise to the Métis. Further, a noteworthy number of these males would appear to be characterized as assertive in terms of their behaviour with others. An example is Jean Dumont, the founder of the Dumont family among the Métis in western Canada. Having "turned off" his country wife, Suzette, the Sarcee-Crow woman, and family to another freeman, Paul Durand, Jean left for Lower Canada in 1802, only to return two or three years later to challenge Durand for his family: "mais Paul Durant [sic] refusait de rendre la femme a son premier propriétaire, Jean Dumont dut la prendre de irve force."[10] Durand's name would disappear from documents until his son by Suzette reached maturity and married. Quite possibly a similar assertiveness expressed itself in the family lives of these men and in their relations with their children, particularly sons. Whether or not such assertiveness in family life constituted "patrifocality" or "man centrality," it does argue for significance in terms of the circumstances in which the young in such families were enculturated. Arguing the importance of the husband and father in proto-Métis households is not to imply the unimportance of the wife and mother.

In attempting to identify the particular historical circumstances and processes which gave rise to the western Plains Métis attention is directed to the wintering villages which first captured Giraud's attention.[11] Within a generation of their first appearance, numbers of these villages dotted the western Plains. Among the most westerly was Buffalo Lake in what is today the province of Alberta. At its height as a wintering village of Métis buffalo hunters it had over eighty cabins, numbering close to 1,000 inhabitants.[12] It is to wintering in the fur trade, not in the 1870s, however, but in the 1770s that scholars must look to identify the circumstances and the processes which gave rise to the Métis on the western Plains.

Wintering in its broadest sense is the complex of individual and community behaviours invoked in response to factors rooted in climatic circumstances. The behaviours are those necessary for survival when on occasion a benign or challenging environment can become threatening. But wintering behaviours involve more than simple survival: they involve the full interplay of individuals and groups in small, face-to-face communities. In the context of the St. Lawrence-Great Lakes fur trade in the 18th century, wintering differentiated *les bons hommes* who wintered in the interior from *les mangeurs de lard* who bound themselves to the constraints of society in the environs of Montreal and elsewhere in French Canada.[13] Those *engagés* who remained in the interior were *les hivernants*. They met the challenge of wintering in the Indian country, not simply by surviving but by becoming persons of consequence among their fellows and in the Indian bands. Thereby they gained reputation and full entry into the adult male fraternity of the St. Lawrence-Great Lakes fur trade. For the officers wintering was the prerequisite, after appropriate social circumstances, for membership in the famous, and at times infamous, Beaver Club.[14] Others of their social and ethnic milieu could be guests at the club's functions, but only winterers of appropriate social circumstances could be members. For those officers and servants in posts in the North Saskatchewan River valley, in the last quarter of the 18th century, *hivernement* (wintering) had an even more specialized meaning.

While the discussion of the circumstances and processes of wintering is sparse in the fur trade literature, it is noteworthy that Giraud provides the most detail. The image of wintering that emerges in Giraud suggests two cardinal factors determining circumstances. The first factor is the *en dérouine* trading system, developed in the St. Lawrence-Great Lakes trade during the closing decades of the 17th century.[15] Jacqueline Peterson has explained that the system involved small parties of men sent from a regional trading fort to trade with Indians on their home hunting and trapping territories. These peddlers would find winter a most appropriate time for their travel not only because the season facilitated travel in areas away from canoe-navigable rivers, but because it would be the best circumstance in which to encourage Indians to emphasize trapping activities. Giraud explains:

> the employees of the Canadian companies, as soon as they reached their wintering places, provided themselves with trade goods and scattered among the Indians in the hope of securing their furs and gaining their allegiance through the mutual sympathy that was born of such a shared experience. … the Canadians already had recourse to this procedure, which they found to their advantage as well as to that of the Indians. … The "coureur de dérouine," as such an employee-trader was called, became the essential cogwheel in the trading post. Many of the Canadians shared … the

> life of the natives, choosing to live over winter in their tents,
> next to their families, without caring about the rigorous
> cold or the uncomfortable quarters. … such a dispersion
> might have an added importance of conserving the fort's
> scanty resources of food.[16]

In effect, wintering in the posts of the *en dérouine* fur trade system involved travel to the Indian bands and some period of residence among them.

The practice of *en dérouine* trading in winter provided the bourgeois of the trading post with a means of addressing the perennial problem of the cost of surplus labour during the winter months.[17] *Engagés* were hired primarily to transport trade goods into the interior and furs out to market. With winter this labour force had to be directed towards other activities. Those *engagés* with crafts such as carpentry and smithing could be profitably employed in most instances. Others less technically skilled could be directed for a time to such activities as cutting firewood. As extensive as this activity might be during a Plains winter the usual course of action was to have as much wood as possible cut, transported and stacked before the onset of cold weather. In effect a number of *engagés* could be relatively idle for extended periods during the winter months; and thus, they would be a drain on the post's stores of provisions and, of course, on the profitability of the trade. While hunting activity could be encouraged for a few appropriately skilled servants, it could be cost effective as well to dispatch small parties of men with a limited supply of trade goods to winter with residential bands of Indians. Their trade goods would permit them to exchange goods for food and other necessities from the Indians. In effect the *en dérouine* system could be combined with the practice of encouraging small parties of men to winter with the bands. Such parties could encourage the bands to act in a manner that favoured their home fort. In competitive circumstances they could direct furs and provisions to their *bourgeois* at the trading post. At the same time they would provision themselves through their own efforts and/or through the efforts of the band with whom they were temporarily residing.

Such wintering practices involved *engagés* intimately in the affairs of the band. On first contact the leader of the trading party would lay the basis for a trading relationship, using all of his social and political skills and his knowledge of Indian ways. In most instances his actions could be described as an "assertive bonhomie" in which gifts were offered and conversation would introduce the names of personages who could be said to offer a link between the *commis* and the adult males of the band.[18] As with many cultural traditions, hunting Indians seemed to have preferred conducting trade with "family." The trader would emphasize conversations that would serve to have him considered in this context. Preferably a common kinsman would be discovered in the course of conversation. In the early period both parties would have to be satisfied with a social link to an Indian or trader of well-deserved reputation. It was out of a successful initial meeting that a social relationship could emerge between the *coureur de dérouine* or *commis* and the adults of the band. A country marriage to an eligible woman of the band would cement this relationship. Although evidence is very sparse, other circumstances at a later date suggest that women of the band were not necessarily simply passive observers in this decision.[19]

Other members of the *en dérouine* party might form marriage relationships with women of the band; but the continuation of these relationships in succeeding winter seasons was far more problematic. Members of the trading party other than the *commis* would be much less likely to have the status that would keep the country wife's interest when the winter and the trade ended. Similarly the *engagé*, should he have the inclination, would be less able than the commis to persuade his *bourgeois* to allow him in succeeding winters to return to the band of the previous year's country wife. The country marriages which led to the Métis appear in large measure to be those that were sustained over several trading seasons.

The country marriage was critical to the *commis*'s trading success because it included him in the social system of the residential band. Kinship determined appropriate privileges and responsibilities in relations with others. By virtue of his marriage the *commis* was enmeshed in this social system. Every person in the residential band and in the surrounding "neighbourhood" was a *"parent"* (relative) who owed him obligations and to whom he owed obligations. A failure to behave appropriately in this area could be fatal to a *commis*'s commercial interests and, in some instances, to himself and his compatriots.[20] The advice of a country wife on this subject as well as others could be critical to the long-term success and health of the commis and his compatriots.

At first glance the spousal relationship involved in wintering suggests "bride service," that is, the newly married couple living with the bride's parents until the birth of the first child. The advantages for the males involved in this practice were the opportunity for the outsider male to learn a new hunting and trapping territory under the skilled tutelage of the bride's male relatives, and the opportunity for the males of the band to acquire an ally who could further their economic and political interests. The advantages for the bride were equally obvious. The new "country husband's" skills as a "provider" could be evaluated while she was still close to the bosom of her natal family. No doubt for many young brides the birth of a first child among female relatives in whom she had confidence was far more preferable than a birthing experience away from her kinswomen. Should the outsider male be found wanting either as a provider or as a work mate and ally of her kinsmen, the spousal relationship could be terminated. On the other hand, relationships which emerged and endured over the course of several winters could be said to have some depth and stability.

The gender-based roles and skills of the woman in the freeman family were crucial to its survival and success. Perhaps as critical as this spousal relationship was the relationship between the outsider adult male and his country wife's male relatives. In point of fact the two relationships were intertwined. A spousal relationship with a woman of consequence which was established in intimate association with the band required her relatives to accept the outsider country husband as a kinsman. Such an acceptance would always be conditional on the outsider's appropriate behaviour towards his wife's kin. In time, instances of genuine affection between the outside male and his "in-laws" could emerge. In most instances the relationship no doubt remained somewhat formal and distant. The lack of harmony in some instances may have led to violence.[21] For the successful freeman and his family, however, the essential requirement accompanying a country wife was the acceptance of his presence by her kinsmen and their neighbouring connections. The tragic fate of the twelve Iroquois and two *Canadien* freemen who journeyed to Chesterfield House in the autumn of 1801 is clear testimony to the sociopolitical understandings that were necessary for survival.[22] The fourteen were a trapping party hoping to base themselves at Chesterfield House near the confluence of the Red Deer and South Saskatchewan rivers, when they were set upon by Atsina, sometimes known as Gros Ventres, who viewed them as interlopers.

A critically important relationship in the emergence of the Métis was that involving two or three outsider males. With the adult males of this wintering group functioning as hunting, trapping and fishing work mates and partners for extended periods of the year, their families came to constitute a social milieu in which the succeeding generation would choose marriage partners. A perusal of some freeman genealogies demonstrates that individuals did marry into indigenous Indian bands, but the large majority in most regions would appear to have taken spouses from other freeman families and bands.[23] It is noteworthy that the families of freemen who failed to form these work mate partnerships became part of the indigenous Indian tradition. Two particular examples are George Sutherland, said to be the founder of the Willow People among the Down-River Plains Cree, and Alexis[?] Piché, the progenitor of several prominent families among the Rocky Mountain-

Beaver Hills People of the Up-River Plains Cree.[24] Without the relationship with other outsider males a winterer and his household might well enjoy success, but the generational legacy in the 19th century would be over-whelmingly in an Indian, not a Métis, tradition.

Among the distinguishing behaviours of some freemen descendants in the North Saskatchewan River valley was the practice of a "folk" Roman Catholicism which predated the appearance of Roman Catholic missionaries by more than half a century.[25] Roman Catholic missionaries after 1840 encountered infant baptism and Roman Catholic prayer among Native laity who had had no previous experience with church-sanctioned religious instruction. Such practices originated in an earlier generation of work mates who sustained some behaviours of the community of their origin, Lower Canada. They were shared among families who shared similar progenitors. In time some of these families would become distinct communities. In terms of ethnogenesis the work mate or outsider male relationship was as impor-tant as the other two relationships.

The cultural significance of the processes involved in the three relation-ships of the first step should not be underestimated. If these processes are ethnogenesis, what then is the relationship between particular experiences in wintering and the emergence of the Métis as a distinct sociocultural entity in the fur trade West? The anthropologist Fredrick Barth suggests a useful "model" to depict the interconnection of behaviour and culture:

> The simplest form of this interconnection would seem to depend on sharing: individual behaviour produces experi-ence, a confrontation with reality which may or may not seem consistent with pre-existing conceptualizations and thus may sometimes tend to confirm, sometimes falsify them. If a number of persons in communication share a sim-ilar opportunity situation, experience the same confronta-tions with reality, and have the same conceptualizations fal-sified, one would expect them to develop shared under-standings and modify their collective culture and expecta-tions in accordance with this.[26]

The shared experiences in wintering were the behaviours involved in establishing the three critical relationships: the country marriage between an outsider male and an Indian woman of the band, the sociopolitical alliance relating the outsider male to the male kinsmen of the woman and the friend-ship that bound outsider males in an economic and social relationship. All of these relationships and the experiences that engendered them and the experiences that they in turn engendered constituted the first stage in the two-stage process of Plains Métis ethnogenesis.

While Giraud's description of the factors determining the circumstances of wintering appears to be clear, the historian will find the process of wintering far more problematic. Brief references to particular activities at the trading post can be found in the various trading post journals. But life outside the trading post in the wintering bands is much more dimly perceived. In order to garner some insight into this experience, the first of two stages in the ethnogenesis of the Plains Métis, it is necessary to examine the second stage, the time when the Métis were emerging as a distinct cultural entity.

The opportunity of going free or becoming a freeman was not an option that would be available to many *engagés*. Most would lack the technical and sociopolitical skills necessary for survival. Not only would a freeman have to know how to hunt, fish and trap successfully while living apart from the fort and the Indian band, but he would require the sociopolitical skills necessary to have the surrounding bands view him as one of themselves in so far as the resources of the region were concerned. Strangers were interlopers who were not tolerated. Such survival skills were acquired over time and required appropriate circumstances for their expression. For several "eastern Indians" who had been hired by the Montreal-based fur trade companies and who were numerous in the Athabasca country, particularly the Lesser Slave Lake and Jasper House neighbourhoods, freeman status proved to be a quick and natural process.[27] Their skills as hunters and trappers and their ability to achieve acceptance on the part of neighbouring Indians suggested they would be more profitable to the fur trade as free trappers and hunters rather than as contracted servants. Similarly, Euro-Canadian servants who contemplated freeman status would have to have the necessary skills to function as a hunter and/or a trapper and to negotiate acceptance on the part of neighbouring Indians.

A critical factor in the transition from *engagé* to freeman was motivation. Elsewhere I have argued the existence of an adult male ethos among French Canadian males of this era that emphasized the necessity of being a man of consequence in one's own eyes and in the eyes of one's fellows.[28] A most dramatic expression of this sense of consequence is found in Alexander Ross's familiar account of the words of an old *engagé* whom Ross met in 1825 *en route* to the Red River Settlement:

> I have now been forty-two years in this country. For twenty-four I was a light canoe man. ... No portage was too long for me; all portages were alike. My end of the canoe never touched the ground till I saw the end of [the portage]. ...

Fifty songs a day were nothing to me, I could carry, paddle, walk and sing with any man I ever saw. ... No water, no weather, ever stopped the paddle or the song. I have had twelve wives in the country; and was once possessed of fifty horses, and six running dogs, trimmed in the first style. I was then like a Bourgeois, rich and happy; no Bourgeois had better dressed wives than I; no Indian chief finer horses; no white man better harnessed or swifter dogs. ... I wanted for nothing; ... I should glory in commencing the same career again. I would spend another half-century in the same fields of enjoyment. There is no life so happy as a voyageur's life; none so independent; no place where a man enjoys so much variety and freedom as in the Indian country.[29]

Enduring status as a lowly *engagé* was incompatible with the ethos of a man of consequence. The expression of such an ethos in *le pays sauvage* required in time promotion, possibly to the rank and status of interpreter, and subsequently for some, freeman status. Others might become freemen earlier in their careers. It would appear that a similar if not identical ethos influenced those eastern Indians who chose to remain in the West to live as freemen. It is the existence of such an ethos which may well explain, in significant part, why the majority of freemen chose to live apart from indigenous Indian bands. Some of the particulars of their sense of a man of consequence would not be shared with the males of the indigenous Indian bands. While each could acknowledge kinship with the other, their respective expressions of consequence limited the time that they and their families could spend in each other's company. A successful freeman as well as his "in-laws" may well have understood the limits of each other's tolerance of "different" behaviours. Living apart from kinsmen for significant periods could well have been an important element in a successful freeman's repertoire of behaviours. In living with his family apart from the Indian band and the trading post, the freeman laid the basis for his children to be enculturated in circumstances distinct from that of the band or the post. The process of enculturation in such circumstances was the second stage of a two-stage process which gave rise to the Plains Métis.

Wintering in the fur trade in the valley of the North Saskatchewan River and its tributaries in the latter decades of the 18th century was the basic context in which, for some Métis, processes of Métis ethnogenesis began. In all probability similar experiences marked behaviour in the valleys of the Red, Assiniboine and Athabasca rivers. The *en dérouine* trading tradition and the *bourgeois*'s interest in controlling labour costs were the twin wintering factors that encouraged the formation of the three essential relationships. These relationships in turn were critical to the success of the freeman and his family or, if you will, the proto-Métis. The first and foremost of these relationships was the country marriage between the servant, who by virtue of reputation and favour led the *en dérouine* party, and an Indian woman closely related to the prominent males of the band.[30] The second critical relationship was that between the leader of the *en dérouine* party, and the adult males of the band. Resting upon the marriage relationship with the Indian woman, the relationship with the males of the band would determine the level of acceptance extended to the outsider. For purposes of exploiting the resources of the region it was essential that adult Indian males view the outsider as one of themselves. The third critical relationship that would see the freeman's family emerge distinct from the Indians was the relationship formed among some of the members of the *en dérouine* party. While examples can be found of freemen and their families living with Indian bands, the overwhelming impression from the sources emphasizes freeman families neighbouring with each other for extended periods of the year.[31] Such second-stage associations suggest friendships built up over time, dating from a period when circumstances encouraged close cooperation among some outsiders. While such associations reflected mutual self-interest in terms of economic activities, they also reflected the freeman's preference for those with whom he shared a similar ethos and all that such sharing entailed.

The second stage in the process of Métis ethnogenesis in the Saskatchewan country emerged with the decision of the experienced *engagé* to become a freeman. With the support of his *bourgeois* who encouraged his pursuit of the material markers of consequence, the freeman claimed his family from the band or possibly the fort and began his assiduous pursuit of provisions and furs in surplus amounts. His ethos and the behaviour that manifested it made him and his family distinct from the indigenous Indians. He naturally grouped with those who suggested compatibility with his ways. With the marriage of his children to the children of other freeman families and with their pursuit of his ways, the process of Métis ethnogenesis on the western Plains, as early as the first quarter of the 19th century, was complete.

Gabriel Dumont the elder, the eldest son of Jean Dumont and Suzette, the Sarcee-Crow woman, witnessed the Métis of the upper North Saskatchewan becoming a community. He married Suzanne Lussier, the daughter of freeman Francois Lussier, the subject of a Paul Kane portrait. Members of his extended family were residing at Lac Ste-Anne when the Roman Catholic missionary Reverend J. Thibault visited there in the 1840s. In 1861 some followed the mission to Big Lake (St-Albert), a few miles north of Fort Edmonton. Already the Métis of the region were responding to the opportunities becoming apparent in the buffalo robe trade. From their base at St-Albert the Métis hunted south and southeast through the parkland to the prairie. In the 1870s at Buffalo Lake they established one of the largest *hivernement* villages. The husband of a grandaughter, Louison Montagnais, became the principal *Chef Métis* in the village. Kinsmen from the lower South Saskatchewan River at *Petite Ville* (ancestral to the village of Batoche) joined them at Buffalo Lake some winters. Dumont himself witnessed the demise of the village when the robe hunt swept southward and the resource on which it was based collapsed.[32] An aged patriarch at the time of his death in 1880, he was finally laid to rest a few miles south of Buffalo Lake on a bluff overlooking another wintering village site at the confluence of Tail Creek and Red Deer River. In his lifetime he would have witnessed the events that marked the processes that constituted the birth of a people.

The foregoing analysis has focussed on the outsider adult male in the circumstances and processes of becoming western Plains Métis. In this process no single act has more consequence than the individual *engagé*'s decision to go free. The action is a powerful statement of self-definition and self-assertion. In this light concepts of partifocality and male centrality suggest explanative insight into which freeman families would succeed as Métis. The bias of the historical sources themselves encourages this focus. What remains to be addressed in more detail is the nature and consequence of the wife and mother from the indigenous Indian band in the process of Métis ethnogenesis.

7. The Market for Métis Lands in Manitoba: An Exploratory Study (1991)

Thomas Flanagan

The fate of Métis land and scrip in Manitoba in the troubled 1870s and 1880s has led to a lasting controversy over the issue of victimization. The argument presented here is that fairness prevailed, associated as it was with the two main tenets of the capitalist free market: non-racist economic competition, and information made available to all. There were winners and losers on every side, but governments acted as constitutionally as could be expected.

The Manitoba Act provided extensive land grants to the Métis of Manitoba.[1] Section 31 set aside 1.4 million acres for distribution among "the children of the half-breed heads of families," while section 32 confirmed the titles of old settlers, Métis or white, who had possessed land in Manitoba prior to 15 July 1870. Subsection 32(5) promised commutation for the rights of hay and common in the outer two miles that had accompanied many of the old river lots. Additional legislation in 1874 granted $160 scrip, redeemable in Dominion Lands, to all Métis heads of families, husbands and wives alike.[2]

What happened to all this land and scrip is one of the enduring questions of Métis history and is also of current legal and political interest now that the Manitoba Métis Federation has commenced litigation on the subject.[3] The Métis case relies to a considerable degree on the thesis of D.N. Sprague that the federal government never intended all this land to pass into Métis hands and therefore structured the grants so as to encourage fraud, misappropriation, and hasty sales at low prices.[4] Gerhard Ens has recently criticized certain aspects of Sprague's dispossession thesis pertaining to the river lots mentioned in section 32 of the Manitoba Act. The data reported by Ens show that the Dominion Lands surveyors recognized Métis occupancy of these lots and that the Department of the Interior faithfully issued patents to the Métis occupants or to those to whom they sold their rights. Difficulties in obtaining title to river lots did not play a major part in encouraging Métis emigration from Manitoba in the 1870s.[5]

This article addresses other aspects of the dispossession thesis—the fate of the Métis children's land grants and of the scrip for heads of families. According to Sprague, most of these benefits were taken from the Métis through deception:

> But a group of about 500 speculators, usually from Ontario, operated from the same lists as the commissioners and worked just as systematically through every parish. Frequently, they told people that it was necessary to have an attorney now that the government was processing claims. Thus they secured powers of attorney. Sometimes they told claimants the government was not to be trusted, no land would ever be granted but twenty-five dollars was offered for the claim on the chance some small portion would be granted. In this way they procured assignments of claims. Occasionally the powers of attorney or assignments were completely fraudulent; they were made up without contacting the claimant at all. ... The culpability of the government in this farce was two-fold. First, they failed to provide an institutional means for validating contracts between literate confidence men and illiterate claimants. Secondly ... the civil servants and elected officials who were closest to these proceedings ... seized upon the opportunity and joined in the bonanza themselves. As a result, virtually all of the money scrip which was supposed to have been awarded to Half-breed heads of families never reached the claimants. As soon as it arrived at the Dominion Lands Office in 1876, assignees and attorneys picked it up instead.[6]

Sprague's account elaborates upon the early reports of Giraud and Stanley that the desperate Métis, discouraged by government delays, were poorly informed and often defrauded; that they sold their rights at trivial prices; and that they received little long-term benefit from the transactions. Stanley wrote: "Despairing of ever receiving their land patents, many disposed of their rights for a mere song. Some gladly sold their scrip for trifling sums to smooth-tongued speculators. ..."[7] Giraud conveyed the same impression:

> Unaware, because of their habits of life, of the true value of the land, they could not resist the temptation of trading their scrip for a sum of money which, no matter how small it might be, would appear to them in the foundering of their traditional activities, as the sole capital likely to save them from poverty. A few dollars were often enough to secure their agreement. Alcohol, whose distribution was no longer subject to any restriction, contributed greatly to the despoilment of the Métis. Often the speculators, abusing their credulity, would make off with the scrip without paying the promised sums.[8]

Both Stanley and Giraud saw the Métis as a more or less primitive people, doomed to extinction in their conflict with expanding civilization,[9] so it is not surprising that they emphasized the supposed inability of the Métis to look after themselves in the market. More recent writers such as Sealey and Lussier, Taylor, Friesen, and Boisvert and Turnbull paint a similar picture of the market, even though they no longer see the Métis as a primitive people.[10] Against this consensus, the author once suggested that the Métis, not only in Manitoba but also later in the North-West Territories, followed a rational course in the market. They sold their land and scrip because money was more useful to them than land at that moment, and they received the value of what they sold as determined by a freely functioning market.[11] This argument was based on *a priori* reasoning and was not substantiated with systematic empirical data at the time.

The earlier hypothesis is now followed up by presenting empirical evidence about the market for Métis land and scrip in Manitoba in the 1870s and 1880s.[12] Three bodies of data are considered: prices for children's allotments, scrip for heads of families, and military bounty warrants. The information casts further doubt upon the dispossession thesis.

Children's Allotments

Section 31 of the Manitoba Act provided for a grant of 1.4 million acres to the "children of the half-breed heads of families" residing in Manitoba as of July 15, 1870:

> 31. And whereas, it is expedient, towards the extinguishment of the Indian Title to the lands in the Province, to appropriate a portion of such ungranted lands, to the extent

of one million four hundred thousand acres thereof, for the benefit of the families of the half-breed residents, it is hereby enacted, that, under regulations to be from time to time made by the Governor General in Council, the Lieutenant-Governor shall select such lots or tracts in such parts of the Province as he may deem expedient, to the extent aforesaid, and divide the same among the children of the half-breed heads of families residing in the Province at the time of the said transfer to Canada, and the same shall be granted to the said children respectively, in such mode and on such conditions as to settlement and otherwise, as the Governor General in Council may from time to time determine.[13]

When the federal government appointed A.G. Archibald lieutenant governor of Manitoba, it requested him to offer advice on the implementation of section 31. That advice was substantially incorporated into the order in council of April 25, 1871, which established the first regime for Dominion Lands.[14] The order provided that the lieutenant governor would conduct a lottery to carry out the Métis children's land grant. Following Archibald's advice, the order loosely interpreted the wording of section 31, allowing all Métis persons, whether children or adults, to participate in the lottery. That meant that individual allotments would be 140 acres, since there were about 10,000 Métis in the province.

By the summer of 1872, the Dominion Lands survey was sufficiently advanced that the selection could begin. Consulting with the Métis parishes over a period of several months, the lieutenant governor and other federal officials chose blocks of townships totalling 1.4 million acres. These were located for the most part immediately behind the parishes among whose inhabitants they were to be distributed. Lieutenant Governor Alexander Morris, who had replaced Archibald, began drawing lots for 140-acre grants on February 22, 1873.[15]

This beginning, however, proved unsatisfactory to some of the leading spokesmen of the Métis. It had become apparent that many Métis were making advance sales of their rights, and their children's rights, to participate in the lottery. Robert Cunningham, editor of the *Manitoban* and member of Parliament (MP) from Marquette, raised the matter in the House of Commons, urging the government to comply strictly with the wording of section 31 and restrict the grant only to "the children of the half-breed heads of families." In later years, exclusion of the adults would discourage immediate speculative sales, since children would not receive their patents until they turned 18.[16] Sir John A. Macdonald quickly complied with the request and introduced the necessary legislation to restrict the grant.[17] His action received the approval of Archbishop Taché, Father N.-J. Ritchot, and Louis Riel.[18]

Exclusion of the adults meant that fewer recipients would share the 1.4 million acres, so the allotment size had to be enlarged. Drawings for 190-acre allotments were recommenced in August 1873,[19] but complications continued to arise. There were many problems with the precise location of the 1.4 million acres as well as uncertainty about how to verify applications for the land. The Dominion Lands agent in Winnipeg advised that his small staff could not handle the approximately 7,000 applications expected.[20]

When the Liberals came to power after the Pacific Scandal caused the fall of Macdonald's government, David Laird became Minister of the Interior and, after making a first-hand investigation in Manitoba, decided a fresh start was necessary. An order in council of April 26, 1875 provided that a special commission would receive applications to share in the lottery. The size of the allotments would be finally determined after the number of participants was fixed, and only then would the lottery be carried out.

The commission consisted of two lawyers, John Machar of Kingston and Matthew Ryan of Montreal. They toured Manitoba over the summer of 1875, approving 5,088 children's claims. Making an allowance for about 500 claims still to be received, the government set the allotment size at 240 acres,[21] and drawings began in the last week of October 1876.[22] In the meantime, Matthew Ryan's commission was extended to allow him to receive applications in the North-West Territories from eligible recipients who had left Manitoba before 1875.[23]

For reasons that are not fully understood, the drawings, which were conducted parish by parish, were not completed until February 1880. Patents, however, were issued in batches as phases of the drawings were finished. The first batch arrived in Winnipeg on August 31, 1877,[24] while others were delivered at irregular intervals into the early 1880s. In the end, 6,034 patents for 240-acre allotments were issued to Métis children, for a total of 1,448,160 acres.[25]

Speculative sales had begun even before the first drawings in February 1873, leading to the exclusion of the Métis adults from the grant. Another result at the same time was passage of the provincial Half-Breed Land Grant Protection Act, allowing Métis who had sold their claims to repudiate their bargains without penalty, as long as they repaid the purchase price.[26] The Manitoba legislature tried to weaken this protection in 1875, but the federal cabinet disallowed the amendment.[27] In 1877, however, the legislature removed the revocation provision prospectively for sales made after July 1,

1877; this time the federal government did not intervene.[28] Subsequent provincial legislation allowed Métis children to sell their grants at age 18 if they had parental consent.[29] Provision was also made for judicially approved sales by children under 18 upon parental application to the Court of Queen's Bench.[30]

Sales thus took place in several forms. Many of the recipients were over 21 by the time patents were issued in 1877 and afterwards, so their sales were normal real estate transactions between adults. In some cases, however, the land was sold before the patent was received or issued, or even before the lottery was conducted. In such cases, vendors sold their right to the proceeds of the lottery. Federal regulations tried to ensure that the patent would be issued directly to the Métis child, but purchasers circumvented this barrier by getting the seller to sign a power of attorney empowering the purchaser to pick up the patent at the Dominion Lands Office.

About 560 allotments were sold under judicial supervision because the sellers were under 18 at the time.[31] A provincial investigation of these sales in the fall of 1881 revealed that the courts were not scrutinizing these cases thoroughly, and judicial sales were discontinued.[32] But this was only a delay, since the children could sell with parental consent when they turned 18, and with no restriction when they turned 21.

This study began by drawing a 1% random sample of sixty allotments from the registers kept by the Department of the Interior.[33] One instance of duplication in the sample left fifty-nine cases to be investigated. Using sources at the National Archives of Canada, the recipient's name and number, the legal description of the allotment, the date of the grant, the date of the recipient's eighteenth birthday, the father's name and parish, and sometimes the name of a spouse were determined. From abstract books in the provincial land titles offices, information was collected about the disposition of the allotment by the recipient, including when it was sold, who bought it, how much was paid, and whether complications ensued.

Table 1 is an overview of the disposition of the fifty-nine allotments. The data confirm the popular impression that the children's allotments were sold rather than kept; only five (about 8%) were retained past 1890. But it is not true that most of the land was sold when the recipients were still children. Because of the long time taken to carry out the distribution, and because judicial sales were terminated in 1881, over 90% of the land was disposed of by people over 18, and more than 60% by people over 21.

The sales took place according to the chronology shown in Table 2. Prices increased rapidly through the late 1870s, shot up in the boom years of the early 1880s, and levelled off thereafter. One should note the spate of

Table 1. Disposition of Sample of Children's Allotments		
Disposition	Number	Percentage
Recipient deceased, sale by heirs	6	10
Recipient seller over 21	24	41
Recipient seller between 18 and 21	16	27
Judicial sale	5	8
Land kept by recipient past 1890	5	8
Sold for taxes	1	2
Information not available	2	
Total	59	

sales at the beginning of the decade: six each in 1880 and 1881. The collapse of the great real estate boom in May 1882[34] had a marked effect on sales of allotments—there were only two in 1882, one in 1883, and none in 1884.

The data contradict the stereotype that most allotments were sold quickly for derisory prices. The early sales that are so often referred to in the literature must have been repudiated under the Half-Breed Land Grant

Table 2. Sales Chronology of Children's Allotments		
Year	Number	Average Price ($)
1875	1	40.00
1876	0	n/a
1877	10	100.00
1878	4	177.50
1879	4	147.50
1880	6	286.66
1881	6	230.00
1882	2	175.00
1883	1	400.00
1884	0	n/a
1885	2	270.00
1886	3	233.33
1887	2	175.00
1888	5	211.00
1889	2	247.50
1890	1	325.00
Total	49	

Table 3. Average Sale Prices of Children's Allotments by Five-Year Periods

Year	Number	Average Price ($)
1875-79	19	123.16
1880-85	17	258.23
1886-90	13	211.54
Total	49	193.47

Protection Act, or were at any rate never carried through, for only one lot in the sample was sold before 1877. It is true that prices prior to 1877 were low; evidence was found elsewhere of four sales from this period at prices of $25, $35, $40, and $55.[35] It is understandable that the stereotype of sales at absurdly low prices arose, but in light of the facts it cannot serve as an overall generalization. For convenience, the data are smoothed out in Table 3. The mean for all forty-nine cases for which a sale price could be ascertained was $193.47.[36]

The lawyer M.B. Wood told the provincial Commission of Inquiry in 1881 that "one thing is to be remembered, that a halfbreed can never get as much money for his land as a white man; for everyone in town are all beating the halfbreeds down.[37] In one sense, Wood's statement was obvious—white speculators would not have traded in Métis lands unless they could sell them for higher prices than they had paid. But interesting problems arise both in documenting these higher prices and in interpreting them.

It is usually impossible to discover the resale price of children's allotments, even though there are entries in the abstract books. Many subsequent transactions were not at arm's length because business partners sold lands back and forth for $1 or other nominal prices. A more fundamental problem with the data is that sellers often grouped allotments into larger batches before reselling them, in which case only aggregate prices were recorded in the indentures and abstract books. There is no doubt, however, that quick "flips" at substantial profits did take place. In one verified instance, John McNab bought the allotment of James Larocque for $200 on March 15, 1881 and sold it for $360 on April 9, 1881.[38]

Another factor to be kept in mind in evaluating resale prices is the boom market of the early 1880s. Until the crash, everyone was a speculative genius; one only had to wait to make money. But things were much tougher afterwards, and sales records for later years contain examples pointing to losses and even bankruptcy for investors.

There were two types of ultimate purchasers: immigrants streaming into Manitoba looking for farms on which to settle, and speculators looking for a long-term investment. Some were individual investors, but there were also land companies, such as the Scottish, Ontario and Manitoba Land Company, for which the MP A.W. Ross was a principal buyer. M.B. Wood testified to the Commission of Inquiry that Ross "is authorized to buy for his clients, and has money from them to enable him to do so."[39] Ross may have sometimes bought directly from sellers, but he also depended on "claim runners" such as Napoléon Bonneau and R.P. Wood to buy and resell to him.[40] Lawyers like Ross did the paper work; they aggregated lands into batches that might interest an external buyer, and funneled money from outside the province into the local market.

From the time the allotment was made, there was usually a chain of two, three, or even more sales before the land came to rest with a person or company prepared to settle on it or hold it for a long time. Each of the intermediate sellers had to be able to cover costs and make some money in order to remain in the market. The land had been granted to Métis who wished to sell it but lived in remote rural locations, often could not read or write, sometimes spoke no English, and had few contacts with potential purchasers. By acting as middlemen, the speculators conveyed land to those who wanted to farm it, or at least hold it for a longer period. Speculative profits were the inducement leading them to perform this useful but risky service.

To understand the chain of relationships and the profit margins at each stage, the Métis might be compared to producers of land, the middlemen to wholesalers, the land companies to retailers, and the settlers to consumers. It is, therefore, misleading to compare the prices that Métis sellers got against the prices later paid to the intermediaries. The Scottish, Ontario and Manitoba Land Company would not have wanted to deal directly with local inhabitants or even with claim runners. A distant company needed to deal with an established lawyer or other businessman who could offer some reliability in unfamiliar conditions. Goods and services are most useful if they are made available at the right place and time, with appropriate labelling, information, and guarantees attached to them.[41] The same is true of land, even if that commodity does not physically change place.

Another important function performed by the middlemen was to absorb risks, which were particularly high for a claim sold before the allotment sheet was posted. Not only might the land turn out to be worthless swamp, there might not be any allotment at all. A seller might be ruled ineligible for technical reasons—for example, living outside Manitoba on July 15, 1870— or he might have applied so late that the land for his parish was exhausted and he would get only $240 scrip. The risks are illustrated in the papers of

David McArthur, a Winnipeg businessman who dealt extensively in Métis lands. His files contain half a dozen letters from the Department of Interior, dated 1888, concerning Métis whose allotments McArthur had bought ten years earlier but who had ultimately received scrip instead of land and had sold it elsewhere.[42]

Another threat was that the vendor might sell his allotment more than once. Chief Justice E.B. Wood wrote that the Métis felt "at liberty to sell as often as they could find a purchaser and make him believe he had not already sold." Fear of multiple sales resulted in a "race to the registry," in Wood's words: "And so soon as the allotment came up there was such a race to the Registry office with the conveyances to get registered first, that horses enough could not be found in the city of Winnipeg for that purpose."[43] Wood's statement is confirmed by a newspaper report:

> The Ste. Agathe allotment was received this morning—and of course there was a rush of those interested to the Lands Office. The fastest horseflesh in town was engaged, but one chap outwitted his rivals by sending a telegraph operator up to the Ste. Agathe registry office, where he tapped the wire, and receiving the description of the allotments by telegraph from here, had them registered before the less 'cute' claimants appeared at the office.[44]

Registration of a deed, power of attorney, or other instrument was not in itself sufficient to secure title, but it did constitute notice to other purchasers: "The registry of any instrument under this Act, or any former Act, shall in equity constitute notice of such instrument to all persons claiming any interest in such lands subject to such registry."[45] In Sutherland *v.* Thibeaudeau, decided March 28, 1879, Chief Justice Wood held that the assignment of an unallotted claim might be validly registered, and constituted notice to other parties.[46] Prior to passage of the Real Property Act, 1885, registration was the best available safeguard of title.

Why did the Métis sell their allotments? Since only five of fifty-nine subjects in the sample kept their allotments, it might be better to begin by asking, "Why did those few keep them?" Interestingly, three of these five cases can be identified as members of the Métis upper class. Jemima Murray was married to Samuel L. Bedson, a white man who was the first warden of the Manitoba Penitentiary. She died in 1886, and he kept her allotment until 1890, when he sold it for $1,440.[47] Timoleon Tait was the son of Robert Tait, a prosperous Métis farmer, miller and businessman. Young Timoleon's allotment was mortgaged, perhaps to provide capital for the father's business enterprises. James Ross, Jr. was the son of James Ross, who had attended the

University of Toronto, and the grandson of Alexander Ross, the historian of Red River. His allotment was kept until 1897, when it was sold for $500. These Métis from educated and well-to-do families seem to have kept their allotments for business and investment purposes.

There is little direct evidence about the motivation of less well-off Métis for selling their lands. One exception is the testimony of Elie Carrière and his children, Joseph-Adolphe (aged 16) and Angelique (aged 13) to the Commission of Inquiry. Carrière testified that he had sold his children's allotments to pay his debts and buy more cattle. "When I got the money I knew it was for the children; and ... when I invested in cattle I thought I was doing well for the children and that these cattle would revert to them."[48] He also outfitted another son "to enable him to start work on the road."[49] Both children agreed that they had wanted to sell their allotments to help the family.

In the absence of such direct statements, one must try to infer motivation from what we know about the Métis. First, although there were important exceptions, most Métis were not commercial farmers. Their small-scale farming, more like horticulture than agriculture, was an adjunct to their economy, not the basis of their way of life. Ens has shown how the Métis came to depend increasingly on the buffalo robe trade after the 1840s.[50] In any event, cash farming on the Manitoba prairie was hardly profitable for anyone prior to about 1880. New strains of wheat and new farm implements were required to make modern agriculture feasible.[51]

Ens has also shown how the buffalo robe trade induced many Métis to leave the Red River colony and move further west, where they could winter on the plains and hunt when the robes were at their prime. Beginning in the 1850s, this movement continued through the 1860s and into the 1870s.[52] Although the desire to participate in the buffalo robe trade was the original inducement, the wish to emigrate was reinforced in the early 1870s, particularly for the French Métis, by conflict with the new English-Protestant settlers in Manitoba.[53] Selling their children's allotments was an obvious way to finance a departure from Manitoba.

There was another peak of Métis emigration from the Winnipeg area in the years around 1880. The buffalo robe trade was largely played out by then, and Ens attributes this wave of emigration to the desire of the remaining Métis to obtain larger tracts of land for farming, compounded by a loss of power and prestige in the political crisis of 1879.[54] Many went to the North-West Territories, while others founded new settlements in Manitoba.[55] But even those who wanted to remain in Manitoba to become commercial farmers did not necessarily want to settle on their particular children's allotments. The Métis tended to move in large, clan-like groups of relatives,

sell = raise # #

consisting of parents and children, brothers and sisters, and in-laws. The partition of reserve land into 240-acre parcels made it difficult to resettle as a group; it would only be chance if a group of relatives happened to get allotments near each other. Sale of the children's allotments was a way to raise money to move to a preferred location.

Keeping the land for a long-term investment was probably not an attractive option for most Métis. They would have to pay property taxes, and the eventual sale would be particularly difficult for those leaving the province. If they were going to sell anyway, they did better to sell in the boom years than to wait. Let us make the more or less realistic assumptions that a given allotment could be sold for $300 in 1881, and that if it were not sold, property taxes would be $3 per year beginning in 1883. Ten years later, compound interest at approximately 3% would have turned that $300 into $403, to which one would have to add $30 in avoided taxes. That means one would have had to sell the same lot for $403 + $30 = $433 in 1890 to do as well as was possible in 1881, but in fact prices in 1890 were not at that level. (The average price of the eight allotments from this sample sold in the years 1888–90 was $234.)

Of course, not everyone was smart or lucky enough to sell during the boom. Only fifteen of forty-nine allotments in the sample, or 31%, were sold in the years 1880–83. Many sellers who took the lower prices prevailing in the 1870s probably wished, with the benefit of hindsight, that they had waited longer. But such situations are universal in a market economy. The Métis did what they did for reasons which seemed good to them at the time.

Scrip

The government made separate provision for the approximately 3,000 Métis heads of families who were removed from sharing in the 1.4 million acres after Cunningham's protest in the spring of 1873. Legislation passed the next year authorized grants of 160 acres, or $160 scrip redeemable in Dominion Lands, to the heads of families.[56] The Machar-Ryan Commission received their applications at the same time as it enumerated the children.

After the government opted for scrip rather than land, the first scrip now was signed on May 1, 1876.[57] In the end, 3,186 scrips were issued to Métis heads of families,[58] while an additional 800 scrips were issued to the original white settlers of Manitoba and their descendants. The Métis heads of families and the white settlers received identical $160 scrip notes, distinguishable only by the serial numbers. There was no difference from the purchaser's point of view.

Fewer formalities attended scrip, so the Métis sold it even more quickly than they sold the land. As with the 240-acre allotments, much of it was sold before it was ever received. It is impossible to gather first-hand data about prices because no legal sales records exist, but there are many references to the price of scrip in the newspapers of the day and other contemporary documents.

Land speculation is often long-term, but speculation in scrip was probably short-term—for example, holding it over the winter to try to take advantage of next spring's immigration. Holding it for long periods would have made little sense, for scrip was in effect a special kind of currency, denominated in dollars and redeemable against Dominion Lands. Its value to the speculator could never rise above the face value of the scrip, and it was liable to radical devaluation if the Department of the Interior should raise the price of Dominion Lands.

Although scrip did not begin to reach Manitoba until the end of June 1876, $46,115.29 (including a small amount of hay scrip granted in commutation of claims under section 32(5) of the Manitoba Act) had been redeemed by the end of the year—equivalent to about 280 claims. By the end of 1877, the equivalent of another 1,000 claims had been redeemed.[59] The records do not show who was locating the scrip; but whoever was doing it, was doing it quickly.

The scrip market became highly developed in a short period of time. Investors from inside and outside the province placed blocks of money with agents who did the actual purchasing. Real estate brokers, lawyers, and other merchants printed advertisements in local newspapers offering to buy and sell individual scrip notes as well as larger quantities. The newspapers also quoted going prices. The brokers printed standardized forms for assignments and powers of attorney, to try to reduce legal complications to a minimum. Some merchants would even accept scrip as payment for merchandise; scrip was, in effect, a land-backed currency, like the famous *assignats* of the French Revolution. In other words, there was a competitive market with a lively flow of information. No one had to accept a take-it-or-leave-it price dictated by a monopoly buyer.

Claims for scrip seem initially to have sold for about $40 or less. The lawyer W.B. Thibeaudeau paid $35 for a claim in 1875.[60] The *Manitoba Free Press* carried an ad on October 9, 1875, offering claims for sale at $40 each. A buyer wrote to John Schultz around the same time: "What are the prospects of the scrip market? Can you buy at $40?[61] On October 21, 1876, Isabella Bird sold her claim to scrip for $40.[62] To put these low prices in context, one must remember that the Manitoba real estate market was depressed after the worldwide business crash of 1873 and after the Liberal government's decision to bypass Winnipeg with the transcontinental railway.

The price seems to have gone up as the issue of scrip actually took place. In the letter cited above, Schultz mentioned prices as high as $65. On November 1, 1876, the *Free Press* reported that the Métis were "desperate under the repeated delays, and they are daily sacrificing their rights for a nominal sum … their assignments may be purchased in trade at a little more than half the cash value of the scrip [$80]." However, *Le Métis* (which repeatedly lectured its readers not to sell and may therefore have perceived the price as lower) said scrip was selling at $40 to $50 on November 23.

There may well have been considerable variation in price in the fall of 1876. Scrip was just coming out, and old assignments were still being traded. It is not always clear whether quoted prices refer to assignments or actual notes; the latter were more valuable because they were not as risky as assignments. In any case, the real estate market had begun to recover somewhat in 1876 as new varieties of wheat made agriculture more profitable.

Prices took a jump in the spring of 1877, perhaps coinciding with a rush of incoming settlers, who often came in early spring, located on land, and tried to get in a crop for fall harvest. Thibeaudeau's scrip was allegedly worth $100 around Easter 1877.[63] Le Métis reported on May 17: "Les scrips de chefs de famille Métis qui se sont vendus jusqu'a $115 et $125 ont baissé de prix. Ils sont maintenant a $100."

Prices seem to have held around $80 throughout 1877, as shown by Table 4. Then there was another rise in the spring, as shown in Table 5 (compiled from price reports in the *Winnipeg Free Press*). Only one more reference to price was found after this, in the *Free Press* of April 22, 1879: "Holders of scrip are asking from $125 to $130 for it." Considering the rate at which scrip was redeemed, notes must have been relatively rare by that time.

Assignments were cheaper than actual scrip notes, so prices quoted out

Table 4. Scrip Prices 1877–1878	
Date	Price ($)
July 12, 1877	80.00*
August 18, 1877	85.00**
August 23, 1877	85.00*
September 22, 1877	80.00**
December 1, 1877	80.00**
January 2, 1878	80.00**
Source: *Le Métis; **Winnipeg Free Press.	

Table 5. Scrip Prices, Spring 1878	
Date	Price ($)
April 20, 1878	120.00
April 25, 1878	105.00
May 10, 1878	108.00
May 23, 1878	102.00–103.00
May 29, 1878	103.00
June 12, 1878	95.00
June 14, 1878	92.00

Table 6. Land Taken Up in Manitoba, 1875–1878	
Year	Amount (Acres)
1875	163,777
1876	154,533
1877	400,424
1878	682,591

of context have to be treated with caution. Those Métis who waited to draw their own scrip probably benefitted more than those who sold their claims early. There was a tendency for the price to surge ahead in the spring of the year and another tendency for the price to rise over time, possibly because the issue of scrip came during the run-up to the great Winnipeg land boom. The annual reports of the Winnipeg lands agent show the growth in land taken up during this period (Table 6, compiled from *Canada Sessional Papers*). The secular rise in the price of scrip accompanied a rise in the price of land caused by immigration. It may also be true that the availability of scrip, by making land cheaper *de facto*, encouraged more of it to be taken up, and the issue of scrip may have been a causal factor in the onset of the Winnipeg land boom.

Military Bounty Warrants

We can get a comparative perspective on the market for scrip and children's allotments through study of the 1,599 military bounty warrants distributed to Canadian soldiers serving in Manitoba between 1870 and 1875. Legally, warrants resembled land scrip rather than money scrip. Like land scrip, warrants were vouchers for 160 acres of Dominion Lands, not $160 to be spent on Dominion Lands. Because they were denominated in acres rather than dollars, they were considered real estate rather than personal property, and their sale required the formality of written assignments and affidavits of execution. The Department of the Interior retained the located warrants and any attached assignments, thus creating a convenient body of data on sales and prices.[64]

A probe of 100 randomly chosen files yielded a sample of eighty-four usable cases in which the sales history of the warrant was complete, or nearly so. Only 6% of the warrants in the sample were located by the recipient; the others were sold for cash. In three-quarters of these sales, the recipients sold the warrants before they received them, giving their discharge certificates to the purchasers, who then applied to the Department of the Interior for the issue of the warrants. Some militiamen sold their warrants or rights after they returned to Ontario or Quebec, but most sold them in Winnipeg shortly after discharge. It was a way of raising money to go back to the east or to make a new start in the west.

Once in the market, the warrants were often resold before being located. Only twenty-three of the sample were located by the first purchaser, the rest being resold at least once. The statistical average was 2.02 sales per warrant, with a median and mode of 2, and a maximum of 6.

Price tended to climb with resale. The average price of all first sales, in which the money went to the discharged militiaman, was $77.56 (n = 78),[65] whereas the average price of all last resales, immediately before location of the warrant, was $128.82 (n = 54). In practice, an immigrant looking to purchase a quarter-section would pay very close to $160 for a warrant, for that was the cost of purchasing 160 acres from the Dominion Lands Office.

An investor had to put out money in advance, hold the warrant, then seek out new purchasers. In most cases, he also had to undertake the burden of dealing with the Department of the Interior. Significantly, the twenty militiamen who waited to receive their warrants before selling them received a much higher average price ($102.40) than the fifty-eight who sold the bare right to draw a warrant ($68.99).

As shown in Table 7, the average price of warrant sales by militiamen started low, reached a peak in 1873, then receded and levelled off thereafter. This time series makes sense in the light of known facts of Manitoba history. In 1871, military bounty warrants were still unfamiliar (the first ones were not actually issued until summer 1872), and there were not yet many immigrants to create demand for them. There was a rise in immigration through 1873, until the worldwide economic crash of that year caused the pace to slow. By 1875, sellers of warrants also had to face stiff competition in the market from Métis heads of families selling their rights to $160 money scrip. Warrants and scrip, however, were different instruments with different

Table 7. Sales Chronology of Military Bounty Warrants		
Year	Number	Average Price ($)
1871	11	35.09
1872	23	68.07
1873	9	105.33
1874	7	90.71
1875	21	93.57
1876	2	105.00
1877	2	65.00
1878	n/a	n/a
1879	3	103.33
Total	78	77.56

legal characteristics. Almost all sales were in different time periods, because scrip flooded into the market in 1876 after warrants had virtually disappeared. Whereas the data for warrants are quite good, consisting of complete sales histories, information about scrip sales must be gleaned from newspaper reports and other fortuitous sources.

In spite of the need for caution, several similarities between the two markets stand out. Recipients of both warrants and scrip generally sold at a deep discount, particularly if they sold their rights before actually obtaining the document. Intermediaries who were willing to wait for appropriate customers obtained higher prices upon resale. Prices in general tended to rise over time as the instruments became known and as the flood of early sales was cleared out of the market. Prices also varied in correlation with known historical factors such as booms and busts or the tendency of immigration to peak in the spring.

It is possible that Métis selling their rights to scrip before receiving it had to accept a deeper discount than militiamen in the same situation with respect to warrants, because there was probably more risk attached to the scrip. Scrip was issued in one great wave, starting in June 1876, to thousands of applicants bearing a relatively small number of family names and Christian names that were often repeated across generations. Whether true or false, rumours abounded that many Métis were selling their claims more than once. And the procedures under which scrip was to be distributed were uncertain because of the confusion over children and heads of families in section 31 of the Manitoba Act. Under such circumstances, a buyer of scrip claims must have perceived some risk that the money for any particular purchase might be wasted.

Warrants probably seemed less risky in comparison. They were issued in small batches as groups of soldiers were discharged. The militiamen must have often been personally known to the merchants who speculated in warrants, and in any case a discharge certificate was good evidence of eligibility to receive a warrant. There were some interim changes of the rules, as when those who had been invalided out of service before finishing their terms of enlistment were made eligible for warrants; but such adjustments were small in comparison to the massive changes that affected Métis land and scrip.

However, the data suggest that, in general terms, militiamen and Métis heads of families realized similar prices from selling their benefits. The early prices of warrants ($35.09 in 1871, $68.07 in 1872) were broadly comparable to the early prices reported for scrip ($30 to $40 before issue, rising to about $65 when it actually appeared). Prices received by militiamen in 1873 and afterwards, in the range of $90 to $100, were also similar to the prices reported for scrip in 1877 and 1878.

Conclusions

Each of the three bodies of data presented here—on allotments, scrip, and warrants—is relatively small, but they all point toward the same conclusions about the Manitoba real estate market in the 1870s and 1880s. The market for Métis lands and scrip was open and highly competitive, with many buyers and sellers actively seeking to make bargains. Sophisticated institutions arose to channel outside money into the market. Local people, some of them Métis, were hired as claim runners to bring buyers and sellers together. Information about market prices was readily available in newspapers and by word of mouth.

Some Métis entered the market with initial disadvantages: a desire to emigrate, which led them to sell quickly; unfamiliarity with the complexities of the new legal system; difficulties in reading or speaking English; and lack of contacts with prospective buyers. On the other hand, the process of buying and selling went on for years, so there was some opportunity for those unfamiliar with real estate transactions to observe and learn how the game was played. Experience with scrip should have enabled parents to advise children about their allotments. The provincial Half-Breed Land Grant Protection Act rendered unenforceable all allotment transactions entered into before July 1, 1877, thus extending the learning period. The allotments themselves were released in batches over a period of years, so that relatives and friends could learn from each other's experience.

Generally speaking, those who sold their rights to receive scrip or allotments fared more poorly than those who waited to rec⌐ documents; and those who waited to sell until the great land boom or ⌐ early 1880s did particularly well. Shrewdness and luck were not the monopoly of any one race. Métis scrip and original white settlers' scrip were indistinguishable and were treated equally in the market. Some white militiamen sold their warrants, and some Métis sold their scrip and allotments, at foolishly low prices. Many white investors overplayed their hand and lost large amounts of money after the boom collapsed in 1882. At that point in time, Métis children who had taken $100 in cash for their allotments would have looked like winners.

The amounts that the Métis received for their allotments and scrip seem small today, but they must be evaluated in the context of contemporary prices. A basic workman's wage was about $1.25 a day in the early 1880s, or $375 a year for a six-day week with two weeks off. Letter carriers in Winnipeg made $400 a year, prison guards $600. The average allotment sale price of $193 was thus the equivalent of several months wages from a full-time job. By the standards of the 1870s or 1880s, these were considerable sums of money. They should have been of real benefit in improving the existing river lots of those Métis farmers who stayed near Winnipeg; purchasing new farms elsewhere for those who chose to relocate; buying guns and horses for those who wanted to follow the buffalo; and acquiring horses and oxen for those who wanted to expand the traditional Métis business of cartage.

These findings shed useful light on the dispossession thesis. They show that the Métis, as a group, received significant sums of money for their land and scrip. Some individuals may have been foolish or may have been cheated, but others did exceptionally well in the boom market of the early 1880s. On average, the Métis could resort to a lively market in which cash, not race, was the primary consideration. They had many reasons for wishing to sell their benefits, including the pull of the buffalo robe trade, the push of English-Protestant immigrants to Manitoba, and the desire to found new communities where they could get better land for farming while preserving their social homogeneity. As Ens has shown with respect to the river lots of the Métis, the decision to sell out and move on did not arise primarily from the federal government's land policies as administered by the Department of the Interior.

These findings also cast considerable doubt on Sprague's account of the fate of children's allotments and scrip for heads of families. However, the dispossession thesis is a complex theory with many ramifications, and further research is required to test all the hypotheses associated with it.

cop out??

8. Dispossession vs. Accommodation in Plaintiff vs. Defendant Accounts of Métis Dispersal from Manitoba, 1870–1881 (1991)

D.N. Sprague

From the perspective of the preceding chapter this is the other side of the coin. Examined from a different angle, the historical data appear to point in three parallel directions: there was no Red River Métis dispersal before the 1870s; the sale of lands was subjected to unfair speculation and the use of a lottery system; and cynical young governments (Canada and Manitoba) used administrative delays to further dislocate the aborted Métis Nation.

According to well-established Métis oral tradition, the Red River Resistance of 1869–1870 was more than Canada could bear. Riel was driven from power; his people lost their land; and the Red River Métis were forced to ever more remote parts of their own homeland by hostile invaders. They were classic victims. Such is the stuff of oral tradition—it simplifies and deifies, but reduces complex reality to the nub of some usable memory, not necessarily false.[1] An oral tradition is an inherited approximation, a collective editing of fact. For people without written history or archives, the importance of maintaining such touch with the past is perhaps most well developed.

For academic historians, oral traditions are useful for formulating questions in documentary investigation. From the 1930s George Stanley, for example, was alert to evidence of victimization and confirmed the injustice done Riel.[2] At the same time, he reiterated the legend of the wholesale swindle of the general population, but without elaborate documentation of the process, nor did Stanley impugn the essential good faith of Canada's negotiators of the Manitoba Act, or of the administration of the land-promise provisions of the statute by the Department of the Interior. Nor did W.L. Morton or the other academic historians touching upon the subject in the 1950s and 1960s. The novelty of the dispossession-preceding-migration explanation of the turnover of population in Manitoba in academic history appearing in the 1980s was the suggestion that Métis dispersal was fostered by "government lawlessness," processes of legislative amendment and administration that unfolded more or less without regard to legal propriety.[3]

The reckless amendment aspect of "government lawlessness" was found in the evisceration of the land-promise provisions of the Manitoba Act by amending statutes and orders in council (as if the law were any ordinary statute, rather than an integral part of the constitution of Canada). The other aspect of "lawlessness" appeared in the records of the Department of the Interior showing its discriminatory administration of land claims. Since the two patterns of evidence together are the basis for allegations in a lawsuit still pending,[4] the "government lawlessness" version of the story is fairly characterized as the plaintiff account of Métis dispersal.

Historians Gerhard Ens and Thomas Flanagan have been retained by the Canadian Department of Justice since 1986 to defend Canada from the plaintiff's claims. Both have published what they consider a better view of the same evidence.[5] As the defendants' defenders they argue that the dispersal of the Red River Métis after 1870 was simply an acceleration or accentuation of disintegration evident for at least a decade before the transfer of Rupert's Land to Canada. In 1870 (continuing to about 1872) many conflicts are admitted to have occurred between old settlers and newcomers, especially between the French-Catholic Métis and Ontario-origin Protestants. Such conflict (said to be completely beyond the control of Canada) is regarded by Flanagan and Ens as tipping the balance in the minds of many Métis who were already tempted by the pull factors that are supposed to have become almost irresistible by the 1860s. The assertion Ens and Flanagan stress is that virtually all persons who wanted to remain on the land they occupied in 1870 had merely to corroborate their claims to occupancy with the testimony of neighbours, and their titles would eventually be confirmed as free grants by Canada. So powerful was the temptation to sell, however, particularly in the context of escalating land values during the boom of 1880 to 1882, that even many confirmed landowners sold out and moved on. At the same time, of course, they liquidated other assets. Flanagan argues that the prices received reflected fair current values. On that account, if descendants of the original settlers in poor circumstances today identify the root of their problems with the imaginary dispossession of their ancestors in the last century, they dream a "morally destructive"[6] nightmare in Flanagan's characterization. According to Ens and Flanagan, Canada fulfilled and over-fulfilled the land promise provisions of the Manitoba Act. Some small mistakes were made, but as errors in good faith; the assertion of an overall pattern of *deliberate* discouragement conflicts with what Flanagan calls "over-whelming" evidence proving nearly the exact opposite was the case.[7]

What follows is a comparison of the evidence of the two sides on the issues for which a central claim and counter-claim have emerged to date.

Migration History

Did the pattern of the 1870s represent a dramatic accentuation? or abrupt departure from previous trends?

The position taken by Ens on migration, 1870–1881, is basically a continuity thesis. Table 1 exhibits some figures reported by Ens in support of his argument. A quick glance at the population trends in St. Andrew's and St. François Xavier (SFX) shows that both parishes sustained phenomenal growth rates even with considerable out-migration for his first period of observation, 1835 to 1849. The population of the Protestant-Métis parish increased 195% in that fourteen-year period. The Catholic-Métis example grew slightly less rapidly in the same interval (180%) because SFX sustained a higher rate of outmigration. Still, the base period was one of unsurpassed *rates* of growth for both areas of the Red River settlement.

Table 1. Population Trends, Whole Settlement vs. Select Areas						
Year	St. Andrew's		SFX		Whole Settlement	
	Observed	Expected	Observed	Expected	Observed	Expected
1835	547	—	506	—	3646	—
1849	1068	—	911	—	5391	—
1856	1207	—	1101	—	8691	—
1863	—	2082	—	1640	—	7979
1870	1456	—	1857	—	11960	—
1877	—	4060	967	2952	—	11809
1881	947	—	743	—	—	—

Explanation: "Expected" figures are based on the rate of increase for each area observed in the interval between 1835 and 1849 (195% in 14 years for St. Andrew's, 180% in 14 years for St. François Xavier, and 148% in 14 years for the whole settlement).

Sources: The St. Andrew's and SFX "Observed" values are in Ens, "Dispossession or Adaptation," 128, 136, and 138 (footnote 62); Whole Settlement "Observed" values are the totals from the Red River Census of 1835 and 1849 in the Hudson's Bay Company Archives, Provincial Archives of Manitoba and the tabulation of the 1870 census of Manitoba reported in the Canadian Sessional Papers, No. 20 (1871).

The new pattern, allegedly extending into the 1870s, is supposed to be evident from the 1850s and 1860s. According to Ens, there was a steady increase in out-migration in response to a dramatic change in the economy, a shift away from summer-autumn pemmican production (with people maintaining a home-base claim to their river-front properties at Red River) towards winter harvest of buffalo for their hide and fur when the coat of the beasts was thickest. With more people chasing fewer animals at a different time of year, the result was expansion of the trade at the expense of the population of the Red River settlement. Ens argues that "scrip records" of the Department of the Interior, 1885–1921, show an ever-increasing exodus which began in the 1850s.[8]

The most serious difficulty with the attempt to locate the beginning of the great dispersal before 1870 is that the argument relies on population trends in two parishes taken in isolation from the rest of the settlement. When the focus shifts to the larger picture, the "Whole Settlement" column of Table 1, the obvious conclusion is that the older parishes began to exhibit declining rates of increase in the 1850s and 1860s as they became crowded and more and more people moved to well-timbered vacant land in nearby satellite parishes. As a result, the rate of increase in the older areas began to level off, but population increase for the settlement as a whole (projected as a figure from the overall rate of growth observed for the 1835–1849 period) continued unabated. Indeed, the whole-settlement population expected for 1863 and 1877 (on the sustained rate calculation projecting the 1835–1849 rate to 1877) was in fact exceeded by the observed figures for 1856 and 1870. In other words, while the rate of increase in the over-populated parishes slowed, that of the newer areas in Red River accelerated because the population surplus from the old spilled over to vacant land in the new. The hypothesis of an increasing *rate* of outmigration to distant destinations is not sustained by the undiminished growth of the community taken as the old parishes and their nearby satellites. Net migration plus natural increase sustained the same rate of growth for that entity from 1850 to 1870, as from 1835 to 1849. Table 1 shows that the dramatic change from the pattern—the real break in continuity—dated from the 1870s, not the 1860s.

Persistence to 1875

Large or Small?
While the population data show that the great dispersal began sometime before 1877, the same figures do not show the precise timing and, of course, the reasons for migration between 1870 and 1877. Ens and Flanagan admit that certain push factors were present in August 1870. They deny that the

pushes—formal or informal—were as powerful as the lure of the new fur trade dating from the earlier period. They agree that a "reign of terror"[9] began with the arrival of Canada's peacekeepers and continued until 1872[10]; they do not hold Canada responsible for the lawlessness. Nor do they see delays of Métis land claims during the terror period (along with encouragement of newcomers to take up land wherever they found apparently vacant locations)[11] as part of an unstated policy of deliberate discouragement to original settlers. Ens and Flanagan insist that the outcome was an inadvertent rather than an intended result. From that standpoint, it is important to show that large-scale migration began before a single claimant was disappointed in his land claim.

Late in 1873 Canada finally opened the door to wholesale consideration of Métis claims to river lots, and more than two thousand applications for letters patent confirming ownership came forward over the next twelve months. The surveyor general reported in December 1874 that "2059 applications under section 32, and subsequent amendment[s] of the Manitoba Act, have been received and filed, of which, 614 have been examined and recommended for patent."[12] Over the next several years Canada completed the examination of several hundred more claims. Table 2 shows that by the end of 1877 approximately 850 river lot claims had passed through the process of application, consideration, and confirmation. The same tabulation also makes clear that roughly one-third (282 of 855) represented cases of purported buyers claiming the land of occupants who may have sold out *before* 1875. According to Ens, "This early glut of river-lot sales would seem to contradict Mailhot and Sprague's assertion that 90 per cent of those Métis found in the 1870 census were still in the settlement in 1875."[13] In fact, the record of the "early glut of river-lot sales" exhibited in Table 2 is evidence of something completely separate from the issue of the persistence of an increasingly discouraged Métis population.

The data supporting Mailhot and Sprague's "assertion" of large-scale persistence are census returns reported in 1875 permitting comparison with the pattern of 1870. The 1870 figures, printed in the *Sessional Papers* of 1871,[14] indicate that the Métis population then was 9,800 people (9,778 according to the enumeration of the whole province by "English" enumerators, 9,840 according to the "French"). The comparison number for 1875 is found in the returns of commissioners who took affidavits from Métis and descendants of "original white settlers" to enrol both for Canada's revised concept of the benefit of section 31 of the Manitoba Act and its amendments. Their lists of diverse categories of claimants have survived for nearly every parish.[15] Table 3 shows that Commissioners Machar and Ryan accounted for more than

Table 2. Manitoba Act Grants of River Lots by Parish and Year

Year	French Parishes				English Parishes				Totals
	Old		New		Old		New		
	Owner	Buyer	Owner	Buyer	Owner	Buyer	Owner	Buyer	
April–June 1875	57	10	2	—	102	11	28	—	210
June 1876–March 1877	78	46	9	15	124	34	29	20	355
March–November 1877	44	52	24	45	41	33	35	16	290
Totals	179	108	35	60	267	78	92	36	855

Explanation: "Old" parishes are the areas included in the HBC survey in the 1830s. "Old French" are St. Boniface, St. Charles, St. Vital, St. Norbert, and SFX. "New French" are Ste. Anne, St. Laurent, Ste. Agathe and Baie St. Paul. "Old English" includes St. Johns, Kildonan, Headingly, St. Pauls, St. Andrew's, and St. Clements. "New English" are Portage la Prairie, Poplar Point, High Bluff and Westburne.

Until 1878, special forms were used for different kinds of Dominion Lands grants. "D.L. Grant (33. Vic)" distinguished Manitoba Act grants from all others. Each such patent described the land, named the owner in 1870 as well as the patentee.

Source: Government copies of the Manitoba Act grant patents are in the National Archives of Canada, microfilm reel C-3992, C-3994, and C-3996. The confirmation that the three cited locations embrace every "D.L. Grant (33 Vic)" is the Alphabetical Index, Parish Land, Manitoba (1875–1883), also in the NAC, microfilm reel M-1640.

9,000 of the persons enrolled in the 1870 census. However, Machar found about 500 "half breeds" in the 1870 enumeration of the Protestant parishes ineligible for Canada's concept of benefits under section 31 in 1875 (mainly because they had "taken treaty" since 1871 and become "Indians," or because they were absent at the time of the transfer on July 15 but present for enrolment in the census in October, or because they were children whose birth dates fell between the date of the transfer and time of the census, between July and October 1870). Ryan's list of claims "disallowed" in the French Catholic parishes has not been found. But assuming a rate of disallowance in the Catholic parishes that was at least half as much as the Protestant (because French "half breeds" were less likely to have "taken treaty"), the number of disallowed claims for the Catholic parishes by reason of absence from Manitoba on the date of the transfer and disqualifying birth date was probably no less than 250 persons, making an overall total of 9,334—"half breeds" and "original white settlers"—in 1875. Since 714 of the claimants were in the "original white settler" category, the persistent Métis component would appear to be 8,620 persons, or 88% of the 1870 figure.

Table 3. Enrolment of Manitoba "Half-Breeds" and "Original White Settlers" by Commissioners Machar and Ryan, May–December 1875

	Categories of Claimants				
	"Half breed"			Whites	Totals
	"heads"	"children"	disallowed		
Protestant Parishes					
St. Peters	35	61	270	—	366
St. Clements	132	251	3		420
St.Andrew's	392	798	116	29	1335
Kildonan	23	58	5	369	455
St. Johns	44	106	27	38	215
St. Pauls	66	133	11	27	237
St. James	87	157	6	21	271
Headingly	56	156	11	45	268
High Bluff/Pop. R.	160	360	27	22	569
Portage/White Mud	78	178	33	24	313
Catholic Parishes					
St. Boniface	283	526		19	828
St. Vital	72	171		44	287
St. Norbert	252	562		19	833
Ste. Agathe	135	240			375
Ste. Anne	81	226		32	339
St. Charles	97	190		3	290
SFX/Baie St. Paul	495	897		22	1414
St. Laurent/Oak R.	80	189			269
Totals	2568	5259	543	714	9084

Machar canvassed the Protestant parishes, Ryan the Catholic. Sources: See footnote 15.

The situation of many persisting families with unresolved claims puts in question migration estimates based on purported sales of land by "landowners" where a landowner population is still indeterminate. The census of 1875 provides a more appropriate statement of the facts regarding persistence to that time. There were approximately 2,000 Métis families in the Red River settlement in 1870, and approximately 1,800 were enumerated again in 1875. River lot claims establish that 2,059 persons represented themselves as "landowners" by 1874 but 1,200 were still unconfirmed as late as December 1877. Since the beginning of the great exodus would appear to fall between 1875 and 1877, Canada's delays and denials might account for far more migration than Ens and Flanagan are willing to concede.

Canada's Confirmation of Titles to River Lots

Every occupant seeking accommodation? or systematic denial of the customary rights guaranteed by the Manitoba Act?

Ens's analysis of land occupancy and sale presupposes a system of formal survey and documentary evidence establishing a chain of title from date of survey to most recent recorded owner. No survey, no land description or record of ownership. No record of ownership, no owner. Sprague's discussion of Métis land tenure assumes a system of customary demarcation of boundaries and descent of rights by community consent. People allotted what they needed. They owned what they used. The obvious point of potential conflict between the two historians was also the point of disagreement between the Métis and Canada in 1869. Métis leaders recognized that the transfer of Rupert's Land to the new Dominion would bring a transition from the customary to the formal system of land tenures, and there was no assurance when Canada's surveyors started their work even before the transfer that the existing population would not be "driven back from the rivers and their land given to others."[16] What made the potential for conflict all the more ominous was that the Red River settlement already had a system of land survey and registry that covered enough of the population that some future authority might be tempted to assert that everyone who deserved protection was already registered.

The system of survey and registry that was partially in effect dated from the mid-1830s. Always eager for a new way to turn a shilling, the Hudson's Bay Company (HBC) had authorized subdivision of the settlement almost as soon as the company clarified the matter of overall title with the heirs of Lord Selkirk. The surveyor hired for the task of confirming the boundaries of the lots occupied by Selkirk settlers (to receive free land), other settlers (expected to pay), and room to grow (lot by lot as succeeding generations of established settlers and newcomers bought land from the HBC) was George Taylor. He laid out 1528 river lots of approximately 100 acres each by 1838 and the HBC capped the project with the opening of a land registry that most settlers cheerfully ignored.[17] In effect, the settlement developed on a dual-track basis—customary as well as formal, especially as the population expanded beyond the limits of the Taylor survey in the 1850s.

By 1860 the HBC abandoned any pretense of enforcing payment for lands. That year, the local Council of Assiniboia adopted a homestead ordinance affirming the legitimacy of the customary, unrecorded system, but required a survey and registration of ownership (in the territory beyond the Taylor survey) where disputes arose. To be sure, settlers with some knowledge of the paper mysteries surrounding formal land tenure did order such surveys in advance of their occcupation of vacant land. R.A. Ruttan, the commissioner of Dominion Lands in Winnipeg in the late 1880s, explained the practice to Archer Martin, a jurist-historian trying to make sense of Red River land tenures in the mid-1890s:

> The Council of Assiniboia authorized two surveyors [probably the only ones in the settlement] Goulet and Sabine, to make surveys for parties desiring to take up land *outside the H.B. surveys.* A survey made by one of those gentlemen defined the land which you or I might hold: gave us a facility for recording too. There was no limit other than that imposed by custom to the river frontage (the country distant from the rivers wasn't considered of any value in those days) which might be taken, excepting the Minute of Council which prescribed 12 chains as the limit in cases of dispute which practically enabled one to take possession of part of the property if anyone were trying to hold more than 12 chains.
>
> I cannot learn that there ever was a dispute before "the transfer."[18]

Unfortunately for the Métis, Canada took the formalities of ownership more seriously than the pattern of residency. Mailhot and Sprague were careful to point out that "the land surveyors were not part of a conspiracy to overlook most Métis while recording a few."[19] They do suggest, however, that the surveyors were more interested in running the boundaries of lots than mapping the locations of persons in the haste to complete everything quickly.[20] The result was many families included in the 1870 census are not found in the surveyor's field notes,[21] even though most such persons enrolled in 1870 were enumerated as residents again in 1875 by the "Half breed commission." Subsequently, any such resident faced two obstacles in establishing his claim by occupancy under the amendments of the Manitoba Act. The first was proving his residency notwithstanding the surveyor's returns to the contrary. Ens and Flanagan correctly point out that supporting affidavits from nearest neighbours were sometimes sufficient to establish occupation overlooked by the surveyor. They conclude too readily, however, that officials at the first level of consideration (Dominion Lands Office, Winnipeg) were willing to accept claims without evidence of "really valuable improvements." No amount of neighbourly corroboration could establish a Métis claim in the mid-1870s if the level of improvements was considered insufficient proof of "occupation."[22] And no level of improvements by "squatters" could establish their title if a non-resident "owner" produced documentation of a chain of title predating the tenure of the actual resident.[23] Table 4 exhibits the scope of vulnerability. What makes the tabulation especially interesting is that the labelling and numbers (except for the "Whole Settlement" column) are Ens's own words and data.

Table 4. Recognition of 1870 Occupants by Canada						
	St. Andrew's		SFX		Whole Settlement	
Occupancy Status	Number	(%)	Number	(%)	Number	(%)
Owned or were recognized as being in possession.	161	56	174	52	959	53
Residing on lots owned by other members of the extended family or squatting on others' land.	126	44	160	48	849	47
Total	287	100	334	100	1808	100

Sources: The Occupancy Status labels and data for St. Andrew's and SFX are from Ens, "Dispossession or Adaptation," 136 (footnote 50) and 128 (Table 1); Whole Settlement data are from Mailhot and Sprague, "Persistent Settlers," 11 (Table 1).

The key issue pertains to the half of the population that Ens and Flanagan consider justifiably outside the claims process. The observation that Canada eventually accorded direct or indirect recognition of everyone except the half of the population in Ens's "squatter" category begs the question of the accommodation or denial of "squatter" rights. A better view of the data in Table 4 (in comparison with Table 2) is that almost half of the entire population of the Red River settlement were excluded from the outset. Such a suggestion is supported by testimonial evidence as well.

Joseph Royal, member of Parliament representing the French parishes of Manitoba, wrote numerous letters to officials in Ottawa from the mid-1870s through the early 1880s seeking "more liberal" treatment of "squatters" claims. In the spring of 1880 his appeal took the form of a concise history intended to persuade the prime minister that the administration of such cases since 1870 had been anything but accommodating. Royal asserted that "hundreds of claims are disallowed, *not having this or that*, which was never required by the Act of Manitoba." The especially difficult cases involved settlement without survey, and occupancy with little "improvement":

> We easily understand the difficulty for officials to recognize
> the condition of things [before the transfer] which admitted
> of nothing official, and it was in fact with a foresight of that
> difficulty that the people of Red River dreaded a loss of
> their property. They knew perfectly well that their right to

the portion of the Settlement Belt regularly surveyed and occupied could not be disputed, but they apprehended that the same right to the land they possessed outside of the surveyed Settlement Belt might be contested: consequently that they would be, more or less, at the mercy of the New Government that might refuse to accept or understand the former condition of this country.[24]

Royal was not alone in making the same complaint. The principal spokesman for Métis interests in the negotiations for the Manitoba Act, Noël Ritchot (parish priest of St. Norbert), also appealed to Macdonald, in Ritchot's case as one negotiator of the Manitoba Act to another. Ritchot reminded the prime minister that they both knew that the law was

> not intended to say that all persons having a good written title and duly registered, etc etc that he shall have continually resided and cultivated so many acres of land yearly and for so many years before the Transfer to Canada, and that he shall cultivate and continually reside during the period of ten years after the Transfer to Canada, so many acres etc etc to be entitled to letters Patent for lands so cultivated and inhabited, [but] ... this is what is required today by the Government through their employees.[25]

Both quotations from credible sources confirm a pattern of discouragement by delay and denial. As early as 1876, large numbers of such discouraged "squatters" were liquidating their assets and moving on. Speculators purchased rights to their claims, evidently confident that additional documentation from them would assure eventual confirmation of even the most "doubtful" cases.

Scrip and Childrens' Allotments

Valuable asset disposed of at fair market prices? or ephemeral benefit sold for derisory return?

The most plausible interpretation of the Métis people's understanding of the land promises they won in the Manitoba Act was that they had an assurance from Canada for continuity where they were already established, and additional scope to expand freely for at least one more generation onto the unoccupied terrain along the rivers and creeks of the new province. One part of the Manitoba "treaty" (section 32) protected the tenure of land already occupied. Another part (section 31) assured heads of families that they might select vacant land for their children. Such a view was not inconsistent with the assurances outside the "treaty" given in writing by Cartier in the name of Canada to Ritchot in May 1870 and by Lieutenant Governor Archibald to Métis leaders when he invited them to designate areas from which families might select their land in 1871.[26] A great deal of claim-staking followed accordingly. Commissioner Ruttan joked about the proceedings in his correspondence with Martin:

> They moved with wonderful alacrity and unanimity. Since '62 or about that time the [French Métis] had been in the habit of wintering stock along the Seine, Rat and La Salle Rivers. These lands naturally offered the favourite playground for the staker who in short order had the entire riverfront neatly staked off. A man didn't confine himself to 1 claim. He frequently had 2 or 3. Sometimes for children, present and in expectancy, he would have the riverside dizzy with "blazes" and "stakes."

> Venne, whose first name was most pertinently Solomon, must have staked 15 claims and, being of uncommon ambition, laid them down along the Red River.[27]

Notwithstanding Archibald's encouragement, the Dominion government refused to recognize any such arrangement as an appropriate administration of section 31 of the Manitoba Act.

In 1875 Canada launched its substitute. In the new arrangement, married adults—with or without recognized claims to river lots—were to receive a special monetary gratuity called "scrip," redeemable for 160 acres of Dominion Lands open for homestead. The population of unmarried persons (not "heads of families" therefore "children" regardless of their age) were to have access to a lottery for drawing 240-acre rectangles of open prairie, no closer than two or four miles to the "settlement belt" along the rivers. Neither benefit was of great value to the Métis, especially as the proposed method for distributing the 1.4 million acres was random selection by lottery. Flanagan observes that "the partition of reserve land into 240-acre parcels made it difficult to resettle there as a group; it would only be by chance if a group of relatives happened to get allotments near each other." The value of both "children's" allotments and "heads of family scrip" was, therefore, as liquidated assets, in Flanagan's characterization, "to finance a departure from Manitoba."[28] From that perspective, the Métis would have been more justly served (and at considerably less trouble to the bureaucracy) if Canada had simply handed each head of family $160 and each "child" $240, and ordered them to move. Instead, the government called the residents of all of the parishes to meet with commissioners in the summer of 1875 to swear to their residency in Manitoba on July 15, 1870. Each person whose claim was corroborated by at least two neighbours was assured future consideration. In the meantime, on-the-spot speculators were willing to pay $30 or $40 instant gratification to secure power of attorney to collect whatever reward should arrive in the future.[29] The government then offered deliberate or inadvertent protection to such speculators by requiring every claimant "not known personally to the Dominion Lands Agent" to hire an intermediary who was known to the man behind the counter to do the actual collecting of the land or scrip.[30] The holder of the power of attorney thus had the edge over the claimant. Still, an important element of risk remained for "attorneys" because individual "half breeds" were said to have sold their claims more than once. Consequently, when the first scrip arrived in Winnipeg in June 1876, there was a great rush on the land office by the speculators to claim their property. They had to rush because Canada distributed the paper to the first "attorney" in line for the claim. Later arrivals were simply denied their reward (Canada did not wish to investigate frauds).[31]

The process of separating recipients of the 240-acre allotments from their land was somewhat more orderly. Moreover, since allotments were of land rather than a specialty currency, their distribution had the fuller cover of documentation that necessarily surrounds all transactions in real estate. More documents mean more room for conventional historical debate as well.

Flanagan does not question the propriety of Canada's substitution of scrip and bald prairie for the benefit the Métis preferred but he does state the facts of enrolment and allotment clearly and correctly: by the end of 1875 more than 5,000 "children" were enrolled, drawings began in 1876, continued in 1877, then became stalled in 1878, according to Flanagan, "for reasons that are not fully understood."[32] Table 5 shows the pattern—Protestant parishes first, the large French-Métis parishes last. The sequence has considerable analytical significance because the timing meant that the allotments for SFX, for example, were not available until that parish had begun wholesale dispersal of its 1870 population (compare Table 5 with Tables 1 and 2).

Still, the migration of recipients was no impediment to the sale of their land. Table 6 shows that in a random sample of 289 allottees whose parentage and sale history have been traced, French-Métis children with landless parents (probably the first to migrate) were also the most likely to become separated from their land within one year of allotment. Nor was age a barrier: almost 60% of a larger random sample of "vendors" were under the legal age of 21 (the age of majority in general application). Flanagan's sample of fifty-nine cases shows that a smaller proportion of land recipients were

Table 5. Timing of Grants by Parish, October 1876–February 1880						
Parishes*	1876	1877	1878	1879	1880	Totals
Portage la Prairie	183					183
Kildonan	55	11	11			77
Ste. Anne	163	58				221
St. Peters		68				68
St. Clements		264				264
St. Andrew's		840				840
St. Pauls		133				133
St. Johns		113				113
Headingly		163				163
High Bluff		359				359
St. Laurent		194				194
St. James			179			179
Ste. Agathe			279			279
St. Charles			186			186
St. Boniface			768	24		792
St. Norbert					631	631
St. François Xavier					1319	1319
Totals	401	2203	1423	24	1950	6001

*Poplar Point probably included with High Bluff, St. Vital with St. Boniface and St. Norbert, and Baie St. Paul with SFX.

Source: National Archives of Canada, "Register of Grants to Half-Breed Children," RG 15, volume 1476.

under age when they became separated from their allotments,[33] in part because Flanagan uses age 18 as the appropriate threshold, and partly because his sample is too small to test the relationship between age and date of sale. Table 7 shows that the ages of the overall population are so skewed beyond 21 years by the time most allotments occurred, that a much larger sample than Flanagan's is needed to draw a population of minors large enough for meaningful statistical generalization.

Given customary preferences as to location and patterns of occupancy, the issue of sale versus retention was settled as soon as Canada devised the lottery scheme from section land on open prairie. No better system for encouraging immediate sale could have been invented. The more open question concerns value received. Table 8 exhibits data from sales records supporting Flanagan's contention that the proceeds to Métis vendors were

Table 6. Tenure of Children's Allotments by Land Status of Parents

Parents' Status	Children's Tenure (in years)			Totals
	less than 1	1 to 5	5 or more	
landless French Métis	72	5	4	81
landless English Métis	27	9	11	47
French Métis patentees	63	7	9	79
English Métis patentees	35	30	17	82
Totals	197	51	41	289

Sources: Every tenth grant starting with grant 10 drawn from the Grants Register (NAC RG 15, vol. 1476) yielded a sample of 626 cases. Linkage with a separate register of "Manitoba Half Breed Children" (NAC RG 15, vol. 1505) yielded information on parentage enabling linkage with the land tenure data compiled from the "Census of Manitoba, 1870" (MG2 B3) and land patent data cited in Table 2. Information on tenure of the children's allotments was taken from the Abstract Books in the Winnipeg and Morden Land Titles Offices.

Table 7. Ages of Recipients of Children's Allotments at Date of Separation from Land Grant

Ages	Sale Periods				Totals
	1876–78	1879–81	1882–84	1885 and later	
8	1				1
9	1				1
10	3	4			7
11	2	4			6
12		14	1		15
13	1	12	4		17
14	2	7	1		10
15	1	4	4	1	10
16	1	9	3		13
17	1	7	4	1	13
18	4	23	19	23	69
19	2	16	9	11	38
20	6	15	2	12	35
21	8	16	1	13	38
22+	40	51	15	26	132
Totals	73	182	63	87	405

Sources: Grant registers and Abstract Books cited under Table 6.

Table 8. Average Recorded Sale Prices of Children's Grants by Chronological Period of Sale and Ethnicity of "Vendor"

	Chronological Period		Overall Averages (Totals)
Ethnicity	1876–78	1879 and later	
"French" vendors (74% illiterate)	$213 (N=31)	$394 (N=245)	$374 (N=276)
"English" vendors (44% illiterate)	$126 (N=76)	$317 (N=119)	$242 (N=195)
Overall Averages (Totals)	$151 (N=107)	$369 (N=364)	$310 (N=471)

Sources: Literacy information taken from Powers of Attorney in NAC, RG 15, volumes 1421–1423. Ethnicity and sales price data are from grant registers and Abstract Books cited under Table 6.

more than reasonable, an overall average exceeding $1 per acre (approximately the same value obtained by sellers of other unimproved lands distant from the rivers).

On closer scrutiny, however, a surprising anomaly becomes readily apparent. It is known that the exodus from the French-Métis parishes such as SFX was well on its way by 1877, and nearly complete by the time of the allotment of that parish in 1880. There is also reason to suggest that almost three-quarters of the "children" in the French parishes could neither read nor write to the extent of signing their own names on the sales documents. Notwithstanding the two disabilities of absenteeism and illiteracy, the anomaly is that they appear to have received the very best prices for their land—almost $400 per 240-acre allotment.

One possible explanation is the rapidly rising land values after 1879, but the other anomaly is that the recipients of land in the English parishes in 1876 and 1877, who held on to their allotments waiting for just such a speculative return, fared remarkably more poorly than the illiterate, absentee recipients of land in the French parishes purportedly selling in the same period after 1879. Is it possible that the documents filed at the Land Registry and Dominion Lands Office were fictional covers for much less respectable—or even nonexistent—sales?

According to the sworn testimony of the chief justice of the Manitoba Court of Queen's Bench before a provincial commission inquiring into the sales of "half breed lands" in 1881, actual prices were $40 to $80 per 240-acre claim. The reason for the discrepancy with the documentary evidence, in Justice Wood's testimony (and he was in an excellent position to know because he and three of his sons played important roles in claim running), is that almost anything was possible in the construction of the paper trail from allottee to the land office:

All sorts of conveyances were resorted to. Deeds were executed beforehand in blank. A power of attorney was taken
to fill them up, or they were filled up without it. And so
soon as the allotment came up, there was such a race to the
Registry Office with the conveyances to get registered first
that horses enough could not be found in the City of
Winnipeg for that purpose. In some cases, a man would be
at the Registry Office with his deed, and they [his accom-
plices] would telegraph him the number of the section [as
soon as it was posted in the parish outside Winnipeg], when
he would fill it in, and thus be enabled to put in his deed
fast—five or ten minutes perhaps before half a dozen others
would come rushing into the office with deeds for the same
lands. The Halfbreed lost all moral rectitude and would sell
to every man as fast as they possibly could—all the contest
was as to registering the papers first.[35]

While Wood blamed the allottees for multiple "sales" of the same property, the absence of hundreds if not thousands of "vendors" from the
province at the time of the purported transactions would suggest many
instances of "sales" with no involvement of the owner at all. Either way,
however, the risks to buyers were great and would predict low prices for
Métis lands. Quite simply—why would a claim runner pay "retail" prices
for land he was acquiring "wholesale," especially considering that the
"wholesale" buyer had little assurance that his paper was going to be the
first conveyance registered? Flanagan concedes that such purchases were
risky, and his selective quotation of testimony from the record of the provincial commission of inquiry impugning the veracity of all such documents
suggests deep skepticism is warranted.[36] Inexplicably, however, Flanagan
concludes that the sales contracts all "appear normal."[37] The conclusion
strains his credibility, to say the least.

Conclusions

Undisputed statistical data impugn the hypothesis of accommodation on
four central points:

   1. *The Red River settlement sustained the phenomenal growth of the 1830s
   to 1870.*

Crowding of population was a problem in the older parishes, but the pull
of migration before the transfer was mainly to nearby river frontage rather
than to the smaller settlements in the distant west and north. Red River

remained the central location of the Métis "nation." To be sure, profound internal divisions developed along lines of religion and economic interest. Even so, the shared fear of disruption by colonization from Canada united Red River in one effective community, the provisional government of 1869-1870. The success of negotiating the "Manitoba treaty" with Canada in April appeared to guarantee continuing political autonomy and adequate land to assure continuity for the Red River settlement as a province of Canada after 1870.

2. Almost 90% of the Métis population enumerated in the autumn of 1870 persisted to 1875, evidently waiting for the terms of the "Manitoba treaty" to come into effect.

Flanagan concedes that Métis patience was bound to be disappointed, however, because Canada had "no intention of establishing a Métis enclave,"[38] no intention of administering the Manitoba Act as understood by the Métis leadership. Nor did Canada sustain Lieutenant Governor Archibald in his similar understanding of the law and its appropriate administration. The Government of Canada regarded the Métis as a "semi-barbarian," "insurgent" population in need of rule by a "strong hand until ... swamped by the influx of settlers."[39] For two years the population was terrorized by a Canadian "peacekeeping" force. For four years, not one Métis claim to a river lot was confirmed in accordance with section 32, not one Métis reserve was established "for the benefit of the families of the half-breed residents" in accordance with section 31.

3. Once Canada did devise a process for administering claims through the Department of the Interior in 1873, the Lands Branch received 2,059 applications for titles to river lots by the end of 1874, but confirmed less than 42% as late as 1878, moving especially slowly on the claims to river lots in the parishes that had developed without general survey before 1870.

Registered owners of lands surveyed under the authority of the HBC were most likely to obtain their patents within one or two years from date of application. A "squatter" improving vacant land registered in the name of another person had to disprove the competing title to establish his own; a "squatter" on vacant Crown land with improvements overlooked by surveyors faced enormous frustration proving occupation contrary to surveyors' returns. Anyone discouraged by the process (for whatever reason) became increasingly tempted to sell his land (at discounted value) to the growing army of land sharks willing to pay at least some pittance for a claim, no matter how "doubtful." Then, after submission of appropriate supplementary documentation a patent would eventually issue to the speculator. As more and more lots passed from original occupants to apparent newcomers, Canada relaxed its criteria concerning the kind of improvements needed to establish a "squatter's" claim. Virtually any type of land use that had routinely disqualified a Métis claim in the mid-1870s was allowed purported buyers of such lands pressing their claims in the 1880s. By that time, the dispersal of the original population was so advanced that there was no longer any threat of a significant Métis enclave remaining. By that time, Flanagan agrees, much of the "agitation carried on in the name of Métis rights had little to do with the actual interests of the Métis."[40] By the same admission, of course, most of the patents conceded after 1878 had little to do with accommodating the Métis and their claims. On that account, the observation that Canada eventually patented 1,562 river lots in the old surveyed part of the Red River settlement, and 580 in the newer, outer parishes[41] does not prove that the Métis migration was "not caused by any inability to obtain Manitoba Act patents"[42] nearly so much as the statistic documents Canada's willingness to reward the informal agents of Métis dispersal. Flanagan's interpretation mistakes long-term results (river lots were eventually patented) for what should have occurred many years earlier (when the lands were still occupied by Métis claimants).

4. Discouraged by harrassment and unreasonable delays, most Métis people dispersed from their river lot locations in the 1870s before the 1.4 million acres of reserve lands were distributed.

The value of the 1.4 million acres went to claim runners who collected patents at the Dominion Lands Office as "attorneys" of the allottees. Many nominal recipients may have known of their grants and intended to sell: some may have realized substantial considerations. The sales documents were certainly intended to create such an impression. However, the testimony of knowledgeable claim runners, lawyers, and jurists concerning transactions in Métis lands in November 1881 suggests a different reality. The sworn testimony of several witnesses impugned the veracity of the documentation generated routinely by most rapacious speculators. Since the same small population of claim runners were at the forefront of transactions in the transfer of claims to river lots as well, a cloud of suspicion must remain over all of the evidence generated by claim runners. In sum, it would seem that the "cascade of benefits"[43] concerning Métis lands in Manitoba fell upon land sharks and their cronies with connections in the bureaucratic apparatus created by Canada more than upon the people who rallied to the provisional government in 1869, and cheered the triumph of their collective resistance in 1870. By 1877 most of that population had become "desperate under the repeated delays"[44] and began selling out to finance retreat west and north. Interpreting the exodus as a reasonable adaptive response states the obvious; asserting that the migration had nothing to do with the frustration of land claims in Manitoba before 1877 is completely contrary to fact. In the case of the dispersal of the Red River Métis, justice delayed was quite literally justice denied.

9. Métis Land Claims at St. Laurent: Old Arguments and New Evidence (1987)

Thomas Flanagan

1885: the year the last spike was driven on Canada's first transcontinental railway; also, the year of the Métis Resistance. In a still pre-modern age when administrative and political communication had to contend with geographical constraints and widespread Métis illiteracy, potential governmental goodwill could be severely hampered. But to what extent should a young immature government be forgiven its all-too-frequent lapses?

*R*iel and the Rebellion: 1885 Reconsidered[1] occasioned a minor flurry of controversy, including demands by the Métis Association of Alberta, that the author be fired from the University of Calgary.[2] Several reviewers made rather extreme statements about the book. "For pure nastiness and vengefulness," wrote Murray Dobbin, "it is unmatched in recent literature. It is not simply flawed, but fundamentally flawed."[3] Ron Bourgeault, calling it "a condemnation of a people and their struggle for democracy and national rights," compared the author's views to Jim Keegstra's holocaust denial.[4] Dennis Duffy, on the other hand, called *Riel and the Rebellion* "a superb and timely work."[5] Most reviewers fell between these extremes, seeing some useful new information in the book but finding themselves unable to agree with all the author's interpretations and conclusions.[6]

Polemics are momentarily entertaining, but the most important thing in the long run is to advance historical knowledge of the Rebellion and related events. This brief article takes another look at two aspects of Métis land claims at St. Laurent: scrip and river lots. On both topics there has been continued writing, and in some instances new documentary evidence has been discovered. This article is thus an attempt to update my earlier analysis in the light of ongoing research by myself and others. My conclusions have had to be modified in certain respects, resulting in a clearer and more balanced explanation of why the Métis took up arms in 1885.

Scrip

Riel and the Rebellion argued essentially that, after many delays and administrative errors, the government was proceeding to fulfill the substance of Métis demands before the resort to arms. That is, plans were being made to administer a land grant in the North-West Territories similar to that which took place in Manitoba pursuant to Section 31 of the Manitoba Act. The chief evidence for this view is the order in council of January 28, 1885, which authorized the minister of the interior to appoint a commission of three to enumerate the North-West Métis

> with a view of settling equitably the claims of half-breeds in Manitoba and the North-West Territories who would have been entitled to land had they resided in Manitoba at the time of the transfer and filed their claims in due course under the Manitoba Act, and also of those who, though residing in Manitoba and equitably entitled to participate in the grant, did not do so.[7]

Several writers have contended, in the words of George Woodcock, that "this did not—as Flanagan seems to assume—promise a resolution of Métis grievances; it merely constituted an undertaking to look into them..."[8] Ken Hatt writes: "In this order there was no commitment to extinguish the claims of the Métis."[9] Hatt also sees the order as defective since it referred to the Manitoba Act rather than Section 125 of the Dominion Lands Act, 1879, which had provided for a land grant to the Métis of the North-West. Hatt and others go on to conclude that nothing of significance occurred until after the battle of Duck Lake, thus implying that a resort to arms was necessary to galvanize the government into action.[10]

Let us examine these contentions. First, as to timing, there is evidence that the government was moving ahead even before the Rebellion broke out. We know from the memoirs of W.P.R. Street, chairman of the Commission, that he was approached by the government in the second week of March. The other members—Roger Goulet, a Métis surveyor from St. Boniface, and A. E. Forget, secretary of the Legislative Council of the North-West Territories—were approached on March 18 and 19.[11] This is well before the battle of Duck Lake on March 26 and is consistent with the only practical plan, i.e., to put the Commission in the field after the spring thaw.

Hatt's query about the wording of the order can also be answered. Section 31 of the Manitoba Act had set aside 1.4 million acres in the province for distribution "among the children of the half-breed heads of families residing in the province at the time of the said transfer to Canada [July 15, 1870]..."[12] This meant that Métis residing outside the province at that date were not eligible for the grant. A second group of Métis excluded from the grant arose in the course of the actual distribution in the years 1875–80, for by that time some Métis who were legally eligible had moved away and could not receive their allotments. Analysis of the order in council of January 28, 1885 shows that it was intended to address the needs of both groups. The "half-breeds in Manitoba and the North-West Territories who would have been entitled to land had they resided in Manitoba at the time of transfer" were the first group, i.e., the Métis who had been outside Manitoba on July 15, 1870. "Those who, though residing in Manitoba and equitably entitled to participate in the grant, did not do so" were the second group, i.e., those who were omitted for administrative reasons, chiefly for being absent when the distribution was actually made.

Hatt is correct that it would have been better to refer to Section 125 of the Dominion Lands Act, 1879, which was the statutory authority for distributing land to the North-West Métis[13]; and this mistake was subsequently corrected in an order in council of March 30, 1885. But there is no reason to see in the oversight anything more malign than administrative confusion. Analysis of the wording of the order of January 28 shows that it was intended to reach the right target groups.

Finally, it is clear that the Commission was more than another investigation that might have no tangible result. Its mandate was not merely to investigate matters. Rather, it was appointed "with a view of settling equitably the claims" of the Métis. It was instructed to "enumerate" them, i.e., to conduct a census and collect the information necessary to determine eligibility for each individual. This was an exact repetition of the procedure followed in Manitoba, where a commission composed of J.M. Machar and Matthew Ryan had enumerated the Métis prior to distribution of the land grant.[14] By way of improvement, two members of the North-West Commission were to be French-speaking and one a Métis.

If everything was fine, why were the Métis of St. Laurent not pacified? The answer seems to lie in faulty communication. The minister of the interior, Sir David Macpherson, telegraphed to Governor Dewdney on February 4, 1885: "Government has decided to investigate claims of half-breeds and with that view has directed enumeration of those who did not participate in grant under Manitoba Act..."[15] This was a very weak expression of the contents of the order in council of January 28, as shown above. *Riel and the Rebellion* erroneously states that Dewdney "sent a copy of the telegram to Charles Nolin."[16] In fact, Dewdney realized that the brief telegram from Macpherson would not satisfy the Métis. He wrote back to Sir John A. Macdonald: "I feared to send the Telegram as worded by Sir David as it would at this season when they have nothing else to do seem to the bulk of the French Half Breeds who are making demands that they have nothing to expect."[17] Instead, Dewdney sent a new telegram to D.H. Macdowall of Prince Albert, a member of the North-West Territories Council, who had been acting as an informal intermediary between Riel and the government: "Government has decided to investigate claims of the Half Breeds and with that view has already taken the preliminary steps."[18]

Dewdney had made two important changes in content. First he had removed the statement that the government would deal with "those who did not participate in grant under Manitoba Act." Dewdney knew full well that most of the Métis of St. Laurent had emigrated only recently from Manitoba, had participated in the distribution of land and scrip in that province, and thus would not be eligible for consideration by this commission. He did not believe they should receive anything further, and he was not trying to do anything for them; he merely wanted not to disappoint their hopes until they had scattered for the freighting season and were no longer capable of uniting to make a disturbance. This alteration in the telegram was not particularly honest, but it was at least consonant with his goal of preventing trouble over the winter. However, his second alteration worked against his own objectives; for in omitting to mention in his telegram that there would be an enumeration, he had made the government's initiative seem like a mere investigation, perhaps only another delaying tactic.

A final disruption of communication occurred when Macdowall gave the telegram to Charles Nolin. It is not clear why Macdowall passed it on to Nolin, but the explanation is probably not sinister. Nolin and his brother-in-law Maxime Lépine, using money advanced by Macdowall, bid to supply telegraph poles for a telegraph line between Duck Lake and Edmonton.[19] Nolin was frequently in Prince Albert in connection with this business deal, and Macdowall perhaps gave him the telegram out of sheer convenience. In any case, Riel, who was also in contact with Macdowall over his claims for an indemnity from the government, probably felt slighted by the way the telegram was transmitted; we know he reacted emotionally when he saw it on February 8.[20]

The net result of these successive lapses in communication was that the government's decision to proceed with the long-delayed Métis land grant in the North-West was perceived by Riel and the Métis as yet another evasion and delay. It was tragically like the classic experiment in which people are asked to whisper a bit of news to their neighbours around a circle. What emerges at the end may be unrecognizable or even the opposite of what was first said.

River Lots

On the question of river lots at St. Laurent, *Riel and the Rebellion* argued that, as with scrip, the federal government was guilty of administrative mistakes and delays but did ultimately accede to the substance of Métis demands before the Rebellion. However, two important questions could not be fully answered on the basis of the evidence presented at the time: 1) Why was only one stretch of land on the South Branch surveyed into river lots, producing seventy-one such lots at St. Laurent? Why were other areas surveyed on the rectangular principle? 2) On what terms did the Department of Interior offer entry to the Métis of St. Laurent in early 1885? Since the official schedule of recommendations had not been found at the time of writing of *Riel and the Rebellion*, the Department's decisions had to be inferred from later records, leaving open the possibility that the relatively generous treatment ultimately accorded had not been envisioned before the Rebellion.

Surveys

Subdivision of the St. Laurent area began in the summer of 1878. Working on the east side of the river, Montague Aldous marked out a river-lot reserve embracing all of T.43, R.1, W.3 and half of T.44, R.1, W.3, thus creating seventy-one river lots. Standing instructions for surveyors were to create river lots wherever they found substantial numbers of settlers already on the land who desired this system. Aldous's notebook shows that he regarded only twenty-four of the seventy-one lots as occupied, almost all of these lying towards the northern end of the settlement.[21] By his own standards, he was apparently tolerant in recognition of claims. For example, he entered the claims of the Carrière family in his book, while noting: "Lots Nos. 20 to 27 (inclusive) are only claimed by the Carriers [*sic*]—they are not at present in occupation."[22] Aldous may have missed some claimants; several other Métis stated in 1884 that they were cultivating land there as early as 1877.[23] But such oral, retrospective statements are not necessarily accurate to the exact year, and in any case the issue here is what degree of settlement had to be perceived by the surveyor in order to justify a river-lot survey. The answer in this instance seems to be about one-third.

The same summer, Duncan Sinclair was surveying north of the river and east of the great bend (T.45 and T.46, R.28, W.2; T.45, R.27, W.2; T.45, R.26,

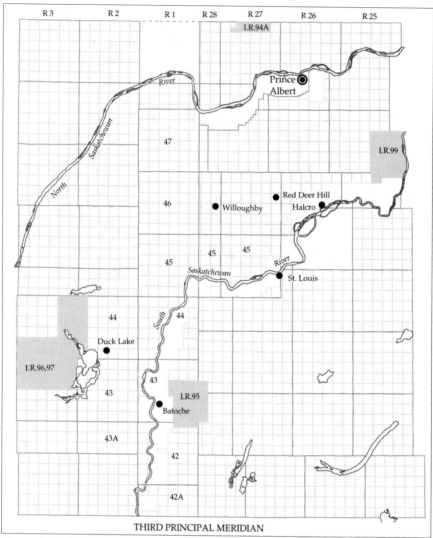

Figure 1. Early Surveys in the Saskatchewan Valley, 1878-82. Cross-hatched areas were surveyed on the sectional system; blank areas, apart from Indian Reserves, were surveyed into river lots. Note that, around Batoche, river lots were drawn only on the east side of the South Saskatchewan River in T.43 and T.44, R.1, W.3. The west side of the river was square-surveyed, even though some French Métis were already settled there before survey. Around St. Louis, only the north side of the river, settled by English half-breeds, received river lots (T.45, R.28, R.27, and R.26, W.3). The south side, where French Métis were settling in numbers around the time of survey (1882), was done on the rectangular principle. The map is adapted from Public Archives of Canada, National Map Collection, V1/502 (1903)

W.2), i.e., across from what would become the parish of St. Louis de Langevin. This area, to the extent that it was settled at all in 1878, was inhabited only by a few Scottish mixed bloods. Sinclair's notebook for T.45 and T.46, R.28, W.2 stated: "There are five settlers on it already that made a beginning last year and are doing well"; it mentioned the names McLean, McKay, and Cameron.[24] His maps show no prior settlers at all in T.45, R.27, W.2 and only five in T.46, R.26, W.2, again with English or Scottish names.[25] In spite of this thin occupancy, Sinclair obligingly drew river lots throughout the townships. This generous treatment of an English-speaking area would later seem like unfair partiality to French Métis who did not receive the same privilege.

River lots were not so readily granted in 1879. In that year J. Lestock Reid surveyed T.42, R.1, W.3 (the Fish Creek area) on both sides of the river as well as T.43 and T.44, R.1, W.3 on the west bank, directly across from the St. Laurent river-lot reserve created the preceding summer by Aldous. Regarding T.42, Reid noted: "There are a few families of French Halfbreeds at present living in this township and from the number of plough furrows marking out the boundaries of claims I am led to suppose a large number are about breaking here."[26] In spite of this observation, he must have used a strict criterion for recognition of claims, for his sketches and final map show only four claims: Dubois, Poitras, Vandal, and Dumont.

A similar contradiction marked Reid's surveying as he worked his way up the west bank. In T.43 he noted: "Both banks of the River are settled by French halfbreeds"[27]; yet he recorded the presence of only two claimants. In T.44 he wrote: "The South Saskatchewan River runs diagonally through this township ... both banks of the river being settled by French Half breeds whose chief occupation has been trading and hunting on the Plains but who are now turning their attention more to farming."[28] Even though his sketches and map show half a dozen instances of settlement, covering almost all sections fronting on the west bank of the river, he still did a square survey rather than river lots.

Although one cannot give a precise quantitative measurement, it seems clear that Reid was operating on a different basis than Aldous, and that Aldous would certainly have created river lots in T.44, and probably in T.43 and T.42. Unfortunately, the available documents do not explain this difference between the surveyors; but since there is no evidence of a shift in official instructions, one can only infer that it was a personal difference in outlook.

Roughly the same situation occurred in St. Louis de Langevin. Whereas in 1878 Duncan Sinclair had surveyed the north bank of the river into river lots, in 1882 Hugh Wilson surveyed the south side into quarter-sections, even though he encountered a higher incidence of settlement than Sinclair had found in 1878. Wilson encountered four river-front claimants in both T.45, R.28, W.2 and T.45, R.27, W.2, not as many as in the St. Laurent area but still far from negligible. Also there is other evidence that Métis were coming in to settle in St. Louis precisely at this time.[29] They may not have had a chance to make visible improvements by the time of survey, but Wilson should have known what was happening.

All this evidence substantiates the conclusion reached in *Riel and the Rebellion*: "it was an error not to have extended the river-lot survey to comprise the whole St. Laurent colony in the first place."[30] There is no evidence to show the mistake was other than a matter of surveyors' judgement in the field, but it nonetheless had serious long-term consequences.

Entry

In spite of many requests, the government refused to resurvey quarter-sections along the river into river lots. Instead it proposed the administrative compromise of allowing squatters to make entry for *de facto* river lots by adding together twenty-acre legal subdivisions. In May 1884 Prince Albert lands agent George Duck collected evidence from ninety-nine Métis claimants at St. Laurent, and on the basis of these submissions made recommendations to the Dominion Lands Board. After some further delays, the Métis were notified between February 26 and March 7, 1885, of the terms on which they could make entry. *Riel and the Rebellion* depicted this process as a reasonable solution to the difficulties created by the original mistake of not having surveyed all of St. Laurent into river lots.

There was, however, a weak link in the book's evidence. Since the schedule of cases investigated by Duck had not been located, it was necessary to infer the substance of the Lands Board decisions from actions recorded in later homestead files. D.N. Sprague used this lacuna in the evidence to propose an alternate interpretation, according to which "what most people received was a provocative denial of their demand for title to the lands they had occupied for years."[31] Sprague pointed out that most claims to *de facto* river lots on quarter-sections involved odd-numbered sections; indeed this was inevitable, since creating a river lot by means of legal subdivision meant that it had to cross two or sometimes three contiguous sections, at least one of which had to be odd-numbered. Now according to Dominion Lands regulations, odd-numbered sections were not open for homestead but were reserved for preemption, i.e., purchase at a favourable fixed price, so that successful homesteaders could expand their landholdings. Reasoning from precedents in other parts of the west, Sprague argued that the St. Laurent

Métis would have been informed that they could make homestead entry on odd-numbered sections but would have to purchase them outright, at one dollar or two dollars per acre, depending on the date of first occupation.[32]

The missing schedule of St. Laurent cases investigated by Duck has now been found, and it shows unequivocally that Sprague's theory is wrong.[33] Squatters whose claims involved odd-numbered sections were indeed allowed to make homestead entry for up to 160 acres. If their claim encompassed more than 160 acres, as sometimes happened with river lots because of the river's irregular course, they could purchase the surplus at one dollar or two dollars per acre, depending on the date of first occupancy. All of this was recommended in 1884, long before there was any question of taking up arms.

Sprague's criticism has, however, been fruitful in another respect. It has drawn attention to the fact that, while the Métis had asked for immediate free patents, the Department of the Interior offered in almost all cases only the right of entry. By 1885, the Métis had generally been on the land more than the requisite three years, but their improvements were not usually sufficient to qualify for patents. *Riel and the Rebellion* did not take sufficient note of this important distinction. Entry required a fee of $10, not in itself an insuperable obstacle for most Métis. But entry did not carry with it the rights to mortgage or sell the land; these rights came only with patent. With the end of the buffalo hunt, the Métis were looking for new sources of cash to increase their intensity of farming or to invest in businesses such as woodcutting and freighting. There may have been many who were disappointed with receiving only entry rather than patent, thus helping to explain why the notification between February 26 and March 7 did nothing to prevent a resort to arms.

Another question that still nags, even if it is of secondary importance, is what form the notification took. *Riel and the Rebellion* asserted that "a letter was sent to each of the claimants stating the terms on which he could make entry,"[34] but this may have been an overstatement. If so many letters were actually sent, it is odd that not even one has ever been found. Two homestead files contain specific notations that letters were sent,[35] but others merely report that claimants were notified to make entry.[36] Even if letters were sent to everyone, it is possible that many Métis did not fully grasp their significance, since hardly any of them could read. With the advantage of hindsight, it seems too bad that a French-speaking employee of the Prince Albert Lands Office did not make a trip to St. Laurent to explain precisely what was being conceded.

Conclusion

Although clichés are always suspect as explanations, it truly seems that a "breakdown in communications" was crucial to the outbreak of the North-West Rebellion. On the two main grievances of scrip and river lots, slow and awkward governmental attempts at explanation were vitiated even further by the intrinsic difficulties of communicating in mid-winter with a non-literate francophone group living in a remote place. If government is to be faulted, it is primarily for not taking extra effort to explain its actions rather than for the substance of its actions.

Collateral support for this interpretation comes from André Lalonde's careful study of the Prince Albert Colonization Company. Lalonde has shown that, in spite of many allegations, the Prince Albert Colonization Company did not present the slightest threat to the Métis living on the South Branch.[37] The parish of St. Louis de Langevin did grow up on land bought by the Company, but the latter had no power to evict settlers and no steps were ever taken in that direction. And yet at least some Métis had the impression that the Company was a threat to their lands. Louis Riel wrote after the Rebellion:

> La Puissance arriva à ne plus garder aucune modération. Elle vendit à une société de colonisation une paroisse métisse toute ronde, le prêtre etait là. Elle vendit la paroisse de St. Louis de Langevin avec la terre de l'église, sur laquelle était une chapelle en voie de construction; elle vendit la terre de l'école et les propriétés de trente-cinq familles.[38]

Even if in reality there was no threat to the Métis from the Company, the perception of a threat may have reinforced the feeling that a resort to arms was necessary.

There are essentially three views about the federal government's role in the origin of the Rebellion. First, that Sir John A. Macdonald deliberately provoked the Métis into taking up arms so that he could crush their power in the west while simultaneously securing funding for the Canadian Pacific Railway. This is the conspiracy theory suggested by A.-H. de Trémaudan,[39] sketched by Howard Adams,[40] and expanded to great lengths by Don McLean.[41] Second, that the government unintentionally drove the Métis into rebellion by grave delays and mistakes in lands policy. This is the standard view in the tradition of George F.G. Stanley. Third, that the government's policy should have satisfied the Métis but did not because it was not properly communicated to them. This is the view developed in *Riel and the Rebellion* and presented here with certain refinements and new information.

10.　Thomas Scott and the Daughter of Time (1998)

J.M. Bumsted

Villain or scapegoat? The Thomas Scott affair has never ceased to haunt Métis history since its denouement in the winter of 1870, and will probably never be explained satisfactorily. A nemesis at Louis Riel's own trial fifteen years later, it raises issues of faulty communication, political misjudgement, and sheer tragic fatality. An original perspective is offered here in an attempt to revisit history and challenge some of its assumptions.

"Truth is the daughter of time"—an old proverb

In 1951 the Scottish author Elizabeth MacKintosh, writing under the pseudonym of Josephine Tey, published one of the most celebrated detective novels of all time, *The Daughter of Time*. In this novel Tey's Scotland Yard detective Allan Grant becomes fascinated by an historical mystery while recovering in hospital from a serious illness. This work has long fascinated historians. Unlike most historical detection, Tey's book does not attempt imaginatively to re-create either the historical personalities or the time period involved, but rather focusses on a modern detective re-examining a mystery from the historical past. This investigation proves very much like the research done by the historian, since it involves working with old books and documents. The mystery Grant investigates in the mid-20th century is the deaths five centuries earlier of two princes of the realm in the Tower of London, an evil deed attributed to their uncle, King Richard III. Grant quickly discovers that Richard III was a character with an ambivalent reputation, a curious mixture of many positive attributes and the villainy in the Tower. As Grant's research continues, he learns that the evidence on which posterity has convicted Richard of the death of the princes is extremely dubious, consisting of a combination of hearsay assumptions and the assertions of his worst enemies. Grant reads the documents looking for the "one unqualified fact" buried within them, and is a sworn enemy of "Tonypandy," which an associate describes as "someone blowing up a simple affair to huge proportions for a political end."[1] Grant himself adds that the point is not simply that the story involved was nonsense, but that everyone there knew it was nonsense and it was never contradicted.[2]

Thomas Scott, who was executed in Red River in 1870, was hardly Richard III. But the historical problem of Scott's reputation has much in common with that of the English king. The Scott execution is unquestionably the most notorious public killing in Canadian history—a mixed jury of Francophones and Anglophones in Manitoba unanimously found that it was "murder." Unquestionably the Scott affair is surrounded by "Tonypandy" on all sides. Most of what we think we know about Scott comes to us in two ways. In the first place, there are unwarranted extrapolations by historians (professional and amateur) from very limited hard evidence. Scott was a young man, and apart from his unexpected involvement in stirring events, was quite an obscure figure. Alexander Begg initially referred to Scott in his journal without giving his first name, and it is likely that some of what little we think we know about Thomas Scott is really information about Alfred or James Scott, both of whom were also in Red River in 1869. Both Thomas Scott's arrival in Red River and his social origins probably help account for his victimization. To a considerable extent, extrapolations from insufficient data are repeated and even improved upon by subsequent historians, as well as influenced by our information from the second source: the evidence about Scott's character and behaviour in captivity as presented by his executioners, particularly by Louis Riel. If we stop and think about this captivity evidence itself for a minute, it presents a number of problems. For the most part, it cannot be substantiated from other sources since Scott's fellow prisoners did not actually witness many of the events which led to his trial, and the trial itself was conducted in camera by a small group of Métis without any outside observers. The details of the tribunal's actions themselves are the subject of considerable confusion, despite its centrality in the subsequent murder trial of Ambroise Lépine in 1874.[3]

From the beginning, anything involving Louis Riel has been the subject of enormous controversy. The contemporary disputatiousness of the death of Scott—a highly partisan business—has helped obscure the fact that much of what we know about Thomas Scott comes mainly from those who executed him. The reasons for that execution have always been shrouded in mystery, and under normal circumstances we would appreciate that it would be in the best interests of those responsible to make their victim out to be as villainous as possible, in order to justify their actions. Why this appreciation appears never to have happened with Scott is an interesting question. For some reason, both contemporaries and subsequent historians seem to have accepted without question the Métis account of Scott's behaviour which served as an explanation for his death, questioning mainly the severity of the response to the charges rather than the charges themselves.

The final problem Scott presents is in the very nature of the assertions about his character and behaviour. Louis Riel described the behaviour of Scott which led to his execution not once, but a number of times over many years. These explanations were not always the same. The charges against Scott that were accepted by his contemporaries in 1870 were certainly not the same accusations levelled against Scott in later years by Riel and then by others. In short, the Métis case against Scott escalated. As the years went by, the charges became progressively more detailed, and Scott became an increasingly nastier character. Many of the secondary accounts of Scott's life and death became based, not on the original 1870 version of his misdeeds, but on the subsequent elaborations, some of which entered the oral traditions of the Métis. Even when the assessment of Scott was based on contemporary evidence, more than one historian has managed to make it sound worse.[4] Overstatement passing well beyond the limits of the evidence is characteristic of much of the writing about both Scott and Riel.[5]

The present study is in the spirit of Josephine Tey's novel. It attempts to untangle the surviving evidence about Thomas Scott's life, fully conscious that much of what we think we know about Scott has been influenced by unsubstantiable accounts of his behaviour in the days and weeks before his execution, as well as by partisanship. It is not concerned with explaining why Scott died; that is a separate study involving the psychology of Louis Riel, among others. It seeks to strip Scott from the legend, to establish the facts of Scott's life and to offer some reassessment of his character. In the process, we may discover a good deal about a variety of related matters. To begin, let us examine what we know about Thomas Scott apart from the evidence of his captors and executioners.

The principal impression to be gained from the testimony of Thomas Scott's anglophone colleagues is that he was a gentle, well-mannered and personable individual, although as we shall see, there was also a minority view that he could be outspoken. Admittedly, most of this testimony was recorded after Scott's death. Whatever its import, this evidence has frequently been neglected or discounted, probably because it has been regarded as part of the closing of ranks of the Canadian Party after the event and in response to the Métis charges at the time of Scott's execution that he was a bad man who deserved to die. Such evidence may well be biased, but it is entitled to as much attention as that of those who killed him. It certainly sets up Scott as a potential dual personality, with one face shown to his friends and another to his enemies.

Scott According to His Anglophone Contemporaries

Thomas Scott's Irish origins are obscure. He was apparently born sometime in the early 1840s in County Down. Lord Dufferin, governor general of Canada in 1874, wrote that Scott "came of very decent people—his parents are at this moment tenant farmers on my estate in the neighbourhood of Clandeboye." Dufferin then added, "but he himself seems to have been a violent and boisterous man such as are often found in the North of Ireland."[6] These two assertions need to be separated. Dufferin undoubtedly knew first-hand that the Scotts were his tenants, but the statement about violence and boisterousness is qualified with the give-away verb "seems," suggesting that the governor-general has extrapolated a stereotyped character from what he had heard about Scott rather than from personal knowledge. There was a good deal of such extrapolation with Scott. In any event, Scott came to Canada in the early 1860s, probably to join his brother Hugh in Toronto.

One of the few surviving records of Scott's Ontario sojourn is a testimonial from one Captain Rowe, of Madoc, Ontario, of the Hastings Battalion of Rifles at Stirling. In a letter to the commanding officer after Scott's death, Rowe wrote:

> I have to inform you that the unfortunate man, Scott, who has been murdered by that scoundrel, Riel, was for a time a member of my company, and did duty with the battalion at Sterling in 1868. He was a splendid fellow, whom you may possibly remember as the right-hand man of No. 4, and I have no hesitation in saying, the finest-looking man in the battalion. He was about six feet two inches in height, and twenty-five years of age. He was an Orangeman, loyal to the backbone, and a well-bred gentlemanly Irishman.[7]

The Reverend George Young, who attended Scott in his last hours, reprinted this testimonial in his 1897 memoir, noting that after the execution he had forwarded Scott's papers to his brother, Hugh. These papers included "many commendatory letters of introduction, with certificates of good character, from Sabbath-school teachers and the Presbyterian minister with whose church he had been connected in Ireland, as well as from employers whom he had served faithfully."[8] Among the material forwarded to Hugh Scott were savings of $103.50.[9] Young also quoted from a journal kept by Scott in 1869. It noted that he and his brother had rowed on Belleville Bay, and wondered "where we shall both be ten years from to-day." Unfortunately, Young apparently did not copy the full texts of all the documents before returning them to the family, and could only refer to most of them in the most general of terms. Nevertheless, Young's evidence indicates that Scott had a Presbyterian upbringing and connection, as well as some education. The presence of substantial savings do not suggest a riotous lifestyle.

The letter from Captain Rowe is also one of the few first-hand pieces of evidence that Scott was not only a northern Irishman or Ulsterman, but "an Orangeman," a term used by contemporaries both to refer to all Protestant Ulstermen who were of anti-Catholic persuasion and to those who were actually members of the Orange Order founded in 1795 to defend the British sovereign and the Protestant religion. In 1989 George Stanley reproduced a resolution of the Orange Lodge of Toronto, which supposedly came from the Toronto *Globe* of April 13, 1870. I have been unable to find the resolution anywhere in the *Globe* or in other contemporary newspapers, but have no reason to doubt that Stanley unearthed it somewhere, probably in another Toronto newspaper unavailable to me. It read:

> Whereas Brother Thomas Scott, a member of our Order, was cruelly murdered by the enemies of our country and religion, therefore be it resolved that while we sympathise with the relatives of our deceased Brother, we, the members of L.O.L. No 404 call upon the Government to avenge his death, pledging ourselves to assist in rescuing the Red River Territory from those who have turned it over to Popery, and bring to justice the murderers of our countrymen.[10]

Note that the Toronto Lodge does not claim Scott as a member of L.O.L. no. 404, but only that Scott was "a member of our Order"; the local lodge to which Scott belonged never stepped forward, however, perhaps because it was in Ulster.

At the same time that the Orange Order claimed Scott, there is no evidence that he ever claimed the Orange Order. Despite the massive response of Orange Ontario to the death of a "brother," orchestrated by the Canada First movement, Scott has left no record—even in the Métis-inspired accounts—of anti-Catholic sentiment. Even if Scott had been a fervent anti-Catholic, of course, there is no reason to regard him as any more a "bigot" than millions of other Americans, Canadians, and Britons who shared with him an antipathy to "Popery" in the 18th and 19th centuries. According to Linda Colley, extreme Protestant anti-Catholicism was part of the glue that held the "British nation" together in the early years of the 19th century.[11] There was no reason to expect such sentiments to disappear by 1870. Whatever Scott's attitude toward Catholicism, as we shall see there is some evidence to support his brother's assertion that "where principle and loyalty to his Queen & country were at stake" he was "a thoroughly brave and loyal man."[12] Loyalty to monarch was another Orange attribute, of course, perhaps as important as hostility to the Pope.

In 1869 Thomas Scott decided to head west. He collected up his papers, doubtless including the introductions and testimonials later left by him with Reverend Young. According to an 1870 private letter of S.H. Harvard, reprinted by Young in 1897, he and Scott travelled from St. Cloud by coach in the summer of 1869.[13] Since St. Cloud was the head of the railway at the time, Scott presumably had gotten there by train. Harvard described Scott as "a fine, tall, muscular youth of some twenty-four years of age," who "behaved properly" and whose bearing was characterized by "inoffensiveness" to "those with whom we came in contact." Harvard made such observations in full appreciation of Scott's execution. The two men shared a bed at a roadside inn outside Abercrombie. Scott told Harvard that he was heading toward the Cariboo to try his luck at the gold mines. If what Scott told Harvard really revealed his plans, his sojourn in Red River may have been intended to be brief.

Shortly after his arrival in Red River in the summer of 1869, Scott took a job with the Canadian road-building crew headed by John Allan Snow. Snow had experienced considerable trouble over the construction of the road from Lake of the Woods to Upper Fort Garry, both within the settlement and on the site. Residents in the settlement were unhappy that the road was being built by the Canadians in advance of the transfer, under the cloak of providing work for famine-ravaged Red River. The settlers were also restive over Snow's efforts to buy land from the Natives. The labourers themselves were unhappy both over their wages and their provisioning. Alexander Begg in his journal had earlier reported that Snow was charging more for provisions than he was paying for them in the settlement, and in 1874 Charles Nolin testified that Scott and other workmen did not like the food they were given, speculating this was perhaps because it was being improperly prepared.[14] According to Nolin, Scott led a three-day strike against Snow, which concluded with the strikers—Scott at their head—marching seventeen miles to Snow's office on 1 October to demand pay both for the time they had worked and for the time they had been on strike. Snow was prepared to pay the former, but not the latter. The men seized Snow and threatened to "duck" him. Snow paid up, but then had warrants issued against four of the men for aggravated assault.

The subsequent court case, the Queen *v.* W.I. Allan, Thomas Scott, Francis Moggridge, and George Fortnay, was heard before Mr. Justice John Black at the quarterly court of the District of Assiniboia on November 19. The court record is tantalizingly brief. It merely notes that Moggridge and Allan were found not guilty, while Fortnay and Scott were given 30 days to pay a fine of 4£ sterling each, their counsel Joseph Coombes acting as security for the payment.[15] Alexander Begg observed in his journal that the case had been badly handled by the defence, suggesting that, given a better presentation by defence counsel Coombes, all four men would have been found innocent. He also added that Scott was overheard commenting before leaving the court "that it was a pity they had not ducked Snow when they were at it as they had not got their money's worth."[16] This comment is interesting both for the use of the term "duck," which suggests something different than "drown," and for the evidence that Scott had something of a dry sense of humour. We will see further evidence of the sense of humour later.

Much has been made of the Snow incident, particularly by Riel and the Métis, as an illustration of Scott's "troublemaking" and general willingness to employ violence and intimidation to gain his ends. Perhaps so. But it seems fairly feeble evidence on which to brand a man either a troublemaker or a bully. Scott was part of an organized worker protest against an employer regarded as having been exploitative and oppressive. He went to some lengths to confront that employer, and while he may have issued threats, no violence was actually employed. From what little is known of the affair and Scott's reaction to his court appearance, it would appear likely that he threatened John Snow with nothing more than a dunking, hardly a serious offence on the 19th-century frontier.

Scott presumably ended his employment with John Snow on October 1. According to Charles Mair, who regarded himself as a friend of Scott, the young man returned to Winnipeg and took up employment as a bartender.[17] If Scott did work as a bartender in Winnipeg, there was bound to be some confusion between himself and the American Alfred Scott, who was also employed as a bartender and was known to be a drinker. There is certainly no real evidence that Scott drank heavily, if at all. A large part of the supposed evidence for Scott's drinking is in testimony by one of his fellow prisoners in the Lépine trial that Scott was on one occasion "apparently half drunk." George Stanley uses this testimony—Scott was even drinking in confinement!—as the only evidence to support his assertion that Scott "drifted into Winnipeg where he drank and fought."[18] Apart from the fact that Stanley attributes the evidence to the wrong prisoner—William Chambers instead of Alexander Murray—it is clear from Murray's statement that he was referring to Alfred Scott, who was visiting Fort Garry with Hugh McKenny and Bob O'Lone for electioneering purposes. The only other contemporary reference to Thomas Scott and drink comes in the Lépine trial testimony of Alexander McPherson on October 15, 1874. He and Scott were taken prisoners together in February 1870, said McPherson, and when they arrived at the Fort, "Scott spoke to me, said it was very cold, let us go down and have a glass; started to go out, when we came near the gate we were pressed back by men of the Fort, Riel's men." This little incident tells us more about Scott's insouciance and sense of humour, however, than it does about his relationship with alcoholic beverages, since Scott must have known full well how unlikely it was that the Métis would let the two men saunter off to the saloon.

If there is little hard evidence to label Scott a drinker, there is even less to substantiate the story that he and Riel had, in 1869, come to blows over a woman. This tale first makes its appearance in 1885, in a little work written by Toronto journalist Joseph Edmund Collins entitled *The Story of Louis Riel the Rebel Chief*. Opposite the title page in this book is an engraving of an Indian attack on a log cabin, clearly showing stereotyped eastern rather than western Indian warfare. Thus is the tone set for the account that follows. The female, a métisse named Marie but given no surname, had supposedly been rescued from flooding waters by the brave Scott, who subsequently helps the girl and her family to hide from Riel and his clumsy courtship of her. After Scott is condemned to death, Riel attempts to get him to reveal the whereabouts of Marie. Scott refuses, of course, and Riel turns on him. "'She shall be mine!' he hissed, 'when your corpse lies mouldering in a dishonored traitor's grave'."[19] There is no contemporary evidence to support any part of this story.

In December of 1869 Thomas Scott joined a number of other residents of Red River, most of them Canadians or members of the so-called "Canadian Party," in an armed defence of the home and storehouse of Dr. John Schultz. In some quarters Scott has been regarded as a henchman or bully boy of Schultz, so it is important to emphasize that there is no contemporary evidence outside the accounts of his executioners to suggest that Scott and Schultz were even acquainted, much less close collaborators. That Scott gravitated to Schultz's house in December of 1869 does not particularly mark him out as under the influence (evil or otherwise) of the good doctor.

Schultz was the acknowledged leader of the Canadian Party in Red River. All Canadians gravitated to him as the Métis stepped up their military activities, and the December 1 date was chosen for the Canadian takeover of Red River (the postponement by Ottawa of this event was not known in the West). Some Canadians, like the Graham brothers, apparently did not know Schultz at all when they "enlisted" to guard the stores and provisions stored at his house.[20] Others of the party, like J.H. O'Donnell, obviously did not like Schultz very much.[21] The party of defenders were buoyed up by the circulation by John Dennis of Governor William McDougall's proclamation of the Canadian takeover dated December 1, 1869. McDougall, of course, had jumped the gun, but the Canadians at Red River were not to know this fact for several weeks. In early December they could legitimately see themselves as the local supporters of the Canadian government and opponents of Louis Riel as a rebel leader.

Scott only emerged out of the crowd at Schultz's house when he was appointed by the band of loyalists on December 7, 1869 as one of the delegates in a "deputation to Riel under a flag of truce, to endeavour to make terms."[22] The Reverend George Young subsequently wrote that these delegates bore "a request to Riel that the ladies then resident in Dr. Schultz's besieged buildings should be permitted to retire therefrom, as they were suffering from prolonged excitement and alarm."[23] According to the account in the *Globe* of April 15, 1870, Scott and "Mr. McArthur" were the two chosen. Peter McArthur in 1934 recalled that the two delegates were Scott and his brother Alex McArthur.[24] According to A.W. Graham's diary, however, the delegates were Scott, McArthur, and William Hallett.[25] Whoever the delegates, the Canadians had no bargaining power whatsoever. Riel had the house surrounded with armed Métis, backed up by cannon from the fort trained at the flimsy wooden structure, and he felt no need to make a deal. All three sources agree that Riel held Scott and sent McArthur back to report that the only terms were total surrender. The sort of spin that could be put on such actions is demonstrated by Major Boulton's account in 1886. Although Boulton appears to confirm Young's account of Scott's peace mission, he probably heard the story from the Methodist clergyman in the first place:

> Scott, it ought to be said, was not taken prisoner with arms in his hands. On the first occasion, before the prisoners were captured in Dr. Shultz's house, he had gone boldly down to the Fort to ask Riel to give safe conduct to the ladies and children who were in danger there, and Riel's only answer to his peaceful mission was to thrust him into prison.[26]

After the unsuccessful negotiations, a party from the town headed by A.G.B. Bannatyne met with the Canadians to advise unconditional submission. What happened to Scott is a matter of some disagreement among the sources, however. Both Graham and McArthur suggest simply that Scott had been made prisoner a few minutes earlier than the remainder of the Canadian party. The account of Coombes and Allan is far more detailed, however. "Aha! says the sneaking Louis" to Scott, "'you are just the man I was looking for,' and with deep malice gleaming from his treacherous and sinister eyes, he ordered his men to seize him. Scott was a man of great stature, six feet two inches in height, of goodly symmetry, and of an ardent and rather impetuous nature, freely expressing his opinions. The act of the despot was prompted by the pettiest motives of personal revenge. Scott had always treated him with marked contempt. Once in the town of Winnipeg he [Scott] got into an altercation with him [Riel], in a saloon, and threw him by the neck into the street."[27] Scott's service as a "bartender," an occupation that often included "bouncer" duties, might explain this contretemps. But the confrontation must have occurred between early October (when Scott left Snow's employ) and early December, a period in which Riel, who was not a drinking man under any circumstances, would have been unlikely to have spent much time in Winnipeg saloons. Indeed, the constant alcoholic consumption of Riel in the account of the Red River uprising according to Allan and Coombes leads one to suspect that they were already engaging in their own version of myth-making and character assassination. Nonetheless, another version of this story had been reported unattributed to anyone by the *Globe* a few days earlier: "Mr Scott, we are told, was a quiet and inoffensive, but at the same time, very powerful and determined man. Before his arrest, Riel stopped him on some road he was going and Mr. Scott with a strong arm thrust him aside and told him to mind his own business."[28] Like the later story of rivals in love, more obviously a total fabrication, these accounts seek to provide an explanation for the later behaviour of Riel towards Scott, which might otherwise appear inexplicable. But these stories are contemporaneous—the tale of Allan and Coombes coming from men who were imprisoned for six weeks with Scott—and therefore cannot be totally ignored.

In any event, Scott became a prisoner at Upper Fort Garry. Incarcerated with the great crowd of Canadians in an upper-storey flat normally used by Hudson's Bay Company clerks, Scott had no opportunity for contact with Dr. Schultz, who was imprisoned in one of the officer's houses below along with his wife, and who subsequently escaped separately from the others. Scott does not appear in any of the first-hand contemporary accounts of prison life until January 9, 1870, when he was one of a number of prisoners who escaped from the Fort. Several of his fellow prisoners subsequently commented on Scott's first incarceration in Upper Fort Garry. In 1914 George Winship sent a manuscript account of the first imprisonment to James Ashdown for comment. In it Winship had characterized Thomas Scott as a "pugnacious fellow" who "believed in the arbitration of violence to settle disputes," although how much such a description owed to Scott's subsequent reputation is open to question. In any case, Ashdown commented, "I do not consider that Scott was very 'Pugnacious': he was a big strong fellow and used language somewhat freely, but was not a bad fellow in any sense of the word."[29] Twenty years later, Peter McArthur in his "Recollections" of 1934–35 wrote that "Scott's death was a great shock to us; he had said loudly and openly what the rest of us quietly thought."[30] Unfortunately, McArthur was not more specific about what either Scott said or the other prisoners thought. On the other hand, A.W. Graham, in the course of reporting the death of Scott as a reason for his family's hasty departure from Red River in 1870, recorded in his diary somewhat closer to the event: "Let me say here that I was over four weeks in Scott's company in Fort Garry jail and I found him quiet, civil and always gentlemanly. Why Riel should say he was a bad man I could never learn."[31]

We do have an account of Scott's escape from Upper Fort Garry in the journal of Henry Woodington, who accompanied him out of the window that cold January night. According to Woodington, the sound that night of the wrenching of a window frame out of the wall in the prisoners' room was covered by the noise of the prisoners "piling on" Joseph Coombes. "Piling on" was, along with chess, cards, and checkers, one of the principal games played by the prisoners in confinement. It was indeed their special favourite. "It begins," explained Woodington, "with one catching hold of another and throwing him down or against the wall, yelling 'pile on.' Then there is a general rush to the scene, and pity the poor fellow that gets under."[32] The popularity of such schoolboyish antics in captivity reminds us that most of the prisoners at Upper Fort Garry were, like Scott, young men with their hormones in full flight. Apart from going down the hall to relieve themselves, this was apparently the only exercise the prisoners got. What the Métis guards made of "piling on," which must have happened so frequently that they did not bother to check on the noise the night of the escape, is another matter. The game may well have produced a general Métis perception that the prisoners were all crazy men of violent proclivities.

In any event, Scott and Woodington by prior arrangement started a brisk trot to Headlingly upon their escape from the Fort. The snow was deep and they were weak from confinement, but they hurried on. They called at the home of William Hallett about two and one half miles from the Fort, and then raided a stable for horses. But they could find no tack. Scott tried to ride without saddle, harness, and reins, but was pitched off the horse into a deep snowbank. "Just imagine the sight," recalled Woodington. "Scott is over six feet in height, with a short body and very long legs, sticking in the snow, with his legs almost straight up in the air." The two men lost the horses and resumed walking. The impression Woodington leaves of the affair is one of great jocularity. The majority of the twelve escapees were easily recaptured, and one of them (Walton Hyman) was badly frostbitten. Thomas Scott was one of the five who remained at large.

Scott eventually made his way to Portage la Prairie. This village was technically outside the jurisdiction of the Council of Assiniboia and beyond the reach of Métis armed authority. It had originally been settled mainly by Canadians, and many other Canadian refugees, including Major Charles Boulton, had gathered there after the imprisonment of the party at Dr. Schultz's house. Another escapee from Upper Fort Garry, Charles Mair, had ended up in Portage at about the same time as Scott, although independently of him. In his 1886 memoirs of the North-West Rebellions, Boulton offers us a glimpse of Scott at Portage. "He gave graphic accounts of his imprisonment and escape, and once more the question was raised to organize a party to effect the release of the other prisoners," wrote Boulton.[33] Boulton's words give us no reason to conclude that Scott was particularly active in organizing the rescue operation; the use of the passive mood in the second part of the sentence on Scott is instructive. There is corroboration on this point. In the 1874 trial of Ambroise Lépine, William Chambers testified that Scott had come to Portage after the question of liberating the prisoners had already been raised.[34]

Nor does Boulton suggest in any way that Scott was a leader of the Portage expedition. In fact, he specifically lists the expedition's "officers," a roster that does not include Scott. Several of the witnesses at the Lépine trial emphasized that Scott was not a leader of the Portage party. According to William Chambers, for example, "Scott had no position in the force, was a full private."[35] Alexander McPherson recalled that the Portage party "seemed to act spontaneously"; he added, "Thomas Scott was with us; he was not a principal actor; there were none."[36] Alexander Murray testified of the Portage expedition: "there was not much commanding by any one."[37] Boulton did record that it was Scott who—on the party's passage through the village of Winnipeg on its way to Kildonan—helped him call at a house looking for Louis Riel: "Thinking we might make a timely capture, we surrounded the house, and Scott and I entered to search for Riel; but the host assured us he was not there; so we passed on without disturbing the family."[38] As we shall see, this incident became an important part of the Métis indictment of Scott.

None of the contemporary Anglophone evidence even mentions Thomas Scott's presence at Kildonan, where Norbert Parisien was badly beaten after he had shot Hugh John Sutherland. The only eye-witness glimpse we have of Scott at Kildonan comes from Donald McLeod, in a memoir of 1942 written when he was 84 years old. Born in 1858, McLeod in 1870 had carried bread to the soldiers at the Kildonan schoolhouse. Scott was among them. "As clothing he wore a Pea Jacket, Beaver cap and leather britches and a gold ring in his left ear," Mcleod recalled.[39] This is the only place where the gold earring appears. It is such an odd recollection that one wants to believe it. Although hundreds of Anglophones gathered at Kildonan in mid-February of 1870, the assemblage quickly dispersed when it was announced that Riel was already releasing the prisoners held at Upper Fort Garry. The Portage party, including Thomas Scott, decided to make its way back to its point of origin. Unfortunately, it returned via a route that took it all too near Riel's stronghold at Upper Fort Garry, and it was easily captured by Riel's forces. Many of the party insisted that Riel had promised them safe passage, but whatever the reason for the blunder, Thomas Scott found himself once again a prisoner of Louis Riel. Apart from Alexander McPherson's story about Scott's jocular walk for a drink, there were no other anecdotes told about Scott at this particular juncture. According to William Farmer, at the moment of capture "Scott offered no resistance."[40]

Anglophone evidence from Scott's second incarceration is both limited and confused. Two points stand out. First, the time period between the capture of the prisoners and the court-martial of Scott—especially after the time taken up with the threatened execution of Charles Boulton is excluded—was relatively short, less than two weeks. Secondly, none of the fellow prisoners or clergymen whose testimony has survived appear to have spent much time with Scott over the course of his captivity, and none, except Alexander Murray and George Sanderson in a much later oral account, offered much account of his behaviour. Sanderson claimed that Scott had been offensive to everyone, including his fellow prisoners, but from what vantage point in Upper Fort Garry he made these observations is not clear.[41] According to Alexander Murray, Scott was initially kept in a room in the same range as the other prisoners, but he was eventually put in another room on the opposite side. Certainly Scott ended up in solitary confinement. Murray added, "I heard that Scott had difficulties with the guards more than once, but never saw it."[42]

Few of the Anglophone prisoners witnessed any persistent confrontations between Scott and his guards. George Newcombe dated Scott's troubles from only the day before his execution.[43] So Alexander Murray, who offered one of the most detailed fellow-prisoner accounts of Scott's confrontation with his guards:

> I saw Riel, Lépine and O'Donolme on the night previous to Scott being shot; they were in the guard-room; Riel came and asked me if I was a Canadian; I told him no! but I belonged to that party; I went back to my room; he followed me up and apparently looking [sic] in my room; I closed the door and said, "Boys, keep quiet, for Riel, O'Donohue and Lépine are in the guard-room." I knelt on my knees and looked through the key-hole; I heard a knock on the door where Scott was confined; the door was opened slightly by one of the guards; Scott said, "I want to get out"; the door was opened a second time; Riel stepped up to Scott, and Scott said he wished to be treated civil; Riel said he did not deserve to be treated civil and called him a dog; Scott asked for his book, I think a pocket-book; Riel said he hadn't it; the door was then shut; I understood it to be a call of nature.[44]

Charles Boulton told a similar story in his memoirs. Although the events he describes happen over a shorter time frame, there are several confrontations between Scott and his guards. About a fortnight after the capture, Boulton recognized Scott's voice in the guardroom, demanding his pocket-book. A considerable scuffle ensued and Scott was locked up in a room. Boulton investigated, and learned that Scott had just advised the prisoners to have nothing to do with Alfred Scott and others who had solicited their votes. The visit of Alfred Scott dates this confrontation in late February. Later Scott asked leave to go outside (presumably to the lavatory) and was refused, which led to another altercation. Riel and O'Donohue visited Scott that same afternoon and evening, "and used violent language against Scott." According to Boulton, he did not manage to visit with Scott until the court-martial had been completed. "I found that similar questions had been put to him as had been put to me, and the same mode of passing sentence had been passed upon him as had passed upon me. I told Scott to be very careful what he said, as I felt sure that Riel meant mischief and would take his life if he could. By then such advice was too late."[45]

The evidence of the several Protestant clergymen who dealt with Scott's final hours was potentially quite confusing. The Reverend John McLean testified at the Lépine trial that he "saw Scott one day, found him handcuffed and his legs ironed; asked him how he was and why he was there; he said he had some trouble with the guards; had some conversation with him about his spiritual wants and when I was coming away I asked permission to call upon him again, but that night he was brought up, and on the following day he was shot; I was totally ignorant of his danger; I afterwards learned that that was the last day of his life."[46] In the wake of the threatened execution of Charles Boulton, McLean told the court he had spoken to the prisoners about the deal he and Donald Smith had made with Riel to save Boulton's life (to visit the Anglophone parishes and convince them to send representatives to the new provisional government). He wanted to gain their consent, and admitted he did so by telling the prisoners "that I thought they were in danger of their lives."[47] But this warning was not particularly directed at Scott. McLean's recollections are quite compatible with (although not identical to) Donald Smith's report of his meeting with Father Joseph Jean-Marie Lestanc on March 4, at which Lestanc had commented on the bad behaviour of the prisoners. According to Smith, "I expressed much surprise at the information he gave me, as the prisoners, without exception, had promised to Archdeacon McLean and myself, that seeing their hopeless condition they would endeavour to act so as to avoid giving offence to the guards, and we encouraged them to look forward to being speedily released, as fulfilment of the promise made by Mr. Riel." Smith added that a prisoner named Parker had been described as quite obnoxious, but not one word had ever been said to him about Scott.[48]

The Reverend George Young in his 1874 trial testimony insisted that he had no conversation with Scott before March 3, by which time he had been tried and was out of irons, but added that when he had visited Scott the previous Saturday—presumably without exchanging any words worthy of the label "conversation"—the young Irishman had been in irons.[49] Young's account in 1897 was quite different: "On Sabbath, February 27th, while visiting the various prisons, I was pained to learn that Scott had been sent into solitary confinement, and going at once to his room, found him in a most pitiable condition—a dirty arid fireless room, a single blanket to rest on or wrap himself in, and with manacles on both wrists and ankles. No marvel that he shivered and suffered under such circumstances. On my asking if he knew the reason of this increased severity, he assured me that he did not, and readily promised to carefully avoid, in action and utterance, whatever might be offensive to the guards."[50] These clerical accounts (and that of Alexander Murray) can be more or less reconciled by assuming that Scott's first confrontation with his guards (as reported by Murray and Boulton) had occurred on Saturday, February 26, and that Scott was in irons from at least the Saturday to the Thursday, when he was tried and then unshackled in preparation for his execution. But the chronology never entirely hangs together.

In any event, Thomas Scott was brought before a military court on the evening of March 3 and tried for his life. At the 1874 trial of Ambroise Lépine, the adjutant general's private secretary Joseph Nolin was the star prosecution witness, offering the only eye-witness account of that trial available. Why Nolin testified in 1874 is not clear from the court records, although the Nolin family had been opponents and critics of Louis Riel for many years. None of the other participants in the event, including Ambroise Lépine, testified in 1874, presumably for fear of self-incrimination. Because it remains the fullest account, and because there is so much confusion in the secondary literature over the details of the trial, Nolin's evidence (as given by unofficial court reporters) must be quoted in full.[51] He was reported as testifying:

> Scott was tried on the evening of the third of March; at the council that tried him Lépine presided; the other members of the council were Janvier Richot, André Nault, Elzear Goulet, Elzéar Legemonière, Baptiste Lépine, and Joseph Delorme; I was secretary of the council; Scott was not present at the beginning; some witnesses were examined to state what evil Scott had done; these witnesses were Riel, Ed Turner, and Joseph Delorme; don't recollect any other witnesses; do not recollect nature of the evidence; Scott was accused of having rebelled against the Provisional Government and having struck the captain of the guard; Riel made a speech, I think against Scott; after the evidence had been heard Scott was brought before the council; Riel asked me to read to Scott what had passed before the council; did not, as I had written nothing; Riel then explained the evidence to Scott, and asked him if he had any defence to offer? Scott said something but I forget what; Riel did not ask Scott whether he had any witnesses; there was no written accusation against Scott; the work of the Council was done in about three hours; the Council sat about 7 o'clock; took some notes of the evidence; wrote them out regularly and gave them to the Adjutant General; Richot moved and Nault seconded that Scott deserved death; Lépine said he would have to be put to death—the majority want his death and he shall be put to death; that closed the business of the

council; Riel explained to Scott his sentence; and asked him if he had any request to make or wanted to see a minister? I do not remember what answer Scott made; Riel said if the minister was at the Stone Fort he would send for him; Riel said he would send Scott up to his room, that his shackles would be taken off, and that he would have pen, ink, and paper to write what he wished to; Riel then told Scott he would be shot next day at 10 o'clock; I do not know what Scott said; he was then taken to his room; when the vote was taken Baptiste Lépine objected to taking the life of Scott; he said they had succeeded so far without shedding blood and he thought it better not to do so now; Ed Turner took Scott to his room; saw Lépine the next morning about 8 o'clock; Lépine told me to write a verbal report of the proceedings of the Council; Riel came to see the report and said it was not formal; Riel then dictated the report; it was made from notes of the evidence; don't remember what Riel changed; gave it to Lépine when written.[52]

Under cross-examination by defence attorney Joseph Chapleau, Nolin observed that during the entire trial he heard Lépine say nothing against Scott:

After the vote had been taken on the execution of Scott, by the words Lépine used and his demeanor during the whole trial, I understood him to be against the death of Scott, but his words were "the majority being for his death, he must die."

The witness then added,

the prisoner [Lépine] did not order me to write the sentence, nor did he write judgment then; Riel was the person who explained what was the sentence, and where and when it was to he performed; Riel was Scott's accuser; Scott was accused of having taken up arms against the Provisional Government, after taking an oath not to fight against it; he was also accused of striking one of the guards, and Riel himself; Edmund Turner one of the witnesses was an Irishman; Turner and Joseph Delorme were witnesses, Joseph Delorme was also one of the Council; do not know what position Turner held; believe Riel was first accusator and also witness; Riel made the charges against Scott verbally; Riel was sworn to prove his charge by me; Riel was the only accuser; don't think Scott asked to examine witnesses; I think he said something, but do not know what he said; Riel was speaking English; Turner was speaking English. The charge of striking Riel and the guard referred to the scuffle in the guard room.

Nolin then told the chief justice that he was "not sure that evidence was produced to show that Scott had taken the oath to the Provisional Government," adding: "I do not know if any book was produced; the 'taking up arms' referred to his coming down with the Portage party." At the close of his testimony, Nolin also told the chief justice that escaped prisoners had never taken any oath.[53] The impression he left in his testimony was that there had been one or two incidents involving Scott rather than a persistent pattern of offensive and insulting behaviour. However, Scott's behaviour toward Riel and his guards was only part of the indictment against him.

Leaving aside all questions about the legal propriety of or possible legal models for these proceedings, exactly what—according to Joseph Nolin—had happened there? Before attempting to answer this question, two points must be made about Nolin's account of Scott's trial. One is that Nolin was a key witness for the prosecution in a murder trial of 1874. The second, however, is that he was under oath and subject to full cross-examination. While what we have of his testimony are unofficial reports rather than an official verbatim transcript, it is clear from these that defence counsel Chapleau cross-examined Nolin extensively, and the chief justice himself asked questions of clarification as well. Nolin is not necessarily the definitive witness on Scott's trial, but his testimony must be accepted as credible as far as it goes. His account is quite clear that Scott was not present for a most important part of the proceedings, the presentation of the evidence in support of the charges against him.[54] Those charges and the evidence for them (emanating partly from Louis Riel) were subsequently summarized to Scott in English by Louis Riel. Later commentators such as A.H. de Trémaudan, who have tried to insist that Riel was not present at all at the trial, must contend with Nolin's evidence.[55] On the other hand, whether Nolin's account fully supports George Young's assertion that "Riel acted as prosecutor, witness, and judge" is for the reader to decide.[56] Certainly Nolin emphasized that it was Riel who had written up the report of the tribunal, although this official account has not survived.

Scott was not condemned entirely unheard. He was offered some opportunity to respond to the charges, although not to examine the witnesses. According to the Reverend Young in 1874, Scott said afterwards he had "objected to the trial as it was conducted in a language he did not under-stand, but was told it made no difference; he was a bad man and had to die."[57] Scott's objection was only partially correct. While he was present before the tribunal Scott was dealt with in English, but he was not present the entire time, and especially had not heard any of the testimony against him, at least some of which was given in French. A better objection would have been that much of the trial had been conducted in his absence. Scott certainly had no legal advice at any point and was, according to subsequent reports, quite stunned by the entire proceedings. Whether the young Irishman was actually present for the vote on his case, which was not unan-imous, is not clear from Nolin's statements, but the sentence was subse-quently "explained" to him by Riel and he was offered what amounted to "last requests" of the condemned, including the services of a clergyman.

The Métis Evidence of Scott's Character and Conduct

Métis explanations for Scott's death began before the firing squad had begun its work. The chief Canadian commissioner to Red River in 1870 was Donald A. Smith, who had been kept under virtual house arrest at Upper Fort Garry since his arrival in the settlement several months earlier. On March 11, Smith was visited by the Reverend George Young about 11 A.M., and informed of the intended execution of Scott at noon. Young then went to plead with Riel, unsuccessfully, first for Scott's life and then for delay on the grounds that the young Irishman was not prepared to die. The minister sent a messenger to inform Smith of his failure. Smith, accompanied by Father Lestanc, then called on Riel himself. The Métis leader turned to Smith and said, "I will explain to you." In his report to Ottawa, Smith transcribed what Riel then said. According to Smith, Riel

> said in substance, that Scott had, throughout, been a most troublesome character, and had been ringleader in a rising against Snow, who had charge of a party employed by the Canadian Government during the preceding summer in road making, that he had risen against the Provisional Government in December last, that his life was then spared; that he had escaped and had been again taken in arms, and once more pardoned (referring no doubt to the promise he had made to me that the lives of the prisoners were secured), but that he was incorrigible, and quite incapable of appreciating the clemency with which he had been treat-ed; that he was rough and abusive to the guards and insult-ing to him (Riel), and that his example had been productive

of the very worst effects on the other prisoners, who had
become insubordinate to such an extent that it was difficult
to withhold the guards from retaliating.[58]

Riel further told Smith that Scott had admitted to him that he and the
Portage party "intended to keep you [Riel] as a hostage for the safety of the
prisoners." Smith, who had never met Scott, argued that the worst case Riel
had made out was that the Irishman was a "rash, thoughtless man, whom
none could desire to have anything to do with." This statement represented
Smith's summary of what Riel had recounted, rather than his own assessment, and was hardly evidence of Scott's character or personality.[59] The
charges Riel raised against Scott, Smith more than implied, did not deserve
a death sentence. In this assessment it is difficult not to concur. The Snow
affair was irrelevant, the searching of the Winnipeg house a natural by-product of the internal conflict of the time, and Scott had never taken an oath of
good conduct. Obviously prisoners should be well-behaved, docile, and easily manageable, but prison authorities might well expect other behaviour,
especially in the course of a civil war.

At the end of this lengthy interview, which delayed the execution beyond
its appointed time, Donald Smith noted that the insurrection had to this
point been bloodless, and that bloodshed might make the negotiations with
Canada more difficult. To this Riel replied, "We must make Canada respect
us." Riel then offered one more example of Scott's offensive behaviour.
When Alfred Scott, at Riel's behest, went to see the prisoners to look for their
vote in the Winnipeg election for councillor to the provisional government,
it was Thomas Scott who had come forward to advise against such support,
saying "My boys, have nothing to do with those Americans."[60] Riel and
Smith then jousted about the Americans. Why Riel thought Scott's comments and actions here could serve as part of the indictment against him
was not clear from the conversation as reported by Smith. Charles Mair, who
was not present at the second incarceration, reported an alternate version of
this incident, based on a later account he received from Murdoch McLeod.
Alfred Scott had been accompanied by the Fenian Dan Shea in the solicita-
tion of the prisoners' votes. According to McLeod, Thomas Scott had shout-
ed, "Boys, you can do what you like, but I won't consent." He was thereupon "ironed with irons which had been taken off Boulton."[61] In any event,
Riel closed the discussion by observing to Smith, "I have done three good
things since I have commenced. I have spared Boulton's life at your instance,
and I do not regret it, for he is a fine fellow; I pardoned Gaddy, and he
showed his gratitude by escaping out of the bastion—but I do not grudge
him his miserable life; and now I shall shoot Scott." The impression Riel left

with Donald Smith was that Scott had been condemned as much for defying Louis Riel as for his behaviour with his guards.

The explanations given to Smith were quite compatible with Joseph Nolin's 1874 testimony in the Lépine trial about the charges levied at the military tribunal against Scott. They were also more or less compatible with two subsequent statements emanating from the friends of the provisional government at the time of the execution. The first appeared in the Red River newspaper controlled by Riel, *The New Nation*, dated the very day of Scott's death. *The New Nation* described the deceased as "Private T. Scott," giving him (and the Portage party) formal military standing and turning the affair into a proper military execution. It reported that from Scott's second capture, he was "very violent and abusive in his language and actions, annoying and insulting the guards, and even threatening the President." It then provided a more detailed discussion of Scott 's threats against Riel: "He [Scott] vowed openly that if ever he got out he would shoot the President; and further stated that he was at the head of the party of the Portage people who, on their way to Kildonan, called at Coutu's house and searched it for the President, with the intention of shooting him."[62] Donald Smith had reported Riel's assertion that Scott had admitted he would have held him to ransom if he had managed to capture him, but there had been no mention of further violence. Now, according to *The New Nation*, Scott actually had threatened to shoot Riel on several occasions! The emphasis of this newspaper account seemed to be on Scott's threats against Louis Riel.

The second contemporary statement appeared in the Quebec clerical newspaper the *Courrier de St. Hyacinthe* in March, and was translated and reprinted in the *Globe* on April 7. The correspondent began: "I send you the following details so that you may be able to use them in reply to the attacks which will doubtless be made." According to this account, Scott had "led the conspiracy against Mr. Snow," whose life had been saved by the Métis. When the Portage people "rose in insurrection against the Provisional Government, he was a strong partisan and entered a house in Winnipeg, where the President often passed the night, while others surrounded it, doubtless with the intention of killing Mr. Riel." Reimprisoned, he had "insulted the President, attacked a captain and a soldier, his insolence was so great that one day Capt. Boulton asked to be admitted to his room so as to make him quiet."[63] The *Courrier* letter insisted that Scott's behaviour had negatively affected the other prisoners. The execution was both to give an example and to "certainly prevent a great loss of life."[64] The correspondent went on to claim that although Scott had been allowed to see a clergyman, he had told Reverend George Young "that he did not belong to any religion." Riel thereupon ordered all the soldiers in the Fort to pray for Scott's change of heart. This letter was very probably written by Father Lestanc, who, according to the text, had interceded for this unfortunate man "who had rebelled and taken up arms against an authority recognized by the two populations." It did not claim that Scott had actually threatened Riel with shooting, however. Scott's prison behaviour was only a part of his offence against the provisional government: his real problem was that he was neither religious nor a Catholic. The *Globe*'s editorial writers had a field day with this letter, particularly with the collective prayers by the rebels that Scott would experience a last-minute conversion.

As for Louis Riel, he turned again to Scott in 1872, when he drafted "Mémoire ayant trait aux difficultés de la Rivière-Rouge."[65] In this document Riel associated Scott with "Schultz et Co." Riel reported the searching of the house of Henri Coutu with the intention of capturing him, but did not here claim that Scott had threatened to shoot him. He noted the deaths of Sutherland and Parisien, but did not attribute blame to anyone for these occurrences. Scott was very violent in his second incarceration, wrote Riel, who focussed on the Irishman's prison behaviour in this document. On the last day of February Scott had really upset the guards, wrote Riel, beating on the "prison gates" and insulting them. The guards had taken him outside and were preparing to "sacrifice him" when a French councillor saved him. Riel quietened the guards a day later, but Scott continued to be offensive and the guards continued to demand a council of war, which they finally got on March 3. The impression Riel left in this document was that he had been pressured into acting against Scott by the insistent demands of his guards and Scott's refusal (or inability) to cease being offensive to them. The exact nature of Scott's offensive behaviour was never specified. Riel and Ambroise Lépine presented a slightly different argument in their famous memorial to Lieutenant-Governor Morris in January 1873, although the focus was still on Scott's prison behaviour.[66] Scott and "Mr [Murdoch] McLeod" had "beat their prison gates and insulted, and went so far as to strike their guards, inviting their fellow-prisoners also to insult them." Only a punishment could "restrain these excited men," and so, said Riel and Lépine, "we had recourse to the full authority of Government."

The same themes reappeared in an 1874 account by Riel entitled "L'Amnistie. Mémoire sur les causes des troubles du Nord-Ouest et sur les négotiations qui ont amené leur règlement amiable," which he probably wrote while in exile in New York State.[67] This document rehearsed the events of the entire rebellion from the perspective of both Riel and the Métis. Here Scott was described as "one of the most dangerous partisans of Dr. Schultz,

McDougall, and Dennis." His involvement in the search for the president of the provisional government in Winnipeg was clear evidence that he was in arms against that authority. Once again imprisoned, he and fellow prisoner Murdoch McLeod "forcèrent les portes de leur prison, se ruèrent gardes, invitant leurs compagnons à faire comme eux." "Tous" demanded that Scott be brought before the "conseil de guerre," and when the Irishman persisted in his "mauvaise conduite" he was finally summoned, against a background of rising new troubles which were not specifically described. Scott was examined on "témoignages assermentés," was convicted and condemned to death. On March 4 the authority of the provisional government, which had the goodwill of the Anglophone colonists, was used to "disarm our enemies."

"L'Amnistie" was published by *Le Nouveau Monde* of Montreal as a pamphlet early in 1874, and quickly drew a response—in the form of a lengthy letter published by various newspapers—written by Dr. James Spencer Lynch, one of the most extreme of the Canadian Party in Red River during the rebellion.[68] Lynch was one of the prisoners taken at Dr. Schultz's house in December of 1869, and he played an active role in the anti-Métis and anti-provisional government campaign in Ontario in the spring of 1870. Lynch's letter objected to Riel's interpretation of the events of 1869–70 on a variety of fronts, including the execution of Thomas Scott. Lynch's principal complaint about the trial of Scott was that it had been quite improper, conducted as it was in French, a language that the accused did not understand. He also criticized the manner and timing of the execution. Riel responded to Lynch's rambling critique in an equally rambling document that was printed in *Le Nouveau Monde* on March 12, 1874.[69] Regarding Scott's trial, Riel denied categorically that it had been conducted in French: "Durant le procès, tout ce qui a été dit en francais, a été traduit en anglais: et tout ce qui a été dit en anglais a été traduit en français." Given Joseph Nolin's subsequent description under oath of the proceedings of the tribunal, this categorical denial may have been a bit disingenuous.

Riel also denied that Lynch had managed to rehabilitate "le caractère de Scott" by asserting that Scott was a decent man of steady habits. Riel's response was noteworthy for the introduction of a new level of attack on the character of Scott. Riel brought several new charges against Scott. "It is said" ("il est dit"), he wrote, that Scott had tracked down Norbert Parisien after the shooting of Hugh John Sutherland, attached a belt ("une ceinture") to his neck, and dragged him behind a horse for a quarter of a mile. Scott was now well set on his way to becoming "the bad man who had to die." That the young Irishman had sought to assassinate ("voulu assassiner") Mr. Snow in 1869 at Pointe des Chênes was an old accusation. What appeared now for

the first time about Pointe des Chênes was the assertion that the community still recalled the disorder created by Scott and his companions during
riotous evenings. While the men were away, the women and children had
guarded their doors and windows against the Canadians. Riel closed his
text: "Here is what the entire parish of Pointe des Chênes knows. Scott was
reasonable? He was of regular habits? Let the reader decide."[70]

Over the next few years, Riel returned more than once in his writing to
the Scott execution, which he appeared to realize full well had been a disastrous misjudgement. In one fragment of 1874–75, for example, he wrote, "Si
j'ai mal fait de faire exécuter Th. Scott, ô Divin esprit, daignez me le faire
connaître parfaitement afin que je vous en demande pardon, que j'en
implore contrition parfaite et que j'en fasse penitence; afin que j'en demande
pardon aux hommes; afin que j'avoue hautement cette faute, si je l'ai faite."[71]
But nothing new was introduced by Riel on the Scott front until, on a return
visit from Montana to Winnipeg, he gave an interview with a reporter from
the Winnipeg *Daily Sun* in June of 1883.[72] It is difficult to know what to make
of this interview, which in its frankness was quite different from another Riel
gave a reporter from the Winnipeg *Daily Times* only a day later.[73] In the *Sun*
interview Riel categorically included the execution of Thomas Scott among
those acts he would do again. He insisted that Archbishop Taché's presence
would not have stopped the execution, "because I was really the leader, and
whenever I believe myself to be right no man has ever changed my opinion." In the *Daily Times* interview, on the other hand, he insisted, "I don't like
to speak about political matters at all, and only do so because I do not like
to refuse to answer your questions."

Riel insisted that Scott was an important loyalist leader "in influence and
prominence, among Métis opponents behind only Schultz, Dennis, and
Bolton [sic]. Schultz and Dennis were beyond the reach of the government,
Riel admitted. "They were more guilty, too," thought Riel, "although Scott
was guilty enough." Riel told the *Sun* reporter that Scott came close to being
killed by the Métis for trying to murder his guard. The Irishman had "seized
a bayonet that was in the room and endeavoured to slay the guard by plung-
ing it into him through an opening in the door of the guard room. He was
always hot-headed and violent." As an example of one of his "crazy acts,"
Riel repeated the story of Scott's dragging Norbert Parisien with a horse, one
end of a scarf tied around Parisien's neck and the other tied to the tail of the
horse. When Riel pleaded with Scott to be quiet in the Fort, Scott had
replied, "You owe me respect; I am loyal and you are rebels." From Scott's
perspective, of course, this observation was indisputable. From Riel's, it was
apparently another illustration of Scott's insulting attitude.

According to a third-hand report reprinted in many Canadian newspapers in 1885, Riel purportedly told his confessor, Father Alexis André, shortly before his execution that he now saw the death of Scott as a "political mistake" but not a crime.[74] Riel added that Sir John A. Macdonald was executing Louis Riel for the same reason that Riel had executed Scott, "because it is necessary for the country's good." He continued, "I admit Scott's shooting was mismanaged, but I commanded it because I thought it necessary. He tried to kill his guards. They came to me and said they could do nothing with him. The rebellion was on the eve of breaking out all over the country, but as soon as Scott was killed it subsided."

Further stories about Scott's bad behaviour, mainly drawn from the oral traditions of the Métis community, appeared in the years after Riel's death, often in work produced within the Manitoba Francophone historiographical tradition. A.H. de Trémaudan recounted in a footnote of great detail Scott's mistreatment of Norbert Parisien, based on an interview of 1923 with André Nault, who sat on Scott's court martial and voted for his execution. Nault gave as his source "Parisien himself, while he was lying on his sick bed."[75] Trémaudan also reported a story told him by Paul Proulx, a councillor of the provisional government in 1870 and a frequent visitor to Upper Fort Garry, about an interview between Riel and Scott, after the guards had told Riel that if Scott was not executed, they would shoot Riel himself.[76] "Riel went to warn Scott, who sneeringly said: 'The Métis are a pack of cowards. They will never dare shoot me.' Then Rich asked him again, 'Ask me anything at all for a punishment.' 'I want nothing,' retorted Scott, 'you are nothing but cowards'."[77] A.G. Morice, without giving a source, wrote in 1935 that "such was the fury which the very sight of the Métis chief could arouse in his [Scott's] breast that, having one day seen him pass by the half-open door, he sprang at him as would a wild beast and, knocking down in his excitement the stool on which he had been sitting, cried out to him with a significant gesture: 'Ah! son of a b—, if I ever recover my liberty, it is at these my hands that you shall perish!'"[78] This is one of the few instances where Scott is recorded as using obscenity, and it is not documented to a first-hand source. In none of Riel's accounts does Scott employ a single swear word, although it is true that Riel may have been too prudish to reproduce any.

There was an Anglophone oral tradition about Scott as well, some of which was reported by George MacBeth in his *The Romance of Western Canada*: "In their cold quarters in Fort Garry, the prisoners used to keep themselves warm by wrestling and sparring. Scott is said to have taken a few rounds out of the guards, and Riel treated that as contempt of his high authority; and so a kind of trial was held…"[79] MacBeth also reported that

Scott's body had been dumped in the river, weighted down with chains, "as I learned in later years from one who was there when it was done."[80] Another local story dealt with the failure to find Scott's body. It had Scott released by the Métis at the last minute, and paid to disappear into the United States, as the authorities hoped to do with Riel and Ambroise Lépine a year later. The execution was then faked.[81]

The tendency to view the killing of Scott as a political act, although not everyone would agree on the politics involved, has dominated the historical treatment of Scott since 1870. While on one level such a perspective is quite legitimate, what has gotten lost in the process is the question of the character of Thomas Scott himself. While not everyone has accepted the propriety or legitimacy of Scott's execution, few have come forward to question the Métis characterization of him as a "hard case," at the very least "hot-headed and violent" and at the worst a singularly villainous man.[82] We shall never be able to get at the unvarnished truth: what we can do, however, is to appreciate the nature of the problem of evidence regarding Scott, and seek to avoid some of the worst excesses of the treatment of Scott's character resulting largely from the ongoing partisanship of the events in which he found himself enmeshed.

What can we say about Scott's character? Many of our conclusions must be negative, rejecting features that have most often received attention from the secondary literature. No contemporary first-hand evidence exists to suggest that he was a heavy drinker. The stories from Pointe des Chênes are about all the Canadian workmen, not about Scott. No evidence survives that he was a henchman of John Schultz, that he was a leader of the "Portage Boys" or the Canadian Party, or even in Riel's many statements, that he was either an extreme anti-Catholic or a master of profanity. Ironically enough, given his subsequent enshrinement as Orangist martyr, Scott's Red River contemporaries never mentioned his Orange Order affiliation. Apart from the stories about his treatment of Norbert Parisien—which are not substantiated in any of the many Anglophone eye-witness accounts of affairs at Kildonan in mid-February 1870, including that of Charles Boulton, who claimed to have saved Parisien from his tormenters after he shot Sutherland—there is precious little evidence that Scott was a bully. Aside from his ducking of John Snow—which could well have been an instance either of frontier justice or boyish high spirits—and the dubious tales of his early confrontations with Riel, there is little evidence from the Anglophone side of Scott's use of physical violence. Alexander Begg wrote sympathetically of Scott in the Snow affair; and certainly nothing from the Métis side suggests that Riel and Scott had ever met before December 1869. George

MacBeth, who was a young man in Kildonan in 1870 but not personally acquainted with Scott, summarized the Anglophone memory when he wrote in 1898: "There is no need now to canonize Scott, nor to claim that he possessed all the virtues and none of the vices of life; but so far as we can gather from those who knew him well, he was a young man of rather quiet habits, indisposed, as most men of Irish blood are, to be trodden upon, but not given to aggressive and unprovoked offending."[83]

As MacBeth's comments suggest, most of his Anglophone contemporaries saw Scott as a well-mannered young Irishman, who had a sense of humour and may perhaps have had a bit too much of a tendency to speak his mind. James Ashdown was the only one who suggested that Scott might have made frequent use of profanity, if we assume that was what was meant by being "free with his language." Although the Scott of the later secondary literature often employed foul language, Louis Riel himself never suggested that this was what Scott's "insults" were about. It is possible that Riel's objections to profanity meant he could not bring himself to repeat what Scott had actually said, although such a position seems too puritan even for Riel. Scott was certainly fearless: there are hints that some of the actions that brought him to the forefront—the negotiations with Riel in early December, the searching of the Winnipeg house in mid-February, perhaps even the standing up to his Métis captors—were the result of his willingness to do things that others were afraid of doing. Scott was also a loyal Canadian, critical of the Americans and an acknowledged opponent of the provisional government of Riel and the Métis. Perhaps—as much of the secondary literature suggests—Scott had nothing but contempt for half-breeds. But insofar as the actual language he used can be substantiated from first-hand testimony, it suggests that he was chiefly contemptuous of rebels. The lionization of Riel has tended to obscure the fact that loyalty to Canada was quite legitimate in the context of the Red River of 1869–70, and that Riel and the Métis could indeed be perceived as rebels against the Queen. Scott ought not to be made out a villain simply because he opposed Louis Riel and the provisional government, or because many Anglophone contemporaries rather simplistically saw his loyalty as the sole cause of his execution.[84]

Nor ought Scott to become a martyr solely because of the poignancy of his last few hours. The details of the death of Scott were, from the very beginning, the stuff of legend, particularly since it was never clear who actually had been an eyewitness to the event. Most of the written accounts came years later from men who had not been present at the time. There were approximately 150 eyewitnesses to the actual execution, however, mostly residents of the village of Winnipeg. The testimony of many of them, taken

PAM N5953

Sketch of the execution of Thomas Scott, by R.P. Meade.

at the 1874 murder trial of Ambroise Lépine, demonstrated mainly how lacking in precise observational powers and memory most eyewitnesses could be; they even disagreed over exactly what the time was when Scott was shot.[85] George Young was certainly present at the execution, but his detailed account of it, written years later, was hardly definitive.[86] Much of it was confused with Donald Smith's 1870 report to Ottawa, which Young had obviously read.

Among the various eyewitnesses, there was general agreement that Scott was led out of the east-side gate at Upper Fort Garry and shot against the wall there. Reports varied as to whether he emerged blindfolded or was blindfolded later. Scott apparently prayed continually while in the open air. According to Donald Smith, who was inside the fort and heard an account from others, the condemned man told Reverend Young, "This is a cold-blooded murder." Young's much later report was that Scott had said, "This is horrible! This is cold-blooded murder. Be sure to make a true statement." Scott then knelt in the snow and said, "Farewell." A firing squad of six men, according to some witnesses intoxicated, then shot him. Reports of the number of shots varied, although several narratives (including Young's) agreed that the Irishman did not die instantly after the initial volley. Some said he was dispatched on the spot by a revolver bullet through the head.[87]

As we have seen, there was a bad Thomas Scott; he was almost entirely a product of Métis evidence, however, especially that of Louis Riel. That testimony is almost entirely unsubstantiated on the Anglophone side, either in specifics or in tone. It is possible that Scott turned into a monster around the Métis, and especially under confinement. But as was pointed out earlier, it would seem fairly problematic to accept without question the executioners' unsubstantiable accounts of the victim's bad character and behaviour when this bad character and behaviour was mainly what was used to justify his execution. Moreover, the evidence of Scott's bad character did become progressively blacker and more detailed as time progressed, especially in the later Métis oral tradition and in the burgeoning secondary literature. Louis Riel, for example, saw Scott as a man of incorrigibly violent behaviour, but never suggested that Scott used profanity, was contemptuous of Métis, or was bigoted against Roman Catholics. André Nault, who had been tried and acquitted of Scott's murder, was the source for several of the later stories, recounted to earnest researchers after an afternoon or evening of conviviality.[88]

One of the many mysteries surrounding the execution of Thomas Scott was what had become of his body, which had supposedly been buried in a plain wooden coffin within the walls of Upper Fort Garry. The question took on special piquancy because of the insistence of several witnesses, mainly Métis guards, that the firing squad had not actually killed him. Noises and talking were heard from the coffin by several passers-by after the execution. Moreover, when the grave was finally dug up after the arrival of the Wolseley expedition in the autumn of 1870, it was found to be empty. The defence in the trial of Ambroise Lépine made much out of this absence of a body, although most contemporaries were satisfied with trial testimony which suggested that the corpse had been disinterred in the middle of the night a few days after the execution and dumped in the Red River.[89] Louis Riel went to his grave without disclosing the final whereabouts of Scott's body, which was one of the last questions asked him.[90]

Instead of becoming obsessed with the disposition of Scott's physical remains, however, it might have been more useful if more of his contemporaries had been concerned with his reputation. Thomas Scott was not only a victim, he was also a perfect illustration of the way historians, or the twists of history, can blame the victim. That he was young, a stranger to Red River, and without social connections, all contributed to the unfortunate end result.

11. The Charismatic Patterns: Canada's Riel Rebellion of 1885 as a Millenarian Protest Movement (1985)

Manfred Mossmann

Millenarianism has been a common phenomenon in the Third or, perhaps more precisely, the Fourth World (that of oppressed minorities). Acculturation leads to social anomie, at which point economic forces give way to spiritual forces: visionaries emerge and appeals to spirituality prevail, soon compounded by reliance on the supernatural and the forging of legends. It is in such a charismatic context that the Riel saga can be profitably examined.

The Wider Context

On October 20, 1982 the police in Maiduguri (North-Eastern Nigeria) who tried to arrest members of an Islamic sect named "Dan Kabarv" were met by gunfire. The following three-day battle cost more than 500 lives. The group's leader, prophet and spiritual father, Mallan Muhammad Marwa, had been killed during riots in December 1980. The sect was outlawed by the Nigerian government.[1] This has been the most recent example of a millenarian protest movement.

These movements, which have emerged in many parts of the world over the centuries, usually occur during an era of rapid and intense socio-economic change. The intrusion of a "colonizing people" into the living space and way of life of a "native people"[2] usually precipitates a "culture clash." The symptoms are: decline of group identity, loss of self-respect, élite displacement, decline of social status and economic well-being (often seen in close connection with destruction of traditional ways of life and imposition of heavy taxes), disruption of community units and kinship bonds leading to growing frustration, violent resistance and a simultaneous rise of a prophetic leader.[3]

Historical publications in Canada have depicted Louis Riel as a rebel and traitor, a French-Canadian martyr, a frontiersman, and a Métis hero and saint.[4] In Thomas Flanagan's book *Louis "David" Riel*, the author stresses the socio-economic side of the Riel Rebellions and the millenarian aspects of Riel's philosophy, or *Weltanschauung*. Flanagan suggests that Riel should be placed in the context of medieval visionaries, such as Joachim of Fiore and Bridget of Sweden, and notes that the Métis resistance was similar to "religious resistance movements of the Third World."[5]

In his study of millenarian protest movements against the European colonial order, Michael Adas[6] establishes a number of structural elements common to those movements and their prophetic leaders. The Métis and Riel almost ideally fit into the general pattern. This becomes clear when Riel is compared to Birsa Bhagwan, Saya San, Te Ua Haumene and Antonio Conselheiro,[7] four major leaders of millenarian prophet-inspired protest movements in India, Burma, New Zealand and Brazil.

The Socio-economic Context

In all of these examples the prophetic leader's people inhabit a relatively isolated, homogeneous, inaccessible and sparsely populated area. Following the intrusion of a foreign culture their (aboriginal) land rights are endangered.

Originally a valley people, the Mundas (Birsa's people), under pressure from various invaders, had been pushed to the highlands of Chota Nagpur in Central Eastern India. Following the establishment of British control, "landlord exactions merely increased and the position of the Mundas ... worsened as long-standing methods of exploitation were intensified."[8] There were riots and a resistance movement culminating in continuous rebellious agitations among the Mundas in the 19th century.

In the second half of the last century Lower Burma was rapidly transformed from a frontier/wilderness country into a prosperous province of the British Empire. After an initial economic improvement the local population was faced with a web of problems, the question of land rights being among the most important ones. Economic depression and sociocultural disruption (including the running out of living space and the loss of control of the peasant over his land) were main factors out of which Saya San forged his rebellion.[9]

The Maori (Te Ua's people) had lived in virtual isolation on the North Island of New Zealand, where they had developed a sophisticated tribal system. The impact of Europeans upon them was sudden. After an initial short period of adjustment and well-being, the Maori became impoverished, were driven into emotional despair, and had to witness the factual abolition of their land rights:

> Even government agencies created to protect Maori inter-
> ests fed the settler's seemingly insatiable hunger for Maori
> land. In 1852, the Colonial Office hesitantly granted repre-
> sentative government to the people of New Zealand, which
> effectively meant the European settlers. It became increas-
> ingly obvious to the Maoris that they must organize and
> resist further encroachments or perish.[10]

In the Manitoba Act of 1870 the Métis were offered 1.4 million acres of land as a compensation for aboriginal rights. There were, however, practical problems: the Act did not state how the land was to be distributed, only Métis of the "third generation" and later generations were eligible, survey-ing had to be completed, the old river lot system was ignored, and distribu-tion of land did not begin till March 1873.[11] In 1876, when the final regula-tions were issued, those Métis who had endured often became the easy vic-tims of land speculators. It seems fairly obvious that the vast majority of Métis, with their "simple characters"[12] as Bruce Sealey calls it, were not in a position to resist the discrimination of the white governmental and bureau-cratic machine. Sealey sums up the situation of the 1870s:

> It is clear that the law was prepared for the benefit of set-
> tlers who understood the value of the land, or for the prof-
> iteers in a western society based on capitalism. There was
> very little left for many Métis but to move away and
> attempt to re-establish the old way of life based on trapping
> and hunting.[13]

Just like the Mundas, the Métis were pushed out of their original area of settlement by land-hungry foreigners. Many Métis went across the border to the United States, others went west, where they set up new settlements in northern Saskatchewan. That migration only eased difficulties for a short period of time. The basic problems, however, remained unsolved.

By 1884 the situation in the Métis communities in Saskatchewan paral-leled the one in Manitoba after 1870: decreasing employment opportunities, economic decline, insecurity about land titles, and an increasing influx of white settlers meant potential threats to Métis land ownership. As Flanagan notes, all in all the situation was even more desperate than in 1870: "the half-breeds resident in the North-West had been allocated nothing, even though the Dominion Land Act of 1878 had allowed a distribution of land in the North-West."[14] Furthermore, there was the problem of those Métis squatting on land reserved by the government for the Hudson's Bay Company (HBC) and the Canadian Pacific Railway (CPR).

The question of land, of effective (legal) control over "Native" lands, was regarded by the native groups as essential to guarantee survival. Moreover, for some the land seems to have been more than just a source of income; it was associated with a way of life and identity. That those people had an understanding of the value of land, even if not all the legal implications, seems to be clear from the fact that they were willing to fight and die for their *Lebensraum*.

Economic order among the peoples considered here was basically pre-industrial and agrarian (or semi-agrarian/nomadic). Self-supply was the primary, yet not the exclusive goal. Socio-economic life was strongly community-orientated. The continuous impact of the colonizers brought accelerated change and relative deprivation for the Native people. The deprivation stemmed from a feeling among the colonized "that a gap existed between what they felt they deserved in terms of status and material rewards and what they possessed or had the capacity to obtain."[15] A people which had had little contact with industrialized culture was suddenly overwhelmed by it and was forced to prove its identity on a collective and individual basis against that foreign culture, which was not willing to accept the "Native" culture as equal.

The Métis were an idiosyncratic product of the fur trade and by the beginning of the 19th century they had established a distinctive way of life that was semi-agrarian/nomadic, combining petty farming with hunting. Others worked as HBC employees, salt miners, freighters or lime makers.[16] The core of the Métis economy was the buffalo. The annual hunts were carried out according to strict rules and were both economic and social events.

The last century in Western Canada was a time of enormous and continuous socio-economic changes, and until about the 1870s the Métis had been well able to adapt to changing circumstances. The disappearance of the buffalo, though, was a most serious blow to the Métis economic system. Furthermore, the coming of the railroad made the old means of transportation largely superfluous. Those Métis who had migrated west were now further removed and in some cases completely cut off from the prosperous trade centres, most notably Winnipeg. The only alternative offered within the new Canadian way of life was to become a settler. That was the point where the Métis, product of social change, ironically became also victims of social change.

It is hard to assess why the Métis seemed unwilling and/or unable to adapt to the post-1870 capitalist system. They were illiterate, and legal proceedings necessarily involved written correspondence. Thus, most Métis had to leave it to their leaders to draft petitions for them, many of which were delayed in a slow governmental machine and in some cases not answered at all. The conclusion is that the Métis tried, but had no real fair chance, because (a) their starting position, against the white settlers for example, was weaker, and (b) they were discriminated against in a number of vital areas, religious, racial, economic, linguistic.[17]

The Prophetic Leaders

The lives of Birsa, Saya San, Te Ua and Antonio Conselheiro show remarkable parallels. As far as social background is concerned, Adas establishes two major types of prophetic leaders:

> At one pole are indigenous authority figures whose position is threatened by changes introduced by the agents of alien civilizations... At the other pole of the continuum are men of low birth, who are exposed to a high degree to alien but dominant civilizations. On the basis of my sample, this is the more common background for prophetic protest leaders.[18]

The four prophetic leaders outside Canada can be placed around that second pole: Birsa was born as the fourth son of a poor peasant family in Chota Nagpur. Since his parents were unable to support him as a young child, he was sent to live with his uncle. Te Ua, who belonged to the Taranaki tribe, was kidnapped at the age of three and was kept as a slave among another New Zealand tribe, the Waikato. Saya San was born in Shwebo in 1882. Early in his life he moved away from his family and made a fairly poor living from fortune-telling and working as a medical healer. Conselheiro surrounded himself with the notion of the mysterious past of a mythic hero. He seems to have been wandering in the Brazilian backlands in his early life, living on alms.

Riel's early years have been covered in various biographies. For this chapter, suffice it to repeat that he was born in 1844 in St. Boniface where his father "farmed and raised livestock on a modest scale; he also operated at various times a grist mill... But he was always in debt to the Hudson's Bay Company, and his best efforts did not succeed in elevating him above the bottom layer of the Métis bourgeoisie."[19]

As far as family background is concerned, Riel had a divided class identity of upper class (through the Lagimodière connection) and middle class (through his father). His social status was continually shifting. For example, during his time in Montreal he experienced a decline in social status and would have to be placed closer to the lower classes. As the other lower class prophets of Adas's system, Riel was exposed to a high degree of foreign civilization throughout his life. By 1870 he had certainly also become a Métis authority figure whose position was challenged. He could at that point be placed around Adas's first pole.

The prophetic leaders of millenarian movements are relatively well-educated and well-travelled. The leaders considered here received an uncommon, special education away from their original homes, an education which put heavy stress on religious matters. Besides that, the four leaders outside Canada studied with Native people and acquired an extensive knowledge of native cults and shamanistic rituals as well as of Christian religions.

While attending school in his home village, the special abilities of Birsa were recognized and he was sent to higher education in the town of Burja. "At Burja he became a Christian and was baptized with the name David. He soon advanced to a larger mission school, where he came into close contact with European teachers for the first time."[20] Te Ua was educated at the Methodist mission school at Kawhia Harbor on the West coast of New Zealand, where he too was made a Christian. Before that he had learned the magic art from one of the tribal priests.

Bishop Taché had arranged for Riel to be sent east to the Collège de Montréal with rich people covering the expenses. He was supposed to become a Catholic priest and return to the West as one of the first Métis missionaries.

Quite often the education is broken off or the overall result is not inclusive enought to secure the future prophetic leader a permanent place in the "colonizers'" society. Birsa was expelled from mission school after seven years. Te Ua too came back to his home village. Riel was dismissed for breaking the house rules, and after finally giving up his intention of becoming a priest and having unsuccessfully tried to enter law, he returned to Red River.

These disappointing experiences left the future leaders with a feeling of ambivalence towards the colonizers' education and made them largely mistrust their culture and religion. After that initial rupture they came to regard their "Native" culture and surroundings as their primary physical and spiritual home. Familiarity with both their own people's and the colonizers' culture and way of life enhanced the prophetic leaders' authority among their own people and enabled them to act as cultural middlemen, or as Adas calls them "cultural brokers."[21] Education was also an important factor, since the followers of the five prophets considered here, including the Métis, were in their vast majority illiterate people, and among such people literacy "was also frequently seen as a sign of his [the prophet's] capacity to master the secrets of the European overlords."[22]

The question of the sociology of charisma is important. Bryan Wilson states that "Charisma is not a personality attribute, but a successful claim to power by virtue of supernatural ordination."[23] Since it is extremely hard to find objective criteria for the validity of such a claim to divine sanction, recognition by the prophet's followers becomes the decisive factor.[24] The successful relationship between prophet and followers can be described as "one of supreme personal trust"[25] or, better and simpler: faith. That the prophets considered here had that trust and faith seems evident,[26] and it makes them truly charismatic. To prove that point with Riel, witness an excerpt from a letter of Father Fourmond: "Notre population ... dans sa simplicité, voyant ce singulier personnage, Métis comme eux, prier presque jour et nuit ... elle avait en lui une confiance aveugle et le prenait pour un saint."[27]

Traditionally, charismatic leaders arise in times of social unrest and change. "Charisma is undoubtedly a case of social change: but it also appears to be a response to it, a response to social disruption."[28] Max Weber goes one step further by saying: "Within the sphere of its claims, charismatic authority repudiates the past, and is in this sense a specifically revolutionary force."[29] Riel did not repudiate the past, but there was a revolutionary trait about him, in that he combined the role of prophetic leader opposed to the Catholic priests in Batoche with the role of political leader opposed to established governmental authorities.

As far as the prophetic leaders' *Weltanschauung* is concerned, they developed a somewhat simplistic view of the world which they wrote down and/or preached to their followers with considerable success. Its core is a binary system made up of such primary dualities[30] as man/God, earth/heaven, good/evil and friend/enemy—a system which was evidently very appealing to the mostly peasant followers, especially as a strong in-group/out-group feeling, a feeling of solidarity, could thereby be established.

A so far neglected part of Riel's *Weltanschauung* is his "Monadism." In his typical philosophically distortive manner, Riel developed a crude mixture of Leibniz,[31] primitive Christian thinking, and electromagnetism as discovered by Oersted in 1820. In Riel's world, which is made up of "essences," the "monades" are the smallest indivisible entities:

> Les essences se composent de 'Monades'... Les 'Monades' sont de deux genres; elles sont, les unes mâles, les autres femelles... Une monade est une électricité... Une monade mâle est une électricité positive. Une monade femelle est une électricité negative... Les monades sont de deux sortes. Les unes sont actives et les autres sont passives.[32]

In another document, probably a draft for a book on his religious/ philosophical principles,[33] Riel writes more along the same lines and defines the relationship between man and God as a sort of magnetic field where the tension between the active essences of God and the passive essences of mankind contain the world in harmony. Religion is the magnet which draws together the divine and the human essences, which has been disrupted by man's original sin.[34] Living in harmony is a divine gift and a divine prerogative:

> L'homme étant créé d'essences passives, ne peut pas, quand il a complètement rompu avec les essences actives, se remettre par lui-même en harmonies avec elles. Car cette harmonie est un don des essences divines.[35]

Man has both negative and positive forces in him. Sin and rupture from God stem from man bringing up his negative forces against the negative commandments of God:

> Et comme les électricités de même nom se repoussent, l'homme entre en dispute avec son Dieu. Lorsque les élec-tricités *Négatives* divines nous defendent quelque chose, si nous nous interdisons toute autre chose que celle-là, nous mettons aussi au jeu nos ˉélectricités Négatives; et comme les électricités de même nom se répugnent nous nous querellons avec les essences divines.[36]

There can be no doubt that in Riel's system of repulsing and attracting forces, of active and passive electricities, God remains the "magnet number one."

The Prophetic Leaders and Their Special Missions

As pointed out above, prophetic leaders derive their primary and principal legitimacy from divine authority. In most cases, though, additional "secular" and other assistance is sought. Consequently, the five leaders considered previously were eager to attain the support of local and/or other authori-ty figures. In Riel's case a letter from Bishop Bourget was of particular importance:

> Mais Dieu qui vous a toujours dirigé et assisté jusqu'à présent ne vous abandonnera pas au plus fort de vos peines. Car il vous a donné une mission qu'il faudra accom-plir en tous points.[37]

In addition, both Saya San and Riel claimed to be of royal descent, thus enhancing their claims to power and leadership:

> Celui que le monde attendait dans la personne d'Henri cinq
> se trouve dans le Prophète du Nouveau Monde, Louis
> 'David' Riel qui par sa mère Julie de la Gimodiere est un des
> princes descendant de Louis XI.[38]

To keep up their prophetic claims the prophets had to "deliver," that is to say, they had to perform some sort of magical acts.[39] That Riel was very much aware of the nature of his prophethood and its wider implications can be illustrated by the following quotation from one of his writings in Regina prison:

> C'est Dieu qui, par la grâce et la force divine de Jésus-
> Christ, a soin des missions extraordinaires. Les hommes
> envoyés du Saint-Esprit ne se caracterisent pas eux-mêmes.
> Ils sont environnés et accompagnés de marques qui les car-
> acterisent. Leurs bons désirs, leur bonne volonté ont des
> sanctions indubitablement bonnes et saintes. Le doigt visi-
> ble de Dieu les designe par les resultats de leur conduite.[40]

Four of the prophetic figures considered here experienced an initial vision or a series of visions triggered off in an unusual situation. After having been shunned from his village, Birsa was struck by lightning while walking through a forest. "This incident was followed by a series of dreams, the content of which Birsa interpreted as injunctions for him to return to his people and rescue them from their misery."[41] Te Ua had his first vision during a serious illness and claimed that the angel Gabriel had spoken to him.

Riel later stated that his mission began in St. Patrick's Church in Washington on December 8, 1875 with a sudden experience of a mystical ecstasy and a following powerful vision.[42] This in Riel's view marked the beginning of a new era, the *Heilswende* (turning point of salvation) leading to the Métis fulfillment of God's providential plan and to the second coming of Christ, a day so important that it marked the redemption of man's original sin in the Garden of Eden.[43]

In these visions the prophetic leaders were told by God or some other supernatural power that they had a special task to perform in the world, a sacred mission which would lead to the redemption of their people and their own personal glory. An important means to reach that goal was the establishment of a form of new church, and generally speaking a new religious-political order.

Both Riel and Te Ua established parallels between the Jews and their own people, the Métis and the Maori, both seeing them as the new chosen people of God. Riel even created a mythic genealogy which made the Métis relatives of the Jews in both spirit and blood.[44] Another interesting parallel between Riel and Te Ua lies in the fact that both were considered to be insane by some of their friends and fellowmen at the time: Te Ua was taken away in chains and Riel was confined in the asylum at Longue Pointe.

An essential part of the visionary contents and the prophetic mission claim was the renaming process. The prophets adopted special names for themselves[45] and their world.[46] This re-naming of course was not an end in itself, but meant redefining, re-evaluating, attributing new meaning[47] and creating a utopian alternative to the modern world.

The renaming factor corresponds with the futuristic tendency Guglielmo Guariglia discusses in his study of prophetic movements. He establishes three basic tendencies: a tendency towards the past, e.g. nativism; one towards the present, e.g. syncretism; and one towards the future, e.g. millenarianism.[48] Those major tendencies can be detected in the "missions" of all five prophetic leaders: that is to say, they were all looking back to a past golden age, working for the present which was to be seen as a time of hardship and testing, and looking ahead in the future to a perfect utopian-millenarian state.

W.E. Muhlmann gives the following definition of nativism:

> Wir verstehen also Nativismus als einen kollektiven Aktionsablauf, der von dem Drang getragen ist, ein durch eine uberlegene Fremdkultur erschüttertes Gruppen-Selbstgefühl wiederherzustellen durch massives Demonstrieren einen "eigenen Beitrags." Das "Eigene" liegt in dem Wunsch und Willen, sich abzusetzen gegen den Eindruck ubermächtiger Fremdkultur, es liegt in der Manifestierung des Gefühls: "Wir sind auch etwas!"[49]

Through the prophet's personal appeal and divine authority, a restoration of the shattered group identity and the overcoming of inferiority feelings were temporarily possible. Due to their superior intelligence and rhetorical abilities the prophetic leaders were able to restore their peoples' pride and give them a "voice."

The prophetic leaders were intelligent enough to know that they could not restore the past and were instead working to preserve certain well-respected values of the past and integrate them into their new system. All five prophets considered here mixed aspects of their "Native" tradition with European thought and tradition, especially as far as religion is concerned.

That leads us to our next point, syncretism. The new religious doctrines and religions/political orders were basically eclectic, and the truly original ideas in them were minimal.[50] Following the classic definitions of millenarian movements established by Talman and Cohn,[51] the Riel Rebellion of 1885 was typical insofar as salvation was to be

    a. collective, to be enjoyed by all the nations of the world and especially the Métis as a community, God's faithful and chosen people to redeem all peoples of the world;

    b. terrestrial, in the sense that Riel's theocratic utopian state was to become reality in Canada;

    c. imminent, insofar as the mission of Riel and the special task of the Métis had already begun on 8 December 1875. Final salvation though was still many years away (to come in the year 4209);

    d. total, in the sense that everyone would be thoroughly affected and the final result would be a radical change in way of life for everyone. Again, that final stage of perfection would be the result of a process of continuous moral reform throughout many years;

    e. miraculous, because it would be brought about with the help of God. Riel's belief in the direct influence and his complete trust in divine providence are evident from a large number of his writings.

A common factor in the prophetic act are apocalyptic visions concerning the forces of the enemy who are opposed to the prophet and not among the "chosen." Te Ua was talking about a great flood that would destroy all Europeans. Riel had similar visions in Beauport, but became more moderate later.[52] Conselheiro was the most radical of the prophets considered here, since in his millenarian visions the final catastrophe and the second coming of Christ were imminent:

    In 1899 the waters shall turn to blood, and … the earth some place shall find itself in heaven. There shall be a great rain of stars, and that will be the end of the world.[53]

After the apocalyptic times of extreme hardship and testing, probation and purification, the preparation time for the millennium or the millennium itself would begin. Except for the famous land division scheme,[54] we have little knowledge of how in Riel's case that preparatory millenarian state was supposed to look. The remark "Jesus Christ wants to perfect the government of His church and to make His apostles able to exercise charitable coercion on men"[55] gives us some idea of a theocratic oppression system. Further clues can be found in a notebook where Riel establishes an elaborate ecumenical council system:

> les trois conseils districts dans chaque nationalité pourraient se saluer et s'édifier en convention une fois tous les trente ans. Et ce triple conseil de toutes les nations du nouveau monde ferraient un grand acte d'amitié chrétienne et un grand pas vers la concorde universelle... Les chefs des chevaliers de chaque pays formeront un conseil à part... Les chefs des prêtres et ministres solitaires de chaque nation constitueront un autre conseil... Les dénominations religieuses du nouveau monde ont besoin d'être reliées ensemble d'une maniere étroite. Il n'est pas impossible qu'elles entrent à cet effet dans une entente générale et qu'elles consentent toutes à former un ordre religieux dont le but serait de réformer sans cesse le clergé, les soldats et la congrégation et les simples fidèles appartenant à chaque denomination.[56]

Obviously, like many other utopian states, Plato's Republic for example, Riel's future society was to have three major classes: *prêtres, chevaliers* and *simples fidèles*. It is not clear what he means by *"chevaliers,"* probably people with military and police functions. It seems evident though that the church's hierarchical system was to be imposed upon the society as a whole and there would be *"gouvernement des chefs,"* government from the "top." Also note the idea of a special religious reform order devoted to continuous reform in all spheres of the different social groups.

Like Riel, Birsa and the other prophets made it clear that victory over the colonizing powers was only the first step towards a new social, political and religious order. Generally speaking, that new society would be theocratic in essence, and free of foreign oppression, moral digression, social injustice and economic hardship. In that respect all prophets thought in global terms and envisaged what Riel in the quotation above calls *"la concorde universelle."* In Saya San's millenarian ideology: "The totality of Burma's people shall be made happy through an abundance of gold and silver and gems. [And the] people of the entire world shall equally become Buddhist... people will be pious, freed from illness and shall have peace of mind and body."[57] Saya San combined pagan/native, Buddhist and biblical thought. The prophetic leader Birsa acted similarly. Riel, Conselheiro and Te Ua, on the other hand, had a preference for biblical models. In Riel's case we can speak of "biblical model-syncretism," since he combined the roles of prophet, priest and messiah and saw himself in line with David, Daniel, Moses, and, especially towards the end of his life, with Jesus.[58]

Here is one of Riel's typical visions from October 2, 1885, which articulates this biblical model:

> [margin] C'est la main de Dieu qui m'a fait faire mon chemin autour de la montagne sainte ... l'italien vertueux et le canadien français m'aident a faire route dans les vallées et les endroits bas de l'humanité. C'est l'église qui parle en moi. [main text] Dieu m'a fait voir que je montais par degré la montagne sainte ... les puissances mettaient le pied sur quelque machination internationale; passaient quelques foyers de conspiration diabolique ... ce chemin était étroit... Le Dieu tout puissant en avait soin. "J'arrive au bout de mes difficultés..." [margin] L'italien humble et vertueux est d'une amabilité et d'une simplicité admirables. Il peut me conduire a une paix glorieuse.[59]

Both the margin and the main text start off with a special prophetic *Botenformel* ("announcing formula"): "*C'est la main de Dieu*" and "*Dieu m'a fait voir.*"[60] The prophet thereby announces the following words as being of divine origin.

As Northrop Frye has recently pointed out, "the image of a Messianic figure flanked by two others"[61] is one of the well-established patterns of the Bible. Just like other prophets in the Old Testament,[62] Riel is fascinated with the concept of trinity.

One picture immediately springs to mind here: the transfiguration of Christ.[63] Moses and Elias as the precursors and supporting figures of Jesus have counterparts in the French-Canadian and the Italian, who are the assisting figures for Riel's New Church in the New World. As allegorical figures the French-Canadian represents French culture and the Catholic Church in Canada, the Italian represents the European immigrant who is willing to accept French superiority in Northern America. Besides that, his extreme friendliness and simplicity make him the ideal "*simple fidèle*" in Riel's thinking. The Italian's virtue probably refers to the virtuous state Riel believed the Roman Catholic Church and the Vatican were in before 1870. Frenchman and Italian, who together form the basis for Riel's new order and new church, are allegorically its moral support and individually its potential members. Riel seems very much aware that he needs human co-operation for his endeavours to "progress" and that only in harmony between man and the almighty God, faithful co-operation between the two, lies the key to overcome the devilish conspiracies and achieve true salvation.

Another biblical image immediately comes to mind: the ascent of Moses to Mount Sinai.[64] Riel further enhances that parallel by saying: *"C'est l'église qui parle en moi."* Like Moses on Sinai receiving God's commandments and thus establishing the basic minimal norms for the Jewish religion, Riel hopes through ascending his visionary mountain to achieve communion with God above and to establish some fundamental rules for his new church.

The mountain in general and the holy mountain in particular were favourite images of the biblical prophets,[65] and the latter was often seen as the home of God.[66] Riel's description of the setting gives this vision a distinct mystical touch. Talking of high and low, God and humanity, devilish conspiracy and glorious peace, mountain and valley, he creates the basic antagonism so typical of medieval visionaries.[67] Another biblical/mystical image is the *"chemin étroit,"* the narrow path of redemption.[68] Riel's ascension step by step fits into the pattern of the medieval visionaries' gradual ascension towards the *unio mystica*, the union with God.[69] At the end of the vision Riel can be seen as being on the *via illuminativa*, one step closer to God, and it is his semi-transfigured ego which now speaks.[70] The time of earthly hardship is coming to its end and paradise looms ahead.[71]

Rebellion

Before the rebellious movements were triggered by the prophetic leaders, their people were in an emotionally agitated state of mind. The leaders were able to exploit that state of mind, and without this sort of special relationship the movements would not have been possible. Confronted with a highly critical state of affairs, or at least with a perception of things being catastrophic, the people turned towards their prophet as a person who supplied both security and identity. Furthermore, the prophets were said to have supernatural powers[72] and were thus predestined to perform the extraordinary measures that seemed to be needed.

Prophetic leaders experienced their most ardent support and a willingness to go to war in times when, due to basically economic hardships and the general feeling that something is "wrong," their people were in a psychological state which manifested itself in feelings of sadness, desperation and inferiority complexes combined with romantic dreams of a golden past.[73] That is exactly the state of mind the Métis were in in 1884–85, and it explains their devotion to Riel.[74] Flanagan describes the state of affairs thus:

> The buffalo … vanished altogether after 1878, adversely
> affecting numerous trades in which the Métis had been

prominent: buffalo hunting, trading with the Indians ... and transporting these goods to market. The Métis cart trains and boat brigades also suffered from the advent of railways and steamboats in the Canadian West. Deprived of much of the income from traditional occupations, the Métis had to rely more on agriculture. As they began to make this transition, they were struck, as were all western farmers, by the economic depression and fall in grain prices which began in 1883.[75]

Besides that, "Their language and religion were jeopardized by massive English and Protestant immigration... And the benign neglect of the Hudson's Bay Company in local affairs was replaced by the stricter control of the Canadian state."[76]

Three main factors are involved in bringing on violence in a millenarian protest movement: (a) the decision of the prophetic leader, (b) the prophet's loss of authority, and (c) the failure of established authorities.[77] The first two were of minor importance, if not irrelevant in the Rebellion of 1885, since Riel had not originally intended to start a second rebellion and since he remained the undisputed leader at Batoche. Although Flanagan is right in describing the controversy as a "train of mistakes, misjudgments and misperceptions on both sides,"[78] the inefficiencies of the Department of the Interior and the failure of the local missionary priests to function as "advisers and link"[79] constituted the decisive factors. In the end the government must take the blame, because it was basically the mishandling of the whole affair by the Canadian government and the tragic misunderstanding at Duck Lake which sparked the consequent violence. There can hardly be any doubt that Riel's principal and initial intentions were non-violent, directed at repeating the successful negotiation of 1869–70.[80] In July 1884 Father André described him in the following words:

> Il a agi et parlé avec calme et bon sens... Tous ses efforts ...
> tendent a faire comprendre au peuple qu'en ré pondant à
> son appel il n'avait d'autre objet en vue que de l'aider par
> des moyens lé gitimes et pacifiques.[81]

Riel acted in full conviction of his prophethood and, as pointed out above,[82] thought in wider terms than the Métis did: global salvation was the final goal. Therefore Flanagan is right in saying that "Preexisting local grievances were only pawns in a complex series of maneuvers aimed at vindicating Métis ownership of the North-West as a whole,"[83] and that Riel wanted "a massive settlement of aboriginal claims."[84] Louis Riel in 1885 was primarily a millenarian leader, not a political one. It was only after "constitutional" order and other agitation had proven fruitless that force was employed as an additional means by the "Native peoples" considered here to make their pleas heard.[85]

For the sake of the "cause" Riel finally agreed to use force to fight force, and at one time even threatened a "war of extermination," but even after open violence had begun, his view of the confrontation remained distinctly religious/prophetic.[86] In a vision from April 1885 he again evoked the image of the road leading up a mountain:

> L'esprit de Dieu m'a fait voir le chemin d'en haut… C'est le chemin des Métis qui vont aux victoires d'ici bas : c'est aussi la route céleste qui conduit au paradis les âmes de ceux que le Seigneur a choisi sur le champs.[87]

Riel leaves no doubt that he thinks God is actively involved on the Métis side and in the last sentence he seems to proclaim a concept close to that of the crusades and the Islamic notion of the *jihad*, or "Holy War."[88]

In the vast majority of millenarian protest movements there is what we might call "job-splitting" between the prophet and a military leader or a group of military leaders. As Adas has pointed out this often leads to internal fights for leadership, and in the course of mounting violence "secondary leaders" often take effective control of the movement.[89] As far as Conselheiro and Riel are concerned, they both seem to have been in firm control over the entire movement till the end of the resistance. Even such a prominent leader as Gabriel Dumont asked Riel first to give him men when he wanted to make a military move,[90] and against his better judgement gave up his guerrilla tactics to follow Riel's trench warfare. "I yielded to Riel's judgement, although I was convinced that, from a humane standpoint, mine was the better plan; but I had confidence in his faith and his prayers, and that God would listen to him."[91] Dumont clearly states the point that in a millenarian movement "humane standpoints" are of secondary importance and belief in the prophet and his supernatural powers are absolutely imperative.

The job-splitting between Riel and Dumont had a tradition among their Indian relatives[92] as well as in the biblical/Judaic tradition of the Métis' European forefathers, where the prophets of the Old Testament hardly ever involve themselves in military activities.

Failure and Aftermath

After having instigated their movements the prophetic figures were faced with official persecution and were often forced to operate underground. After the Red River Rebellion, Riel was driven into exile in the United States and even there had to fear for his life. In May 1885 he surrendered, obvious-ly hoping to present his ideas to new and possibly sympathetic audiences.[93]

A common factor in the lives of the prophetic leaders seems to be what we might call "the big mistake," a crucial blunder which severely shattered their individual and sometimes also their peoples' reputation. Driven by hunger, Birsa robbed a grave to steal jewels and was caught in the act. He was shunned from the village for this sacrilege. Te Ua failed to gain substan-tial and lasting respect among his fellow tribesmen and was rebuffed. In Riel's case his military strategy in 1885 can also be regarded as a major mis-take in judgement.

In view of the superiority, both in military/logistic and in economic/political matters, of the colonizing peoples, final failure of the rebellious movements was inevitable. Although guerrilla tactics often brought initial and impressive victories for the rebels,[94] it merely helped to prolong the movements for a limited period of time and raised the overall number of casualties.

Much has been written about Riel's failure to form a workable alliance with the Indians. Although this would have certainly enhanced Riel's posi-tion, resistance through legal means appears to have been the only viable solution:

> For all the rebel leaders with any vision … recognized that the day when they could sweep the white man from the prairies was gone, if it had ever existed. What they hoped for was that a strong alliance of native peoples, willing to take decisive action, could force the Dominion government to negotiate…[95]

Whereas some of the Native peoples revived their rebellions, legal action has been and still is the way in which the Métis continue to struggle for their rights.[96]

After the prophetic leader's arrest or death, the movement for the time being is defeated and the leader later tends to become a sort of folk hero. Birsa was arrested in February 1900 and died in prison: "The prophet's cap-ture ended the last and most serious Munda attempt to forcibly expel the invaders of their highland home."[97] Te Ua was captured in March 1866. Saya San was executed in August 1931. Antonio Conselheiro died in Canudos in August 1897. Clearly, "neither movement survived the loss of their prophet-instigators."[98] Prophets have always had a scapegoat and victim image,[99] and it was imprisonment and death which finally turned four of the five prophets considered in this chapter into martyrs and allowed them to become legends and folk heroes among their people:

There is, however, no doubt that Birsa is still remembered by the Mundas. His exploits are a popular theme of the Munda folk songs and stories. Many boys are named after him in the Munda country. By some Indian nationalists Birsa is hailed as an early "freedom fighter" and ardent Indian patriot.[100]

Something similar happened to Riel in Canada. As Margaret Atwood says: "Riel is the perfect all-Canadian hero—he's French, Indian, Catholic, revolutionary and possibly insane, and he was hanged by the Establishment."[101] He also fits in well with the classic tragic hero in Canadian literature who dies in the end resisting stronger powers—nature, Indians or the Mounted Police. Besides that, a minor but profitable folk industry of "Rieliana" has developed,[102] which takes Riel into the realm of an *Oberammergau* religious tourism.

Conclusion

Riel can then be seen as a prophetic leader of a millenarian protest movement with strong bonds to the Bible and biblical mysticism. While almost all of the traditional elements of classical Third World resistance movements can be identified in the rebellion of 1885, it was also unique. It was modern in its attempt to integrate the means of political resistance, such as drafts of bills and petitions, with the establishment of a provisional government. It was also modern in its ambivalence about the use of violent militant force. In its national context it was typically Canadian, because it was built upon the participation of both Métis and Indians, and because it produced quite different reactions in English-speaking Canada and in Quebec.

Millenarian movements all over the world work according to similar patterns because they are all born out of similar socio-economic circumstances of deprivation, cultural disruption, loss of economic wealth, political power and social status of a "Native people," caused by the intrusion and discriminations of an industrialized, "colonizing people." These movements see the rise of a prophetic leader, who through his charisma strikes a supernatural chord in his mainly peasant or semi-nomadic followers, and through his exceptional personality is able to inspire his followers with a desperately needed hope for the future and with the firm belief that with the help of God or god-like powers armed resistance will lead to the coming of a new era of peace, justice, wealth and universal harmony—a new golden age.

12. Louis Riel and Sitting Bull's Sioux: Three Lost Letters (2007)

David G. McCrady

Three little-known letters addressed by Louis Riel to the command-
ing officer of Fort Assiniboine in March of 1880 afford us a glimpse
into the 'political Riel,' who was trying to secure the removal of
Sitting Bull's Sioux from the Canadian-American borderlands in
order to strengthen his own position as recognized leader of the
Métis community in Montana. From his strictly American stance,
Riel places much blame on the Mounted Police.

In 1985, a major documentary project culminated in *The Collected Writings of Louis Riel*, a publication intended to collect and edit all of Riel's known works. As is generally the case in projects of this scope, some writings were overlooked or unknown at the time of publication.[1] Three important letters of Riel's came to my attention when I was researching 19th-century Sioux-Métis relations in the Canadian-American borderlands.[2] A draft of one of the three appears in *The Collected Writings*, but the other two have not been published previously. Dated in March 1880, the three were written to Lieutenant Colonel Henry Moore Black, the commanding officer of Fort Assiniboine, at his request. The United States Army had established the post in 1879 primarily to patrol the Canadian-American boundary and prevent unwanted incursions by Canadian Indians and Métis into American territory, but also to keep watch over Sitting Bull's "hostile" Sioux, who had fled to Canada following the Custer fight on the Little Bighorn in June 1876. Riel had gone to Fort Assiniboine to talk to Black about the Sioux, and Black had asked him to put this information in writing. Today, these three letters are located in the records of the United States Army's Adjutant General's Office at the U.S. National Archives in Washington, DC.[3]

The basic events of Louis Riel's political career are well known. The leader of the Red River Resistance of 1869–70, Riel argued the case of the Red River settlers who opposed the unilateral sale of Rupert's Land to Canada and negotiated the creation of the Province of Manitoba. Exiled for his participation in these events, and the execution of Thomas Scott in particular, Riel lived for several years in the eastern United States before moving to Montana in 1879. In June 1884, the Saskatchewan Métis invited him to come north and speak on their behalf to Canadian government officials. Riel attempted to recreate his success of fifteen years earlier, but his North-West Rebellion failed and he was hanged in Regina in November 1885 for treason.

We eagerly accept Riel's return to the Canadian North-West as a "homecoming," but, by the mid-1880s, Riel's home was Montana. His involvement in local politics, his attempts to secure land grants for the Montana Métis, his marriage in Carroll, Montana, to Marguerite Monet *dit* Bellehumeur (herself a migrant from Manitoba), his decision to become an American citizen in 1883, his work as a school teacher at St Peter's Mission and, as we shall see, his negotiations with the Sioux, all point to his incorporation into the Montana Métis community. While the years Riel spent in the United States are discussed in the literature, his biographers have tended to look more to the events of his life that took place on the Canadian side of the Canadian-American boundary.[4]

During the winter of 1879–80, Louis Riel was living on the Fort Belknap Reservation, home to the Gros Ventres and Upper Assiniboines and one of the last refuges of the buffalo herds. No doubt the Métis had been invited to hunt on the reservation as many of them had relatives among the Gros Ventres and Assiniboines. They were not alone. Several thousand Aboriginal people from Canada, where the herds had failed completely in the autumn of 1879, had come south to hunt, as had Sitting Bull's Sioux. Sitting Bull and other Sioux leaders had taken some 3,000 followers north to Canada in the aftermath of the Great Sioux War and now, with the buffalo virtually extinct north of the boundary, many were travelling south to hunt.

Always the politician, Riel saw the issue of the Sioux refugees as an opportunity to advance the interests of the Montana Métis. Riel spent the winter of 1879–80 along the Missouri River trying to convince refugee Sioux leaders to surrender to American authorities. In this endeavour, he was motivated by two complementary goals: his concerns for Métis sustenance, and his hope of deflecting US authorities from evicting the Métis from the Fort Belknap Reservation. The Montana Métis, along with their Gros Ventre and Assiniboine kin, were competing with Sioux hunters for the same diminishing herds. Convincing Sioux leaders to surrender to American authorities would remove hungry Sioux mouths from Montana to reservations further down the Missouri River in Dakota Territory. In addition, by helping to "bring in" Sitting Bull, Riel hoped to curry favour with the United States Army, which was charged with removing squatters, such as the Métis, from Indian reservations.

The two heretofore unpublished letters that Riel wrote to Black speak of his attempts to convince Bull Dog, the leader of fifty-seven lodges, perhaps some 300 people, to surrender. They offer glimpses into Riel's larger strategy to remove all of Sitting Bull's Sioux from the Canadian-American borderlands and help position Riel as a leader of the Métis community in Montana.

Riel arrived at Fort Assiniboine on March 18, 1880 and informed Black of his discussions with Bull Dog and his chief soldier, Red Elk. They had been forced by hunger to come south of the boundary to hunt and took the opportunity to ask Riel to find out on their behalf what terms the Americans would grant their people if they surrendered. American policy was to disarm and dehorse any Sioux who wished to surrender. Riel argued against this policy, claiming that "The moral effect" of leniency "would enivitably [*sic*] be to bring in all the Titons [Tetons, an alternate name for the Western, or Lakota Sioux] and Sitting Bull himself in the course of a few weeks."[5]

As symbols of their intentions, Bull Dog and Red Elk gave Riel a pipe and a knife to give to Black. But, not having instructions from Washington to deviate from standard policy, Black could not accept the gifts. He told Riel to inform Bull Dog and Red Elk that the surrender had to be unconditional. Talks then broke down.

These three letters also refer to Sitting Bull, whom Riel met in late January 1880. Two rather dubious accounts of that meeting survive. One was written by Jean L'Heureux, an enigmatic Canadian who lived with Crowfoot's Blackfoot band in the 1860s and 1870s and who was on the government payroll as an interpreter in the 1880s.[6] According to L'Heureux, Riel's discussions with Sitting Bull revolved around a plan to gain support from Canadian Indians for a general uprising in the Northwest. According to the plan, the Métis would capture two North-West Mounted Police posts—Wood Mountain Post and Fort Walsh—and the European settlement of Battleford (then the capital of the North-West Territories). They and the Blackfoot would together take the police force's Fort Macleod. After this, Riel was to proclaim a provisional government and argue the Aboriginal people's case to the Canadian government. "'Sitting Bull' and all American hostile Indians were to be invited to join, with promises of plunder and horses."[7]

A similar account, supposedly in Crowfoot's words, parallels this story.

When asked whether Riel had ever asked him to join in revolt, he said, "Yes; over in Montana in the winter of 1879 or the spring of 1880. He wanted me to join with all the Sioux, and Crees, and half-breeds. The idea was to have a general uprising and capture the North-West, and hold it for the Indian race and the Métis. We were to meet at Tiger Hills, in Montana; we were to have a government of our own. I refused, but the others were willing; and then they reported that already some of the English forts had been captured. This was a lie. Riel took [Plains Cree leader] Little Pine's treaty paper [i.e., his printed copy of Treaty 6] and trampled it under his foot, and said we should get a better treaty from him. Riel came also to trade with us, and I told my people to trade with him, but not to listen to his words. Riel said he had a mighty power behind him in the east."[8]

The story that Louis Riel hoped Sitting Bull would join him in an invasion of Western Canada was accepted by the official historian of the North-West Mounted Police, John Peter Turner, in the 1950s. It has appeared from time to time since, and in its most abbreviated retellings historians note Riel's attempts to form an Indian-Métis confederacy without specifically naming the Sioux.[9] This story provides a misleading account of the relationship between the Montana Métis and Sitting Bull's Sioux. Whatever Riel's intentions were with respect to Canadian Indians, he did not intend forming any alliance with the Sioux. In December 1879, Commissioner James Macleod learned from a North-West Mounted Police mail-carrier that Riel had forged an agreement with Native leaders along the Milk River, granting both the Métis and Native people access to the herds on both sides of the boundary. Significantly, the mail carrier told Macleod that the proposed agreement specifically did not include the Sioux.[10]

Edward Lambert, a mixed-blood who worked as an interpreter for the North-West Mounted Police until July 1879 and who then became a trader among the Sioux, reported a far more convincing account of Sitting Bull's and Riel's conversation. In February 1880, Lambert returned from trading among the Sioux and informed North-West Mounted Policeman L.N.F. Crozier that Riel had offered to intercede on Sitting Bull's behalf with the American government. "Keep the peace and do not get yourselves between two fires until Spring at any rate," Riel had supposedly told Sitting Bull. "If you want then to go back and live in peace with the Americans I will see the President and arrange everything for you."[11]

Sitting Bull turned down Riel's offer. Instead, he chose to work out an arrangement with James Morrow Walsh of the North-West Mounted Police to have Walsh communicate with the Americans on his behalf. Sitting Bull asked Walsh in May 1880 to tell the Queen and the American president that he was ready to make peace with the Americans. He indicated that he wanted to go to Ottawa to meet the "White Mother's daughter" (one of Queen Victoria's daughters, Princess Louise, was married to the Marquess of Lorne, then Canada's governor general) and then to Washington to meet the president.[12] In the end, Riel was unable to convince any Sioux leader to surrender to the Americans. Bull Dog did not surrender to American forces at Fort Keogh until the spring of 1881. Sitting Bull followed suit in July.

Riel blamed his failure on the "underworking influence of the Canadian Mounted Police," and not without some cause.[13] While official Canadian policy was to use persuasion to encourage the Sioux to surrender to American authorities, relationships between individual rank-and-file policemen and the Sioux were more complicated. Some half-dozen Mounties were married to Sioux women, while others had casual liaisons with them. One police deserter, Charles Thompson, lived in the Sioux camps, "adopted Indian habits even to the extent of wearing the breech clout and paint," and had one or more Sioux wives.[14] American army commentators complained of surreptitious visits by police to Sioux camps on American territory and that various policemen used their influence to convince the Sioux to remain in Canada. Some indicated that the policemen were working on behalf of traders at Wood Mountain who did not want the Sioux to surrender as that would deprive them of their greatest customers.[15]

More than any other Mountie, Riel blamed James Morrow Walsh. "That officer of the canadian Police," Riel wrote, "takes advantage of the presence of Titons around him, both to gratify his national pretension that the english are good to indians while the americans are not; and to exagerate [sic] his personal usefulness in the Northwest."[16] Walsh was rumoured to have been involved with various Sioux women, and to have wanted to put Sitting Bull on exhibit in eastern cities (just as Buffalo Bill Cody did, in fact, do later).[17] The Canadian government, including the prime minister, shared Riel's view that Walsh was manipulating the situation for his own benefit and, to end his contact with Sitting Bull, forced him to return to eastern Canada on "sick leave" in July 1880.

When stringing together the pieces of Louis Riel's life, historians tend to focus on the events that transpired in Canada. These letters, brief glimpses into Riel's attempts to negotiate the removal of the Sioux from the borderlands, reveal that the decade Riel spent in the United States deserves more attention. When he headed to Saskatchewan in 1884, Riel told the Métis that he hoped to return to the United States by September.[18] His intention was to remain awhile and then go home, and there is no reason not to believe him.

The Letters

1. Louis Riel to Henry Moore Black, Fort Assiniboine, March 16, 1880
Fort Assiniboine, March 16th 1880.
   Colonel H.M. Black.
Colonel,
  according [to] your wish, I have informed the Metis hunters of the Big Bend of Milk River, that you requested them to leave the [Fort Belknap] indian reservation, as soon as possible; and without any delay which would necessitate further action from the government. Their answer is this: they thank you for having stated their condition last fall, to your superiors; they acknowledge that your true and kind representations have helped them a great deal; and that the government have been very liberal towards them and that they have conferred a great favor on their children, on their families and on themselves, in allowing them (the Metis hunters) to winter at the Big Bend of Milk River.
  Having no other way of acknowledging efficiently such a favor, those metis have exerted themselves during the whole winter to pacify the hostile Sioux; Sitting Bull himself and all his band; they have prepared, as much as they have been able to do it, those indians to change and to become friendly: The fact is that the most part of the hostile Titons do now regret the bad reception they have given to Bishop Martin,[19] and it may be just to suppose that, if Sitting Bull himself had not been falsely advised on the other side of the boundary line, he would not have been so obstinate,[20] and I have the honor to inform you, colonel, that in compliance with your request, the greater part of the hunters who have wintered at the Big Bend, have already dispersed. Some of them have gone north of the Boundary line. A greater number of them are going south of the Missouri.
  Those who have not yet left, will also go away, as soon as their too poor horses will have become strong enough.
  I know six or seven cases of sickness amongst those who are yet in their wintering place, at the Big Bend. And if any one remains there a little later than you have [a] right to expect, I have not doubt, it will be on that account.
  I have the honor
   to be,
    Colonel,
   Your humble and obedient serv[ant].
    Louis Riel.

2. Louis Riel to Henry Moore Black, Fort Assiniboine, March 18, 1880

The "Bull Dog" chief of the Brulees Sioux[21] and his first soldier "Red Elk" send the Calumet and Knife to fort Assinaboin and ask for peace.

What they ask for their fifty seven lodges they ask it for the whole camp.

They want to go back to their country and demand a reservation there.

They ask for provision, blankets etc and common ammuniion for small game.

They love their horses and arms.

But many of their horses have died and are now dying by disease.[22] Good many others have been killed to be used as food; and they have sold another quantity of them.

What remains of their band of horses are perhaps hardly worth the trouble to be taken and sold by the government. as to their arms, they cannot make much use of them, for want of improved ammunition.

The Brulees seem to have been send [*sic*] forward by the others to feel the ground. Sitting Bull and the other chiefs are in council on frenchman's creek[23] and probably waiting for the answer which the government is expected to give to their brethren, the Brulees.

Would it not be good policy to receive the Brulees and grant liberally their demands and to extend the same advantages to the rest of the tribe?

A rejection of the demands of the Brulees would throw the whole camp back to their former hostile attitude.

If the demands are rejected, Sitting Bull and [*illegible and struck out*] the main part of the tribe will, it is reported, go and plant their lodges along the lakes of the Northwest, to live on fish, whence small parties of war, travelling at night will very likely continue, in spite of any force, to infest Montana by horse-stealing and by murdering.

Would it not be better to bring the whole tribe at once, as there are chances to do it now, under the control of the government? Sitting Bull and the others could be treated liberally and at the same time watched very closely.

A gift of provisions at the present moment would go far to win them all completely.

A liberal gift and the granting of their demands would not cost half as much as an expedition against them.

Another consideration seems to be in favor of such a policy: on account of the absolute desappearence of Buffalo in the British Northwest, the British indians have already begun to make irruption on our indian reservations and in other sections of this territory. We do not know how and when that irruption of the english indians will end.

Would it not be well to take advantage of the ouvertures of the Brulees, to do away with Sitting Bull and his tribe.

I have the honor
     to be,
          colonel,
       Your obedient serv[ant].
         Louis Riel
Fort Assinaboin
      March 18th 1880.

3. Louis Riel to Henry Moore Black, Fort Assiniboine, March 18, 1880
fort Assinaboin. March 18th 1880
      Colonel H.M. Black
Colonel,

The Sioux of Sitting Bull are presently gathering at or near "Mud House"[24] on frenchman's creek with the good intention of smoking, as they say, the tobacco of Peace with the americans, if possible.

The Brulés, a party of fifty seven lodges amongst them have entrusted me with a pipe and a knife which I bring, in their name, to you as to commanding officer of this post: the pipe is a demand of reconciliation and the knife a mark that they want no more fighting with the americans. At the same time they address the government through you; and they say: give us good reservations on our lands which you have conquered. We wish to go back thither, because we love our native soil.

Give us some provisions, blankets and some of the other things that we want, because we are poorer than ever.

Give us shot and balls to hunt our small games: a few cartridges to kill a Buffalo once in a while, so that we may take, in peace again, meals out of that good flesh and enjoy its taste.

Do not take from us the horses and the arms that we have.

We want you to feel good in seing [seeing] this pipe and this knife: take them: if you take them, it will be the way to prove that you are going to act with us, according [to] our demands.

Colonel, when the chief of the Brules, named "Bull Dog" and his first soldier "Red Elk" charged me to convey thus their wishes to you, they appeared to be confident that you would receive their pipe and their knife and that the government would not reject their demands.

The Brulés seem to have been sent forward by the whole tribe to feel the ground. and I believe the camp of Sitting Bull are only waiting to see the result.

If I dare express any opinion about it, I think it would be good policy to receive the Brulés. and to grant liberally their demands. The moral effect would enivitably be to bring in all the Titons and sitting Bull himself in the course of a few weeks.

As they have sold many of their horses; as they are now eating many of them; as they have lost and are now loosing a quantity of their ponies by disease, I know that the Sioux of Sitting Bull have at this present time a comparatively small band of horses. and it would not be a very great advantage for the government to take their horses away from them as they propose to do.

Besides, the horse amongst the indians is a religious item, because a young man cannot get married, without giving a horse to the father of his bride.

as to their arms, they cannot make much use of them without ammunition. and the cartridges with which they had been supplied last fall and during December last, by the english trader at Wood Mountain have completely been spent and given away for provisions.

If the Brulés were refused, it would have a bad effect on the whole tribe. Small parties would no doubt surrender. But the brulk [bulk] of the camp would go over the boundary line and remain hostile. Good soldiers and brave officers would probably have no other success than the one of keeping them there.

I have been told that, if the government do not accept their demands, the Sioux intend to go and locate themselves along the lakes of the Northwest and there to subsist as long as long as possible on fish.

Meanwhile, small parties of war travelling only at night might in spite of any force continue to infest Montana, by horse stealing and possibly by murdering in the territory several of our pioneers.

For those reasons, it would also be a good policy, I think, to receive Sitting Bull as well as the other chiefs of the tribe.

Had he not been under the false and jealous influence of the Northwest Mounted Police, Sitting Bull would have undoubtedly come and made peace long ago.

The advantage of taking the ponies and the arms away from the Sioux is, in my humble opinion, not as great as the advantage of bringing Sitting Bull and his whole camp under the control of the government at once.

Disposed as they are now and taking advantage of the 57 Brulés lodges, the government can safely settle the "Sitting Bull" question. A present of some thousands dollars in provisions would reconcile all the Sioux of Sitting Bull without any exception and a gift of that kind with the granting of their simple demands would not cost half as much as an expedition against them.

    I have the honor
        to be
            Colonel
      respectfully
Your obedient servant
           Louis Riel

13. The Battle of Batoche (1985)

Walter Hildebrandt

A minor event in military history, the battle of Batoche was a trau-matic turning-point for the Métis. To understand what went on during those few days between a cautious Canadian army and about 300 Métis led by a good tactician (Gabriel Dumont) and an incompetent commander (Louis Riel), it is necessary to map the troops' movements in all their details, and to heed contemporary military handbooks as well as the Métis perspective.

The Battle of Batoche has been the subject of numerous scholarly and pop-ular studies.[1] This interest, however, has been focussed on the signifi-cance of the battle, its consequences, and its importance as a watershed in Canadian history and as a symbolic victory of Anglo-Canadian forces over those resisting the new economic order. The earliest publications, Major Boulton's *Reminiscences of the North-West Rebellion,* and C.P. Mulvaney's *The History of the North-West Rebellion of 1885,* were based on first-hand accounts of North West Field Force participants anxious to explain their victory. Immediately after the appearance of the official account of the rebellion, published in the Canada Sessional Papers in 1886, little analytical work was attempted.[2] Early accounts made almost no reference to sources that might have provided perspective to the Métis actions.[3] This to some extent has been corrected by George Stanley and, more recently, Desmond Morton, but the overall result of past histories of the Battle of Batoche has left the mili-tary actions of the Métis and the Indians vague. The impression that the out-come of the battle was inevitable still remains.[4]

Traditionally, the last day of the battle, when the North West Field Force suddenly and surprisingly broke through weakened Métis lines at the southeastern end of the battlefield, has been emphasized. Yet a detailed narrative shows that the first day had by far the most military action, which included the *Northcote* incident and at least two nearly successful attempts by the Métis and the Indians to outflank the North West Field Force. On this first day the Métis and the Indians put such pressure on Middleton's men that some accounts suggest that only the highly mobile and rapid-fire Gatling gun prevented a serious setback. In fact, according to Reverend G. Cloutier's diary, the Métis considered the first day a victory.[5] They believed that their actions caused Middleton to withdraw into the zareba on the evening of May 9.

One other noticeable imbalance exists in the historic record. The tactics adopted by Middleton bore the brunt of considerable criticism, especially by the Canadian officers, many of whom felt slighted because Middleton preferred British officers. Similar criticism from military historians has been made without reference to contemporary military handbooks such as Garnet Wolseley's *A Soldier's Pocketbook*.[6] Furthermore, none of the well-known accounts of the military actions cite the military manuals of the day, such as Captain Callwell's *Small Wars: Their Principle and Practice*.[7] This last book makes frequent reference to Middleton's actions during the 1885 campaign. Indeed, they are held to be exemplary, given the conditions he encountered. The ten maps which illustrate my article are based on the documents and maps of the period and on many trips to the site to examine the terrain over which this battle was fought.[8] (In this endeavour I am indebted to Jack Summers, who tramped the site with me on numerous occasions over the past two years. Without his insights, much of what is detailed here could not have been accomplished.)

In 1885 there were approximately 48,000 Native westerners in the Assiniboia, Saskatchewan and Alberta territories.[9] Politically, many grievances of these people had been ignored, and fears of an Indian uprising were widespread.[10] The dangers of an uprising by Native westerners were denied by P.G. Laurie of Battleford, editor of the *Saskatchewan Herald*, whose columns frequently contained diatribes against reports from eastern newspapers, whose editors claimed the Western frontier was a lawless and dangerous territory.[11] Laurie thought that such reports might slow the settlement he so desperately wanted. Also known to many was the recent catastrophe at the Little Bighorn. Such factors lent credence to the preconceived but basically irrational notion of a hostile, wild frontier.[12] It was largely for this reason that the North West Field Force organized a careful well-ordered strategy to move into this unknown territory.

Major General Charles F.D. Middleton, CB, Commander of the Canadian Militia and leader of the North West Field Force, was uncertain about the exact number of "savages" his men would be fighting. The experience of British contingents in small wars throughout the Empire showed that caution would have to be exercised. When fighting native forces, there was always the fear that a small group could easily gain momentum with a few early successes against a regular European-type army.[13]

Not all Canadian leaders were confident of a clear early victory. The obstacles of geography, transportation and supply were enormous. Middleton, though armed with a brash confidence, initially showed disregard for the fighting prowess of the Métis and forged ahead to confront them as soon as he could. Only after Fish Creek, the first encounter and a setback for the North West Field Force, did Middleton grudgingly acknowledge that he had underestimated the Métis.[14]

To move against Prince Albert and, later, Batoche, identified as the Métis stronghold, Middleton and his officers agreed to a three-pronged movement into the Northwest. Columns were to march towards what were considered to be potential trouble spots. Middleton would proceed north from Qu'Appelle (Troy) along the South Saskatchewan; Otter from Swift Current towards Battleford; and Strange from Calgary towards Edmonton. Of these columns only two were to be engaged in any serious fighting, and only Middleton's column was involved in more than one battle with the Métis in which any lives were lost.

Essentially there were five significant battles or confrontations during the suppression of the insurrection in the West. The North West Field Force was involved in four of them: Fish Creek, Cut Knife Hill, Batoche and Frenchman's Butte. At Duck Lake the skirmish was between the Métis and the North West Mounted Police, under Superintendent Crozier. One other major event occurred during the campaign: the Frog Lake Massacre, where whites and Métis in the community were killed and the remainder taken hostage by Big Bear's Cree insurgents. Only the Battle of Batoche gave the government forces a decisive victory. The sole clear victory for the Métis came at Duck Lake. The other three conflicts—Fish Creek, Cut Knife Hill and Frenchman's Butte—were all stand-offs in one form or another. At Fish Creek, the Métis retreated after an indecisive battle; at Cut Knife Hill, Otter withdrew pursuant to the resistance of Poundmaker's Cree; and at Frenchman's Butte, Big Bear's Cree retreated from the barrage of fire into their defensive alignment, although the militia were unable to pursue them through the muskeg.

Perhaps more significant than the battles which were fought, were those which were not. Although the newspapers of the time indicate that many whites feared reprisals from Indians during the rebellion, very few took place. At Battleford, some 500 men, women and children were allegedly besieged in the North West Mounted Police fort by Poundmaker's Cree, but the fort was not directly attacked, although the stores of the town, momentarily abandoned by a frightened population, were looted.[15] In Prince Albert, residents protected by the North West Mounted Police were not threatened by Indians or mixed bloods. Trouble was anticipated from the large number of Indians comprising the Blackfoot Confederacy. Crowfoot, their war chief, had received an invitation from Riel to join the resistance, but did not respond. The presence of the North West Mounted Police and the trust the Indians had was certainly partially responsible for their reluctance to participate alongside Riel.[16] A general attack was feared by many whites in the West, however.

The Governor-General and Adolphe Caron, the Minister of the Militia, differed with Middleton over the course of action that would most quickly end the campaign. The target for the first attack remained uncertain. Governor-General Lansdowne clearly believed that after Fish Creek, Prince Albert would be the objective for the North West Field Force. He had written to Lord Derby in London stating that he hoped Middleton would join forces with Otter at Prince Albert and would then advance on Batoche: "Middleton will probably have to fight again on his way to Prince Albert. He would, I gather, prefer not to fight if he could avoid doing so, until after he had reached Prince Albert and perhaps effected a junction with Otter."[17] Lansdowne, who was in touch with Caron on an almost daily basis, appeared to be under the impression that a greater number of troops would finally advance on Batoche.[18]

The correspondence between Lansdowne, Derby and Melgund (later Earl of Minto and Governor-General of Canada) leaves the impression that there were reservations over Middleton's ability to conduct the campaign from the field. Lansdowne intimated these concerns to Melgund. On one occasion he wrote, "The Fish Creek affair has troubled me very much—Even without your private telegrams I could read something very like the word disaster between every line of the General's other accounts. I have thought all along that he and the experts quite underrated the difficulty of the task before him."[19] Other observers saw Middleton as a general too old and reluctant to engage in combat and to advance on Batoche:

> During this tedious delay General Middleton gave all sorts
> of excuses for his reaction. One day it was want of supplies
> then he had not sufficient medical staff to take with him
> after having a suitable force to look after the wounded.
> Then the excuse was that the wounded could neither be left

where they were nor removed up the river to Saskatoon. The truth was that he was afraid to advance on the rebels' position at Batoche until he was materially reinforced.[20]

Whether Middleton actually had a clear plan of attack in mind for Batoche after Fish Creek is not known. According to Boulton, Middleton seldom communicated his intentions even to those in his immediate staff. What is known is that up to April 29, Middleton was heading towards Prince Albert and that he was reluctant to engage his men too hastily after Fish Creek:"Find it would be better to push on to Prince Albert by Hudson's Bay Crossing. Troops behaved well but are raw, officers same. Would not be safe to risk defeat so shall relieve Prince Albert and join with Otter in attacking rebels. Shall send courier to Humboldt or Clark's Crossing … am engaged in bringing column to this side. Will march tomorrow."[21] It was a rather optimistic prediction the day after Fish Creek and it was in fact to be over two weeks before he would march again. Three days later, on April 28, Middleton again reasserted his conviction to move to Prince Albert first. Middleton had mixed reactions to the battle; in his communications to Caron there was only a cautious optimism. "I think we have taught the rebels a lesson and am pretty sure that I would march to Batoche, but their men would harass me all the way, and I lose a great many men and I am very averse to that and do not think it would be politic."[22]

The arrival of the *Northcote* on May 5, with its supplies and two companies of the Midland Battalion on board, coincided with Middleton's change of plans. Middleton's confidence seemed renewed with the appearance of the *Northcote*, and Batoche now became his objective. Reasons for changing targets from Prince Albert to Batoche are unclear, and no evidence exists to suggest that he discussed his change in plans with any of those around him or with Caron in Ottawa. Even those at the front believed he would first move on to Prince Albert. Major Boulton, Commander of Boulton's Scouts, wrote:

> On the 5th of May General Middleton completed his arrangement for a further advance on Batoche. At the time he was, I believe, urged to advance directly on Prince Albert, in order to effect a junction with Colonel Irvine and his corps of Mounted Police, leaving Batoche for future attack; but no doubt feeling that this would be a sign of weakness, the General determined to march on to Batoche, and to attack Riel in his stronghold without further delay, sending a message to Colonel Irvine to cooperate with him from the North.[23]

A new determination now pervaded Middleton's communications and he no longer expressed concern over his shortage of manpower—he certainly dropped the idea of joining forces with Otter for an attack on Batoche. This might have been due, at least partially, to Otter's fall from favour after his battle with Poundmaker's Cree at Cut Knife Hill on May 2. Otter had embarked on his mission to Cut Knife Hill against Middleton's orders but with the approval of Lieutenant-Governor Dewdney. These two events—the arrival of the *Northcote* and Otter's encounter at Cut Knife Hill—coincided with Middleton's determination to move against Batoche. A two-pronged attack was still planned, but Otter would no longer be part of it.

The arrival of the *Northcote* significantly strengthened Middleton's marching capacity. On board the boat were 80 men of the Midland Battalion, together with Colonel Van Straubenzie and Captain Howard of the United States Army. Howard, a representative of the American gun manufacturer, had with him the Gatling gun which was to provide the important fire power on the first day of fighting at Batoche. The cargo also contained the desperately needed food supplies and some ammunition. The steamer itself was also to be used in the attack.[24]

Alterations to the *Northcote* were made by Major Smith of "C" School of Infantry who was placed in command of the steamer. Middleton ordered the upper deck to be made "bullet proof" and placed the following somewhat motley crew on board:

> Thirty-one rank and rifle, two officers C Company School Corps, Captain Bedson, my aide-en-camp, Captain Wise, who, though better, was to my great loss, incapacitated from walking or riding, three sick officers, Mr. Magre and Mr. Pringle, medical staff, several men of supply and transport services, Mr. Gottam, a newspaper correspondent, and some settlers returning to their homes, amounting with some of the crew to about fifty combatants.[25]

Then Major Smith was ordered "to anchor the first night abreast of our camp, remain there the next day, and on the morning of the ninth drop down and meet the column at about 8, just above Batoche."[26]

These tactics were not without critics:

> the commander had conceived the rather ludicrous idea of converting the *Northcote* into a gunboat. She was furnished with clumsy barricades, which were to serve as bulwarks, and as she had no cannon to counter against, the task of rendering these barricades bullet proof was a difficult one. The

utter folly of equipping and arming her in the manner described was seen when she passed down the river and began the fight on May 9.[27]

Obviously, loading down a steamer that had already experienced serious navigational difficulties with sandbars downstream was considered impractical. However, no other sources were critical of this phase of Middleton's strategy for Batoche.

Finally, on May 7, Middleton was prepared to move on from the site of his first battle with the Métis and the Indians. The General had estimated the strength of his force to be 700 but, according to Melgund, 886 men made up his ranks.[28]

Middleton chose to advance with an infantry force which included Boulton's Scouts and French's Scouts (the Dominion Land Surveyors were to arrive on May 11). There was no trained cavalry at the front even though it was available. Middleton's decision not to include Denison's cavalry was one part of his plan for which he later received much criticism.[29]

Four guns or cannon were in the Field Forces' arsenal, two with the Winnipeg Field Battery and two with "A" Battery. All four were RML nine-pounders and were put to extensive use by Middleton, especially at Batoche. Their effectiveness against the elusive Métis and their well-hidden rifle pits has been questioned by some. But it has also been argued that they were effective in psychologically demoralizing the enemy over the four days of fighting.[30]

The more publicized piece of artillery during the campaign was the Gatling gun carried to the front by the *Northcote.* Operated by Captain Howard throughout the campaign, the Gatling gun's effectiveness at Batoche has been the source of some controversy, judging from the reports following the fighting. For many, it was the first time they had ever seen a rapid-fire gun in action and, as a novelty, it attracted considerable attention and commentary both during and after the campaign. Major Boulton, in his reminiscences, was cautious in assessing the contribution the Gatling made to the success of the North West Field Force. While admitting that it was a significant weapon, particularly on the first day of the fighting, he was less effusive than most. Boulton felt that the success attributed to the Gatling detracted from what he considered the brave and solid role played by the infantry and artillery companies.[31]

The Gatling gun's primary advantage was its rapid-fire capacity—it was advertised as being able to fire 1,000 shots per minute. It was also relatively light to transport and easily adjustable for both elevation and direction. Of the gun's ten barrels, five were fired in succession while the other five were being loaded. When the crank which fired the gun was turned, firing, loading and extraction all took place synchronically without interruption.[32]

The entire combat contingent which was to move against Batoche was thus assembled. On the afternoon of May 7, the troops marched from Fish Creek to Gabriel's Crossing, which they reached by 6:00 p.m. Here they met the *Northcote*, which had landed that afternoon. A scouting mission was undertaken to decide on the safest approach to Batoche. Middleton wrote:

> As I had learned there were some nasty places to pass on the river trail, I rode out with some scouts to the east, accompanied by Mr. Reid, the Paymaster of the Midlanders, etc., in this very neighbourhood. With his assistance I marked out a route for next day's march which would bring us on the Humboldt trail to about five or six miles from Batoche.[33]

On the morning of Saturday, May 9, reveille was sounded at 4:00, breakfast was taken at 4:15 and the men were ready to march at 5:00, each with 100 rounds of ammunition.[34] As the column advanced on Batoche, it encountered sporadic rifle fire from two houses along the road. The two houses, not far from the church and rectory and belonging to Ludger Gareau and Jean Caron Sr., were barricaded. One report has the building about 400 yards from the church and rectory.[35] The first house was fired on by the Gatling gun, which caused the men in and around the two buildings to scatter. Boulton's Scouts then fell back and a gun from "A" Battery shelled the second house: "Some rebels immediately ran out of a ravine behind the house into the bush. The two houses took fire and were soon in ashes."[36]

The coordinated attack on Batoche was to take place at 8:00 a.m. with the *Northcote* moving downriver from the south and Middleton coming across land from the east. It is clear that 8:00 a.m. had been agreed upon as the time for the two-pronged advance to begin (see map 1).

The steamer was to remain just downstream from Batoche until bombardment from Middleton's guns was heard. But the *Northcote* was engaged by the Métis before Middleton's troops reached the village defense. As Middleton wrote: "As we got near the river, much to my annoyance we heard a rattling fire and the steamer's whistle, showing the latter was already engaged."[37]

According to Major Smith, the *Northcote* was progressing as planned until shortly before 8:00 that morning. At 6:00 a.m., the *Northcote* had moved to a point just south of Batoche, where she anchored because she was slightly ahead of schedule. The sources describing the progress of the *Northcote* agree that she was fired on immediately after her advance upriver resumed.

There is disagreement, however, over when this advance commenced. One source had it at 8:10, while Major Smith reports it as being 7:40—a difference of some 30 minutes, and enough to spoil the plan.

As the *Northcote* struck out towards midstream she immediately came under heavy fire from both banks. In his reports, Smith indicated that the men on board did not return the fire at first, but as the hail of bullets became heavier his men began "independent and volley firing."[38] The Métis appeared to be lying in wait:

> as we rounded the bend a moment or so later we were raked fore and aft by a fierce storm of bullets coming from both banks. From almost every bush rose puffs of smoke, and from every house and trees on the top of the banks came bullets buzzing. The fire was steadily returned by the troops on board, consisting of C Company School of Infantry; and notwithstanding that the rebels were protected by the brush and timber which covers the banks, apparently some injury was inflicted upon them. Volley after volley was fired and several of the lurking enemy were seen to drop headlong down the sloping bank.[39]

Father Fourmond, who was housed in the rectory throughout the fighting, also remembered the activities surrounding the arrival of the *Northcote*:

> Vers 8 hs. a.m. nous étions sortis… Tout à coup, un … sifflement affreux se fit entendre à nos oreilles, venant du côté haut de la rivière… C'est le bateau à vapeur… C'est le bateau arrivant et sifflant la guerre… L'attaque commença par un parti de Sioux campés proche de la mission… Aussitôt prennent fusils et se précipitent vers le bateau à travers les buissons… La bataille était engagé.[40]

Philippe Garnot recalled Dumont telling him that almost all of the Métis had left their rifle pits along the Jolie Prairie to fire on the *Northcote* as it moved by the village. Garnot himself remembered sending about 20 men to join the assault.[41]

One of the more spectacular events was the decapitation of the steamer's smoke stacks when the ferry cable crossing the river was lowered—sending them crashing to the deck. Major Smith's report suggested that he was unaware of the loss of the stacks and whistle until after the *Northcote* had anchored again downstream, even though he wrote: "As we passed Batoche the fire was especially heavy, and I heard a crash as if a portion of the upper deck had been carried away."[42] This decapitation was engineered by the

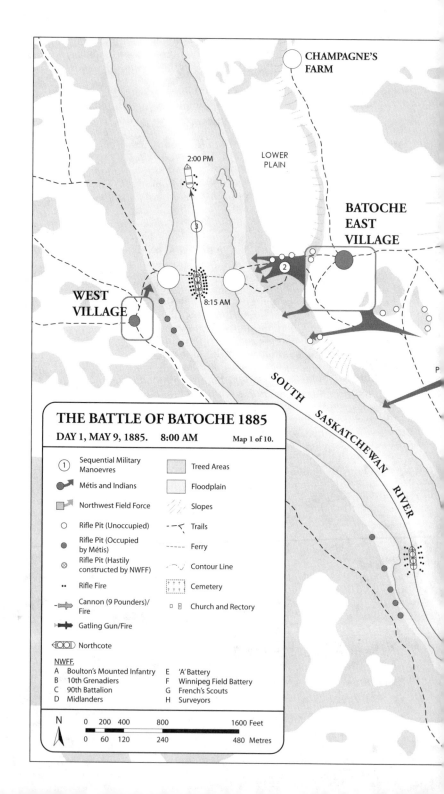

CHAMPAGNE'S
FARM

LOWER
PLAIN

2:00 PM

BATOCHE
EAST
VILLAGE

3

WEST
VILLAGE

8:15 AM

2

SOUTH SASKATCHEWAN RIVER

P

THE BATTLE OF BATOCHE 1885

DAY 1, MAY 9, 1885. 8:00 AM   Map 1 of 10.

①	Sequential Military Manoevres		Treed Areas
	Métis and Indians		Floodplain
	Northwest Field Force		Slopes
○	Rifle Pit (Unoccupied)		Trails
●	Rifle Pit (Occupied by Métis)		Ferry
⊗	Rifle Pit (Hastily constructed by NWFF)		Contour Line
••	Rifle Fire		Cemetery
	Cannon (9 Pounders)/ Fire	□ ▯	Church and Rectory
	Gatling Gun/Fire		
	Northcote		

NWFF.
A   Boulton's Mounted Infantry   E   'A' Battery
B   10th Grenadiers   F   Winnipeg Field Battery
C   90th Battalion   G   French's Scouts
D   Midlanders   H   Surveyors

N

| 0 | 200 | 400 | 800 | 1600 Feet |
| 0 | 60 | 120 | 240 | 480 Metres |

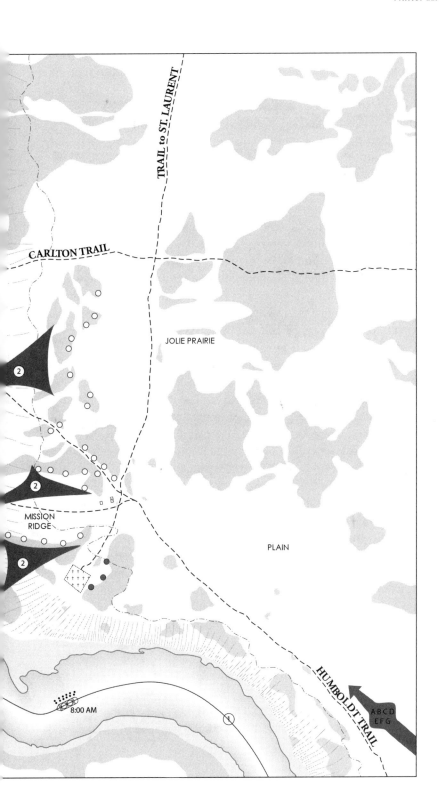

TRAIL to ST. LAURENT

CARLTON TRAIL

JOLIE PRAIRIE

MISSION
RIDGE

PLAIN

HUMBOLDT TRAIL

ABCD
EFG

8:00 AM

ferryman, Alex P. Fisher, who was assisted by Pascal Montour. The consequence of this tactic might have been greater had the Métis been able to corral the steamer at this crossing.

On board the *Northcote* only three minor injuries were reported, including the shot to the heel suffered by Macdonald, the carpenter. Major Smith concluded his report to Middleton by praising the zeal and coolness of his soldiers, while placing the blame for the disastrous fate of the *Northcote* on the near-mutinous crew. "Our weakness lay in the fact that the master, pilot and engineer were aliens, and that the crew were civil employees and not enlisted men."[43] The final assessment published in Mulvaney's history of the North-West Rebellion was less circumspect: "General Middleton's navy project did little more than imperil many valuable lives and withdrew from his forces a considerable number of men who were badly needed on Saturday, Sunday and Monday."[44] This last condemnation perhaps does not take into account the effect the *Northcote* had in distracting the Métis and the Indians away from the eastern front where Middleton's advance took place. The Métis expended much energy and ammunition on the *Northcote*, even after it had been incapacitated. It is remarkable that on May 9, Middleton reached the church and rectory, which he was unable to do the following day—in fact he would not reach this point again until the final day.

The organization of the Métis facing the troops who were advancing towards Batoche is less well known that that of the North West Field Force, though some evidence was collected by W.B. Cameron from Patrice Fleury and Charles Laviolette later.[45] Two scout detachments were formed, one under Fleury and the other under Ambroise Champagne. Fleury was on the west side of the river, while Champagne patrolled the east side. Both had chosen a few good riders to accompany them. Dumont, who was Commanding General, had nine or ten captains who were responsible to him—each of them, in turn, responsible for a troop of men. A Board of Strategy, headed by Louis Riel and Charles Nolin (who had left before the fighting had started), also was formed to advise Dumont. The first secretary of the board was William Jackson, who was later replaced by Philippe Garnot. Remaining members were Albert Monkman, Napoléon Nault (brother of André Nault), John Boucher, Philippe Gariépy, Pierre Gariépy, Old Man Parenteau (father-in-law of Xavier Batoche), Moise Ouellette, Maxime Lépine and Joseph Arcand.

As the *Northcote* floated downstream beyond Batoche the infantry neared the church and rectory. Within 100 yards of the church two rounds were fired from the Gatling gun. Immediately following this burst of fire a white flag, or handkerchief, was noticed and the firing was halted by Middleton (see map 2). He had apparently given "strict injunctions to the force to spare non-combatants as far as possible."[46] From Middleton's recollections the flag was seen being waved by a priest from the opened door of the church. He then approached the church: "I stopped the fire and rode up to the house which I found to be full of people; three or four Roman Catholic priests, some Sisters of Mercy, and a number of women and children, the latter being all half-breeds. They were naturally alarmed, and having reassured them we continued our advance."[47] According to Boulton, only the corner of the rectory had been struck by the bullets. Some of the bullet marks can still be seen in its woodwork.

Fourmond recorded this encounter in some detail:

> En même temps, nous voyons les habits rouges se développer en ligne de bataille tout autour de la mission; profitant des divers accidents du terrain, pour cacher leur marche en avant... Sortons, dit P. Fourmond, ils vont nous reconnaître, et ne pas tirer sur nous... PP. Fourmond et Vegreville sortent et s'adossent au pignon de la maison, faire face aux soldats pour titre reconnus... A peine là, qu'une détonation retentit et une balle frappe au-dessus de nos têtes... Rentrons, il y a danger. A peine entrés ... on entend la mitrailleuse cribler le toit de la maison.[48]

There a decision was made to try to raise a white flag:

> P. Moulin saisit un morceau de coton donné par les Mères et entrouve la porte ouverte et l'agite en face des soldats avancant en ordre de bataille. Au même instant on entendit ce cri retentir de leur côté. "Don't fear! Don't fear!"[49]

After the encounter at the church, Boulton's Scouts advanced. Only a short distance past the church, Boulton's infantry were fired upon from "a sort of low brush about 200 yards or 300 yards ahead."[50] Two companies of the 10th Grenadiers were then ordered to advance in skirmishing order, and these men reached the edge of the ravine on the left; another two companies moved forward on the right near the church. "A" Battery was now ordered forward to the crest of the hill overlooking Batoche with both its nine-pounders and the Gatling gun. The former began to shell the houses at Batoche while the latter was directed at the west bank, "from where a galling fire was being kept up by a totally invisible enemy."[51] This was the farthest the Field Force was able to advance, and it was not until May 12 that they would reach the crest of the hill overlooking Batoche again. Having reached this ridge by the mission, the Grenadiers and "A" Battery came under a

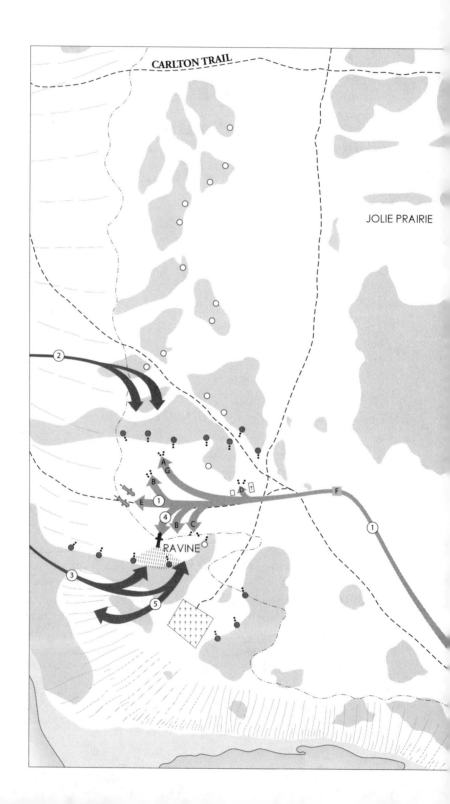

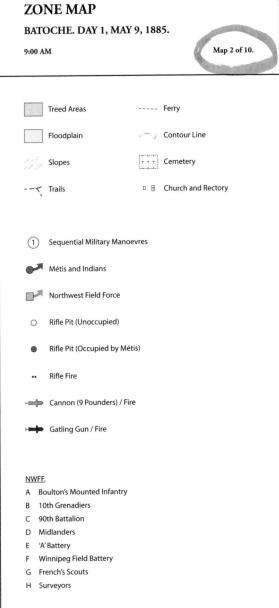

DETAILED BATTLE ZONE MAP

BATOCHE. DAY 1, MAY 9, 1885.

9:00 AM

Map 2 of 10.

Treed Areas ----- Ferry

Floodplain Contour Line

Slopes Cemetery

Trails Church and Rectory

① Sequential Military Manoevres

Métis and Indians

Northwest Field Force

○ Rifle Pit (Unoccupied)

● Rifle Pit (Occupied by Métis)

.. Rifle Fire

Cannon (9 Pounders) / Fire

Gatling Gun / Fire

NWFF.
A Boulton's Mounted Infantry
B 10th Grenadiers
C 90th Battalion
D Midlanders
E 'A' Battery
F Winnipeg Field Battery
G French's Scouts
H Surveyors

PLAIN

AREA WHERE
ZAREBA WILL
BE BUILT IN
AFTERNOON

N

0	100	200	400	800 Feet
0	30	60	120	240 Metres

shower of bullets. Recalling this moment, Boulton wrote, "We had now received a decided check. Immediately in our front lay thick bush, beyond which we could not penetrate. We had been driven by a heavy fire of the enemy from the position which the guns occupied overlooking the village, which was within easy range of the rifle pits that were covered by the bush."[52] At this point Middleton ordered the Gatling gun ahead.

This initial clash has been estimated by some to have been just before 9:45 a.m. As the Grenadiers moved forward the heaviest fire was felt from the left, "and desperate efforts were made to turn our left flank by their men in the bush under the high river bank and on the slope, who fired with great vigour."[53]

Having reached the crest of the hill overlooking Batoche, Middleton noted that "the gun detachments and horses were suffering,"[54] and ordered them to pull back. At this point the heaviest of fire was felt from, as Middleton wrote, "a bluff just below."[55] By all accounts it was here that the Gatling gun made its most memorable contribution by holding off the enemy fire until the Grenadiers could make an orderly retreat. It looked as though the Métis were trying to pinch off the Grenadiers, leaving them cut off from an easterly retreat.

The Grenadiers had previously been ordered to fire from a lying position, but now as they stood up to retreat, drawing the Métis fire,

> The Gatling, which was being worked for a second time and was just getting into action, with Captain Howard at the crank, turned its fire on the concealed foe, and for a moment silenced them.[56]

Although the fire from the Métis was intense, no one was killed during these clashes. At this time the Field Force occupied a position just back from the top of the ravine. The Métis held two positions: one lay immediately to the front and centre in rifle pits and to the left on the heavily wooded crest of the river bank. The right as yet was not defended, and it would not be until May 11 that it became necessary for the Métis to deploy greater numbers to the north.

The Gatling gun was now moved from the left flank towards the lines extending to the church (see map 3). This could be considered the second of three attempts to break through the enemy lines. As Middleton reported, "I brought the gatling round the church and Captain Howard made a dashing attempt to flank the bluff, but could not succeed, as the enemy was ensconced in well made rifle pits."[57] The time was now estimated by one source to have been approximately 9:45 a.m. The Winnipeg Rifles occupied the left flank along the river and graveyard; the 10th Grenadiers were next (going left to right) to the front and centre, while "A" Battery, along with Boulton's and French's mounted infantry, lined the right flank. "The Midlanders were in reserve near the church, near which the General and staff took a position, while the remaining companies of the 90th, aided by the Winnipeg Field Battery and dismounted detachments, were deployed on our right centre, right and right flank."[58]

The Métis made two attempts at encirclement during this early action. The first was made on the left flank. The second attempt came after the Gatling had to save the troops following the initial advance:

> The Grenadiers advanced to the edge of the wood in rear of the school house, and a little to the right of the spot where we first felt the rebel fire… The rebels detected the movement, and desperate efforts were made to turn our left flank by their men in the bush under the high river bank and on the slope, who fired with great vigour; but they had nothing but shot guns, and their fire fell short. Some rebels with rifles on the other side of the river also took a hand in, but the Gatling silenced them.[59]

A planned manoeuvre to capture the Gatling gun on the first day failed. It was described by Elie Dumont as they moved from right to left for their aborted attack:

> Tout droit où mettaient le gatling [*sic*], on se trouvait dans les petits trembles… Alors, Philippe tire et Bap. Boucher tire aussi. Gens du gatling ont commencé à tourner la machine. Le gatling tire sur nous. Quand fini la décharge, je me sauve en descendant les côtés… Une partie de nos gens étaient là et voulaient aller au bord de la riviere … on était comme une 30ne. On a suivi la Rivière à l'abri des écarts pour remonter le courant vis-à-vis le gatling… Voulait ramasser du monde assez pour aller prendre le gatling sur la côte en face de nous … restait encore 100 vgs pour aller au gatling: on n'était pas assez de monde. … On a resté 1/2 hs. là, et retourne par même chemin en courant vite au bord de la rivière pour éviter à nos gens de tirer sur nous… On a été auprès du cimetière. Soldats déjà reculés. On ne pouvait pas tirer les soldats étaient trop loin déjà.[60]

After the first line of skirmishers ran into resistance and retreated a short distance, Middleton ordered the two nine-pounders of "A" Battery forward. No. 1 gun, under Captain Drury, fired a few shells a distance of fifteen

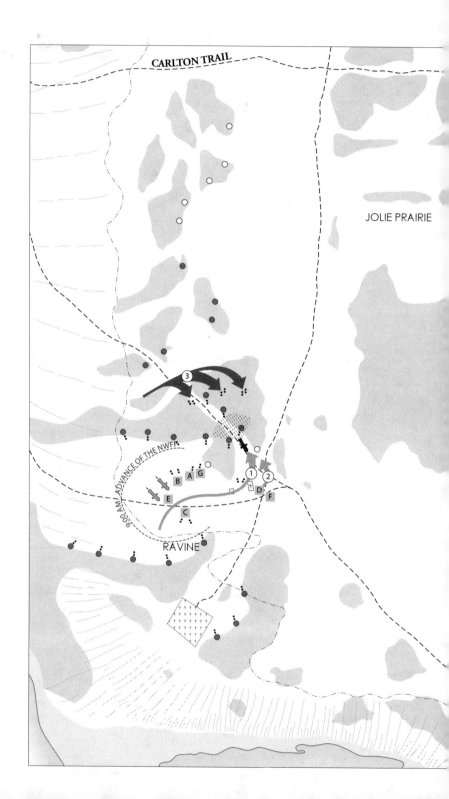

CARLTON TRAIL

JOLIE PRAIRIE

RAVINE

DETAILED BATTLE ZONE MAP

BATOCHE. DAY 1, MAY 9, 1885.

11:00 AM

Map 3 of 10.

Treed Areas	----- Ferry
Floodplain	Contour Line
Slopes	Cemetery
Trails	Church and Rectory

(1) Sequential Military Manoevres

Métis and Indians

Northwest Field Force

○ Rifle Pit (Unoccupied)

● Rifle Pit (Occupied by Métis)

.. Rifle Fire

Cannon (9 Pounders) / Fire

Gatling Gun / Fire

NWFF.

A   Boulton's Mounted Infantry
B   10th Grenadiers
C   90th Battalion
D   Midlanders
E   'A' Battery
F   Winnipeg Field Battery
G   French's Scouts
H   Surveyors

PLAIN

AREA WHERE
ZAREBA WILL
BE BUILT IN
AFTERNOON

N

0	100	200	400	800 Feet
0	30	60	120	240 Metres

hundred yards across the river, and No. 2 gun, under Lt. Ogilvie, also fired at buildings across the river. The fire from the Métis was not particularly intense at this time, and an almost unencumbered shelling by the nine-pound guns was continuing. Dumont was on record as stating later that the initial resistance was less than it might have been since "Those in the pits near the river could not resist the excitement of following the 'Northcote' down stream, otherwise the General and the guns would not have advanced to the position from which they shelled Batoche on the 9th, before clearing out the rifle pits along the river bank, in the cemetery coulee, and on either side of the trail from where it descended the hill."[61] In the intervening time after the *Northcote* had floated downstream, the Métis were again manning the rifle pits along the entire front. During this lull Middleton ordered one of the guns further forward. Unfortunately for Middleton, the gun misfired and Middleton ordered a retreat,

> when with a startling suddenness of a thunderbolt from a
> cloudless sky, a crashing fusillade, it could almost be called
> a volley, swept through the wooden slope at the right front
> ... the bushy slope, which hitherto appeared to be perfectly
> deserted, appeared suddenly to be infested by coyotting
> savages. The guttural 'ki-yi-ki-yi,' the sweeping fusillade,
> and above everything, the startling suddenness of the erup-
> tion, combined to make the new situation a trying one for
> the nerves of the bravest.[62]

At approximately 12:00 noon, after Captain Howard's attempt to out-flank the Métis on the right had failed, Middleton moved back to the left flank where he had left Melgund in command. When he arrived he found Captain Peters had attacked the Métis lines to the west attempting to reach the rifle pits: "I found Captain Peters had made a gallant and vigorous attempt, with a few of the garrison artillery, to drive the enemy out of the bluff below, but had failed and had retired, leaving a wounded man behind [Gunner Philips]."[63]

Shortly after Philips was shot (one source had it at 2:00 p.m.), an attempt to rescue him was organized under the direction of Captain Peters (see map 4). It was believed at first that Philips had only been wounded, and perhaps that was the case. One participant recalled Philips crying out after he was hit: "Captain French, my leg is broken. For God's sake, don't leave me here."[64]

Shortly after Philips was rescued, a second encirclement of the Field Force was attempted, this time from the right flank of their line of defense (see map 5). Middleton makes almost no mention of these threats of being cut off from supplies, but they are detailed at some length in numerous other accounts. Earlier, the Gatling had been effective in repelling an attack on the left flank, but the Métis now employed distracting tactics by taking advantage of the northwesterly wind blowing towards the church. A prairie fire was lit upwind, and it was expected that the Métis would try to attack under the cover of the smoke. The tactic managed to unsettle some of the senior officers; Melgund described the effects of this unanticipated tactic:

> Enemy ... lighted bush fire on our right front, behind smoke of which we expected them to advance, things looked awkward we got wounded out of church into waggons, and had ordered them to fall back to camp. I found that the ammunition waggons were also retiring, and I stopped them, much to Disbrowe's relief, who was in charge of them and had done well all day.[65]

The smoke and fire appears to have alarmed the men sufficiently that the wounded were moved out of the temporary hospital which had been set up in the church. According to another source, however, the troops were never in danger of panicking:

> For a time we were surrounded by fires from the sloughs, the smoke of which rolled along the ground like fog. It was a tight place, but the troops never for a moment flinched. They simply looked to their officers who in turn patiently waited for orders from the chief.[66]

The fire, then, was the cause of some anxiety for the right flank but it appears that it was not followed by any sustained advance from the Métis.

After Philips's rescue and the perceived encirclement had been withstood, the heavy firing on both sides subsided. It was now mid-afternoon: "Towards three o'clock the fire slackened somewhat, though a head shown by either party was a target for a score of bullets."[67] At 3:00 p.m., Middleton decided to send Lord Melgund, his chief of staff, to Humboldt, ostensibly to send a private message to Caron. The documentary sources remain ambiguous, so that the real purpose of the mission remains clouded with controversy. Later, some innuendo appeared in the eastern press to the effect that Middleton was panicking and was anticipating a desultory battle which he feared might be lost by the Field Force. The telegram was never found and, therefore, the issue cannot be definitely settled. In his own account, Middleton states that he sent Melgund simply as a precautionary measure. The order to send Melgund in fact was tied to Middleton's larger problems. The first of these was that he was retreating and he was concerned over the

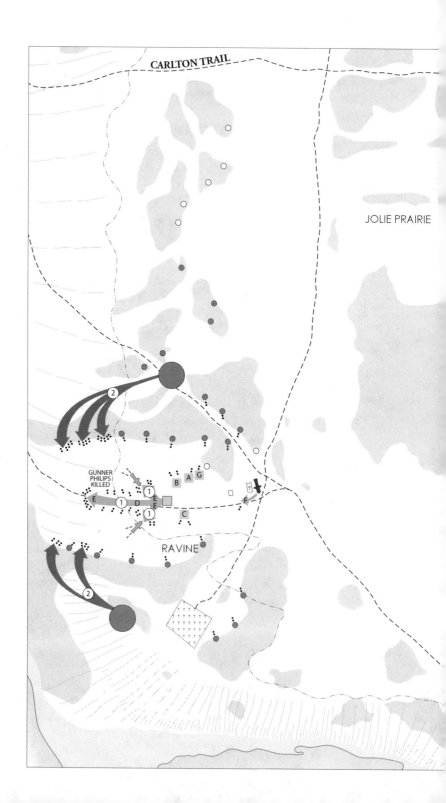

CARLTON TRAIL

JOLIE PRAIRIE

GUNNER
PHILIPS
KILLED

RAVINE

DETAILED BATTLE ZONE MAP

BATOCHE. DAY 1, MAY 9, 1885.

2:00 PM

Map 4 of 10.

Treed Areas	----- Ferry
Floodplain	Contour Line
Slopes	Cemetery
Trails	Church and Rectory

① Sequential Military Manoevres

Métis and Indians

Northwest Field Force

○ Rifle Pit (Unoccupied)

● Rifle Pit (Occupied by Métis)

•• Rifle Fire

Cannon (9 Pounders) / Fire

Gatling Gun / Fire

NWFF.
A Boulton's Mounted Infantry
B 10th Grenadiers
C 90th Battalion
D Midlanders
E 'A' Battery
F Winnipeg Field Battery
G French's Scouts
H Surveyors

PLAIN

AREA WHERE
ZAREBA WILL
BE BUILT IN
AFTERNOON

N

0 100 200   400   800 Feet

0   30 60   120   240 Metres

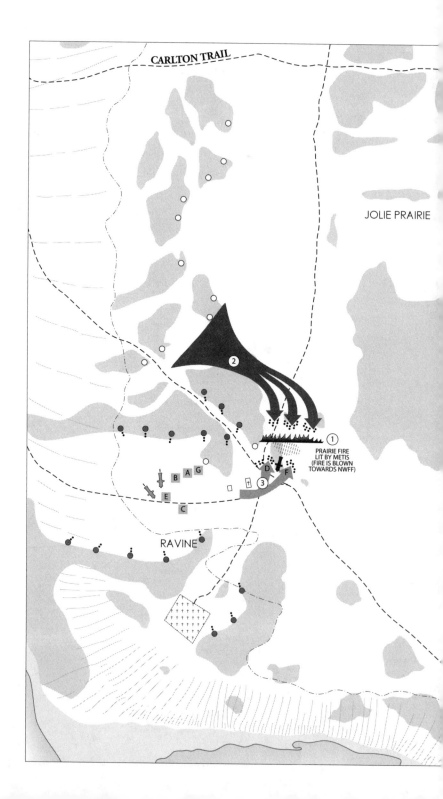

CARLTON TRAIL

JOLIE PRAIRIE

PRAIRIE FIRE
LIT BY METIS
(FIRE IS BLOWN
TOWARDS NWFF)

RAVINE

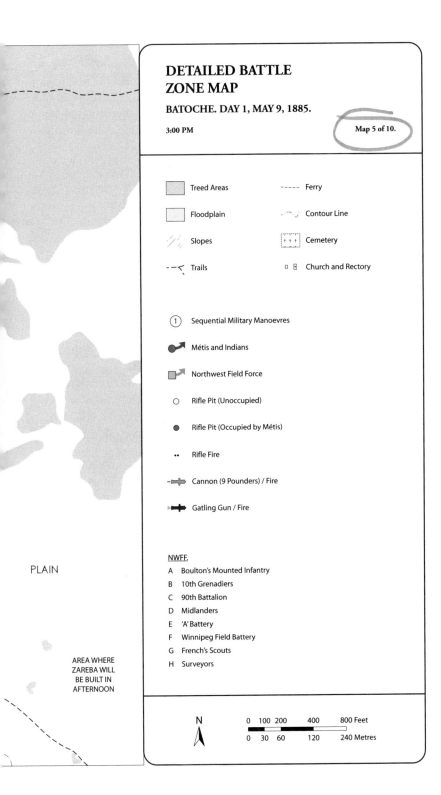

DETAILED BATTLE ZONE MAP

BATOCHE. DAY 1, MAY 9, 1885.

3:00 PM

Map 5 of 10.

Treed Areas	----- Ferry
Floodplain	Contour Line
Slopes	Cemetery
Trails	Church and Rectory

① Sequential Military Manoevres

Métis and Indians

Northwest Field Force

○ Rifle Pit (Unoccupied)

● Rifle Pit (Occupied by Métis)

•• Rifle Fire

Cannon (9 Pounders) / Fire

Gatling Gun / Fire

NWFF,
A Boulton's Mounted Infantry
B 10th Grenadiers
C 90th Battalion
D Midlanders
E 'A' Battery
F Winnipeg Field Battery
G French's Scouts
H Surveyors

PLAIN

AREA WHERE
ZAREBA WILL
BE BUILT IN
AFTERNOON

N

0	100	200	400	800 Feet
0	30	60	120	240 Metres

effect this would have on the enemy; second, he did not know how far to retire. His concern over whether the Métis would interpret the withdrawal as a retreat from weakness (to which the Métis could respond by an attack) was paramount with Middleton.

Melgund's account of this event does not relate any of the atmosphere surrounding the order, or any of the underlying reasons for it. He simply stated:

> About 3 p.m. General told me he wished me to go to Humboldt and send some telegrams for him. He also wished me for several reasons to go to Ottawa. I accordingly started, and found our camp on prairie breaking up in order to move up to General.[68]

By approximately 3:00 p.m. the fighting had subsided. Middleton had sent Boulton and Secretan to strike camp and move it to within a mile of Batoche (about one-quarter mile from the church). Three and one-half hours later the transport carrying the camp forward was arriving and a zareba was formed. The zareba consisted of a transport pulled into a "zareba" shape, with earth and poplar branches filling the space underneath the wagons; a small trench was also dug around the outside of the enclosure.

Zareba warfare is recommended when a long column of transport needs to be guarded and when fighting guerillas. Major Callwell also advocated the use of these tactics, especially when approaching an enemy of unknown strength. It was seen as a defensive tactic within an overall offensive campaign:

> The principle [zareba warfare] is an excellent illustration of defensive tactics superimposed upon offensive strategy. The regular troops invade hostile territory, or territory in temporary occupation of the enemy, and they maintain strategically the initiatives; but when they find themselves in presence of the irregular forces prepared for battle, they form the laager or zareba as the case may be, and either await attack or else leave their impediments in it and go out to fight without encumbrances. In any case they have a secure bivouac and adequate protection during the hours of darkness.[69]

In fact, Callwell recommended such tactics in the terrain of South Africa and North America. The precedent for the use of such tactics originated with pioneers, who came to the frontier in wagons, and used circling formations in face of hostile natives. In regular military strategy this tactic stems from the square. A similar tactic was actually used by the Métis against the Sioux at the battle of Grand Coteau. In North America, pioneers "when operating against Red Indians often formed laagers, or corrals as they were called."[70] Callwell specifically cited the use of zarebas: "During the suppression of Riel's rebellion in 1885, laagers were generally established after each march by the government troops."[71] He furthermore cited Middleton's tactics as an example of a proper use of these tactics: " in the campaign against Riel ... the regular army has adopted it to varying circumstances with great success."[72] And as such Callwell concluded:

> Some think it to be derogatory, some fear its evil moral effect upon the troops. But if kept within limits, and employed only when clear necessity arises, if not permitted to cramp their energies or to check judiciously applied offensive action on the part of the troops there is much to be said for a military system which safeguards the supplies of an army and which grants it temporary repose.[73]

Coinciding with the withdrawal of the troops to the zareba, at approximately 6:30 p.m., was a renewed advance from the Métis. Middleton wrote: "Towards evening the troops were gradually withdrawn, some of the enemy following them up until checked by a heavy fire from the zareba."[74] The Gatling gun was again heavily relied upon to cover the retreat to the zareba (see map 6). From all accounts the retreat was an unpleasant one: "The rebels, well aware of our retirement, took advantage of their safe route under the brow of the cliff, and rising over the brow fired into the zareba."[75] Both the 90th and the 10th Grenadiers were deployed to meet the Métis' pursuit and, as one source noted, "the wonder is that our loss was not heavy. The only reasonable explanations are poor ammunition, poor and hurried marksmanship, greater caution on the part of our forces, and a kind Providence."[76] One man was killed during this final skirmish of the day, however: Private Moor, 3rd Company of the Grenadiers, was shot through the head while defending the zareba.

At dusk, around 7:00 p.m., the fire lessened; "A few of them kept up a desultory long-range fire for a short time, killing two horses and wounding a man."[77] As the fighting waned, fires were lit and men ate supper and prepared for the night. Only the wounded were allowed to sleep in tents, the remainder made do under the open sky. The night was ominous for many, and one man recorded his feelings:

> Night came at length, but tired as we were it was scarcely welcome. We were cooped up, and had the extreme satisfaction of furnishing a good mark for pot shooters. In the

corral were more than six hundred mules and horses, and eight cattle. Men were busy throwing up hasty entrenchments; teamsters, nervous and frightened, were yelling at equally nervous animals; around the hospital tents the doctors were busy dressing wounds, probing for bullets, etc. The bullets were whizzing and pinging overhead, and occasionally when one remembered that a favorite trick among the reds is to stampede the cattle and horses of the enemy. Hoofs would be apt to deal worse wounds than balls, and against afrighted animals, cooped up within a small space, we had absolutely no defense. The anticipations of a mean night were largely realized, though thus far we have escaped a stampede. Few, if any, slept five hours consecutively, and the firing kept up almost all night.[78]

To prevent a surrounding manoeuvre by the Métis during the night, trenches had been dug around the zareba, and the Midland Battalion and one company of the 90th took up positions on a height of land overlooking the river. This did not prevent the dropping fire which the Métis and Indians kept up throughout the night, however.

According to Elie Dumont, the Indians did much of the firing during the first evening:

Grosse gagne se sont assis. On tire des plans pour la soirée. Sauvages disaient on va les tirer ce soir dans leur camp, toute la nuit: vous autres vous travaillerez dans la journée, les métis. Métis disent oui. Au commencement de la veillée, les sauvages ont commencé à tirer, sur le camp, une 10ne de minutes entres les coups, toute la nuit jusqu'au jour.[79]

The resistance of the Métis and the Indians on the first day appears to have momentarily stunned Middleton. His decision to move the camp up to the front showed that he had not entirely lost confidence in the ability of his men to break through the defenses at Batoche—but in spite of this, Middleton's actions during the next few days were cautious and deliberate. Even though his intelligence reports were showing that the Métis were fewer in number than he had estimated and that they were low on ammunition, Middleton was taciturn, unwilling to embark on a bold offensive.[80] He chose this tactic even though he had lost only two men and a few wounded. In effect, he was imposing a partial seige on Batoche. His caution was shown when, according to Boulton, he ordered reinforcements to the front, although Middleton himself did not admit this in his official account published in the *Sessional Papers*.

By the end of the first day of fighting at Batoche, Middleton and the North West Field Force were in a defensive encampment; the men and animals huddled in the zareba spent a fretful night. While the Métis and the Indians by contrast were in an almost victorious mood: having witnessed the uniformed army in retreat, they showed an audacious confidence by keeping up a constant fire into the corral throughout the night. Fourmond recalled that the Métis were in a jubilant mood that evening. As he wrote: "On eut dit l'armée mise en fuite. Et la victoire gagnée par les métis qui alors poursuivit l'ennemi d'aussi près que pouvait le permettre le gatling gun."[81]

The priests who occupied the church through most of the fighting made a number of perceptive observations. The first was that the Canadians appeared to be somewhat disorganized on this first day (a weakness that Middleton himself acknowledged): "Parmi les diverses impressions de la journée, il en est une qui regarde la tenue de l'armée canadienne. Fûmes surpris de son triste accoutrement aussi bien que de son peu de discipline. Nous disions: où sont nos troupes françaises. Quel contraste! Il nous semblait voir des enfants jouant au soldat."[82] Fourmond also noted the shortage of ammunition among the Métis even after the first day: "on voyait Sioux, rôder sur le champ laissé par les soldats, les cartouches abandonnées ou perdues, s'approvisionnant ainsi pour le lendemain."[83] After a cannon ball was fired on the house holding the prisoners, it too was used for ammunition: "Le fils de Michel Trottier ramasse le boulet, va au bas de la côte porter la poudre de dedans et ramasse les balles des soldats et va les faire fondre pour faire des balles pour Métis."[84] One other observation made by the priests was that the Métis may have gained a false sense of security from the method of firing used by the Field Force: "Les Métis souvent induits en erreur sur les morts des soldats par la manoeuvre qui fait coucher le premier rang avant le second tire."[85] The recognition by the Métis that they were killing fewer men than they believed could have demoralized them after the apparent victory of May 9.

The next day, May 10, was a Sunday; the North West Field Force was unable to reach the position left the day before, "as the enemy was in greater force, and now held the high ground about the cemetery and the ground in front of the church. Some of them, apparently Indians from their war cries, had taken post at the end of the point of land below the cemetery…"[86] (see map 7).

Middleton had apparently decided to attempt to demoralize the enemy with heavy artillery fire during the day. Shortly after 5:00 a.m., he began to fire on positions which he had held the previous day: "Two guns were directed against the houses in the basin-shaped depression along the river.

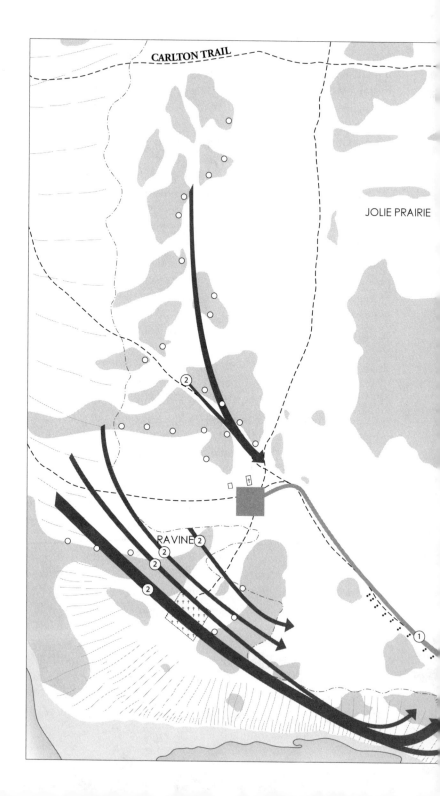

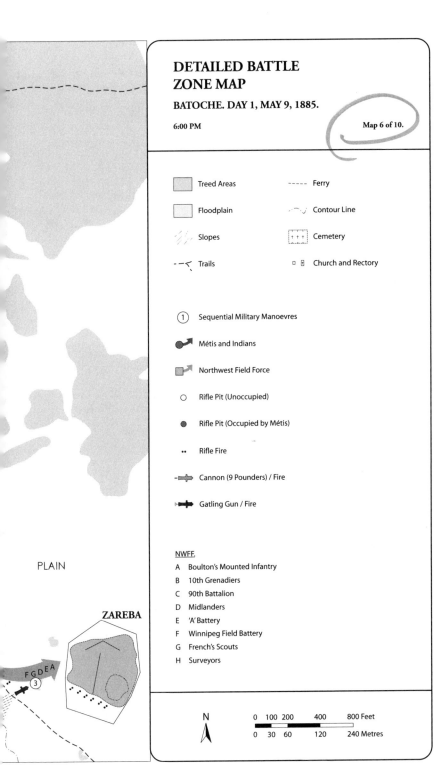

DETAILED BATTLE ZONE MAP

BATOCHE. DAY 1, MAY 9, 1885.

6:00 PM

Map 6 of 10.

Treed Areas

Floodplain

Slopes

Trails

Ferry

Contour Line

Cemetery

Church and Rectory

① Sequential Military Manoevres

Métis and Indians

Northwest Field Force

○ Rifle Pit (Unoccupied)

● Rifle Pit (Occupied by Métis)

‥ Rifle Fire

Cannon (9 Pounders) / Fire

Gatling Gun / Fire

NWFF.
A Boulton's Mounted Infantry
B 10th Grenadiers
C 90th Battalion
D Midlanders
E 'A' Battery
F Winnipeg Field Battery
G French's Scouts
H Surveyors

PLAIN

ZAREBA

F G D E A
③

N

0 100 200   400   800 Feet

0 30 60   120   240 Metres

A few rebels lay behind three log shanties just below the river bank, and the artillery soon drove them out."[87]

On May 11, Middleton appeared more anxious for a direct engagement with the Métis and the Indians (see map 8). But he approached this strategy with caution. Most of the day was spent in reconnaissance, exploring all the possibilities available for a major attack. On this penultimate day of the Battle of Batoche, the fighting escalated, as a consequence of the reconnaissance carried out by Middleton.

It had been reported to Middleton that a space of open prairie, overlooking the village of Batoche, lay just to the north of the zareba. Boulton, whose men accompanied Middleton, described the purpose as follows:

> We marched out about ten o'clock under the command of the General himself, leaving (Alone) Montizambert, Colonel Grasset, Colonel Williams, Major Jarvis, Colonel Mackeand and Colonel Van Straubenzie all discussing the position, and studying a plan of the ground which had been drawn by Captain Haig, R.E. with a view of preparing an attack.[88]

Middleton, accompanied by the Gatling gun, proceeded north through a small swamp, under the cover of bushes lying to the north of the zareba (see map 9). They emerged on an irregularly-shaped clearing "about two miles long and 1,000 yards in the broadest part, with a sort of slight ridge running down the centre and some undulations."[89] As they moved northward they attracted a sporadic fire from the rifle pits which ran along this ridge. In response to the sniper fire, Middleton ordered the Gatling gun to direct two or three rounds into the rifle pits. Middleton then rode further to the north, where he pursued two men he spotted riding across the prairie on ponies and captured another, later discovered to be one of Riel's men, who came out of the bush. According to Middleton, "We also captured some cattle and ponies which we took back to camp with us."[90] Boulton wrote: "Before leaving this point we burned down some log houses that might offer shelter to the enemy, in case further operations were needed here."[91]

Middleton had been receiving intelligence reports which indicated that the Métis were almost out of ammunition. Now that he could see the Métis thinly spread out along their line of rifle pits, he discovered what he needed to know in preparation for his final attack on Batoche: "We could see with our glasses that the enemy had a series of rifle pits all along the edge of those woods, and numbers of them were running up between the woods and disappearing into the pits. Evidently they were prepared for an attack in this direction."[92] It was clear that the Métis had responded to Middleton's manoeuvre of pulling men away from their right flank to reinforce the left where the Field Force "drew a smart fire."[93]

Further evidence that the Métis had followed the Gatling gun to the north awaited Middleton when he returned to camp. There he found that the infantry were able to regain the ground they had held on the first day of fighting: "A party of Midlanders, under Lieutenant-Colonel Williams' command, finding the fire slacken from the Indians' post below the cemetery, and led by him, gallantly rushed it, the Indians bolting leaving behind them some blankets and a dummy which they had used for drawing our fire."[94] Middleton now knew that the Métis could not be certain how many men he might deploy in a manoeuvre to the north because of the cover offered by the intervening bushes. As a consequence of the advances made by the infantry, the artillery were again able to draw up in the vicinity of the graveyard to open fire on the village and on the houses on the opposite bank: "shelling the opposite bank we [observed] that the shells created great consternation among the rebels, making them scatter and get well beyond range, and silenced the long range rifles which were a constant source of annoyance."[95]

It was clear to Middleton that the resources of the Métis and Indians were running low and that his men were gaining confidence.[96] The Métis hardly pursued the Field Force as it retired for the night and there was no fire into the camp that evening; a parapet had been built around the zareba that day to protect against bullets fired into the camp. Late that evening Middleton made his decision: "Our men were beginning to show more dash, and that night I came to the conclusion that it was time to make our decisive attack."[97]

Convinced that the Métis and the Indians would follow his manoeuvre accompanied by the Gatling gun, Middleton again reconnoitred to the open plain north of the zareba. Middleton then told Van Straubenzie to proceed to the original front, and "that as soon as he heard us well engaged he was to move off, and, having taken up yesterday's position, push on towards the village."[98] This manoeuvre engineered by Middleton was commemorated in a major military study of the 19th century, which examined warfare against what were referred to as "savages" throughout the British Empire. Major Callwell cites Middleton's feinting action as particularly successful in the situation confronting him:

> General Middleton found the half-breeds holding a long line of rifle pits; this stretched across the land enclosed by a wide salient angle formed by the Saskatchewan. The Government forces encamped opposite one end of this line of defence and formed a zareba, and they remained facing

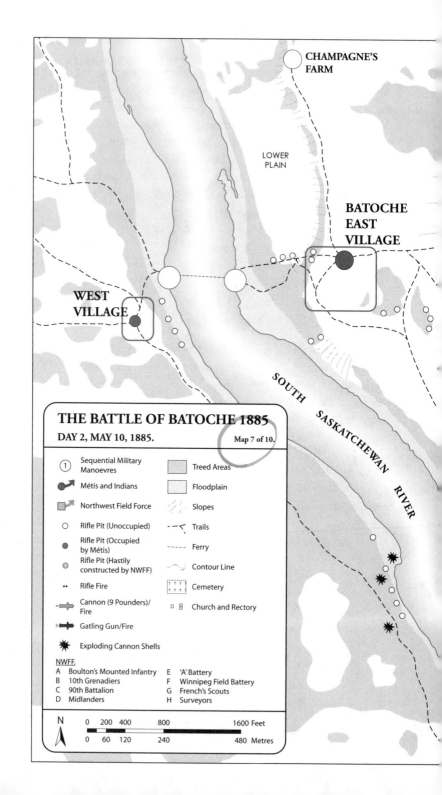

CHAMPAGNE'S
FARM

LOWER
PLAIN

BATOCHE
EAST
VILLAGE

WEST
VILLAGE

SOUTH SASKATCHEWAN RIVER

THE BATTLE OF BATOCHE 1885

DAY 2, MAY 10, 1885.

Map 7 of 10.

①	Sequential Military Manoevres	
	Métis and Indians	
	Northwest Field Force	
○	Rifle Pit (Unoccupied)	
●	Rifle Pit (Occupied by Métis)	
⊗	Rifle Pit (Hastily constructed by NWFF)	
••	Rifle Fire	
	Cannon (9 Pounders)/ Fire	
	Gatling Gun/Fire	
✸	Exploding Cannon Shells	

Treed Areas

Floodplain

Slopes

Trails

Ferry

Contour Line

Cemetery

Church and Rectory

NWFF.
A   Boulton's Mounted Infantry
B   10th Grenadiers
C   90th Battalion
D   Midlanders
E   'A' Battery
F   Winnipeg Field Battery
G   French's Scouts
H   Surveyors

N

0	200	400	800	1600 Feet
0	60	120	240	480 Metres

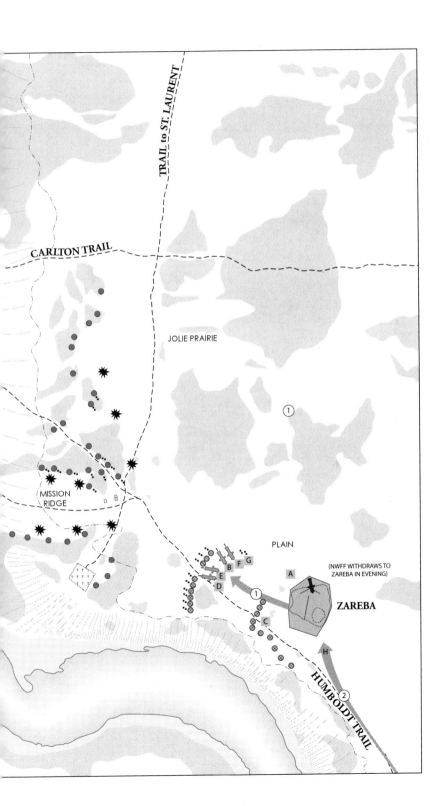

TRAIL to ST. LAURENT

CARLTON TRAIL

JOLIE PRAIRIE

①

MISSION
RIDGE

PLAIN

(NWFF WITHDRAWS TO
ZAREBA IN EVENING)

A

B F G

E
D

C

①

ZAREBA

H

②

HUMBOLDT TRAIL

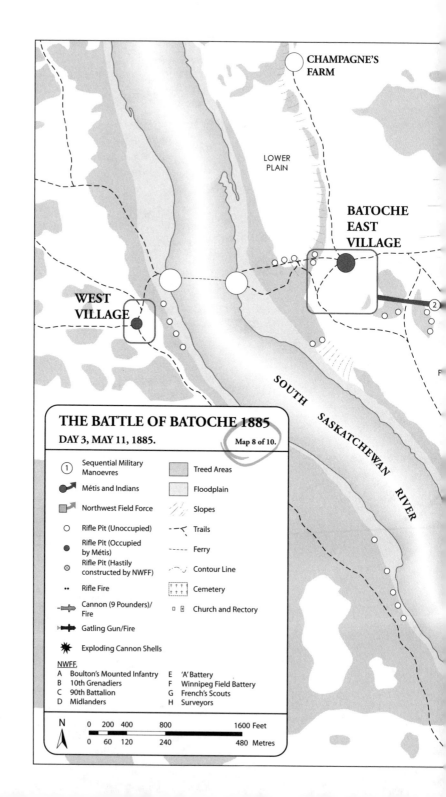

CHAMPAGNE'S
FARM

LOWER
PLAIN

BATOCHE
EAST
VILLAGE

2

WEST
VILLAGE

SOUTH SASKATCHEWAN RIVER

F

THE BATTLE OF BATOCHE 1885
DAY 3, MAY 11, 1885.

Map 8 of 10.

①	Sequential Military Manoevres	
	Métis and Indians	
	Northwest Field Force	
○	Rifle Pit (Unoccupied)	
●	Rifle Pit (Occupied by Métis)	
⊗	Rifle Pit (Hastily constructed by NWFF)	
••	Rifle Fire	
	Cannon (9 Pounders)/ Fire	
	Gatling Gun/Fire	
✳	Exploding Cannon Shells	

	Treed Areas
	Floodplain
/////	Slopes
--⟨	Trails
-----	Ferry
⌒⌒	Contour Line
⊹⊹⊹	Cemetery
▫ ▣	Church and Rectory

NWFF:
A   Boulton's Mounted Infantry
B   10th Grenadiers
C   90th Battalion
D   Midlanders
E   'A' Battery
F   Winnipeg Field Battery
G   French's Scouts
H   Surveyors

N

0	200	400	800	1600 Feet
0	60	120	240	480 Metres

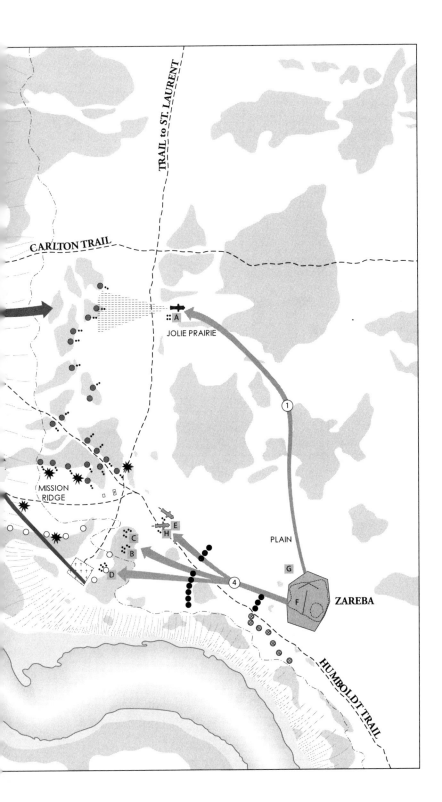

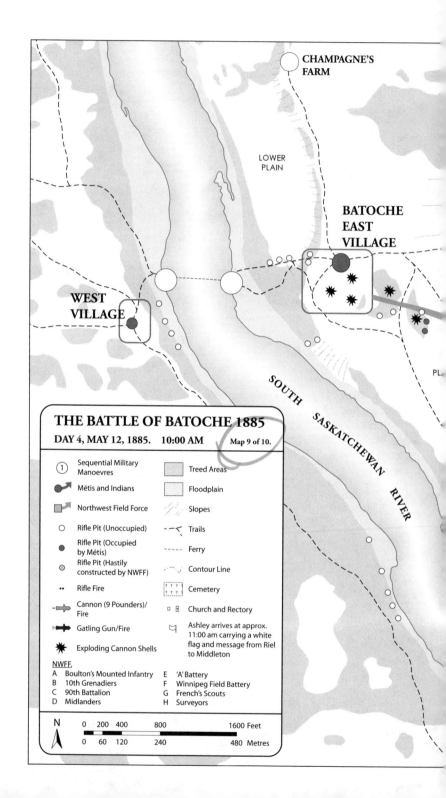

CHAMPAGNE'S
FARM

LOWER
PLAIN

BATOCHE
EAST
VILLAGE

WEST
VILLAGE

SOUTH SASKATCHEWAN RIVER

PL.

THE BATTLE OF BATOCHE 1885

DAY 4, MAY 12, 1885.   10:00 AM   Map 9 of 10.

①	Sequential Military Manoevres	
	Métis and Indians	
	Northwest Field Force	
○	Rifle Pit (Unoccupied)	
●	Rifle Pit (Occupied by Métis)	
⊗	Rifle Pit (Hastily constructed by NWFF)	
••	Rifle Fire	
	Cannon (9 Pounders)/ Fire	
	Gatling Gun/Fire	
✸	Exploding Cannon Shells	

	Treed Areas
	Floodplain
	Slopes
--〈	Trails
-----	Ferry
	Contour Line
	Cemetery
▫ ▣	Church and Rectory
	Ashley arrives at approx. 11:00 am carrying a white flag and message from Riel to Middleton

NWFF.
A	Boulton's Mounted Infantry	E	'A' Battery
B	10th Grenadiers	F	Winnipeg Field Battery
C	90th Battalion	G	French's Scouts
D	Midlanders	H	Surveyors

N

| 0 | 200 | 400 | 800 | 1600 Feet |
| 0 | 60 | 120 | 240 | 480 Metres |

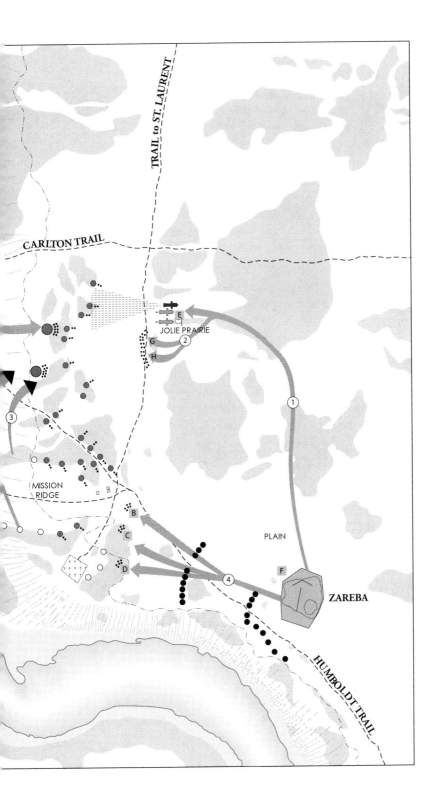

TRAIL to ST. LAURENT

CARLTON TRAIL

JOLIE PRAIRIE

E

G

H

2

1

3

MISSION
RIDGE

B

C

D

4

PLAIN

F

ZAREBA

HUMBOLDT TRAIL

the enemy four days engaged in skirmishes. On the third day the mounted troops made a demonstration against the hostile centre, and it was observed that a part of Riel's followers were withdrawn from the end of the line opposite the zareba to strengthen the threatened point. On the following day this demonstration was repeated by the mounted men with two guns, and these then returned quietly to camp. In the afternoon the whole Government force attacked the end of the rebel line in front of the zareba where it had been greatly weakened, and broke through and reached Batoche. The undulating nature of the ground patched with woods and copses enable the feint to be carried out in very effective fashion.[99]

The strategy was straightforward and simple, even though it failed initially. The attack from the left flank was to be led that morning by Colonel Van Straubenzie's brigade. The men making up the party intended to participate in the feinting manoeuvre were "Captain Dennis' corps, my own corps [Boulton], and Captain French's, in all numbering about one hundred and thirty men, one gun of "A" Battery, under Captain Drury and the Gatling under Lieutenant Rivers, accompanied by Captain Howard, marched off under General Middleton..."[100] The nine-pounder which accompanied Middleton's expedition was pulled up into firing position, and the Land Surveyors, under Captain Dennis, dismounted and advanced in skirmishing order. The Gatling gun was then stationed to the north of this point, and Middleton rode out to within 400 yards of the Métis rifle pits to order the advance of the dismounted surveyors. The rest of the infantry was kept hidden behind the advancing skirmishers. According to one surveyor's reminiscences, it appeared that the Métis were anticipating an attack from the basin where Middleton assembled his men: "The Rebels evidently expected us, for we had only advanced a few yards when they must have caught sight of one of us over the rise, and a volley was fired into our ranks, at the report of which we dropped our faces in the brush, one of us never again to rise again, for poor Kippen fell dead with a rifle bullet in his brain."[101] The nine-pounder and the Gatling also opened fire and there was a brief, but from most accounts, intense exchange. Perhaps the Métis, in fact, had expected the main attack to come from this front.

During the morning's action, another event occurred which suggests that the Métis position was weakening. It also showed that Riel, by sending his message to this front, believed that it was where the main attack would take place. Just as the Gatling was ready to move to a position further to the north, Middleton saw a man riding towards him with a white flag. It turned out to be a Mr. Astley, a surveyor captured by Riel just after the battle at Duck Lake. "He told me he had just come from Riel, who was apparently in a great state of agitation, and handed me a letter from him in which he said, apparently referring to our shelling the houses, that if I massacred his women and children they would massacre their prisoners."[102] Middleton replied that he had no intention of deliberately injuring women and children and suggested that they be placed in a building marked by a white flag. Astley, after having explained Riel's condition for surrender, returned with Middleton's reply. Shortly after this, another man emerged on foot carrying a white flag. He turned out to be Thomas Jackson, later found to be sympathetic to Riel. Jackson was carrying the same note as Astley; however, he refused to go back to Riel's camp and Middleton allowed him, for the time being, to go free.

It was now about 11:30 a.m. and Middleton was prepared to move back to camp. His deployment of troops in the morning seemed to confuse the men in the rifle pits, according to Boulton, "keeping us for a while just out of sight of the enemy, occasionally showing a mounted man or two to puzzle the rebels as to our movements, which always drew a volley from them."[103] Following this, the men returned to camp having lost only one man in what was to be an all-out advance against the Métis and Indians.

That morning Van Straubenzie had ordered the Midlanders and Grenadiers out in quarter column ready for an attack on the left flank. Due to a strong east wind he was however unable to hear any of the artillery or rifle fire from Middleton's contingent. According to a number of accounts, Middleton was furious when he returned to camp at lunch to find that no attack had been made. Middleton himself wrote: "I am afraid on that occasion I lost both my temper and my head."[104] Later, in retrospect, Middleton seemed to believe that it was fortuitous that the charge had been aborted:

> On regaining the camp I was much annoyed at finding that, owing to a misconception of my orders, the advance parties had not, as I had directed, been sent forward to hold the regained position and press forward, as I drew the enemy from their right by my feint; but now I am inclined to think it was a fortunate thing that they had not, for I believe the total silence and absence of fire from my left only strengthened the belief of the enemy that I was going to attack from the prairie ground.[105]

The men of the Grenadiers and Midlanders were just completing their meal, which one man described as "munching the bulletproof discs of that indescribable compound known as Government biscuit that formed our lunch…"[106] Middleton was sitting down to his when he gave a rather vague order to Van Straubenzie to "take them as far as he pleased."[107] It is believed that the order was simply intended to send the men back to the positions they held that morning although it might have been taken as a signal to advance further against the Métis positions.

Conflicting accounts over exactly what happened and who was responsible for the charge at this point are numerous (see map 10). Much of the conflict was motivated by those who sought personal glory, and also by those who either hated or admired Middleton. One observer noted:

> one of the Midland men on the slope of the hill near the cemetery was hit by a volley from the west side of the river, and the ambulance men going to his relief were also fired upon. This seemed to infuriate the men, and their officers saw that there was no holding them any longer. Colonel Williams therefore decided upon charging, and with only two companies of the Midland, he led the way counting on the 90th and the Grenadiers for support.[108]

Others also gave credit to Williams for leading the final charge, though it is not clear whether he proceeded on his own or under orders. Colonel Denison, who was not at the front but stationed at Humboldt, acknowledges Williams as the leader of the final charge. Captain Peters gives credit for the charge to Van Straubenzie, while Boulton tends to credit Middleton and Van Straubenzie with issuing the string of orders which led to the final charge.[109] Middleton's own description, which he wrote closest to the time of the action, indicates that the breakthrough merely happened and was not actually ordered as an advance:

> After the men had had their dinners they were moved down to take up old positions and press on. Two companies of the Midland, 60 men in all, under Lt. Col. Williams, were extended on the left and moved up to the cemetery, and the Grenadiers, 200 strong, under Lt. Col. Grassett prolonged the line to the right beyond the church, the 90th being in support. The Midland and Grenadiers, led by Lt. Cols. Williams and Grassett, the whole led by Lt. Col. Straubenzie in command of the Brigade, then dashed forward with a cheer and drove the enemy out of the pits in front of the cemetery and the ravine to the right of it, thus clearing the angle at the turn of the river.[110]

One theory suggests that because of the turn in the river it was necessary for the line of advance to be equidistant from the rifle pits all along the front and that, consequently, the extreme left had to be ordered slightly forward. When so commanded they advanced without resistance, possibly due to weakly manned or vacant rifle pits (men being now located to the north, where attack was anticipated). Gaining confidence and momentum and encountering little resistance, they broke into a run. Seeing this movement, the rest of the front, extending to the right from the river past the church, now followed suit. This advancing front, made up from left to right of the Midlanders, Grenadiers and 90th, was now joined by men ordered by Middleton to extend the line to the right. This was done by sending out the gun of "A" Battery and by "B" and "F" of the 90th; Boulton's Mounted were then sent to lengthen the line even further. The Surveyors were ordered out to the right of Boulton's men. The artillery were now firing both at the village and at the Métis in rifle pits across the river, whose fire was pouring down on the Midlanders closest to the river. The gun from the Winnipeg Field Battery and the Gatling were ordered to fire at the village from the right extreme on the front.

Loud cheers were heard as the men now broke towards the village. One reporter wrote:

> with a rush and a cheer they were down on the rebels with the fierceness of Bashi-Basouks, the Midland on the left, the Grenadiers in the centre, and the 90th on the right. The advance came sweeping round until a few minutes saw the line of direction at right angles to the original line of attack. The cheering was that of satisfied and contented men, and the enthusiasm was intense. Nothing could have withstood the pace, the force, and the dogged determination of the men. The cheering attracted the General, and, taking in the situation at glance, he came on with the Winnipeg artillery, Gatling and three companies of the 90th).[111]

Just as Middleton heard cheers from the men as they broke through the first line of rifle pits, Astley, Riel's messenger, again appeared. He carried with him a note from Riel which read, "General,—Your prompt answer to my note shows that I was right mentioning to you the cause of humanity. We will gather our families in one place and as soon as it is done we will let you know."[112] It was signed Louis David Riel. On the outside another missive, reflecting a more agitated state of mind, appeared. "I do not like the war, and if you do not retreat and refuse an interview, the question remains the same concerning the prisoners."[113] The message on the envelope, which

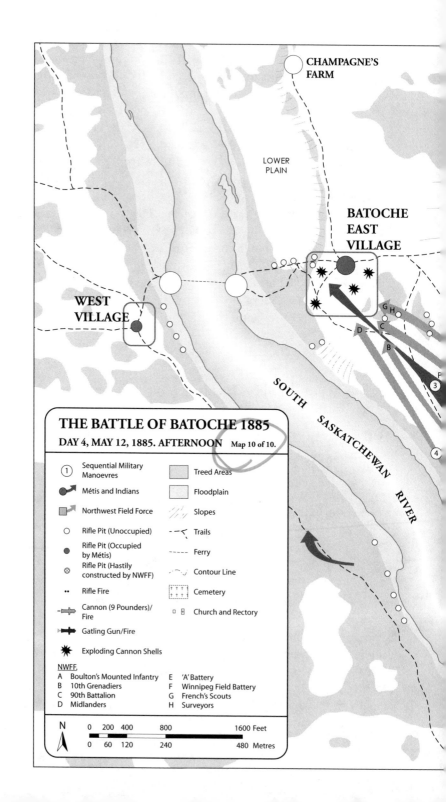

CHAMPAGNE'S
FARM

LOWER
PLAIN

BATOCHE
EAST
VILLAGE

WEST
VILLAGE

SOUTH SASKATCHEWAN RIVER

G H
C
D
B
F
3

4

THE BATTLE OF BATOCHE 1885

DAY 4, MAY 12, 1885. AFTERNOON   Map 10 of 10.

①	Sequential Military Manoevres	
	Métis and Indians	
	Northwest Field Force	
○	Rifle Pit (Unoccupied)	
●	Rifle Pit (Occupied by Métis)	
⊗	Rifle Pit (Hastily constructed by NWFF)	
••	Rifle Fire	
	Cannon (9 Pounders)/ Fire	
	Gatling Gun/Fire	
✸	Exploding Cannon Shells	

	Treed Areas
	Floodplain
	Slopes
- -<	Trails
-----	Ferry
	Contour Line
	Cemetery
□ ⊡	Church and Rectory

NWFF.
A   Boulton's Mounted Infantry
B   10th Grenadiers
C   90th Battalion
D   Midlanders

E   'A' Battery
F   Winnipeg Field Battery
G   French's Scouts
H   Surveyors

N

0	200	400	800		1600 Feet
0	60	120	240		480 Metres

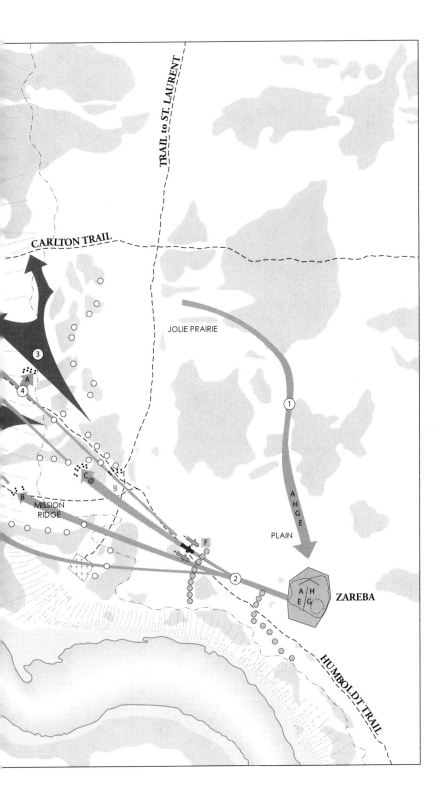

TRAIL to ST. LAURENT

CARLTON TRAIL

JOLIE PRAIRIE

MISSION
RIDGE

PLAIN

ZAREBA

HUMBOLDT TRAIL

contained a veiled threat, was in fact a contradiction of the note inside, an indication of Riel's instability. Middleton ignored both the note and the message:

> Of course no answer was sent, and soon, with the officers well in front, a general advance of the whole line was made with rousing cheers, the place was captured, the prisoners released, and the fighting was over, except for some desultory long-range firing, which was soon put down by two or three parties sent in different directions.[114]

The final offensive did not run as smoothly as Middleton described, and a number of sources indicate that some stiff resistance was met as they moved down the slopes towards the village. One skirmisher recalled the action: "The enemy poured in a hot fire when we started, but I don't think any of our men were hit until we got into the bush. Here many of the men were struck."[115] Most were hit by shots fired from the camouflaged rifle pits.

The well-constructed rifle pits discovered after the attack by the Field Force were praised by Middleton:

> I was astonished at the strength of the position and at the ingenuity and care displayed in the construction of the rifle pits ... In and around the pits were found blankets, trousers, coats, shirts, boots, shoes, food, oil, Indian articles of sleep, one or two damaged shot guns and one good rifle. It was evident that a detachment of Rebels had lived in these pits, day and night, and it was easily understood, by an inspection of them, how perfectly safe the holders of these pits were from the fire of our rifles and especially from the Gatling and artillery.
>
> These pits were also judiciously placed as regards repelling a front attack, but by attacking their right (which was their weakest point) and driving it in, we turned and took in reverse all their entrenchments, along the edge of the prairie ground, and thus caused a rout which ended in a "sauve qui peut."[116]

The Métis, as is now well known, were short of ammunition and fighting men on this last day. Of the original 320 to 350 combatants, Lépine recalled that only 50 to 60 men were fighting during the final battle[117]: "40 environ métis, avaient des carabines, le reste avaient des fusils à canard (2 coups)."[118] Nails were being fired by some in the rifle pits when the metal bullets manufactured from the last of the melted down cannon balls had been exhausted. In addition to the fact that they were poorly armed and lacked ammunition, the Métis, it appears, were also misled by appearances on this last day. Vandale remembered thinking that the peace had been won when Middleton withdrew his men from their left flank in the morning. The Métis, it seems, believed that Riel's messages had succeeded in winning a cease-fire. Vandale wrote: "Le canon arrête et Champagne se sauve et dit c'est la paix... Les Métis se lèvent, s'assient sur le bord des trous ... puis se relèvent et se retirent au camp des familles, une douzaine environ, pensant que c'était la paix."[119] As was evident, however, it was a terrible misunderstanding: "On était à se laver, quand Gabriel vient nous renvoyer aux trous du vieux chemin—s'y sont rendus, et grand bruit dans le camp et coups de fusil—10 minutes plus tard, bataille générale. Quand la bataille recommence, il y en avait 18 qui tenaient bon, et plusieurs se sauvaient un à un quand ils avaient une chance."[120] It is clear that the state of disarray the Métis found themselves in on the last day was greater than has previously been believed. Indeed, the orders under which the Métis were acting were confused and contradictory. The final attack by the Field Force was decisive, therefore, even from the perspective of the Métis:

> On voit l'armée déboucher de tous côtés en ordre de bataille. Infanterie, artillerie, cavalerie, tout à la fois. Avec un ordre et détermination, une rapidité de mouvement que nous n'avions pas vue les autres jours. Du 1er coup d'oeil, on comprit que l'heure decisive était venue; que c'en était fait de Batoche.[121]

At dusk, Middleton ordered that the camp be formed into a zareba. Trenches were dug, but they were not as extensive as before. These precautions turned out to be unnecessary as no other shots were fired at Batoche. The zareba was located just to the north and east of Batoche's house.

During the period after the fighting and throughout the following days, the men with the Field Force, and the reporters accompanying them, made a number of observations about the Métis and recorded statements made by them. While these statements were accurately recorded, whether they were factual remains questionable. One recurring observation was that the Métis and their families were forced to take up arms against their will.[122]

Almost ten years later, when he was reflecting over the events of 1885, Middleton was generous in his praise of the fighting ability of the Métis and Indians. Of the combat on May 12, in particular, he wrote:

> Needless to say, I was well satisfied with the result of the day's fighting, which proved the correctness of my opinion

> that these great hunters, like the Boers of South Africa, are
> only formidable when you play their games, "bush fight-
> ing," to which they are accustomed, but they cannot stand a
> determined charge.[123]

This seems to be an accurate assessment, but begs the question in that the
Métis and Indians were prevented by their own leader from fully engaging
in guerilla warfare. A bold frontal attack was possible not through anything
Middleton or the Field Force did, but through Riel's determination to decide
their fate at Batoche.

For the Westerners who rose or were tempted to rise in arms, there was
a subtle irony in the presence of these Eastern soldiers. Many who had come
obediently and with preconceived notions of the savagery of the Wild West
came to sympathize with the problems of their former foes. The problems of
the administration of the Northwest was apparent to those who marched
into the territory—they too suffered from privations on the frontier. Only
after receiving reports from the distant Northwest did many of the officials
in the East become aware of Western discontent and discover that there was
substance to the complaints.

Melgund, on whose observations both Lansdowne and Derby relied,
believed that there was general discontent in the Northwest among all
groups as a result of inadequate administration and neglect. As he wrote
after the fighting had ended:

> Riel and Gabriel Dumont were not counting only on their
> half-breed and Redskin rifles, but on the support of white
> men who they had been lulled into believing would stand
> by them. Riel put his fighting men in his first line, but in his
> second we may perhaps find the disappointed white con-
> tractor, the disappointed white land shark, the disappoint-
> ed white farmer.[124]

The tragedy of Batoche was that those mentioned by Melgund, and especially the Métis and Indians who fought in the last battle, relied too heavily
on Riel to win redress for their grievances.

14. Another Father of Confederation? (1999)

Allen Ronaghan

> *For all his faults, Louis Riel strikes an exceptional figure in Canadian history. Deprived of his political rights in the Red River settlement by a government eager to affirm its growing independence from England, he developed a paranoia reflecting the siege mentality experienced by the Métis. His alienation, exacerbated by Ottawa's internal colonialism, prepared the ground for the events of 1885 and reflects the lasting conflict between East and West.*

The proposal that Louis Riel should be honoured posthumously with the title "Father of Confederation" has had a mixed reception among the historiographers of our country, and particularly those of the province of Ontario. This is not at all remarkable, given the part played by that province in the affairs which involved Riel.

Should Riel be honoured as a Father of Confederation? Certainly not, if attendance at one or more of the Confederation conferences is the sole qualification for that honour. Riel was unfortunate enough to come from a portion of British North America which was not even invited to be present at Charlottetown, Quebec or London. How is it, then, that his name is mentioned so many years after those conferences, especially since for many of those years he has borne the title of "rebel"?

This is one of the ironies of Canadian history, one of those conundrums which trouble historians from time to time because of the difficulties in obtaining and using sound evidence about what happened. There is no doubt that in 1885 Louis Riel "levied" war "upon her majesty," to use the words of an eminent American historian.[1] History tells us that Riel was tried for treason and hanged in 1885. Can a man who was tried for treason be also a Father of Confederation?

One commentator has used the word "heritage" as something distinct from "history."[2] I can sympathize with this comment. Once, as a young man, I overheard a conversation in which two elderly gentlemen discussed this very point. One of them made the remark that "Riel was tried for treason and hanged for the murder of Thomas Scott." The Thomas Scott in question was executed fifteen years earlier, in 1885, and Louis Riel certainly did not murder him, although Riel was tried for that murder in the Ontario press in 1870 and found guilty. Is it still necessary for us to decide which is history and which is heritage? There is something "passing strange" in this.

The principal events of the resistance of 1869 and 1870 have been well outlined by several of our prominent historians, so it is not necessary to go into detail on those events here. It is well known that the Métis people, still suspicious of those in authority because of the events of the Guillaume Sayer trial in which Riel's father played a leading part, viewed with alarm the actions and words of those sent by Canada to Red River in 1868 and 1869.[3]

It had been comparatively simple in 1849 to organize a group of men and a petition for, among other things, the removal of the bigot Thom from the bench of the Red River Settlement's only court.[4] Mobilizing the Settlement in the face of the menace posed by the boastful young Canadians and in the absence of any statement of policy from Britain, from Canada or from the Hudson's Bay Company at the time of the purchase, was quite another matter.[5] The old Métis councillors looked at the problem and fled onto the plains so that they would not have to face it head on.[6] The void in leadership was filled by younger men. The steps taken by Riel and his companions are familiar to students of our history: the formation of a national committee; the efforts to enlist the support of the English-speaking portion of the Settlement; the stopping of the surveyors; the occupation of Fort Garry; the refusal to allow Lieutenant Governor designate McDougall to enter Rupert's Land; the efforts to form a provisional government and send delegates to Ottawa. Not so well known are the acts of the opposition: the undercover efforts at interference by John C. Schultz[7]; the gathering and surrender of the "enlisted" men at Schultz's houses[8]; the escape of Thomas Scott and others[9]; Scott's part in the march of the Portage men to the rendezvous at Kildonan at a time when the entire Settlement had agreed upon a provisional government[10]; the deaths of Sutherland and Parisien.[11] These attempts at interference at Red River only came to an end with the departure of Schultz, Lynch and Mair, and with the trial and execution of Thomas Scott on March 4. Attempts at interference continued at full speed in Ontario, however, and featured a media campaign in the Ontario press and Colonel G.T. Denison's willingness to use the levers of power in the Orange lodges of Ontario.[12] The result was a thoroughly aroused province of Ontario and a shaken federal government.

In order to keep our perspective about Riel's work in 1869 and 1870, we must remember that the Red River Settlement had not become a Crown colony, but was still under Hudson's Bay Company rule. The natural centre of the Settlement was upper Fort Garry, and here it was that the governor and council met. After the occupation of Fort Garry on November 2, 1869, Riel and the National Committee were the effective, if not the legal, government of the Settlement. They found themselves having to act simultaneously in matters that would later be described as municipal, provincial and federal, while at the same time having to care for the men taken prisoner when "levying war" against the only government in the Settlement. Their success was so evident and acceptance so general that the American observer James W. Taylor wrote that "elsewhere than in an English colony, it would long ago have been recognized at Washington."[13]

Not so generally known are the policies of the Canadian government with regard to the Red River Settlement and Rupert's Land. It was not known, for example, which men or groups of men were to shoulder the rifles which were in transit to Red River at the time McDougall was prevented from entering Rupert's Land.[14] The Métis, of course, had their fears.

We are left wondering, too, why it was that McDougall was so reluctant to speak to the National Committee about Canada's intentions. Could he not, through Provencher, have begun talks with the National Committee? Why did he, instead, send Colonel Dennis to join forces with Schultz in efforts to upset that committee?

A Red River Expeditionary Force was part of Canadian government policy as early as January of 1870—long before the execution of Scott—when contracts were let for the construction of the necessary boats, and preparation went forward steadily from then on. The campaign in the Ontario press about the "murder" of Scott only added impetus to what had already been decided.

Why was an expeditionary force considered to be essential? Rupert's Land was British territory, and there were many ties of relationship between people there and families in old Canada. To answer this question we must read the language of the Cabinet's Minute of Council dated February 11, 1870. This Minute expressed the fear that the insurgent leaders would insist upon demands made in the Manifesto or Declaration of Rights, "several of which are inadmissible." The Minute also expressed the fear that the delegates might return to Fort Garry "smarting under the sense of failure" and, "unless confronted by a Military Force and a strengthened Government, make violent appeals to the people and raise a second insurrection on a more formidable basis." The Minute did not specify which demands were "inadmissible."[15]

Which demands were inadmissible? Several lists of rights composed by Red River people have come down to us for study, and anyone familiar with the British North America Act, as the Métis and their advisors certainly were, must have thought that the admission of Red River to the new Confederation would be almost automatic, once the delegates had had a chance to express their wishes.[16]

One can understand the puzzlement of Riel and his associates, in the winter of 1869–70, at the refusal or inability of those sent to Red River— Thibault, de Salaberry and Smith—to give positive assurances concerning what the people of Red River wished to see guaranteed in any arrangement which allowed them to be a part of Canada.[17] Instead, Smith came equipped with money to enable him to subvert the government at Fort Garry.[18]

The three Red River delegates—Judge Black, Father Ritchot and Alfred Scott—were soon to find out which demands were "inadmissible," and they found this out at roughly the same time that they learned of the sending of the Expeditionary Force. They could see only too well that from that day forward they were negotiating while a gun was being pointed at them.[19]

Cartier and Macdonald were offering to create a province out of a portion of Rupert's Land, a province which, unlike the original four, would not have control of its chief natural resource, its ungranted lands.[20] These lands were to be "vested in the Crown, and administered by the Government of Canada for the purposes of the Dominion."[21] In so doing Cartier and Macdonald were, in effect, crossing a Rubicon—making a change in the British North America Act, a change which they well knew the people of Rupert's Land did not wish to accept.[22]

The three delegates had no way of knowing that at the same time they were objecting to this feature of the arrangement John C. Schultz was threatening to make public his opposition to it. Lionized throughout Ontario as the "suffering loyalist" of Red River, Schultz posed a serious threat to the government's plans. The threat was met with substance and dispatch. Schultz agreed to receive $11,000 in lieu of claims he was making for losses at Red River.[23] This money came not from government funds but from money which Sir Francis Hincks made available privately for the purpose.[24]

The Red River delegates finally accepted a compromise by which a grant of 1.4 million acres was to be made available for the "children of the half-breed heads of families," a compromise which became section 31 of the Manitoba Act. This compromise and the payment to Schultz cleared the way for the passage of the Manitoba Act.

In May of 1870, at the same time that the Manitoba bill was introduced in the House of Commons, Charles Mair and "Canada First" began a process which would bring about an emigration of Ontario farmers to Red River and interfere both with the implementation of government policy and with Métis plans to abide by that policy.[25] The process began with a letter to the *Globe* and continued with the organization of the North-West Emigration Aid Society.[26] The result was that during the winter of 1870–71 farmers all across Ontario began to sell off their farms and chattels, and to prepare for a move to the new province.

Before he left Ottawa to return to Red River, Ritchot asked Cartier who was to govern at Red River pending the arrival of the Lieutenant Governor. Cartier replied that Riel should "continue to maintain order and govern the country as he has done up to the present moment."[27] Cartier also gave Ritchot a letter stating that section 31 of the Manitoba Act would be implemented in such a way "as to meet the wishes of the Half-breed residents.[28]

Meanwhile, the uproar in Ontario and the news of the sending of an expeditionary force were causing some concern at Red River.[29] Men with experience recognized that whatever the Canadian authorities might say— and the Governor General had referred to it as an "errand of peace"—the purpose of the Force could only be punitive.[30] Riel was immediately under pressure to take steps to oppose it.[31] Riel, however, urged everyone to wait until they had heard the report of Father Ritchot. On June 17, the day of Ritchot's arrival by steamboat, the noise of the twenty-one-gun salute and the general jubilation surrounding his return made it a day that Gabriel Dumont never forgot.[32] Yet the news that there was no amnesty cast a shadow over affairs. Dumont and others were certain that the force was punitive and offered help to oppose it at certain key spots on the Winnipeg River. All the prestige that Riel had with these people was necessary to restrain them. The pressure on Riel was so great that on June 28, Bishop Taché left the Settlement on the steamboat *International*.[33] He had quieted the demands on Riel by declaring that he would go to Ottawa and press for an amnesty.[34]

The delegates had been promised an amnesty at the beginning of negotiations[35] and, with the Fenian attack repulsed and the Red River Expeditionary Force under way, Cartier, acting as prime minister during the illness of Macdonald, turned his attention to composing the memorandum which would accompany Father Ritchot's petition for it. This took up Cartier's evenings for more than a week. When he had finished he passed the memorandum to the office of the Governor General for transmission to London.[36] Sir John Young also forwarded to London a letter he had received from Dr. Lynch, one of the " Canadian" party at Red River, which asked that no amnesty be granted.[37] This, along with a note from Young saying that Cartier's memorandum should not be regarded as a minute of a united cabinet, deprived it of all force, and no action was taken.[38] There would be no amnesty.

When Sir Garnet Wolseley failed to send emissaries to the provisional government on August 23, 1870, and made prisoners of the emissaries sent by Riel, his Force ceased to be a "mission of peace" and became an invading army.[39] In so doing Wolseley broke his own word, as well as that of the Governor General, and carried out "Canada First" policy rather than official Canadian or British policy. Also his disposition of the militia units left in the new province carried out Schultz's policy—that the Métis would have to give way[40]—rather than making any serious attempts to maintain law and order.

What the St. Paul press described as a "reign of terror" lasted throughout the time that the Ontario Rifles were at Fort Garry, and caused Lieutenant Governor Archibald no end of trouble.[41] He attempted to put together a viable administration while knowing full well that the man who had the confidence of the majority of the people of the province—who should have been premier—was forced to remain in hiding.[42]

Riel and his supporters had only temporarily interrupted the carrying out of Canadian government policy. Having recuperated in Prince Edward Island and on the Parliament Hill grounds, Macdonald now turned to that policy again. On January 2, 1871, a committee of the Privy Council for Canada approved a memorandum of the Minister of Justice concerning the constitutionality of the Manitoba Act of 1870, and advised the Governor General "to move the Earl of Kimberley to submit to the Imperial Parliament a measure confirming the Act of the Canadian Parliament above referred to, and containing the other provisions enumerated in the said annexed memorandum." The basis for concern was stated to be that doubts had "been entertained respecting the powers of the Parliament of Canada to establish Provinces…"[43] In taking this high ground the Canadian government effectively concentrated the attention of British authorities upon Canada's competence as a new nation to legislate for its own territories. The Earl of Kimberley said, in introducing the bill in the House of Lords:

> The law officers of the Crown were of opinion that these acts [the North-West Territories Act and the Manitoba Act] were valid, as not beyond the powers of the Canadian Parliament: but doubts having been expressed the Canadian Parliament had addressed the Crown for an Act in the Imperial Parliament confirming their validity.[44]

The bill passed both Houses of Parliament of the United Kingdom without debate on 29 June 1871, not long before the end of the confrontation at Rivière aux Ilets de Bois.

This confrontation began in April when the emigration artificially induced by Charles Mair and "Canada First" began to reach Manitoba. It continued through May and June and into July, as Ontario farmers squatted on lands the Métis had looked forward to claiming under section 31 of the Manitoba Act. A less disciplined people would have slaughtered the intruders. However, the influence of Riel and the men in contact with him along with the assurances of Archibald prevented bloodshed, and the Métis had to give way to the Ontario newcomers.[45]

The two orders-in-council of April 25 and May 26 broke the word of Cartier, of Archibald, and of Riel and the men in contact with him. The people were left frustrated, bitter and angry. If, as Archibald pointed out to the Canadian government, there ever was a time when an indication of outside support could have meant abandonment of the Canadian connection by the Métis, this was that time. It was precisely then that word came that Riel's former associate O'Donoghue was on his way through Minnesota with a Fenian force of undisclosed strength.[46]

Archibald saw at once that the situation was critical. If the embittered Métis population between Winnipeg and the border were to rise in support of O'Donoghue and anything like a civil war were to break out, the Fenians among the Irish workers on the two railroads then being built in Minnesota could be attracted by the chance of plundering Fort Garry and Winnipeg. Manitoba could be lost to Canada.[47]

There were differences of opinion among the leaders of these Métis. Some, like John Bruce, saw an opportunity to bring about the annexation of Manitoba to the United States. However, beginning on 28 September, eleven of the men in contact with Riel met with him to discuss strategy. The first meeting lasted seven hours and ended with the decision to declare themselves in favor of the Canadian connection. Meetings were held in the Métis parishes, and in an agonizingly slow process the people were persuaded to give their support to Archibald and Canada. The culmination came on 8 October, when Archibald went to St. Boniface and accepted the support of Riel and his troops.[48] The Ontario press, following the lead of Schultz's *Liberal*, went wild in its denunciation of Archibald for shaking the "bloody hand" of Riel.[49] There were calls for Archibald's resignation and, indeed, when Archibald realized that the government was accepting the *Liberal*'s interpretation of events, his resignation was forwarded to Ottawa.

With the passing of the Dominion Lands Act in April of 1872, the last rivet was in place where federal government policy on the West was concerned. Far from giving the Métis the promised 1.4 million acres priority, the Act made "such lands as ... may be required to satisfy the ... claims created under Section 31" of the Manitoba Act subject to rights "defined or created under this Act."[50] Thus a volunteer who had come to Manitoba in August 1870 was as entitled to a grant of land as a Métis whose family had been in Rupert's Land for decades.

Remarkably enough, the situation in Manitoba in 1872 was not unlike what the arrogant and boastful young Canadians had predicted in the summer and fall of 1869 when the men of the Métis National Committee had been stung into taking action. The Métis were becoming hewers of wood and drawers of water, or were being forced to "give way" and dispersed into the vastness of the West. The chief resource of a province was under the control of a department located not in the provincial capital but in the distant federal capital, and headed by a man who had never seen either that land or the people living in it. To add insult to injury, the land was being used, not for the purposes of Manitoba but for the "purposes of the Dominion."[51] The people of Manitoba had striven to avoid this fate, and their efforts had resulted in so little violence that the whole affair looked peaceful when compared with contemporary popular movements elsewhere. Amnesty, however, was not part of government policy: an "indignation meeting" in Toronto had given a "direction to the settlement of affairs in Red River."[52] Accordingly, the man who should have been premier had to remain in hiding because a government formed by him might have asked awkward questions, and the Canadian government's subterfuge would have been revealed before the steps needed to make the Manitoba Act legal could be taken.

It can be seen now that the severe policies of "Canada First" actually worked in favour of the accomplishment of the policies of Cartier and Macdonald. These gentlemen were more interested in gaining the control and use of western lands for settlers and railway capitalists than they were in other considerations. So we may conclude that under their guidance our country took a wrong turn, a turn which has kept us divided for more than a century.

It is time now for us to look dispassionately at a man whom the Canadian government wronged. Louis Riel opted for Canada again and again, both when in power at Fort Garry and when in hiding in southern Manitoba. It is time for us to honour his memory.

Notes & References

References to Chapter 1

Ablon, J. 1964. "Relocated American Indians in the San Francisco Bay Area," *Human Organization* 23, no. 4: 296–304.

Bakker, P. 1997. *A Language of Our Own: The Genesis of Michif, the Mixed Cree-French Language of the Canadian Métis*. Oxford: Oxford University Press.

Brown, J.S.H. 1985. "Diverging Identities: The Presbyterian Métis of St. Gabriel Street, Montreal." Pp. 195–206 in J. Peterson and J.S.H. Brown, *The New Peoples: Being and Becoming Métis in North America*. Lincoln: University of Nebraska Press.

Campbell, M. 1973. *Halfbreed*. Toronto: McClelland and Stewart.

Card, B.Y., G.K. Hirabayashi and C.L. French. 1963. *The Métis in Alberta Society*. Edmonton: University of Alberta Committee for Social Research.

Cardinal, B. 2002. "Drawn to the Land: An Urban Métis Woman Makes her Connection." Pp. 69–76 in P. Douaud and B. Dawson, *Plain Speaking: Essays on Aboriginal Peoples and the Prairie*. Regina: Canadian Plains Research Center.

Cardinal, D. and G. Melnyk. 1977. *Of the Spirit*. Edmonton: NeWest Press.

Damon, A. 1965. "Stature Increase among Italian Americans: Environmental, Genetic, or Both?" *American Journal of Physical Anthropology* 23, no. 4: 401–08.

Daniels, H.W. (ed.). 1979a. *The Forgotten People: Métis and non-Status Indian Land Claims*. Ottawa: Native Council of Canada.

——. 1979b. *A Declaration of Métis and Indian Rights*. Ottawa: Native Council of Canada.

Dawson, B. 2002. "'Better Than a Few Squirrels': The Greater Production Campaign on the First Nations Reserves of the Canadian Prairies." Pp. 11–21 in P. Douaud and B. Dawson, *Plain Speaking: Essays on Aboriginal Peoples and the Prairie*. Regina: Canadian Plains Research Center.

Deloria, V. 1969. *Custer Died for Your Sins*. London: Macmillan.

De Trémaudan, A-H. 1979 [1935]. *Histoire de la nation métisse dans l'Ouest canadien*. Saint-Boniface, MB: Editions des plaines.

Dickason, O.P. 1980. "A Historical Reconstruction of the Northwestern Plains," *Prairie Forum* 5, no. 1: 19–37.

Dion, J.F. 1979. *My Tribe the Crees*. Calgary: Glenbow Institute.

Douaud, P. 1985. *Ethnolinguistic Profile of the Canadian Métis*. Ottawa: National Museums of Canada.

Douaud, P. and M. Cronin. 1992. "Irish Travellers in Search of an Identity," *Proactive* 11, no. 1: 26–33.

Douaud, P. and B. Dawson. 2002. *Plain Speaking: Essays on Aboriginal Peoples and the Prairie*. Regina: Canadian Plains Research Centre.

Drouin, E.O. 1968. *Joyau dans la plaine: Saint-Paul, Alberta*. Québec: Ferland.

Eccles, W.J. 1972. *France in America*. Vancouver: Fitzhenry and Whiteside.

Flanagan, T. 1979. *Louis "David" Riel: "Prophet of the New World."* Toronto: University of Toronto Press.

Foster, J.E. 1972. "Missionaries, Mixed Bloods, and the Fur Trade: Four Letters of the Rev. William Cockran, Red River Settlement, 1830–1833," *Western Canadian Journal of Anthropology* 3, no. 1: 94–125.

Fraser, A. 1992. *The Gypsies*. Oxford: Blackwell.

Frideres, J.S. 1974. *Canada's Indians: Contemporary Conflicts*. Scarborough, ON: Prentice-Hall.

Giraud, M. 1945. *Le Métis canadien: son rôle dans l'histoire des provinces de l'Ouest.* Paris: Institut d'Ethnologie.

Gray, C. 2004. *The Museum Called Canada.* Toronto: Random House.

Hiernaux, J. and N. Heintz. 1967. "Croissance biométrique des franco-vietnamiens," *Bulletins et mémoires de la Société d'anthropologie de Paris* 12, no. 1: 55–89.

Howard, J.K. 1974. *Strange Empire: Louis Riel and the Métis People.* Toronto: Lewis and Samuel.

Kirk, R.L. 1981. *Aboriginal Man Adapting.* Oxford: Oxford University Press.

Leacock, E.B. 1981. *Myths of Male Dominance.* New York: Monthly Review Press.

Le Treste, J., OMI. 1997. *Souvenirs d'un missionnaire breton dans le Nord-Ouest canadien.* Sillery, QC: Septentrion.

Luna, F. 1993. *Breve historia de los argentinos.* Buenos Aires: Planeta.

Manuel, G. and M. Posluns. 1974. *The Fourth World: An Indian Reality.* Don Mills, ON: Collier-MacMillan.

Marchildon, G. and S. Robinson. 2002. *Canoeing the Churchill: A Practical Guide to the Historic Voyageur Highway.* Regina: Canadian Plains Research Centre.

Morton, W.L. 1969. *The Kingdom of Canada.* Toronto: McClelland and Stewart.

Olivier, G. 1964. "Hétérosis et dominance dans les populations humaines," *Comptes-rendus hebdomadaires des séances de l'Académie des sciences* 259, no. 3: 4357–60.

Peterson, J. 1978. "Prelude to Red River: A Social Portrait of the Great Lakes Métis," *Ethnohistory* 25: 41–67.

Peterson, J. and J.S.H. Brown. 1985. *The New Peoples: Being and Becoming Métis in North America.* Lincoln: University of Nebraska Press.

Podruchny, C. 2006. *Making the Voyageur World.* Toronto: University of Toronto Press.

Preston, R.J. 1976. "Reticence and Self-Expression: A Study of Style in Social Relationships." Pp. 450–94 in W. Cowan (ed.), *Papers of the Seventh Algonquian Conference, 1975.* Ottawa: Carleton University Press.

Price, J.A. 1978. *Native Studies: American and Canadian Indians.* Toronto: McGraw-Hill.

Rivard, G. and P. Parker. 1975. *A Comparative Study of the Status of Indigenous Persons in Australia, Canada, and New Zealand.* Edmonton: University of Alberta mimeograph.

Scollon, R. and S.B.K. Scollon. 1979. *Linguistic Convergence: An Ethnography of Speaking at Fort Chipewyan, Alberta.* New York: Academic Press.

Sealey, D.B. and V.J. Kirkness (eds.). 1974. *Indians Without Tipis.* Agincourt, ON: Book Society of Canada.

Sealey, D.B. and A.S. Lussier. 1975. *The Métis: Canada's Forgotten People.* Winnipeg: Manitoba Métis Federation Press.

Sharp, P.F. 1973 [1955]. *Whoop-Up Country.* Norman: University of Oklahoma Press.

Siggins, M. 1994. *Riel: A Life of Revolution.* Toronto: HarperCollins.

Sprenger, G.H. 1972. "The Métis Nation: Buffalo Hunting vs. Agriculture in the Red River Settlement (circa 1810–1870)," *Western Canadian Journal of Anthropology* 3, no. 1: 158–78.

St-Onge, N. 2004. *Saint-Laurent, Manitoba: Evolving Métis Identities, 1850–1914.* Regina: Canadian Plains Research Center.

Stanley, G.F.G. 1963. *Louis Riel.* Toronto: McGraw-Hill and Ryerson.

Thompson, L. 1967. "Steps Toward a Unified Anthropology," *Current Anthropology* 8: 67–91.

Titley, E.B. 1979. "The Hawthorn Report and Indian Education Policy," *Canadian Journal of Native Education* 7, no. 1: 10–13.

Trevor, J.C. 1953. "Race Crossing in Man: The Analysis of Metrical Characters," *University of London Eugenic Laboratory Memoirs* 36.

Vandervort, B. 2006. *Indian Wars of Mexico, Canada and the United States, 1812–1900.* New York: Routledge.

Endnotes to Chapter 2

1. Joe Sawchuk, *The Métis of Manitoba: Reformulation of an Ethnic Identity* (Toronto: P. Martin Associates, 1978), contains an excellent discussion of this development as it relates currently to Manitoba.
2. See particularly J. Russell Harper (ed.), *Paul Kane's Frontier: Including Wanderings of an Artist Among the Indians of North America* (Austin, TX: University of Texas Press, 1971), 86, 142, 188, 189, 190, 191.
3. See Alexander Ross, *The Red River Settlement: Its Rise, Progress, and Present State. With Some Account of the Native Races and Its General History to the Present Day* (1856; Edmonton: Hurtig, 1972), 245–73.
4. See William Butler, *The Great Lone Land: A Narrative of Travel and Adventure in the Northwest of America* (1872; Edmonton: Hurtig, 1968), Appendix A, p. 386.
5. See Marcel Giraud, *Le Métis Canadien: son rôle dans l'histoire des provinces de l'Ouest* (Paris: Institut d'ethnologie, 1945), 669–92; E.E. Rich (ed.), *London Correspondence inward, from Eden Colvile, 1849–1852* (London: Hudson's Bay Record Society, 1956), Introduction by W.L. Morton. Professor Morton's introduction constitutes the most useful social history of the Red River Settlement in this period. As well, note J.E. Foster, "The Country-born in the Red River Settlement, 1820–1850" (PhD dissertation, University of Alberta, 1973).
6. See Giraud, *Le Métis Canadien*, 1002–41.
7. Trudy Nicks, "Iroquois and the Fur Trade in Western Canada" (unpublished paper, Fur Trade Conference, Winnipeg, 1978) constitutes the most recent and most useful scholarly study.
8. Ibid., 15.
9. Jacqueline Peterson, "Prelude to Red River: A Social Portrait of the Great Lakes Métis," *Ethnohistory* 24 no. 1 (Winter 1977): note 3.
10. Jennifer S.H. Brown, "Halfbreed, Squaw, and Other Categories: Some Semantic Shifts and their Implications in the Northwest Fur Trade, 1800–1850" (unpublished paper, Fur Trade Conference, Winnipeg, 1978). Dr. Brown's study is fundamental to any discussion on terminology bearing on the "mixed-bloods" in Western history.
11. For an explanation of the reasons for the use of this term see J.E. Foster, "The Origins of the Mixed Bloods in the Canadian West" in L.H. Thomas (ed.), *Essays on Western History: In Honour of Lewis Gwynne Thomas* (Edmonton: University of Alberta Press, 1976), 72–73. To date I have encountered "Rupert'slander" only in conversations with scholars seeking a more effective term for this socio-cultural entity.
12. J.M.S. Careless, "Frontierism, Metropolitanism and Canadian History," *Canadian Historical Review* 35, no. 1 (March 1954), details the historical explanation that frequently evokes the metropolitan perspective.
13. Perhaps the most useful examples are the scholarly treatments of Governor George Simpson. See A.S. Morton, *Sir George Simpson: Overseas Governor of the Hudson's Bay Company, a Pen Picture of a Man of Action* (Toronto: Dent, 1944), and J.S. Galbraith, *The Little Emperor: Governor Simpson of the Hudson's Bay Company* (Toronto: Macmillan of Canada), 1976.
14. A.J. Ray, *Indians in the Fur Trade: Their Role as Trappers, Hunters, and Middlemen in the Lands Southwest of Hudson Bay, 1660–1870* (Toronto: University of Toronto Press, 1974), 59–61, 85.

15. C.W. Cole, *Colbert and a Century of French Mercantilism* (Hamden, CT: Archon Books, 1939), 2 vols., and Eli F. Heckscher, *Mercantilism* (London: Allen & Unwin, 1935), 2 vols., present effective studies of the relationship between "commercial interests" and "the national interest" in this period. Also see W.J. Eccles, *The Canadian Frontier, 1534–1760* (Toronto: n.p., 1969), 130–31.

16. Eccles, *The Canadian Frontier*, 116.

17. R.J. Surtees, "The Development of an Indian Reserve Policy in Canada," in J.K. Johnson (ed.), *Historical Essays on Upper Canada* (Toronto: McClelland and Stewart, 1975), 262.

18. Giraud, *Le Métis Canadien*, 312–31. Also see Peterson, "Prelude to Red River."

19. Eccles, *The Canadian Frontier*, 190.

20. Ibid., 55, 57–59.

21. Ibid., 126, 131, 146–49.

22. Grace L. Nute, *The Voyageur* (1931; St. Paul: Minnesota Historical Society, 1955), 93.

23. Pierre Gaultier de Varennes, Sieur de la Verendrye and his sons and nephews are perhaps the most familiar example. As well see Peterson, "Prelude to Red River."

24. A quick perusal of E.E. Rich, *Journal of Ooccurrences in the Athabasca Department by George Simpson, 1820–1821, and Report* (Toronto: The Champlain Society, 1938), "Introduction" by Chester Martin, and materials in the Hudson's Bay Co. Archives such as the post journals, account books, and reports of the Athabasca country for the period 1800–1840 suggest politico-social strategies very similar to the Great Lakes trading families in an earlier period. Note particularly Hudson's Bay Company Archives (HBCA), B. 239/Z/12, York Factory Miscellaneous Items, 1838.

25. The patronyms of several Métis families, such as Sayer, Wilkie, Pongman, McGill and others attest to this development.

26. E.E. Rich, *The Fur Trade and the North West to 1857* (Toronto: McClelland and Stewart, 1967), 109.

27. Ibid.

28. Ray, *Indians in the Fur Trade*, 59-61.

29. J.E. Foster, "The Indian Trader in the Hudson Bay Fur Trade Tradition," in J. Freedman and J.H. Barkow (eds.), *Proceedings of the Second Congress, Canadian Ethnology Society*, Vol. II (Ottawa: National Museums of Canada, 1975), 578.

30. Brown, "Halfbreed, Squaw, and Other Categories," 15.

31. Ibid.

32. HBCA, A. 16/32, "York Servants Accounts, 1738–60," fo. 19, fo. 20.

33. HBCA, B. 239/a/49, "York Factory Journals," fo. 20, January 2–3, 1762.

34. J.E. Foster, "The Home-Guard Cree: The First Hundred Years," in D.A. Muise (ed.), *Approaches to Native History in Canada: Papers of a Conference Held at the National Museum of Man, October 1975* (Ottawa: National Museums of Canada, 1977), 59.

35. HBCA, B. 239/a/49. "York Factory Journals," fo. 20, January 2–3, 1762.

36. Ibid.

37. Brown, "Halfbreed, Squaw, and Other Categories," 4.

38. Ibid., 10–11.

39. Ross, *The Red River Settlement*, 273.

40. A.S. Morton, "The New Nation, The Métis," in *Transactions of the Royal Society of Canada*, Series III, Section 2 (Ottawa: Royal Society of Canada, 1939), 138–39.

41. Giraud, *Le Métis Canadien*, 968–73.

42. Robert Gosman, *The Riel and Lagimodière Families in Métis Society, 1840–1860* (Ottawa: National Historic Parks and Sites Branch, Parks Canada, Dept. of Indian and Northern Affairs, 1977), 1–3.

43. Giraud, *Le Métis Canadien*, 669–91, 1087.
44. Nicks, "Iroquois and the Fur Trade in Western Canada," 3–5.
45. Ibid., 13.
46. Ibid., 14–15.
47. Brown, "Halfbreed, Squaw, and Other Categories," 4.
48. Foster, "The Country-born in the Red River Settlement," 157–63.
49. Ibid., 203.
50. Ibid., 184.
51. Church Missionary Society Archives, Incoming Correspondence, Joseph Cook to the Lay Secretary, July 29, 1846.
52. Brown, "Halfbreed, Squaw, and Other Categories," 8–9.
53. Public Archives of Canada (PAC), MG 17, B1, D13, Society for the Propagation of the Gospel, Rupert's Land, 1850–59, Rev. D.T. Anderson to Rev. E. Hawkins, November 24, 1852.
54. Brown, "Halfbreed, Squaw, and Other Categories," 8–9.
55. PAC, MG 19, E6, Vol. 1, Thomas Cook to Rev. John Smithurst, January 30, 1853.
56. Foster, "The Origins of the Mixed Bloods in the Canadian West," 72.
57. Brown, "Halfbreed, Squaw, and Other Categories," 9–10.
58. Ibid., 4–5, 9–10.
59. Ibid.
60. Ibid.
61. Glyndwr Williams (ed.), *Hudson's Bay Miscellany, 1670–1870* (Winnipeg: n.p., 1975), 227. Initially Simpson had serious reservations concerning Sinclair's abilities.
62. Perhaps the most familiar was Simpson's cousin Chief Trader Thomas Simpson. See Alexander Simpson, *Life and Travels* (London: n.p., 1845).
63. Foster, "The Origins of the Mixed Bloods in the Canadian West," 79.

Endnotes to Chapter 3

1. This research was funded by a fellowship from the Kavanaugh-La Vérendrye Fund at St. Paul's College, University of Manitoba. The authors would like to thank Doug Fast, Geography Department, University of Manitoba, for his cartography on maps 1 and 2. Any errors or omissions are the responsibility of the authors.
2. "The Buffaloe" spelled with an "e" indicates a man rather than an animal. See the family tree of Alexander Henry the Younger in Barry Gough (ed.), *The Journal of Alexander Henry The Younger 1799–1814* (Toronto: Champlain Society, 1988), xx.
3. Linguist John Crawford, one of the first linguists to study the Michif language, also expressed amazement at the documented history of the Jerome family in 2003 which was not available when he taught Jerome's sister at the University of North Dakota Grand Forks in the 1980s. Personal communication, September 20, 2003. See Crawford, "Speaking Michif in Four Metis Communities," *Canadian Journal of Native Studies* 3, no. 1 (1983): 47–53. Other linguists such as Richard Rhodes, David Pentland and Peter Bakker have since expanded the study of this mixed language composed of French nouns and Cree verbs, the language of the bison hunters.
4. Swan and Jerome, "The Collin Family at Thunder Bay: A Case Study of *Metissage*," in David Pentland (ed.), *Papers of the 19th Algonquian Conference* (Winnipeg: University of Manitoba, 1998), 311–21. Swan and Jerome, "The History of the Pembina Metis Cemetery: Inter-Ethnic Perspectives on a Sacred Site," *Plains Anthropologist* 44, no. 170 (1999): 81–94. Swan and Jerome, "Unequal Justice: The Metis in O'Donoghue's Raid of 1871," *Manitoba History* 39 (Spring-Summer 2000): 24–38. Swan and Jerome, "A Mother and Father of Pembina: A NWC Voyageur Meets the Granddaughter of The Buffaloe,"

in John Nichols (ed.), *Actes du 32ème des Algonquinistes* (Winnipeg: University of Manitoba, 2001), 527–51. Ruth Swan, "The Crucible: Pembina and the Origins of the Red River Valley Métis" (Ph.D. dissertation, University of Manitoba, 2003).

5. Jacqueline Peterson, "Prelude to Red River: A Social Portrait of the Great Lakes Métis," *Ethnohistory* 25, no. 1 (Winter 1978): 41–67. Jacqueline Peterson, "The People in Between: Indian-White Marriage and the Genesis of a Métis Society and Culture in the Great Lakes Region, 1680–1830" (Ph.D. dissertation, University of Illinois at Chicago, 1981).

6. A.S. Morton, "La Verendrye: Commandant, Fur-trader, and Explorer," *Canadian Historical Review* (*CHR*) 9: 284–98.

7. Jean Delanglez, "A Mirage: The Sea of the West," *RHAF* 1, no. 2 (1947–48): 541–68. Malcolm Lewis argued that the Sea of the West was not a myth, but a series of mistaken interpretations. See Lewis, "La Gande Rivière et Fleuve de l'Ouest: The Realities and Reasons Behind a Major Mistake in the 18th-Century Geography of North America," *Cartographica* 1 (Spring 1991) 54–87.

8. Lawrence J. Burpee (ed.), *Journals and Letters of Pierre Gaultier de Varennes de la Vérendrye and his Sons* (Toronto: Champlain Society, 1927). The search for the Western Sea is discussed in the biography by Yves Zoltvany, "Pierre, Gaultier de Varennes et de la Vérendrye," *Dictionary of Canadian Biography* (*DCB*), vol. 3 (Quebec and Toronto: Universities of Laval and Toronto, 1974), 247–54.

9. Nellis Crouse, "The Location of Fort Maurepas," *CHR* 9 (1928): 206–22.

10. Gerald Friesen, *The Canadian Prairies: A History* (Toronto: University of Toronto Press, 1984), 53–54. A.J. Ray gives slightly different dates for the establishment of these posts. See Ray, *Indians in the Fur Trade* (Toronto: University of Toronto Press, 1974), 56, Figure 18.

11. Yves Zoltvany, *DCB*, on Pierre Gaultier, Sieur de la Vérendrye, vol. 3. See also Kathryn Young and Gerald Friesen, "La Vérendrye & the French Empire in Western North America," in *River Road: Essays on Manitoba and Praire History* (Winnipeg: University of Manitoba Press, 1996), 16.

12. André Vachon, "Antoine Adhémar de Saint-Martin," *DCB*, vol. 2 (Toronto: University of Toronto Press, 1969), 10–11. Jean-Guy Pelletier, "Jean Baptiste Amable Adhémar," *DCB*, vol. 4: 5–8.

13. René Jetté, *Dictionnaire génealogique des familles du Québec des origines à 1730* (Montreal: Les Presses de l'Université de Montréal, 1983), 598: "Jerome *dit* Beaune, Leblanc et Latour, François, de … Bretagne, 30 ans en 1705; cited 18–11–1698 à Montreal; sergeant de la compagnie de Le Verrier." C. Tanguay, *Dictionnaire Génealogique des Familles Canadiennes*, vol. 2 (Montreal: 1887), 173: "Marriage of François-Jérôme Beaume, [father of François Jr.] b. 1675, de St. Médrias, diocèse de St. Malo [France] and Angèlique Dardenne, b. 1682, 3 novembre, 1705, Montréal." A footnote suggests that his names are "Leblanc *dit* Latour, sergent de M. Leverrier." On page 602 with the Jerome family genealogy, the footnote for François Jerome suggests "Son vrai nom est Beaume." Sometimes, this name was printed "Beaune" or "Bone." In the next generation, that surname was dropped and the son was known as "François Jérôme *dit* Latour." Tanguay lists Jerome family surnames: Baumeleblanc, Beaume, Beaumeleblanc, De la Tour, Latour, Leblanc, Longtin, Patry, Rivière.

14. Jérôme's first voyageur contract is recorded in the Archives Nationales du Québec (ANQ): "François Jerome *dit* Latour, 13 mai, 1727, Notaire: Jean Baptiste Adhémar #3600."

15. See Hudson Bay Company Archives (HBCA) Search File, Gerome Family: Fort Carlton

District Report, B.27/e/2, fo. 2d, May 28, 1819. January 30, 1822: "Samart Gerome and Battoches Son [Letendre] arrived from Dog Rump Creek's House…" Martin Jerome was also known as "St. Martin Jerome" or "St. Matte Jerome" after he moved to Red River Settlement in the 1820s; see for example Census Returns, Red River Settlement (HBCA: E.5/2, #906, 1828 Census: St. Martin Jerome, age 28). This tradition was carried on in Red River by Martin's son, André Jerome and his sons. Also, National Archives of Canada (NA), R.G. 15, v. 1505, General Index to Manitoba and NWT Half-Breeds and Original White Settlers, 1885: 8 children listed of André St. Mathe and Marguerite Gosselin, listed in Ste. Agathe Parish. Public Notices of "Children of Half-breeds" also list the children of André Jerome and Marguerite Gosselin as "St. Mathe" and "Martin Jérome alias St. Math"; Provincial Archives of Manitiba (PAM), MG4 D13. In PAM, MG2-B4-1: District of Assiniboia, General Quarterly Court: "André Jerome St. Matthe, found not guilty on charge of levying war against the Crown; charged 24 November, 1871." In Red River, the family was more commonly known as "St. Mathe" than "Jerome" which can make it difficult to follow them in the records.

16. Tanguay, *Dictionnaire Généalogique des Familles Canadiennes*, Jerome Genealogy, p. 603. This volume includes Jerome entries to 1785.

17. Voyageur contract information is published in the Rapport de l'Archiviste de la Province de Quebec (RAPQ). The Detroit contracts were for François Bone/Baune/Beaune. The complete name in the voyageur contract has been included to show how François was identified in the records, as there is some variety. But genealogical sources such as Tanguay and Jetté suggest they were the same person. His father François Sr. was too old to carry on this type of energetic livelihood.

18. RAPQ, "Sea of the West" (1929–30), 429. In a report on "La Famille Jerome," Alfred Fortier, Director of the St. Boniface Historical Society (SHSB), mentioned that the Jerome family was present in the Canadian West for about 250 years, citing François's contract to sieur de la Vérendrye in 1743 to look for the Sea of the West. He also cited various North West Company (NWC) references as in David Thompson, Masson and Alexander Henry the Younger to Jeromes along the Saskatchewan River. Fortier began his Jerome Genealogy with Martin Jerome Sr., married to Louise Amerindian, parents of Martin Jr. (born about 1800) and Marie-Louise (born 1803), who moved to the Red River Settlement in the 1820s. "La Famille Jerome," *Bulletin, La Société Historique de Saint-Boniface* 4 (été 1993): 5. Edward Jerome had previously researched this information when he brought the family to Fortier's attention.

19. RAPQ, "La Reine and Dauphin" (1922–23): 219–20. Clifford Wilson, "La Vérendrye Reaches the Saskatchewan," *CHR* 33, no. 1 (1952): 39–49.

20. Crouse disputes the location of this post, which may have been near the mouth of the Red or on the Winnipeg River; "The Location of Fort Maurepas," *CHR* 9 (1928): 206–22.

21. RAPQ, "Maurrepas and La Reine" (1922–23): 238.

22. RAPQ, "Wabash" (1931–32): 237.

23. RAPQ, "Beaumayer to Michilimackinac" (1931–32): 352. St. Michel likewise, same volume, p. 351.

24. Yves Zoltvany, "Pierre Gaultier de Varennes et de La Vérendrye," *DCB*, vol. 3: 252.

25. Antoine Champagne, "Louis Joseph Gaultier de La Vérendrye," *DCB*, vol. 3: 242.

26. A.S. Morton, *A History of the Canadian West to 1870–71* (London: Thomas Nelson and Sons, 1939), 233: "In 1742–43, [le Chevalier] and his brother François made their final, if mistaken, attempt to reach the Sea of the West with the assistance of the Gens des Chevaux."

27. Smith, G. Hubert, *The Explorations of the La Vérendryes in the Northern Plains, 1738–43*

(edited by Raymond Wood) (Lincoln: University of Nebraska Press, 1980). Malcolm Lewis, "La Grande Rivière et Fleuve de l'Ouest: The Realities and Reasons Behind a Major Mistake in the 18th Century Geography of North America," *Cartographica* 1 (Spring 1991): 54–87.

28. Morton, *A History of the Canadian West*, 230–31.

29. Champagne, "Louis Joseph Gaultier de La Vérendrye," 241–44.

30. According to Antoine Champagne in his *DCB* biography of Louis Joseph Gaultier de La Vérendrye (Le Chevalier) (*DCB*, Vol. 3: 243–44), he was active in the fur trade on Lake Superior. He went to Michilimackinac and Grand Portage in the spring of 1750 to pay his men and obtain the furs to pay his father's debts. In 1752, he was in charge of Chagouamigon (Ashland, Wisconsin) on the southwest shore of Lake Superior. In 1756, he was made commandant of the poste de l'Ouest and operated out of Michipicoten and Kaministiquia. He drowned off the coast of Cape Breton in November 1762.

31. HBCA, A.11/114, fos. 130–131; York Factory Journal, May 17, 1749, correspondence copied by John Newton, Master. Newton copied a translation of François Jérôme's letter into his journal. It is not the original in French, but it is contemporary and documents his trading activity at Fort Bourbon.

32. Morton, *A History of the Canadian West*, 231.

33. Joan Craig, "John Newton," *DCB*, vol. 3: 482–83. Newton later became famous as the composer of the hymn "Amazing Grace," written after his conversion to Christianity. Having been the captain of African slave ships, the piece expressed his need for redemption.

34. A.J. Ray, *Indians in the Fur Trade* (Toronto: University of Toronto Press, 1974), 89–91. Barbara Belyea, *A Year Inland: The Journal of a Hudson's Bay Company Winterer* (Waterloo: Wilfred Laurier University Press, 2000). Belyea compares four manuscript versions of Anthony Henday's journal, suggesting that there was another "original" source.

35. Note: Friesen erred in his naming of these forts. "Fort la Corne" was Fort St. Louis, established by Louis Chaput, Chevalier de la Corne during the French regime. He was made commandant of the Western Posts in 1753 and according to Morton, "built a new post (possibly with 200 yards on the Fort La Jonquière of 1751) on the Saskatchewan. It stood on the fine alluvial flat on which the HBC built their Fort à la Corne towards the middle of the 19th century. Its remains lie a mile west of the site of the Company's post. It was no more than an outpost of Fort Paskoyac. Fort St. Louis, as La Corne's post was called, was visited by Anthony Henday on his return." A.S. Morton, *A History of the Canadian West*, 238. To clarify these names, Fort St. Louis was the French name before 1763 and Fort à la Corne was the British name for the HBC post.

36. Gerald Friesen, *The Canadian Prairies: A History* (Toronto: University of Toronto Press, 1984), 56. Although Henday did not give a name to the French fort west of "basquea house," it was probably "Fort St. Louis" which was established by Luc à la Corne. This name was later adopted by the HBC in the 1800s in the same vicinity. See map in end of Dale Russell's *Eighteenth Century Western Cree and Their Neighbours*, Archaeological Survery of Canada, Mercury Series Paper 143 (Ottawa: Canadian Museum of Civilization, 1991).

37. Belyea, *A Year Inland*, 188: E.2/II, May 29, 1755, on the return to York.

38. A.J. Ray, *Indians in the Fur Trade*, 91.

39. Belyea, *A Year Inland*, 187: E.2/II, May 25, 1755.

40. Friesen, *The Canadian Prairies*, 56. He based this observation on the comments of A.S. Morton who was critical of the HBC for not building interior posts during the French regime. Morton saw the fur trade as a contest of European empires, battling for

territory: "True to Britain's form, it refused to prepare for the renewal of the crisis [competition with Montreal traders after 1763], and ... it had to develop its organization ... after the way had broken out, slowly, painfully, and ... with great losses." *A History of the Canadian West*, 251–52. For a discussion of the problems of editing the various versions of Henday's journal, see Glyndwyr Williams, "The Puzzle of Anthony Henday's Journal," *The Beaver* 309 (Winter 1978): 41–56.

41. W.S. Wallace, *The Pedlars from Quebec* (Toronto: Ryerson, 1954), 13.

42. Many of these inland traders who travelled with the Cree returned with over 60 canoes full of furs and they succeeded in persuading some of the Blackfeet to trade at the Bay. Morton reported that some of the French traders were reckless in their use of alcohol and were stealing native women which resulted in several attacks on their posts and several deaths. It may have been the fear of these Indian attacks which inhibited HBC masters from building forts in the interior. Morton, *A History of the Canadian West*, 252–53. Jennifer S.H. Brown made the same argument in *Strangers in Blood: Fur Trade Company Families in Indian Country* (Vancouver: University of British Columbia Press, 1980), 82. Readers should be aware that Morton's opinions tended to be anti-French and these behaviours he ascribed to French Canadian voyageurs were shared by HBC men at the bayside posts; for example, Joseph Hemmings Cook was accused of keeping three Indian women under lock and key in his apartment at York Factory, suggesting they were sex slaves (Charles Bourke, PAM, MG2A1: copy of Selkirk Papers, v. 67: 17868, May 1, 1812). The amount of abuse is difficult to estimate because it was not well documented. It could also have been exaggerated as voyageurs like Jean Baptiste Collin in Red River kept to one wife; see Swan and Jerome: "A NWC Voyageur Meets the Daughter of The Buffaloe," *Papers of the Algonquian Conference* (2001), 527–51.

43. See Clifford Wilson, "Anthony Henday" in *DCB* vol. 3 (1974), 285–87. Henday was credited with being the first European to visit Alberta and see the Rocky Mountains, but the latter claim is disputed by modern historians like Glyndwyr Williams and Barbara Belyea. Because historians rely on documentary evidence and most of French exploration was not documented, except for the La Vérendrye expeditions, their accomplishments are unknown. And the fact is that all these outsiders depended on Indian guides who are usually invisible. Neither Henday's *DCB* biographer Wilson or A.J. Ray mentioned Henday's Cree guides, Attickashish [Little Deer] and Connawappa. See Belyea, *A Year Inland*, 345–46.

44. A.S. Morton, *A History of the Canadian West*, 254.

45. *RAPQ* (1931–32): 237, voyageur contract.

46. A.S. Morton, *A History of the Canadian West*, 254.

47. W.S. Wallace, *The Pedlars from Quebec* (Toronto: Ryerson, 1954), 7–10. On May 16, 1769, William Pink from York Factory reported that he met the English Canadian trader James Finlay on the Saskatchewan and planned to take his furs back to Montreal, but two men were left at the "lower house" to trade for the winter. Thomas Corry came from Michilimackinac and wintered at Cedar Lake below Pasquia, then took his furs to Grand Portage. Corry spent a second year on the Saskatchewan and then returned to Montreal, making such a fortune that he was able to retire from the trade.

48. According to Antoine Champagne, Le Chevalier (Louis-Joseph Gaultier de La Vérendrye) obtained permission in the the spring of 1750, after his father's death, to go to Michilimackinac and Grand Portage, "to meet the canoes coming from the west, in order to settle his father's business." He expected to be made commandant of the Western Posts, but did not receive the appointment. In 1752, he was appointed to the post of Chegouamigon (Ashland, Wisconsin, on the southwest shore of Lake Superior)

to conduct the fur trade, but conflicted with other French officers. In 1756, he was given commandant of the *poste de l'Ouest* and remained in the Lake Superior area; the trade became free and he had to buy the appointment. *DCB*, vol. 3: 243.

49. Charles Lart, "Fur Trade Returns, 1767," *CHR* 3 (1922): 351–58. British General Benjamen Roberts, Superintendant at Michilimackinac, wrote in 1767: "This being the first year the traders were permitted to winter amongst the Indians at their Villages and Hunting Grounds, it was fd. Necessary they shld. Enter into fresh security with the Commissary, of this, the only post they had liberty to winter from, for it frequently hapned [*sic*] they made of [*sic*] with their goods, by the Mississipi, and cheated the English Merchants, besides they were restricted from trading with Nations that misbehaved." Presumably if traders went west of this post before 1767, they were operating illegally i.e. without the sanction of the British authorities in the Great Lakes. This illegal trade has not been documented to this point.

50. W.S. Wallace, "The Pedlars from Quebec," *CHR* 13 (1932): 388.

51. A.S. Morton, "Forrest Oakes, Charles Boyer, Joseph Fulton and Peter Pangman in the North West, 1765–1793," *Transactions Royal Society of Canada* (*TRSC*) 2 (1937), 89.

52. HBCA: York Factory Journal: B.239/a/56, William Pink's first expedition, May 16 and May 31, 1767. The Indians told Pink that the first house they passed had been where the French resided 10 years earlier (in 1757) and a second site, seven years earlier (1760). They predicted that "five large canews" would be returning that summer or fall. This oral history suggests that French traders continued to trade in the interior despite the British take-over in 1763.

53. Lart, "Fur Trade Returns," 353. Louis Menard would later be found as a free trader out of the Brandon area trading goods to the Mandan on the Missouri, see W. Raymond Wood and T.D. Thiessen, *Early Fur Trade on the Northern Plains* (Norman: University of Oklahoma Press, 1985), 43–44.

54. A.S. Morton, *A History of the Canadian West*, 268.

55. C. Tanguay, *Dictionnaire Généalogique*, "Jerome," 602–3.

56. August 7, 1767: "This Day Mr. Francis (La Blonc, a trader from Michilimackinac) bound to the northwest, came in and brought some letters from Major Rogers by which we understood we was to have no supplys this year from him…" In John Parker (ed.), *The Journals of Jonathan Carver* (Saint Paul: Minnesota Historical Society Press, 1976), 132. A footnote says that François Le Blanc, also known as "Mr. Franceways" or Le Blancell took six canoes from Michilimackinac to Forts Dauphn and Des Prairies (on the Saskatchewan) in 1767; Marjorie Campbell identified him as an associate of Isaac Todd and James McGill of Montreal and the first trader to reach Lake Winnipeg after 1763. Rogers's letter is published on page 198. A manuscript copy in the British Museum identifies the trader as "Mr. François." C.P. Stacey's biography of Robert Rogers, commandant at Michilimackinac, suggests they were looking for the northwest passage, but were unsuccessful. *DCB*, vol. 4 (1979), 681.

57. The Indians told Tomison there were two houses on Red River, one commanded by an Englishman named Wapestan and a Frenchman named Paquatick. A.S. Morton guessed that these men were Forrest Oakes and Charles Boyer; the latter had been previously on the Rainy River. They also said there were three forts to the westward. In 1767, Thomas Corry, one of the earliest British traders on the Saskatchewan, built the Fort du Milieu on the Assiniboine and Forrest Oakes built the Pine Fort in 1768. The other two earliest British traders were Joseph Fulton and Peter Pangman. See "Forrest Oakes, Charles Boyer, Joseph Fulton and Peter Pangman in the North-West, 1765–1793," *TRSC* 2 (1937), 87–100. The Indians at Rainy Lake plundered Oakes and Boyer in 1765, and it was perhaps this incident which prevented François from getting to the Saskatchewan that year.

58. HBCA: Fort Severn Post Journal: B.198/a/10, June 16, 1767; Tomison's inland journey.

59. John Nicks, "William Tomison," *DCB*, vol 6: 775–77.

60. HBCA: Fort Severn Post Journal, B.198/a/10, 1767–78, October 2, 1767. Cited by Victor P. Lytwyn, *The Fur Trade of the Little North: Indians, Pedlars and Englishmen East of Lake Winnipeg, 1760–1821* (Winnipeg: Rupert's Land Research Centre, University of Winnipeg, 1986), 25–26. See Jonathan Carver's details about the dress of Indianized Frenchmen at Detroit, which are similar, in Parker (ed.), *The Journals of Jonathan Carver*, 66.

61. Archaeologists Alice Kehoe and David Meyer placed François's house near Nipawin, Saskatchewan. See *François' House: An Early Fur Trade Post on the Saskatchewan River* (Regina: Saskatchewan Culture and Youth, 1978), map, Figure 2. Olga Klimko, "The Grant, McLeod, Neufeld Sawmill and Loos Cabin Sites," in David Burley (ed.), *Nipawin Reservoir Heritage Study*, vol. 9 (Saskatoon: Saskatchewan Research Council, 1987), Figure 1.2: Locations of Some Fur Trade Posts on the Upper Saskatchewan River. The François-Finlay Post is upriver from Nipawin.

62. HBCA: York Factory Journal, B.239/a/58, 1767–68, Pink's second journey inland.

63. HBCA: B.239/a/61, 1768–69, May 16, 1769. Pink's third journey inland.

64. Around 1792, a French Canadian named Toussaint Lesieur established what would become a very important provisioning post at the mouth of the Winnipeg River, called Bas de la Rivière Winipic. When the HBC took it over in 1832, they called it Fort Alexander.

65. See Ray, *Indians in the Fur Trade*, 129, Figure 39: Fur Trade Provision Supply Network in the Early 19th Century. Fort Bas de la Rivière and Cumberland House are shown as the two major provisionings posts for the NWC and HBC.

66. See "Saswaus [*sic*] House" on "A Plan of Part of Hudson's Bay and Rivers Communicating with the Principal Settlements by Andrew Graham," in John Warkentin and Richard Ruggles (eds.), *Manitoba Historical Atlas* (Winnipeg: Historical and Scientific Society of Manitoba, 1970), 94.

67. HBCA: York Factory Journal: B.239/a/69: August 23, 1772.

68. "Peter Pangman," *DCB*, vol. 5: 656–57.

69. HBCA: York Factory Journal: B.239/a/69, Ma 20–23, 1773, Mathew Cocking's Journal.

70. Morton, *A History of the Canadian West*, 286. The anti-French bias in primary sources such as Cocking's journal and HBCA post journals persisted in later historical writing. Although people like W.L. Morton could not be described as anti-French, he, like A.S. Morton, tended to emphasize the British traders who entered the North West after 1763 as the British replaced the French bourgeois in the upper levels of the Canadian partnerships. For example, W.L. Morton wrote: "In 1768 James Finlay was on the Saskatchewan, and in 1771 Thomas Corry. The new Northwest traders had all but reoccupied the former fur domain of the French." He did not mention the French Canadian traders like Franceway, Louis Primeau and Charles Boyer. See W.L. Morton, *Manitoba: A History* (Toronto: University of Toronto Press, 1957, 1979), 38. The idea of British replacement after 1760 is reiterated in Plate 61: "Competition and Consolidation, 1760–1825" in the *Historical Atlas of Canada*, vol. 1 (Toronto: University of Toronto Press, 1987).

71. Giraud, *The Metis in the Canadian West*, vol. 1, 584, note 328, cites Thomas Hutchins, Albany Fort, HBCA: A.11/3, p. 29, July 5, 1776. Giraud argued that adoption of native customs by the French helped strengthen their trading relationships with the natives. The French Canadians even adopted powers of divination to impress their customers. See also Bruce White, "Encounters with Spirits: Ojibwa and Dakota theories about the French and their Merchandise," *Ethnohistory* 41, no. 30 (Summer 1994): 369–406. British traders like Cocking found the close ties between French Canadian traders and their Native customers difficult to understand.

72. HBCA: York Factory Journal: B.239/a/69: Cocking's Journal.

73. Bruce White wrote extensively about the symbolic nature of fur trade rituals and argued that the Ojibwe around the Great Lakes perceived French traders, with practical material goods like metal objects and cloth, as other-than-human persons, god-like creatures, with special magical powers whom they called "esprits" (spirits). See White, "Encounters with Spirits."

74 HBCA: B.239/a/69: Cocking's York Factory Journal, August 23, 1772. "They showed me some Brazil Tobacco, saying it was traded from [Thomas] Correy, he had but a small quantity left when they see him, most of it being expended before; however, he traded it at the same rate as the Company's Standard. Virginia Leaf a large Brick as a six Beaver coat. Vermilion, awls, etc., given gratis, also cloathing, several." The most lucrative trade good was alcohol. For the ritual use of alcohol in the trade, see Bruce White, "'Give Us a Little Milk'," *Minnesota History* (Summer 1982): 60–71.

75. Morton, *A History of the Canadian West*, 289.

76. Lytwyn, *The Fur Trade of the Little North*, 11. Cocking also suggested that Franceway had been in the North West among the Indians for 30 years.

77. A.J. Ray, "William Holmes," *DCB* vol. 4: 365–66. In J.B. Tyrrell (ed.), *The Journals of Samuel Hearne and Philip Turnor* (Toronto: Champlain Society, 193), 120, Tyrrell quoted a letter from Samuel Hearne at Cumberland House, October 9, 1774: "Messrs. Paterson and Franceway came in the other Canoe out of curiosity."

78. Morton, *A History of the Canadian West*, 305. Morton cited the Cumberland House Journal, December 16, 1774, as mentioning: "Messrs Paterson Homes and Franceways houses"; two more, probably three, posts were now in operation, presumably Isaac's House (established by Isaac Batt), and one or two of the three contiguous forts some 23 miles farther upstream and about two miles above the present La Corne. Morton estimated they had about 160 men, compared to the eight that Hearne had for the HBC.

79. Ibid., 311.

80. W.S. Wallace, *Documents Relating to the North West Company* (Toronto: Champlain Society, 1934), 45. "Extract of Cocking's Journal, January 22, 1776: 'The Pedler Franceway who has been many Years Trading in these Parts being superanuated is retired'."

81. Tyrrell, *Journals of Hearne and Turnor*, 120, note about François retiring to Detroit.

82. We drop the French accents on "Jerome" with Pierre as he appeared to spend most of his adult life along the Saskatchewan.

83. L.R. Masson, *Les Bourgeois de la Compagnie du Nord-Ouest: lettres et rapports inédits relatifs au Nord-Ouest canadien*, vol. 1 (New York: Antiquarian Press, 1960), 63 and 397, at Fort des Prairies. It is possible that this Cree interpreter was Martin Jerome Sr. as Pierre would have been 60 years old in 1800.

84. E. Coues (ed.), *The Manuscript Journals of Alexander Henry and of David Thompson, 1799–1814*, vol. 2 (Minneapolis: Ross and Haines, 1897), 544. In a footnote, Coues stated: "Mr. Jerome, Jerome or Gerome, of the NWC, was at Fort George with John Mcdonald and Mr. Decoigne, in September 1798, but interpreters are not usually given any title." Co-author Edward Jerome suggests that the "M. Jerome" may have been Martin Jerome, not Monsieur Jerome. Also by Alfred Fortier: "David Thompson cite un M. Jérôme au Fort George, le 18 septembre 1798; un M. Gérôme est interprète pour la NWC au Fort-des-Prairies en 1804." *Bulletin, SHSB* 4 (1993): 5.

85. HBCA: Carlton House Post Journal, B.27/a/11 and district report, B.239/a/1, fo. 50.

86. Tanguay's *Dictionnaire Généalogique* (p. 603) suggests that a Pierre Jerome married in 1840, so that he could have had a son Pierre a year or two later, about the right age of the Pierre who died at Carlton House in 1821.

87. Coues, Henry's *Manuscript Journals of Alexander Henry and of David Thompson*, vol. 2: 545, 584, 587, and 599.

88. Ibid., 555 and 603.

89. HBCA: Carlton House Post Journal: B.27/a/11 and 12 for these dates.

90. E.E. Rich and H. Fleming (eds.), *Colin Robertson's Correspondence Book, 1817–1822* (Toronto: Champlain Society, 1939), 194.

91. HBCA: E.5/2, fo. 8d-9; and E.5/3, fos. 10d-11; E.5/4 and E.5/5.

92. This idea challenges the argument of Cornelius Jaenen that the French failed in assimilating the Amerindians into a new society. Although the Métis were not "assimilated" Frenchmen, they created a new plains or Western culture which spread French Canadian cultural influence around the North West, not by colonial power but by intermarriage. See "The Meeting of the French and Amerindians in the Seventeenth Century," in J.M. Bumsted (ed.), *Interpreting Canada's Past*, vol. 1 (Toronto: Oxford University Press), 27–39.

93. Tanguay, *Dictionnaire Généalogique*, 602–3.

94. Alfred Fortier, Director of the Société Historique de St. Boniface (SHSB) suggested this link in his Jerome family genealogy, which starts with Martin Sr. Bulletin. See *SHSB* 4 (été 1993): 5.

95. Foster's argument was in opposition to the gender analysis of two feminist historians, Sylvia Van Kirk and Jennifer Brown, who argued that Métis identity was linked to the Native mothers who were left to raise their children when their husbands returned to eastern Canada or Europe when they retired. Van Kirk and Brown's argument applied mainly to the officer class and not the voyageurs.

96. John Foster, "Wintering, the Outsider Adult Male and the Ethnogenesis of the Western Plains Metis," *Prairie Forum* 19, no. 1 (Spring 1994): 1–13.

97. Ray, *Indians in the Fur Trade*, 131. Thanks to Toby Morantz for this suggestion, personal communication, October 25, 2003, 35th Algonquian Conference, London, Ontario.

Endnotes to Chapter 4

The author would like to thank the Hudson's Bay Company for permission to consult and quote from its archives. I would also like to thank D.W. Moodie and Keith Ralston for commenting on earlier drafts of this paper. Of course the author is responsible for opinions expressed. Bison have been referred to throughout this paper as buffalo in keeping with historical practices. The term mixed-blood is used for the same reasons.

1. Arthur J. Ray, *Indians in the Fur Trade* (Toronto: University of Toronto Press, 1974), 131–35.

2. Numerous accounts of this process exist. For a recently published observation see G. Charette, *Vanishing Spaces: Memoirs of Louis Goulet*, edited and translated by R. Ellenwood (Winnipeg: Editions Bois-Brûlés, 1980), 55.

3. Ibid., 56.

4. Given this practise, B. Gordon has cautioned against using the hunting schedule of the Métis as a model for the Indians. See, B. Gordon, *Of Men and Herds in Canadian Plains Prehistory* (Ottawa: National Museum of Canada, 1979).

5. Ray, *Indians in the Fur Trade*, 87–89.

6. See, for example, Thomas Kehoe, *The Gull Lake Site* (Ottawa: National Museum of Man, 1973), 22–50.

7. Ibid., 195.

8. Charette, *Vanishing Spaces*, 55, and Alexander Ross, *The Red River Settlement* (Minneapolis: n.p., 1972), 257.

9. Ross, *The Red River Settlement*, 257.

10. Ibid., 256–57.

11. For a discussion of the spread of horses in this area, see Ray, *Indians in the Fur Trade*, 156–62.

12. A.J. Russell, *The Red River Country, Hudson's Bay & North-West Territories Considered in Relation to Canada* (Ottawa: G.E. Desbarats, 1869), 194.

13. L. Ugarenko, "The Beaver Indians and the Peace River Fur Trade, 1700–1850" (MA thesis, York University, 1979), 80–87.

14. For a discussion of this episode, see A.S. Morton, *A History of the Canadian West to 1870–71*, 2nd ed. (Toronto: published in cooperation with University of Saskatchewan by University of Toronto Press, 1973), 537–72.

15. J.J. Hargrave, *Red River* (Montreal: printed for the author by J. Lovell, 1870), 168.

16. C. Sprenger, "The Métis Nation: The Buffalo Hunt vs. Agriculture in the Red River Settlement, ca. 1810–70," *Western Canadian Journal of Anthropology* 3, no. 1 (1972): 159–78.

17. Hargrave, *Red River*, 175–76.

18. Ross, *The Red River Settlement*, 113–14 and 120–24.

19. Ray, *Indians in the Fur Trade*, 132.

20. C.M. Judd, *Lower Fort Garry, The Fur Trade and the Settlement at Red River* (Ottawa: Parks Canada, 1976), Appendix E: 313.

21. Charette, *Vanishing Spaces*, 53.

22. Ray, *Indians in the Fur Trade*, 131.

23. F.G. Roe, *The North American Buffalo*, 2nd ed. (Toronto: University of Toronto Press, 1972), 373–76 and 860–61.

24. Ray, *Indians in the Fur Trade*, 131.

25. Hudson's Bay Company Ration schedules are contained in "Standing Rules and Regulations, Northern Department, 1843–70," Public Archives of British Columbia, Add MSS 220. Red River census data are contained in *Censuses of Canada, 1665–1871*, Statistics Canada, Vol. 4 (Ottawa: Queen's Printer, 1876).

26. Hudson's Bay Company Archives, Public Archives of Manitoba, E 18/8, folio 40.

27. See Ross, *The Red River Settlement*, 258 and P. Erasmus, *Buffalo Days and Nights*, edited by I. Spry (Calgary: Glenbow-Alberta Institute, 1977), 31–33.

28. Roe, *The North American Buffalo*, 404–09.

29. Ibid., 503–05.

30. Ray, *Indians in the Fur Trade*, 210–12.

31. Ibid.

32. Ibid., 212.

33. Hargrave, *Red River*, 174.

34. Robes were processed by the women. The need for this skilled labour prevented large numbers of white hunters from entering into the trade.

35. Ross, *The Red River Settlement*, 267.

36. A.J. Ray, "York Factory: The Crises of Transition, 1870-1880," *The Beaver* (Autumn 1982): 28–29.

37. Ugarenko, "The Beaver Indians and the Peace River Fur Trade, 1700–1850," 117.

Endnotes to Chapter 5

The author wishes to express his sincere appreciation to the Hudson's Bay Company Archives, Provincial Archives of Manitoba for permission to consult and to quote from its extensive collection of thoroughly described documents. The author also acknowledges the helpful suggestions from two anonymous referees. This is a revised version of a paper presented originally at the Northern Great Plains History Conference, sponsored by the Department of History, Brandon University, Brandon, Manitoba, September 29, 1995.

1. Here, except for quotations from primary sources, among the available options "Indian," "Aboriginal," and others, I adopt the terminology for First Nations peoples used in Olive P. Dickason, *Canada's First Nations: A History of Founding Peoples from Earliest Times* (Toronto: McClelland and Stewart Inc., 1992).

2. Paul C. Thistle, *Indian-European Trade Relations in the Lower Saskatchewan River Region to 1840* (Winnipeg: University of Manitoba Press, 1986); and Paul C. Thistle, "Indian-Trader Relations: An Ethnohistory of Western Woods Cree-Hudson's Bay Company Trader Contact in the Cumberland House-The Pas Region to 1840" (MA thesis, University of Manitoba, 1986).

3. Richard Slobodin, *Métis of the Mackenzie District* (Ottawa: Canadian Research Centre for Anthropology, Saint-Paul University, 1966), 7, 14, 159; cf. Jacqueline Peterson and Jennifer S.H. Brown (eds.), *The New Peoples: Being and Becoming Métis in North America* (Winnipeg: University of Manitoba Press, 1985), 7.

4. Jennifer S.H. Brown, "Woman as Centre and Symbol in the Emergence of Metis Communities," *The Canadian Journal of Native Studies* 3, no.1 (1983): 40, 45.

5. Frank Tough, "The Northern Fur Trade: A Review of Conceptual and Methodological Problems," *Musk Ox* 36 (1988): 68 ff.

6. Nancy O. Lurie, "Ethnohistory: An Ethnological Point of View," *Ethnohistory* 8, no. 1 (1961): 90 ff.; James Axtell, "Ethnohistory: An Historian's Viewpoint," *Ethnohistory* 26, no. 1 (1979): 2–3 ff.

7. R.A. Schermerhorn, *Comparative Ethnic Relations: A Framework for Theory and Research* (New York: Random House, 1970), 195.

8. T. Shibutani and K.M. Kwan, *Ethnic Stratification: A Comparative Approach* (London: Collier-Macmillan Ltd., 1965), 134.

9. Wsevlod Isajiw, "Definitions of Ethnicity," *Ethnicity* 1, no. 2 (1974): 111–24.

10. W.S. Abruzzi, "Ecological Theory and Ethnic Differentiation Among Human Populations," *Current Anthropology* 23, no. 1 (1982): 15; C.F. Keyes, "'Towards a New Formulation of the Concept of Ethnic Group," *Ethnicity* 3, no. 3, (1976): 202–03.

11. Shibutani and Kwan, *Ethnic Stratification*, 41; R. Cohen, "Ethnicity: Problem and Focus in Anthropology," in B.J. Siegel et al. (eds.), *Annual Review of Anthropology*, Volume 7 (Palo Alto, CA: American Reviews Inc., 1978), 387–97; E.K. Francis, "The Nature of the Ethnic Group," *American Journal of Sociology* 52, no. 5 (1947): 396–97.

12. Cohen, "Ethnicity: Problem and Focus in Anthropology," 386, 395.

13. Bruce G. Trigger, "Brecht and Ethnohistory," *Ethnohistory* 22, no.1 (1975): 51–56.

14. Cohen, "Ethnicity: Problem and Focus," 385.

15. Jacqueline Peterson, "Many Roads to Red River. Métis Genesis in the Great Lakes Region," in Peterson and Brown, *The New Peoples*, 39; David Stymeist, *Ethnics and Indians: Social Relations in a Northwestern Ontario Town* (Toronto: Peter Martin Associates, 1975),13; Isajiw, "Definitions of Ethnicity," 122.

16. This scholarship, although massively comprehensive, has been thoroughly critiqued by Frank Tough, "Race, Personality and History: A Review of Marcel Giraud's *The Métis in the Canadian West*," *Native Studies Review* 5, no. 2 (1989): 55–93.

17. Marcel Giraud, *The Métis in the Canadian West*, Vol. I (Edmonton: The University of Alberta Press, 1986), 93; Olive P. Dickason, "From 'One Nation' in the Northeast to 'New Nation' in the Northwest: A Look at the Emergence of the Métis," in Peterson and Brown, *The New Peoples*, 30.

18. Dickason, "From 'One Nation'," 30; John Foster, "The Métis: The People and the Term," in A.S. Lussier (ed.), *Louis Riel and the Métis: Riel Mini-Conference Papers* (Winnipeg: Pemmican Publications, 1983), 86.

19. Slobodin, *Métis of the Mackenzie District*, 29.

20. Cited in Giraud, *The Métis in the Canadian West*, 319, 322; Andrew Graham, in G. Williams and R. Glover (eds.), *Andrew Graham's Observations on Hudson's Bay, 1769–91* (London: The Hudson's Bay Record Society, 1969), 145.

21. Jennifer S.H. Brown, *Strangers in Blood: Fur Trade Company Families in Indian Country* (Vancouver: University of Vancouver Press, 1980), 70.

22. This and the following information on Magnus Twatt are derived from the "Biographical Sheets" reference prepared by staff at the Hudson's Bay Company Archives, Provincial Archives of Manitoba in Winnipeg.

23. John Nicks, "Orkneymen in the HBC, 1780–1821," in C.M. Judd and A.J. Ray (eds.), *Old Trails and New Directions: Papers of the Third North American Fur Trade Conference* (Toronto: University of Toronto Press, 1980), 102, 122–23.

24. Philip Goldring, *Papers on the Labour System of the Hudson's Bay Company, 1821–1900*, Vol. I, Manuscript Report No. 362 (Ottawa: Parks Canada, 1979), 181; D. McKay, *The Honourable Company* (Toronto: McClelland and Stewart, 1966), 231.

25. The type of life and work undertaken by Twatt at this post has been described for a slightly later period by Michael Payne, *The Most Respectable Place in the Territory: Everyday Life in Hudson's Bay Company Service York Factory, 1788 to 1870* (Ottawa: Minister of Supply and Services, 1989).

26. Hudson's Bay Company Archives, Provincial Archives of Manitoba (hereinafter cited as HBCA), Cumberland House Journal B.49/a/27b, fol. 20.1.

27. HBCA, Cumberland House Journal B.49/a/25a, fol. 15.

28. HBCA, Cumberland House Journal B.49/a/25a, fol. 22; Thistle, *Indian European Trade Relations*, 55–56, 91.

29. For example, HBCA, Cumberland House Journal B.49/a/25a, foL 35; cf. B.49/a/31, fol. 12. The competitive process of *en dérouine*, adapted from French and later NWC practice, involved taking a supply of trade goods out to Amerindian camps rather than waiting for the trappers to bring their furs into the trading post.

30. HBCA, Cumberland House Journal B.49/a/31, fol. 12.

31. HBCA, Cumberland House Journal B.49/a/31, fol. 13.

32. HBCA, Cumberland House Journal B.49/a/25a, fol. 30.

33. Cf. Edith I. Burley, *Servants of the Honourable Company: Work, Discipline and Conflict in the Hudson's Bay Company, 1770–1879* (Toronto: Oxford University Press, 1997).

34. HBCA, Cumberland House Journal B.49/a/31, fol. 17.

35. Cited in Arthur J. Ray, "Holmes, William," in M.P. Bentley et al. (eds.), *Dictionary of Canadian Biography, Vol. IV, 1771–1800* (Toronto: University of Toronto Press, 1979), 365–66.

36. HBCA, Cumberland House Journal B.49/a/31, fol. 30.

37. Giraud, *The Métis in the Canadian West*, Vol. I, 309, 312, 355; Brown, *Strangers in Blood*, 87.

38. Sylvia Van Kirk, *"Many Tender Ties": Women in Fur-Trade Society in Western Canada, 1670–1870* (Winnipeg: Watson & Dwyer Publishing Ltd., 1980), 4.

39. HBCA, Cumberland House Journal B.49/a/32a, fol. 18.

40. The term "made beaver" refers to the standard unit measuring an amount of any variety of fur equivalent to the value of one prime beaver pelt.

41. Giraud, *The Métis in the Canadian West*, Vol. I, 323, 333; Carol M. Judd, "Native Labour

and Social Stratification in the Hudson's Bay Company Northern Department, 1770–1870," *Canadian Review of Sociology and Anthropology* 17, no. 4 (1980): 308.

42. James G.E. Smith, "Western Woods Cree," in J. Helm (ed.), *Handbook of North American Indians, Vol. 6: Subarctic* (Washington, DC: Smithsonian Institution, 1981), 261.

43. Cf. mention of the families of Charles Isham, William Had (Flett), and Isaac Spence inhabiting the post: HBCA, Cumberland House Journal B.49/a/ 16, fol. 26; B.49 /a /18, fol. 25 6; B.49/a/27b, fol. 27; and also regular mention of "the boys" at work, e.g. HBCA, Cumberland House Journal B.49/a/32b, fol. 15,18.

44. Giraud, *Métis in the Canadian West*, Vol. 1, 323; Judd, "Native Labour and Social Stratification," 308.

45. Samuel Hearne, in R Glover (ed.), *A Journey from Prince of Wales's Fort in Hudson's Bay to the Northern Ocean 1769* (Toronto: The Macmillan Company of Canada Ltd., 1958), 35; cf. Van Kirk, "*Many Tender Ties*," 73.

46. K.G. Davies and A.M. Johnson (eds.), *Letters from Hudson Bay, 1703–1740* (London: Hudson's Bay Record Society 25, 1965), xxv–xxvi.

47. HBCA, Cumberland House Journal B.49/a/25a, fol. 7.

48. For example, HBCA, Cumberland House Journal B.49/a/6, fol. 15.

49. HBCA, Cumberland House Journal B.49/a/27b, fol. 6; B.49/a/32b, fol. 5.

50. HBCA, Cumberland House Journal B.49/a/32b, fol. 11.

51. HBCA, Cumberland House Journal B.49/a/32b, fol. 18.

52. HBCA, Cumberland House Journal B.49/a/32b, fol. 13.

53. HBCA, Cumberland House Journal B.49/a/34, fol. 5.

54. HBCA, Cumberland House Journal B.49/a/34, fol. 32.

55. Thistle, *Indian-European Trade Relations*, 29.

56. Ibid., 29, 58–59, 79, 91–92 *passim*.

57. HBCA, Cumberland House Journal B.49/a/35, fol. 15. Note that Jennifer Brown's "Fur Trade as Centrifuge: Familial Dispersal and Offspring Identity in Two Company Contexts," in R.J. DeMallie and A. Ortiz (eds.), *North American Indian Anthropology: Essays in Culture and Society* (Norman, OK: University of Oklahoma Press, 1994), 205 reports a third son named Robert, and other references to Willock's "brother-in-law" indicate the existence of at least one sister.

58. HBCA, Cumberland House Journal B.49/a/35, fol. 33.

59. HBCA, Cumberland House Report, 1819, B.49/e/2, fol. 2.

60. Thistle, *Indian-European Trade Relations*, 57–58, 75, 81.

61. HBCA, Cumberland House Journal B.49/a/35, fol. 40.

62. For one discussion of the varying terminology used to describe mixed-descent peoples, see John Foster '"The Métis: The People and the Term."

63. Brown, "Fur Trade as Centrifuge," 17-18.

64. HBCA, Cumberland House Journal B.49/a/45, fol. 7.

65. Judd, "'Mixt Bands of Many Nations'," in Judd and Ray, *Old Trails and New Directions*, 138; cf. HBCA, Cumberland House Journal B.49/a/44, fol. 27.

66. HBCA, Cumberland House Journal B.49/a/47, fol. 9.

67. HBCA, Cumberland House Journal B.49/a/37, foL 11.

68. See Smith, "Western Woods Cree," 260.

69. Lewis R. Binford, "Willow Smoke and Dogs' Tails: Hunter-Gatherer Settlement Systems and Archaeological Site Information," *American Antiquity* 45, no. 1 (1980): 10–12 *passim*.

70. Frank Tough, "Research on Fur Trade and Native Economies in the Post-1870 Period: An Historical Geography Approach to the Daily Journals of the Hudson's Bay Company," *Native Studies Review* 3, no.1 (1987): 129–46.

71. HBCA, Cumberland House Journal B.49/a/41, fol. 6, 13 *passim*.

72. HBCA, Cumberland House Journal B.49/a/41, fol. 43.

73. HBCA, Cumberland House Journal B.49/a/41, fol. 37.

74. HBCA, Cumberland House Journal B.49/a/49, fol. 28.

75. Isajiw, "Definitions of Ethnicity," 122.

76. HBCA, Cumberland House Journal B.49/a/40, fol. 41.

77. Smith, "Western Woods Cree," 259–60.

78. Cf. Thistle, *Indian-European Trade Relations*, 72, 79 *passim*.

79. HBCA, Cumberland House Journal B.49/a/36, fol. 7.

80. HBCA, Cumberland House Report, 1919 B.49/e/2, fol. 2.

81. HBCA, Cumberland House Journal, B.49/a/35, fol. 75; Thistle, *Indian-European Trade Relations*, 89.

82. HBCA, Cumberland House Journal B.49/a/36, fol. 12–13.

83. Thistle, *Indian-European Trade Relations*, 57–58, 82, 83–85.

84. "Lower Nipawin" was at the locale the Cree called Nipowiwinihk ("a standing place") in the present day Codette area rather than down river at the place now, to the chagrin of Cree elders, called Nipawin. See David Meyer and Paul C. Thistle, "Saskatchewan River Rendezvous Centers and Trading Posts: Continuity in Cree Social Geography," *Ethnohistory* 42, no. 3 (1995): 429, n. 12. "Upper Nipawin" was located in the Fort à la Corne area.

85. HBCA, Cumberland House Journal B.49/a/41, fol. 6.

86. HBCA, Cumberland House Journal B.49/a/43, fol.15-16.

87. HBCA, Cumberland House Journal B.49/a/42, fol. 32.

88. Leonard Mason, *The Swampy Cree: A Study in Acculturation*, National Museums of Canada Anthropology Papers No.13 (Ottawa: Department of the Secretary of State, 1967), 39.

89. HBCA, Cumberland House Journal B.49/a/49, M. 2-3; B.49/a/51, fol. 1.

90. HBCA, Cumberland House Journal B.49/a/40, fol. 12.

91. HBCA, Cumberland House Journal B.49/a/41, fol. 23.

92. HBCA, Cumberland House Journal B.49/a/42, fol. 15.

93. HBCA, Cumberland House Journal B.49/a/42, fol. 47.

94. HBCA, Cumberland House Journal B.49/a/44, fol. 10.

95. HBCA, Cumberland House Journal B.49/a/47, fol. 10.

96. HBCA, Cumberland House Journal B.49/a/50, fol. 27.

97. HBCA, Cumberland House Journal B.49/a/43, fol. 10.

98. HBCA, Cumberland House Journal B.49/a/51, fol. 1; also quoted in Thistle, *Indian-European Trade Relations*, 91–92.

99. Katherine A. Pettipas, "A History of the Work of the Reverend Henry Budd Conducted Under the Auspices of the Church Missionary Society, 1840–1875" (MA thesis, University of Manitoba, 1972).

100. Alexander Deetz, personal communication.

101. J.H. Richards, "Physical Features of Saskatchewan," in *Atlas of Saskatchewan* (Saskatoon: University of Saskatchewan, 1969), 41.

102. Cf. Richard Slobodin, "Subarctic Métis," in June Helm (ed.), *Handbook of North American Indians, Volume 6: Subarctic* (Washington: Smithsonian Institution, 1981), 362; A. Olmstead, "The Mixed Bloods in Western Canada: An Ecological Approach," in James S. Frideres (ed.), *Native People in Canada: Contemporary Conflicts*, 2nd ed. (Scarborough: Prentice Hall Canada Inc., 1983), 278.

103. David Meyer, "Time-Depth of the Western Woods Cree Occupation of Northern Ontario, Manitoba, and Saskatchewan," in W. Cowan (ed.), *Papers of the Eighteenth*

Algonquian Conference (Ottawa: Carleton University, 1987), 194; Garry A. Dickson, *Prehistoric Northern Manitoba* (Winnipeg: Manitoba Historic Resources Branch and the Manitoba Museum of Man and Nature, 1977), 27.

104. Meyer and Thistle, "Saskatchewan River Rendezvous Centers and Trading Posts," 403–44.

105. David V. Burley, *Structural Considerations of Métis Ethnicity: An Archaeological, Architectural and Historical Study* (Vermillion: University of South Dakota Press, 1992).

106. Van Kirk, *"Many Tender Ties,"* 48, 95; Giraud, *Métis in the Canadian West*, Vol. I, 264–80.

107. Philip Goldring, "Papers on the Labour System of the Hudson's Bay Company, 1821–1900, Vol. II," unpublished manuscript report (Ottawa: Environment Canada, 1980), 12.

108. HBCA, Cumberland House Journal B.49/a/39, fol. 11.

109. HBCA, Cumberland House Journal B.49/a/37, fol. 20.

110. Brown, *Strangers in Blood*, 153.

111. Cf. Thistle, *Indian-European Trade Relations*, 89.

112. Edward S. Rogers, "Leadership Among the Indians of Eastern Subarctic Canada," *Anthropologica* 7, no. 2 (1965): 266; June He, "The Nature of Dogrib Socioterritorial Groups," in R.B. Lee and L. DeVore (eds.), *Man the Hunter* (Chicago: Aldine Publishing Company, 1968), 121; John W. Ives, *A Theory of Northern Athapaskan Prehistory* (Calgary: University of Calgary Press), 298.

113. Jennifer S.H. Brown, personal communication.

Endnotes to Chapter 6

1. Marcel Giraud, *The Métis in the Canadian West*, 2 vols., translated by George Woodcock (Edmonton: University of Alberta Press, 1986), vol. 2: 159. Originally published as *Le Métis Canadien* (Paris: Institut d'Ethnologie, Musée National d'Histoire Naturelle, 1945). Giraud's view is comparable with "the problem of the frontier, namely the clash between primitive and civilized peoples" in G.F.G. Stanley, *The Birth of Western Canada* (1936; Toronto: University of Toronto Press, 1960), vii, and the Red River Settlement as "an oasis of civilization … amid the surrounding barbarism of forest and plain," in W.L. Morton, *Manitoba: A History* (Toronto: University of Toronto Press, 1976), 56.

2. Gerhard Ens, "Dispossession or Adaptation? Migration and Persistence of the Red River Métis, 1835–1890," *Historical Papers* (Ottawa: Canadian Historical Association, 1988), 121–22. Also see "Kinship, Ethnicity, Class and the Red River Métis: The Parishes of St. Francois Xavier and St. Andrew's" (PhD dissertation, University of Alberta, 1989).

3. While terms such as "Aboriginal" and "Amerindian" have received support from academics and political activists, it is my impression that among most elders in a reserve context in western Canada these terms are not used. Further, in many instances they are viewed as needless, ostentatious affectations. Perhaps in time this popular, community-rooted opposition will cease. At the moment, however, "Indian" would appear to be the preferable term.

4. Charles Winick, *Dictionary of Anthropology* (Totowa, NJ: Littlefield, 1968), 193, "ethnogenic. Relating to the beginning of ethnic groups." Also see Jacqueline Peterson and Jennifer S.H. Brown, "Introduction, " in Peterson and Brown (eds.), *The New Peoples: Being and Becoming Métis in North America* (Winnipeg: University of Manitoba Press, 1985), 3–16.

5. In this article French terms and phrases used historically in the western fur trade will be acknowledged with italics.

6. Jacqueline Peterson, "Prelude to Red River: A Social Portrait of the Great Lakes Métis," *Ethnohistory* 25 (1978): 58.

7. *En dérouine* varies in spelling. The form *en drouine*, as used in the original version of this chapter, is used in Giraud, *Métis in the Canadian West*, vol. 1: 216. Also see *Tresor de la langue Francaise: Dictionnaire de la langue du XIXe et du XXe siècle (1789–1960)* (Paris: Editions du Centre national de la recherche scientifiques, 1979), vol. 17: 526a. For the purposes of consistency in the present publication, the term *en dérouine* is used.

8. Jennifer Brown, *Strangers in Blood: Fur Trade Families in Indian Country* (Vancouver: University of British Columbia Press, 1980).

9. Jennifer Brown, "Woman as Centre and Symbol in the Emergence of Métis Communities," *The Canadian Journal of Native Studies* 3, no. 1 (1983): 39–46.

10. Provincial Archives of Alberta (PAA), Congregations des oblats de Marie Immaculée (OMI), Fonds oblat de la province d'Alberta-Saskatchewan, Paroisse Duck Lake, "Liber Animarum des Indiens et Métis ... jusqu'en 1940," boite 1, item 1, p. 725. Suzette, the Sarcee-Crow woman, was also known as Josette. "Turning-off" was the process whereby an individual leaving *le pays sauvage* induced a younger man to replace him as husband and father by turning over to him one's "outfit" such as horses, traps and other accoutrements. Jean Dumont had apparently acquired Suzette in a similar fashion early in the 1790s from a Jean-Baptiste Bruneau. In the process of "turning-off," the country wife was not necessarily a passive participant.

11. Giraud, *Métis in the Canadian West*, vol. 2: 152–58.

12. John E. Foster, R.F. Beal, and L. Zuk, "The Métis Hivernement Settlement at Buffalo Lake, 1872–77," report prepared for Historic Sites and Provincial Museums Division, Department of Culture, Government of Alberta, 1987.

13. Grace Lee Nute, *The Voyageur* (1931; St. Paul: Minnesota Historical Society, 1966), 5.

14. Marjorie W. Campbell, *The North West Company* (1957; Toronto: Macmillan, 1973), 163–64.

15. Nute, *Voyageur*, 93; note the spelling *"derouine."* See Giraud, *Métis in the Canadian West*, vol. 1: 216.

16. Giraud, *Métis in the Canadian West*, vol. 1: 215–16.

17. Ibid., 263.

18. Unfortunately the detailed descriptions of trade negotiations which have survived in the Hudson's Bay Company tradition are not matched for the winter camps in the Montreal-based trade for this period.

19. H.M. Robinson, *The Great Fur Land* (New York: G.P. Putnam's Sons, 1879), 258–59. In describing courtship among the Métis a century later Robinson suggests that the daughter and mother would indicate to the father whether a proposal was acceptable.

20. Giraud, *Métis in the Canadian West*, vol. 1, 200–01.

21. Occasional references to incidents of violence involving peddlers and Indians in winter camps in HBC documents cannot be confirmed.

22. Alice Johnson (ed.), *Saskatchewan Journals and Correspondence: Edmonton House 1795–1800, Chesterfield House 1800–1802* (London: Hudson's Bay Record Society, 1967), 311, 314.

23. PAA, OMI, Paroisse Duck Lake, "Liber animarum," vol. 1: 1, demonstrates this point in the genealogies of the Jean Dumont and François Lucier families.

24. William A. Fraser, "Plains Cree Assiniboine and Saulteaux (Plains) Bands 1874–84," manuscript (n.p.,1963),12–13, copy in possession of author.

25. Foster, Beal and Zuk, "Métis Hivernement Settlement," 65.

26. Fredrick Barth, "Descent and Marriage Reconsidered," in Jack Goody (ed.), *The Character of Kinship* (London: Cambridge University Press, 1973), 5.

27. Gertrude Nicks, '"The Iroquois and the Fur Trade in Western Canada," in C.M. Judd and A.J. Ray (eds.), *Old Trails and New Directions: Papers of the Third North American Fur Trade Conference* (Toronto: University of Toronto Press, 1980), 90.

28. John E. Foster, "The Plains Métis," in R. Bruce Morrison and C. Roderick Wilson (eds.), *Native Peoples: The Canadian Experience* (Toronto: McClelland and Stewart, 1986), 384.

29. Alexander Ross, *The Fur Hunters of the Far West*, 2 vols. (London: Smith, Elder and Co., 1855), vol. 2: 236–37. As quoted in W.J. Eccles, *The Canadian Frontier 1534–1760* (Toronto: Holt, Rinehart and Winston, 1969), 191.

30. Giraud, *Métis in the Canadian West*, vol. 1: 255–56 suggests Indian women preferred marriage relationships with Euro-Canadians. Sylvia Van Kirk, *"Many Tender Ties": Women in Fur Trade Society in Western Canada, 1670–1870* (Winnipeg: Watson and Dwyer, 1980) is a useful corrective.

31. Giraud, *Métis in the Canadian West*, vol. 1: 267.

32. Gabriel Dumont the elder (sometimes Alberta) was the uncle of the more famous Gabriel Dumont the younger (sometimes Saskatchewan). Also see John E. Foster, "The Métis and the End of the Plains Buffalo in Alberta," in John E. Foster, Dick Harrison and I.S. MacLaren (eds.), *Buffalo* (Edmonton: University of Alberta Press, 1992), 61–78.

Endnotes to Chapter 7

The research reported in this article was financially supported by the federal Department of Justice.

1. Statutes of Canada (SC), 1870, c. 3.

2. SC, 1874, c. 20, u. 1-2. The statute provided for a grant of either $160 scrip or 160 acres to Métis heads of families. The government opted for scrip in an order in council, March 23, 1876.

3. Dumont v. A.G. (Canada) and A.G. (Manitoba), 48 M.R. (2d) 4 (1987); 52 M.R. (2d) 291 (1988) (1990) 1 SCR 279. The case is discussed in Donald Purich, *The Métis* (Toronto: James Lorimer, 1988), 74–79.

4. D.N. Sprague, *Canada and the Métis, 1869–1885* (Waterloo: Wilfrid Laurier University Press, 1988); "Government Lawlessness in the Administration of Manitoba Land Claims, 1870–1887," *Manitoba Law Journal* 10 (1980): 415–41; "The Manitoba Land Question, 1870–1882," *Journal of Canadian Studies* 15 (1980): 74–84.

5. Gerhard Ens, "Dispossession or Adaptation? Migration and Persistence of the Red River Métis, 1835–1890," *Canadian Historical Association Historical Papers* (1988): 138–41.

6. Sprague, "The Manitoba Land Question," 79.

7. George F. G. Stanley, *The Birth of Western Canada* (1936; Toronto: University of Toronto Press, 1961), 245.

8. Marcel Giraud, *The Métis in the Canadian West*, trans. George Woodcock (1945; Edmonton: University of Alberta Press, 1986), vol. 2, 383. Ens, "Adaptation or Dispossession?," 121.

9. D. Bruce Sealey and Antoine S. Lussier, *The Métis: Canada's Forgotten People* (Winnipeg: Manitoba Métis Federation Press, 1975), 97; John Leonard Taylor, "An Historical Introduction to Métis Claims in Canada," *The Canadian Journal of Native Studies* 3 (1983): 157; Gerald Friesen, *The Canadian Prairies: A History* (Toronto: University of Toronto Press, 1987), 197-200; Donald Boisvert and Keith Turnbull, "Who are the Métis?," *Studies in Political Economy* 18 (1985): 131–36.

10. Thomas Flanagan, *Riel and the Rebellion: 1885 Reconsidered* (Saskatoon: Western Producer Prairie Books, 1983), 65–67. For a critique and rejoinder, see Ken Hatt, "The North-West Rebellion Scrip Commissions, 1885–1889," in F. Laurie Barron and James

B. Waldram (eds.), *1885 and After: Native Society in Transition* (Regina: Canadian Plains Research Center, 1986), 189–204; and Flanagan, "Comment on Ken Hatt," in Barron and Waldram, *1885 and After*, 205–09.

11. In an unpublished "Southern Interlake Heritage Report" (February 1982), Gerhard Ens compiled the prices for all Métis allotments in the rural municipalities of Rosser and Rockwood. I benefitted from reading Ens's paper but chose not to report his data here because of methodological differences in data collection. As I did, Ens took the prices from the abstract books in the Winnipeg Land Titles Office (LTO); but he did not control for the fact that these prices are sometimes artificially high because they record the sale of multiple allotments in batches. The researcher must check suspiciously high prices against the more detailed information given in the sale indentures, also available in the LTO. Perhaps because he did not make these corrections and also perhaps because he was dealing with a restricted area, Ens found higher average sale prices than I did.

12. SC, 1870, c. 3, s. 31.

13. A.G. Archibald to Joseph Howe, December 27, 1870; National Archives of Canada (NAC), RG 15, vol. 236, file 7220. Order in council, April 25, 1871, confirmed by the Dominion Lands Act, SC, 1872, c. 23.

14. *Manitoban*, March 1, 1873.

15. House of Commons, *Debates*, March 12 and March 24, 1873; NAC, RG 14 D 4, P-58, pp. 16, 35.

16. Order in council, April 3, 1873. SC, 1873, c. 38.

17. A.A. Taché to Robert Cunningham, March 28 and April 16, 1873; Archives of Ontario (AO), MU 762. N.-J. Ritchot to A.-A. Taché,12 May 1873; Archives de l'Archevêché de Saint Boniface (AASB), T 12072-75 (Ritchot went to Ottawa in the spring of 1873 to lobby for the same purpose as Cunningham). Andre Neault and Amable Gaudry to Robert Cunningham, July 23, 1873; AO, MU 762 (letter in Riel's hand). For drafts of this last item, see G.F.G. Stanley et al., *The Collected Writings of Louis Riel* (Edmonton: University of Alberta Press, 1985), items 1–169 to 1–172.

18. *Le Métis*, August 16, 1873.

19. Donald Codd to J.S. Dennis, February 8, 1874: NAC, RG 15, vol. 230, file 829.

20. Order in council, September 7, 1876.

21. *Manitoba Free Press*, October 24, 1876.

22. Order in council, June 14, 1876.

23. Donald Codd to J.S. Dennis, August 31, 1877; NAC, RG 15, vol. 238, file 9321.

24. N.O. Côté, "Administration and Sale of Dominion Lands," NAC, RG 15, vol. 227. Officials had underestimated the number of late applications, so the reserved land was exhausted before all applicants could receive a share. Under an order in council of April 20, 1885, 993 latecomers were given scrip for $240.

25. Statutes of Manitoba (SM), 1873, c. 44. The lieutenant governor reserved royal assent, but the federal cabinet let the act stand. A.-A. Dorion, memo of February 21, 1874. In WE. Hudgins (ed.), *Correspondence-Reports of the Ministers of Justice and Orders in Council upon the Subject of Dominion and Provincial Legislation, 1867–1895* (Ottawa: Government Printing Office, 1896), 779.

26. SM, 1875, c. 37. Edward Blake to Privy Council, October 7, 1876, printed in Hudgins, *Correspondence*, 804–05.

27. SM, 1877, c. 5. A.A. Lash, memo of May 3, 1878, in Hudgins, *Correspondence*, 821–22.

28. SM, 1878, c. W. Amended by SM, 1879, c. 11; SM,1883, c. 29; and SM, 18M, c. U.

29. SM, 1878, c. 7.

30. Entered in volumes labelled C, B, E, X, and Minute Book in Provincial Archives of Manitoba (PAM), GR 462. Records of each judicial sale are in PAM, GR 181, temporary boxes 104–107.

31. The complete transcript of evidence heard by the inquiry is in PAM, RG 7 B 1. Gerhard Ens, "Métis Lands in Manitoba," *Manitoba History* 5 (1983): 2–11, gives an account of these abuses based on the evidence of the inquiry but does not make it clear to the reader that judicial sales occurred in only a small minority (about 560 of 6,034) of the Métis children's land grants.

32. PAC, RG 15, vols. 1476–77. For convenience, I drew the sample from the version of the list printed in Emile Pelletier, *Exploitation of Métis Lands*, 2nd ed. (Winnipeg: Manitoba Métis Federation Press, 1979).

33. George Bryce, *A History of Manitoba* (Toronto: Canada History Company, 1906), 185–96.

34. Indentures filed with powers of attorney are in PAC, RG 15, vols. 1421–23. These sales must also be seen in the context of their own time. Father Ritchot, for example, was buying river lots in St. Norbert in 1871 for $40. Philippe Mailhot, "Ritchot's Resistance: Abbé Noël Joseph Ritchot and the Creation and Transformation of Manitoba" (PhD dissertation, University of Manitoba, 1986), 248–53.

35. With a 5% chance of error, the confidence interval for this estimate is $193 ± $31. That is, there is a 95% probability that the mean sale price for the entire population lies between $162 and $224. See Jerome C.R. Li, *Statistical Inference* I (Ann Arbor: Edwards Brothers, 1964), 162–64. For any given risk of error, the narrowing of the confidence interval is proportional to the square root of the increase in sample size. To reduce the above confidence interval by half would require drawing a sample four times as big. It is a question of the researcher's judgment whether it is worth the cost to collect and process four times as much data in order to produce an estimate on the other of $193 ± $16 rather than $193 ± $31. In my view, the additional precision would not be worth the cost in a study of this type, whose purpose was to estimate broad magnitudes as an aid to historical interpretation. Little would hinge on whether the population mean was really $175, $200 or $225. Historians unfamiliar with statistical theory should also know that the ratio of the sample to population size hardly matters; sample size itself is the relevant consideration.

36. PAM, RG 7 B 1, testimony of November 22, 1881, p. 14.

37. Winnipeg Land Titles Office, documents 3816, 3819. This was a judicial sale approved by the court November 2, 1880. McNab apparently tied up the land with a court order, then went looking for a buyer.

38. PAM, RG 7 B 1, testimony of November 22, p. 19.

39. M.B. Wood and R.P. Wood were sons of Chief Justice E.B. Wood, who approved most of the judicial sales. This relationship helped to provoke the investigation of 1881.

40. Thomas Sowell, *Knowledge and Decisions* (New York: Basic Books, 1980), 84.

41. For example, Department of Interior to David McArthur, December 5, 1888, PAM, MG 14 C 21, box 13. The deeds of purchase are in the same box.

42. PAM, RG 7 B 1, testimony of November 29, 1881, pp. 15-16.

43. *Free Press*, February 5, 1879.

44. SM, 1873, c.18, s. 45, quoted in *Free Press*, May 20, 1881.

45. *Free Press*, May 20, 1881.

46. The high price suggests it may have been part of a batch of lands, but I found no evidence of this.

47. PAM, RG 7 B 1, testimony of November 10, 1881, p. 16.

48. Ibid., 13.

49. Ens, "Dispossession or Adaptation?," 124–26.

50. W.L. Morton, "Agriculture in the Red River Colony," *Canadian Historical Review* 30 (1949).

51. Ens, "Dispossession or Adaptation?," 135.

52. Allen Ronaghan, "Charles Mair and the North-West Emigration Aid Society," *Manitoba History* 14 (1987): 10–14; Allen Ronaghan, "The Archibald Administration in Manitoba 1870–1872" (PhD dissertation, University of Manitoba, 1986).

53. Ens, "Dispossession or Adaptation?," 141; Gerald Friesen, "Homeland to Hinterland: Political Transition in Manitoba, 1870 to 1879," *Canadian Historical Association Historical Papers* (1979).

54. Ens, "Dispossession or Adaptation?," 142.

55. SC, 1874, c. 20, ss. 1–2.

56. The cancelled scrip notes are stored in NAC, RG 15, vols. 1479–1484.

57. Côté, "Administration and Sale of Dominion Lands," NAC, RG 15, vol. 227.

58. NAC, RG 15, vol. 2128, unpaginated (C-14934).

59. "In re W.B. Thibeaudeau, M.L.R. (Temp. Wood)," 149–57.

60. [?] to John Schultz, October 13, 1876. PAM, MG 12E 1, p. 7561.

61. Indenture in PAM, MG 14 C 21, box 14.

62. "In re W.B. Thibeaudeau, ML.R. (Temp. Wood)," 149–57.

63. The warrants are in NAC, RG 15, vols. 1608–1627.

64. The confidence interval is $78 ± $10, with a 5% chance of error.

65. Civil Service List, 1882.

Endnotes to Chapter 8

1. See Jan Vansina, "Oral Tradition and Historical Methodology," in D.K. Dunaway and W.K. Baum (eds.), *Oral History: An Interdisciplinary Anthology* (Nashville: American Association for State and Local History, 1984), 102–06.

2. See Stanley's account of his work in "Last Word on Louis Riel—The Man of Several Faces," in F. Laurie Barron and James B. Waldram (eds.), *1885 and After: Native Society in Transition* (Regina: Canadian Plains Research Center, 1986), 3–22.

3. D.N. Sprague, "The Manitoba Land Question, 1870–1882," *Journal of Canadian Studies* 15 (1980): 74–84; Sprague, "Government Lawlessness in the Administration of Manitoba Land Claims, 1870–1887," *Manitoba Law Journal* 10 (1980): 415–41; Sprague, *Canada and the Métis, 1869–1885* (Waterloo: Wilfrid Laurier University Press, 1988); and P.R. Mailhot and D.N. Sprague, "Persistent Settlers: The Dispersal and Resettlement of the Red River Métis, 1870-1885," *Canadian Ethnic Studies* 2 (1985):1–31.

4. In Dumont, et al. *vs.* A.G. Canada and A.G. Manitoba, Canada's initial defense was a motion for dismissal on grounds that the outcome of the case was so "plain and obvious" that the question was "beyond doubt." In March 1990, the Supreme Court held that the constitutionality of the legislation enacted in the course of administration of the Manitoba Act was "justiciable" and, in the event that judgement went in favour of the plaintiffs, "declaratory relief … in the discretion of the court" was an appropriate remedy. New procedural motions have now been brought by Canada. Rejected in the Manitoba Court of Queen's Bench, Canada has appealed to the Manitoba Court of Appeal.

5. Gerhard Ens, "Dispossession or Adaptation? Migration and Persistence of the Red River Métis, 1835–1890," Canadian Historical Association, *Papers* (1988): 120–44. Thomas Flanagan, "The Market for Métis Lands in Manitoba: An Exploratory Study," *Prairie Forum* 16, no.1 (Spring 1991): 1–20; and Thomas Flanagan, *Métis Lands in Manitoba* (Calgary: University of Calgary Press, 1991).

6. Flanagan, *Métis Lands*, 232.

7. Ibid., 189.

8. Only the general reference appears in Ens, "Dispossession or Adaptation," 131. There is no citation of a particular series.

9. Ens uses the "reign of terror" phrase in "Dispossession or Adaptation," 137; Flanagan prefers less colourful language. The evidence of assault, rape, and murder inflicted on the Métis people by Canada's troops becomes merely a "push of English-Protestant immigrants" in Flanagan's latest characterization of the process, "Market," 17.

10. Fred J. Shore, "The Canadians and the Métis: The Re-Creation of Manitoba, 1858–1872" (PhD dissertation, University of Manitoba, 1991).

11. See Sprague, *Canada and the Métis*, 94–95.

12. Canada, *Sessional Papers*, 1875, no. 8.

13. Ens, "Dispossession or Adaptation," 138.

14. Canada, *Sessional Papers*, 1871, no. 20, 90–93.

15. The missing returns are: Machar's list of "Half breed heads of families" for the parish of St. Johns; the supplementary heads of families list prepared by Ryan in January 1876; and Ryan's claims disallowed in the Catholic parishes. The first deficiency is remedied by the figure of 40 cases for St. Johns appearing in the preliminary tabulation published as Appendix 4 in the "Report of the Surveyor General, October 31, 1875," in Canada, *Sessional Papers*, 1876, no. 9. The second can be estimated from the supplementary children's claims on the assumption that there would be two heads of family per family of claimant minors. Even if such an assumption is somehow defective, the resulting bias is trivial: 30 cases in the Protestant parishes, 76 in the Catholic, for a total of 96 in a universe of 9,000. Thus Table 3 is primarily a tabulation of the "Returns of Half Breed Commissioners" exactly as found on the lists in National Archives of Canada (NAC), RG 15, vols. 1574–1607. Two aspects of aggregation are that heirs are reduced to single descendents and claimants disallowed by reason of double enumeration are not included in the tabulation.

16. NAC, MG 26A, Macdonald Papers, Incoming Correspondence, 40752, William McDougall to Macdonald, October 31, 1869.

17. D.N. Sprague and R. Frye, "Manitoba's Red River Settlement: Manuscript Sources for Economic and Demographic History," *Archivaria* 9 (1978–80): 179–93.

18. Provincial Archives of British Columbia, Archer Martin Papers, Add Mss 630, box 1, file 5, Ruttan to Martin (July 11, 1894).

19. Mailhot and Sprague, "Persistent Settlers," 5.

20. One of the surviving diaries, that of M. McFadden, surveyor of Baie St. Paul from July 29 to September 7, 1871, shows that the survey of that parish occupied him for a total of 31 working days. Only two days, August 4 and 11, were noteworthy for "a good deal of time taken up with the claimants in getting their claims properly defined." PAM, RG 17-Cl, Survey Diary and Report, No. 274: 8–14.

21. McFadden's "Field Notes" recording the names, locations and readily apparent improvements of occupants in Baie St. Paul are in ibid., Field Notebook, No. 533: 3–9.

22. Flanagan does not admit that the level of improvements demanded by officials was fluid and more stringent in the 1870s than in the mid-1880s. The kind of case Flanagan cites as typical of Canada's generosity was dated 1883, but all such claims were consistently rejected in the 1870s. Compare evidence cited in Flanagan, *Métis Lands*, 164, with Sprague, *Canada and the Métis*, 115–20.

23. A particularly instructive example affected the family of Alexis Vivier, in occupation of unsurveyed land in Baie St. Paul between Baptiste Robillard and James Cameron since 1863. One of the first difficulties was Canada's surveyor divided the Vivier claim

into four different lots, with only one showing significant improvements. Still, the Viviers regarded the entire tract as their land, and claimed more cultivation, housing, and outbuildings than that recorded in the survey. A new problem arose in 1878 when documentation purportedly proving the sale of part of the tract by the now absent Robillard to one Isaac Cowie brought Vivier into a conflict with Cowie over title. Cowie's claim prevailed. See documentation in PAM, Parish Files, Baie St. Paul, lots 126-130.

24. NAC, RG 15, vol. 245, file 22638, Royal to Macdonald, March 8, 1880.
25. NAC, MG 26A, Macdonald Papers, Incoming Correspondence, 141514–141526, Ritchot to Macdonald, January 15, 1881.
26. See Sprague, *Canada and the Métis*, 94–95.
27. Provincial Archives of British Columbia, Archer Martin Papers, Add Mss 630, box 1, file 5, Ruttan to Martin, July 11, 1894.
28. Flanagan, "Market," 10.
29. Ibid., 11–12.
30. Order in Council of Canada (March 23, 1876) stipulated that recipients with "proper identification to the satisfaction of the Dominion Lands Agent" might collect their scrip in person; otherwise, they would be required to hire an agent with power of attorney. In practice, however, the route was as stated above. See the form letter from Donald Codd, Dominion Lands Agent, Winnipeg, to Mrs. E.L. Barber (May 10, 1879) in Provincial Archives of Manitoba, Barber Papers (MG 14 C66), item 2954.
31. Sprague, *Canada and the Métis*, 124–25.
32. Flanagan, "Market," 4.
33. Ibid., 5–6.
34. Provincial Archives of Manitoba, RG7 BI, Commission to Investigate Administration of Justice in the Province of Manitoba, Transcript of Testimony, 207–08.
35. Ibid., 210–11.
36. Compare Flanagan's quotation in "Market," 8, with the fuller text of Wood's testimony cited above. See also Flanagan's admission of "artificially high" prices evident by comparing certain sales instruments and figures in the Abstract Books ("Market," 18, footnote 11).
37. Flanagan, *Métis Lands*, 231.
38. Ibid., 229.
39. Sir John A. Macdonald quoted in Sprague, *Canada and the Métis*, 89.
40. Flanagan, *Métis Lands*, 179.
41. Ibid., 186–88.
42. Ibid., 190.
43. Flanagan's ill-chosen phrase, *Métis Lands*, 227.
44. Report in Manitoba *Free Press* quoted in ibid., 147.

Endnotes to Chapter 9

I am grateful to the Research Grants Committee of the University of Calgary for a grant to update my research on the North-West Rebellion.

1. Thomas Flanagan, *Riel and the Rebellion: 1885 Reconsidered* (Saskatoon: Western Producer Prairie Books, 1983).
2. Calgary *Herald*, December 3, 1983, p. 32; *Alberta Report*, January 2, 1984, p. 27.
3. Murray Dobbin, "Thomas Flanagan's Riel: An Unfortunate Obsession," *Alberta History* 32 (Spring 1984): 26.
4. Ron Bourgeault, review in *Labour/Le Travail* 16 (1985): 284–85.

5. Dennis Duffy, *The Globe and Mail*, October 22, 1983, p. E6.

6. See, for example, John Foster in *Great Plains Quarterly* 5 (Fall 1985): 259–60; J.E. Rea in the *Canadian Journal of Political Science* 17 (September 1984): 612–13; Gerald Friesen in *Saskatchewan History* 37 (Autumn 1984): 119–20.

7. Thomas Flanagan, *Riel and the Rebellion*, 70.

8. George Woodcock, "Not Guilty," *Books in Canada* (January 1984): 10. Grammatically, Woodcock's sentence refers to the subsequent telegram to Governor Dewdney and not to the order in council, but in context it is clear he is writing about government policy as a whole and is not distinguishing among different documents.

9. Ken Hatt, "The North-West Rebellion Scrip Commissions, 1885-1889," in F. Laurie Barron and James B. Waldram (eds.), *1885 and After: Native Society in Transition* (Regina: Canadian Plains Research Center, 1986), 191.

10. Ibid.

11. H.H. Langton, "The Commission of 1885 to the North-West Territories," *Canadian Historical Review* 25 (1944): 39, 45.

12. S.C., 1870, c.3, s.31.

13. S.C., 1879, c.31, 8.125(3), cited in Thomas Flanagan, *Riel and the Rebellion*, 67.

14. Thomas Flanagan, *Riel and the Rebellion*, 64.

15. Diane Payment, *Batoche (1870–1910)* (Saint-Boniface: Les Editions du Blé, 1983), 78.

16. Thomas Flanagan, *Riel and the Rebellion*, 71. I must, of course, take responsibility for errors in my book. However, it should be noted that the episode of the telegrams is also inaccurately reported in well-known books such as George F.G. Stanley's *Louis Riel* (Toronto: Ryerson, 1963), 297–98, and George Woodcock's *Gabriel Dumont* (Edmonton: Hurtig, 1975), 155–57. It is to be hoped that the correct version, established by Payment and by Beal and Macleod, and accepted here, will become prevalent in the literature.

17. Diane Payment, *Batoche*, 79; Bob Beal and Rod Macleod, *Prairie Fire: The 1885 North-West Rebellion* (Edmonton: Hurtig, 1984), 131.

18. Ibid.

19. Thomas Flanagan, *Riel and the Rebellion*, 113.

20. Ibid., 71.

21. Government of Saskatchewan, Central Survey and Mapping Agency, Legal Surveys Branch (Regina) (hereafter LSB), Notebook 747. Diane Payment was the first to exploit these notebooks.

22. Ibid.

23. The statements are in Saskatchewan Archives (Saskatoon), Homestead Files, 81184. For example, Daniel Garripie claimed in 1884 that he had lived continuously on lot 37 since 1877, but Aldous did not note his presence.

24. LSB, Notebook 746.

25. All references to township maps are to the complete set of bound volumes in the Provincial Archives of Saskatchewan (Regina).

26. LSB, Notebook 872.

27. Ibid., Notebook 882.

28. Ibid., Notebook 880.

29. Thomas Flanagan, *Riel and the Rebellion*, 37.

30. Ibid., 51.

31. D.N. Sprague, "Deliberation and Accident in the Events of 1885," *Prairie Fire: A Manitoba Literary Review* 6 (1985): 107.

32. Ibid., 103.

33. University of Alberta Archives, William Pearce Papers, MG 9/2/4-4 (Vol. 4), 224-75. It

is embarrassing to have to report that Diane Payment, D.N. Sprague and I had all consulted the Pearce Papers before 1983 without finding this schedule. The letterbooks are difficult to read and not well indexed.

34. Thomas Flanagan, *Riel and the Rebellion*, 47.

35. Provincial Archives of Saskatchewan (Saskatoon), Department of Agriculture, Lands Branch, Ag11, Files 30061 (Father Julien Moulin) and 29800 (Joseph Pilon).

36. Ibid., files 29805 (Jean Caron, Jr.), 29811 (George Ness), 30047 (Isidore Dumas).

37. André N. Lalonde, "Colonization Companies and the North-West Rebellion," in Barron and Waldram, *1885 and After*, 53–65.

38. Thomas Flanagan (ed.), *The Collected Writings of Louis Riel/Les Ecrits complets de Louis Riel*, 5 vols. (Edmonton: University of Alberta Press, 1985), 3: 288. Originally published November 28, 1985, in the Montreal *Daily Star* under the title "Les Métis du Nord-Ouest."

39. A.-H. de Trémaudan, *Histoire de la nation métisse dans l'ouest canadien* (Montreal: Editions Albert Levesque, 1936).

40. Howard Adams, *Prison of Grass* (Toronto: New Press, 1975), ch. 9.

41. Martin Shulman and Don McLean, "Lawrence Clarke: Architect of Revolt," *Canadian Journal of Native Studies* 3 (1983): 57–68; Don McLean, *1885: Métis Rebellion or Government Conspiracy?* (Winnipeg: Pemmican Publications, 1985); Don McLean, "1885: Métis Rebellion or Government Conspiracy?" in Barron and Waldram, *1885 and After*, 79–104. For my review of McLean's book, see *Canadian Historical Review* 67 (September 1986): 462.

Endnotes to Chapter 10

1. Josephine Tey, *The Daughter of Time* (1951; London: Harmondsworth, 1974), 94. Tonypandy is a place in the South of Wales where—according to Tey—a riot which was stopped by unarmed London police was built up as a massacre, by armed troops, of Welsh miners striking for their rights.

2. Ibid., 95.

3. There are two reports of this trial: one in a publication entitled *Preliminary Investigation and Trial of Ambroise Lépine for the Murder of Thomas Scott, Being full report of the proceedings in this case before the Magistrates' Court and the several Courts of Queen's Bench in the Province of Manitoba* (Montreal: Burland-Desbarats, 1874), which was based on the court reports of various reporters for eastern Canadian newspapers; and one in Winnipeg's *Free Press*, which was based on the work of local reporters. The two sets of reports have much in common, particularly because the various participants distributed their set speeches in advance to the press, but also probably because the reporters often pooled their resources. But there is some significant new material in the *Free Press* accounts which has not often been used by historians. In addition to the published accounts, the trial notes of Judge Edmund Burke Wood also survive, in the Provincial Archives of Manitoba. These provide over 160 pages of crabbed judge's notes, often illegible, on the testimony.

4. Easily the most blatant example of such malpractice occurs in Dr. Peter Charlebois, *The Life of Louis Riel in Pictures* (Toronto: NC Press, 1978). He quotes from Mrs. Black's account of her brother's death in William Healy's *Women of Red River* (Winnipeg: Women's Canadian Club, 1923) that his killer Parisien was "lying half-unconscious with the blood streaming from a wound in the side of his head which Thomas Scott had given him with a hatchet." In Healy's text, the original quotation read "which someone had given him with a hatchet."

5. W.B. Osler in *The Man Who Had to Hang: Louis Riel* (Toronto: n.p., 1952), for example, described Thomas Scott as an "obscure young man" who "cursed himself into eternity." Osier continued: "First there was the time—it was months before Riel and his men turned back McDougall at the frontier—when they [Riel and Scott] met on the street in Winnipeg and Scott, cursing, furiously attacked Riel with his fists. Louis, no fighter, was rescued by onlookers. No one ever found out what caused this outburst. Even Riel apparently did not know. Later, when Scott was first captured and imprisoned at Fort Garry, he screamed curses at his guards and beat upon his cell door. Then he escaped, and in the raid on Coutu's home he informed the indignant householder and anyone else within hearing that when he caught Riel he would kill the bastard. Recaptured, he renewed his abuse of the guards. And one day when his cell door was opened as the President walked past he leaped into the corridor, flung himself upon Riel, and screamed: 'You son of a bitch! If I'm ever free I'll kill you with my bare hands!'" (182–83).

6. Quoted in Frances G. Halpenny (ed.), *Dictionary of Canadian Biography*, IX, 1861–1870 (Toronto and Buffalo: University of Toronto Press, 1976), 707.

7. Quoted in Rev. George Young, *Manitoba Memories: Leaves from My life in the Prairie Province, 1868–1884* (Toronto: William Briggs, 1897), 145.

8. Ibid. What survives of this material is in the United Church Archives (Toronto), George Young file.

9. George Young file. W.L. Morton in his introduction to W.L. Morton (ed.)*Alexander Begg's Red River and Other Papers Relative to the Red River Resistance of 1869–70* [hereafter *Begg's Journal*] (Toronto: The Champlain Society, 1956), argues from these savings that Scott was "obviously neither a wastrel nor a drinker" (p. 111). This money may have played an important role in Scott's behaviour during his second imprisonment. According to Alexander Murray in his 1871 Lépine trial testimony, he and Scott were taken prisoner together in February. The two were searched and Murray had his pocketbook containing £60 taken from him. According to Murray, Scott asked for his pocketbook in the course of the final contretemps with Riel.

10. G.F.G. Stanley, *Toil & Trouble: Military Expeditions to Red River* (Toronto and Oxford: Dunburn Press, 1989), 78.

11. Linda Colley, *Britons: Forging the Nation 1707–1837* (New Haven and London: Yale University Press, 1992).

12. Hugh Scott to John A. Macdonald, April 6, 1870, quoted in Morton, *Begg's Journal*, 111n. His brother also described Thomas as "a very quiet and inofensive [sic] young man," an assessment which has traditionally been ignored, presumably because of its source.

13. Young, *Manitoba Memories*, 144. If Scott got to Red River by coach, then he could not have been the "James Scott" who arrived on board the steamer *International* in late June in company with "Wm. A. Allen" and "F.J. Mogridge" *Nor'Wester*, June 26, 1869. It is also possible that the newspaper got the surname wrong; James Robb is a likely alternate candidate.

14. Nolin insisted that the food itself was good, since he had supplied it. Charles Nolin Testimony, October 21, 1874, at Lépine Trial.

15. Provincial Archives of Manitoba (PAM), MG 2 B4-1, District of Assiniboia Minutes of Quarterly Court, Sheriff's Court Book.

16. *Begg's Journal*, 173.

17. Norman Shrive, *Charles Mair, Literary Nationalist* (Toronto: University of Toronto Press, 1965), 94. According to the diary of P.G. Laurie in the Saskatchewan Archives Board, E.L. Storer Papers, Scott was living at "Garrett's" while awaiting trial. According to the

News-Letter of February 1, 1871, he helped collect funds about this time for the welcome of Governor McDougall to the settlement.

18. Stanley, *Louis Riel*, 111 and note 52.

19. *The Story of Louis Riel the Rebel Chief* (Toronto/Whitby: I.S. Robertson and Brothers, 1885), 117.

20. "Diary of A.W. Graham," *The Elgin Historical and Scientific Institute Proceedings* (1912).

21. John H. O'Donnell, *Manitoba as I Saw It. From 1869 to Date* (Toronto: Clarke, 1909), esp. 30 ff.

22. Report of William Allan and Joseph Coombes, in Toronto *Globe*, April 15, 1870.

23. Young, *Manitoba Memories*, 131–32.

24. PAM, MG 11 A1, "Recollections of Peter McArthur 1934–5."

25. "Diary of A.W. Graham," p. 75.

26. Charles Arkoll Boulton, *Reminiscences of the North-West Rebellion, with a Record of the Raising of Her Majesty's 100th Regiment in Canada, and a Chapter on Canadian Social & Political Life, by Major Boulton, Commanding Boulton's Scouts* (Toronto: Grip Printing and Publishing Co., 1886), 133.

27. Report of Allan and Coombes.

28. The *Globe*, April 4, 1870.

29. PAM, MG 3 B15, James Ashdown notes on Winship Manuscript (1914).

30. PAM, NG11 Al, "Recollections of Peter McArthur 1934–5."

31. "Diary of A.W. Graham," 82.

32. PAM, MG; 3 B11, "Journal of Henry Woodington, 22 September 1869–17 February 1870.

33. Boulton, *Reminiscences*, 101 ff.

34. Testimony of William Chambers, *Free Press*, October 15, 1874.

35. Ibid. In his unpublished thesis, Neil Allan Ronaghan argues that after Scott's death, the Canadian Party conspired "to leave the impression that Scott had played almost no part in their affairs." He offers no evidence for this assertion, nor does he explain why such action made Scott a better martyr. In any event, the result, argues Ronaghan, is that "the researcher must regard everything written about Scott after April of 1870 with caution, and everything written after 1885 with suspicion." Ronaghan, "The Archibald Administration in Manitoba—1870–1872" (PhD dissertion, University of Manitoba, 1986), 211–12.

36. Testimony of Alexander McPherson, *The Trial of Ambroise Lépine*, October 14, 1874.

37. Testimony of Alexander Murray, *The Trial of Ambroise Lépine*, October 16, 1874. Nor was Scott one of the fourteen members of the "general council for the force" chosen at Kildonan and listed in the *St. Paul Daily Pioneer*, April 2, 1870.

38. Boulton, *Reminiscences*, 105.

39. PAM, P733 f 110, Memoir of Donald McLeod.

40. Testimony of William Farmer, *Free Press*, October 14, 1874.

41. Irene Spry (ed.), "The Memoirs of George William Sanderson," *Canadian Ethnic Studies* 17 (1985): 115–34.

42. Testimony of Alexander Murray, *The Trial of Ambroise Lépine*, October 16, 1874.

43. Testimony of George Newcombe, *The Trial of Ambroise Lépine*, October 15, 1874.

44. Testimony of Alexander Murray, *The Trial of Ambroise Lépine*, October 16, 1874. Murray continued this testimony by dating this contretemps at nine p.m. on the evening of March 3. We know from other evidence that Scott had already been tried and convicted by this time, so something must be wrong with Murray's chronology.

45. Boulton, *Reminiscences*, 126–27.

46. Testimony of John McLean, *Free Press*, October 20, 1874.

47. Testimony of John McLean, *The Trial of Ambroise Lépine*.

48. Donald Smith to Joseph Howe, April 28, 1870 (no source given)

49. Testimony of George Young, *Free Press*, October 15, 1874. The evidence about the previous Saturday does not appear in the *Free Press* report, however, but only in *The Trial of Ambroise Lépine*.

50. Young, *Manitoba Memories*, 132–33.

51. Donald Gunn and Charles Tuttle, in their *History of Manitoba* (Ottawa: Maclean, Roger, 1885), 396–97, were the only early historians who quoted Nolin's testimony at length, although their earlier discussion of the Scott "court-martial" made clear that they did not entirely understand what Nolin had said.

52. Testimony of Joseph Nolin, *Free Press*, October 17, 1874; *The Trial of Ambroise Lépine*.

53. Ibid.

54. A.G. Morice ignored this point when he cited Nolin's sworn evidence as part of an impassioned demolition of the subsequent "English" criticism of the trial in *A Critical History of the Red River Rebellion* (Winnipeg: Canadian Publishers, 1935).

55. Trémaudan asserted in *The Canadian Historical Review* 6 (1925), "I have it from some of the men who sat on that trial that Riel had nothing whatever to do with the proceedings taken, the decision arrived at, and the execution performed, beyond, of course, the appointment of the tribunal itself, and except, before and after the verdict was rendered, to plead with his people for mercy" (p. 233n).

56. Young, *Manitoba Memories*, 133.

57. Testimony of George Young (no source given).

58. Smith to Joseph Howe, April 28, 1870, reprinted in Morton, *Begg's Journal*.

59. A.G. Morice, in his *Critical History*, wrote in a footnote, "As we have seen, even D.A. Smith called him [Scott] in his Report 'a rash, thoughtless man, whom none cared to have to do anything with'." A number of other writers repeat Smith's remark without noting that it was not Smith's assessment.

60. Smith argued that this was a trifling business, but Riel insisted, "Do not attempt to prejudice us against Americans, for although we have not been with them they are with us, and have been better friends to us than Canadians."

61 Quoted in Shrive, *Charles Mair*, 103.

62. *The New Nation*, March 4, 1870.

63. According to Boulton, this visit occurred only after Scott had been sentenced to death. See Boulton's *Reminiscences*, 127.

64. Letter from Fort Garry in the *Globe*, April 7, 1870.

65. G.F.G. Stanley et al. (eds.), *The Collected Writings of Louis Riel/Les Ecrits Complets de Louis Riel* (Edmonton: University of Alberta Press, 1985), vol. 1: 198–200. This document was originally reprinted as "The Execution of Thomas Scott" with a translation and extensive notes by A.H. de Trémaudan in *The Canadian Historical Review* 6 (1925): 222–36. In these notes, the editor introduced a good deal of information based on recent interviews with Métis involved with Riel in 1869–70.

66. Ibid., 243–57, especially 247.

67. Ibid. 298–319, especially 308–11.

68. See the Montreal *Gazette*, February 18, 1874, and the Montreal *Herald*, February 19, 1874.

69. It has been reprinted in Stanley et al., *The Collected Writings of Louis Riel*, vol. I: 323–49.

70. The original document was written in French. This translation is mine. It is entirely possible that the Scott involved in the drinking bout was James Scott, who according

to the *Nor'Wester* of June 26, 1869 arrived in Red River in late June with Francis Mogridge and William A. Allen aboard the steamer *International*. If it was James Scott who helped terrorize the community, then Thomas Scott was once again being blamed for alcoholic activities not really his fault.

71. Ibid., 421.

72. Reprinted in Stanley, *The Collected Writings of Louis Riel*, vol. II: 413–23.

73. Ibid., 424–26.

74. Ibid., vol. III: 583–84.

75. Trémaudan, "The Execution of Thomas Scott," 228–29n.

76. Ibid., 231n.

77. The Anglophone witnesses concur that Scott could not believe that he would actually be executed. These witnesses suggest that Scott's disbelief was a product of his sense that he did not deserve death for his behaviour, rather than because of his contempt for his captors.

78. Morice, *Critical History*, 283n.

79. R.G. MacBeth, *The Romance of Western Canada*, 2nd ed. (Toronto: William Briggs, 1920), 156–57.

80. Ibid.

81. PAM, MG3 B23, W.M. Joyce Papers.

82. "Issued from a low social stratum," wrote A.G. Morice, "he was of a naturally rough disposition which, in captivity, bordered on actual ferocity," in *Critical History*, 283.

83. R.G. MacBeth, *The Making of the Canadian West: Reminiscences of an Eyewitness* (Toronto: William Briggs, 1898), 82.

84. Captain George Huyshe in his *The Red River Expedition* (n.p 1871), 20, insisted that Scott's "only crime had been loyalty to his Queen and country."

85. Scheduled for noon, the execution occurred nearly an hour later, partly because of the time taken by Donald Smith pleading for Scott's life.

86. Young, *Manitoba Memories*, 131–37.

87. Witnesses at Lépine's trial could not agree on who had fired the revolver shot.

88. See, for example, Trémaudan, "The Execution of Thomas Scott" for an account of the interviewing process.

89. A.G. Morice in 1935 wrote that he had learned from André Nault, who claimed to be one of those who had helped Riel remove the body from the Fort, that it had been buried in an unmarked spot in St. John's Protestant cemetery. Morice, *Critical History*, 293–95.

90. Stanley, *The Collected Writings of Louis Riel*, vol. IV: 583.

Endnotes to Chapter 11

1. Cf. M. Deltgen, "Neuer Mahdi bedrohte den Staat mit blutigen Gewaltakten," *Die Welt*, November 16, 1982, p. 6; *The Globe and Mail*, November 20, 1982, p. 4.

2. The terms "native people" and "colonizing people" are to be regarded in their broadest sense here. They will be used for reasons of simplicity for the Métis and the Canadians respectively, although more appropriate terms would be "semi-native" people and "colonizing-colonized people." "The broad context of the second Riel Rebellion was the intrusion of Canadian society onto the Great Plains and the consequent disruption of the culture of the Métis." T. Flanagan, "Catastrophe and the Millennium: A New View of Louis Riel," in Richard Allen (ed.), *Religion and Society in the Prairie West* (Regina: n.p., 1974), 44.

3. Cf. M. Adas, *Prophets of the Rebellion. Millenarian Protest Movements Against the European Order* (Chapel Hill, 1979), 92 f. "we may expect that agrarian areas subject to repeated

catastrophes, either natural or social, will constitute particularly likely breeding grounds for millenarianism. However, the final necessary ingredient is salvationist doctrine articulated by a prophetic figure." M. Barkun, *Disaster and the Millennium* (New Haven, 1974), 89f; "Any explanation of why the rising occurred must focus on Riel." T. Flanagan, *Riel and the Rebellion: 1885 Reconsidered* (Saskatoon, 1983), 76.

4. For a summary of those developments and a bibliographical survey of the major works see D. Owram, "The Myth of Louis Riel," *Canadian Historical Review* 63 (1982): 315–36.

5. T. Flanagan, *Louis "David"Riel: Prophet of the New World* (Toronto, 1979), 179. Flanagan's article "Catastrophe and the Millennium" (cf. note 2, which was presented at the annual meeting of the Canadian Political Science Association in 1973, was the first work to analyze Riel's millenarianism. The approach was adapted by Gilles Martel who wrote that the Métis in Saskatchewan "réduits à une crise d'anomie suite à une crise d'évolution ambiante, ont réagi par un mouvement social de type plutôt réformiste et moule dans une ideologie millénariste." G. Martel, "Le Messianisme de Louis Riel (1884–1885)" (PhD dissertation, Sherbrooke-Paris, 1976), 2: 632. Flanagan again described Riel as a millenarian leader in chapter 8 of *Louis "David"Riel.*

6. Adas, *Prophets.*

7. Unless indicated otherwise biographical facts about the first three prophetic leaders will be taken from Adas, *Prophets,* about Conselheiro from E. da Cunha, *Rebellion in the Backlands* (Chicago, 1967).

8. Adas, *Prophets,* 23.

9. Cf. ibid., 38 ff.

10. Ibid., 17.

11. Cf. B. Sealey, *Statutory Land Rights of the Manitoba Métis* (Winnipeg, 1977), 67 ff. D.N. Sprague, "The Manitoba Land Question, 1870–1882," *Journal of Canadian Studies* 15 (1980): 74–84.

12. Sealey, *Land Rights,* 95.

13. Ibid. A notion of the original Indian concept of land as the totality of environment, having a divinity about it, also comes in here. On the other hand, both Indians and Métis quickly learned, and at least by the 1860s were pretty much aware of the title issue. Cf. W.L. Morton, *Manitoba, A History* (Toronto, 1967), 105 ff.

14. Flanagan, *Louis "David" Riel,* 122.

15. Adas, *Prophets,* 44.

16. Cf. E. Pelletier, *A Social History of the Manitoba Métis* (Winnipeg, 1977).

17. This analysis is supported by the facts and figures D.N. Sprague gives in "Manitoba Land Question." Cf. note 11. As far as terminology is concerned, the Métis were often discriminatively referred to as simply "breeds." "There is very little talk about Riel... . There is no doubt at all the breeds swear by him and whatever HE says is law with them." Sergeant W.A. Brooks to Crozier, Public Archives of Canada (PAC), Justice, 519.

18. Adas, *Prophets,* 117.

19. Flanagan, *Louis "David" Riel,* 5.

20. Adas, *Prophets,* 107.

21. Ibid., 118.

22. Ibid., 120.

23. B.R. Wilson, *The Noble Savages. The Primitive Origins of Charisma and Its Contemporary Survival* (Berkeley, 1975), 7. See also the classic definition of Max Weber in S.N. Eisenstadt (ed.), *Max Weber, On Charisma and Institution Building* (Chicago, 1968), 48.

24. "His charismatic claim breaks down if his mission is not recognized by those to whom he feels he has been sent." Eisenstadt, *Weber, On Charisma,* 20.

25. Wilson, *Noble Savages*, 6.
26. Cf. da Cunha, *Rebellion*, 180; Adas, *Prophets*, 93 ff; K. Hatt, "Louis Riel as Charismatic Leader," in A.S. Lussier (ed.), *Riel and the Métis. Riel Mini-Conference Papers* (Winnipeg, 1979), 25, is right in saying that the millenarian elements in the Métis resistance were not indigenous to the Métis, but to see the Rebellion of 1885 as basically an agrarian protest is not sufficient as millenarian elements, especially as far as Riel is concerned, became increasingly important during the Rebellion and as in this case charisma and millenarianism are two sides of the same socio-religious coin.
27. P.V. Fourmond to Mère Gertrude de la Visitation, June 15, 1885, Archives Deschatelets.
28. Wilson, *Noble Savages*, 27.
29. Eisenstadt, *Weber, On Charisma*, 52.
30. The notion of duality in religion is well-established, going back to the earliest cults, and in Christianity was most notably established by Augustine who saw the world as eternally divided by the city of the world, ruled by Satan, and the city of God.
31. Cf. G.W. Leibniz, *Monadology and Other Philosophical Essays* (Indianapolis, 1965).
32. Prophéties de Riel, Archives de la Société Historique de Saint-Boniface (ASHSB), Papiers de Riel, 11 f.
33. PAC, Justice, 2312 If. et 2361-65. The individual paragraphs are numbered and subdivided into smaller "thought units."
34. Cf. PAC, Justice, 2312.
35. Ibid., 2315.
36. Ibid., 2314.
37. L. Pouilliot (ed.), "Correspondance Louis Riel-Mgr Bourget," *Revue d'Histoire de l'Amérique Française* 15 (1961): 437.
38. Archives de l'Archevêché de Saint-Boniface (AASB), Fonds Taché, T. 32703. T. Flanagan, *Louis "David" Riel*, 125, is uncertain about that claim. Since here we have it in Riel's own hand, the point can be regarded as confirmed. This document (AASB,T. 32703-10) is also important in another way: the October Diary ends, "Dieu m'a révélé qu'en s'unissant ainsi avec la grande république, l'Angleterre pourrait facilement rendre l'Irlande plus libre; et qu'en s'unissant avec la Grande Bretagne, les Etats-Unis se trouveraient en meilleur position qu'ils ne le sont maintenant de contribuer au bonheur de l'Irlande." T.32703 (after the sentence in quotation 38, which Riel very likely added later and separated from the main text by a line) begins: "Dieu m'a révélé qu'après avoir joui des apogées de sa gloire. L'Angleterre aura à combattre, à chaque génération, des coalitions formidables; qu'elle fera face à ses ennemis pendant quatre siecles et demi…" This document is not included in Flanagan's edition of the diaries. Yet it is evident from its continuity in content, style and handwriting that here we have the direct continuation of the October Diary, which breaks off for the simple reason that Riel's notebook was full. Flanagan's statement, "The diaries end here," in Flanagan (ed), *The Diaries of Louis Riel* (Edmonton, 1976), 1701, should therefore be modified.
39. Te Ua experienced that sort of pressure: after having been given credit for sinking a British ship and failing to produce similar miracles after that his power quickly passed over to his coadjutors and emissaries.
40. ASHSB, Papiers de Riel, 11.
41. Adas, *Prophets*, 108.
42. See description Riel gives in T. Flanagan, *Louis "David" Riel*, 49 f.
43. "Dieu m'a révélé qu'Adam et Eve ne sont sortis du purgatoire que le 8 decembre 1875." Public Archives of Manitoba (PAM), Riel collection MG 3 D1, 525, 74.
44. Cf. ibid., 70.

45. Antonio Conselheiro named himself "counselor." Saya San proclaimed to be the "Sektya Min" (universal emperor).
46. Riel was practically re-naming the whole world. The continents were given new names, and so were certain mountains, the days of the week, the zodiac etc., cf. PAM, Riel, 525, 64 ff, 72 ff.
47. Here the biblical tradition comes in: God re-naming Jacob into Israel, Saul into Paul, and Jesus naming Peter "Rock," thus accenting their new direction in life. Also note this passage from Revelation, the "most millenarian" of the books in the Bible: "Him that overcometh will I make a pillar on the temple of my God ... and I will write upon him my new name." Rev. 3: 12.
48. G. Guariglia, *Prophetismus und Heilserwartungsbewegungen als völkerkundliches und religionsgeschichtliches Problem* (Horn-Wien, 1959), 275.
49. W.E. Muhlmann, *Chiliasmus und Nativismus. Studien zur Psychologie, Soziologie und historischen Kasuistik der Umsturzbewegungen* (Berlin, 1964), 11 f.
50. Cf. Adas, *Prophets*, 92 ff.; T. Flanagan, *Louis "David" Riel*, 73ff.
51. According to Yonina Talman's definition (Y. Talman, "Millenarism" in: *Encyclopedia of the Social Sciences*, vol. 10), millenarian salvation is to be "imminent, total, ultimate, this-worldly, and collective." In this essay we follow the adaptation and slight variation of that definition by Norman Cohn in N. Cohn, *The Pursuit of the Millenium. Revolutionary Millenarians and Mystical Anarchists of the Middle Ages* (New York, 1970), 13.
52. "Londres et Liverpool descenderont au fond de l'eau. Et tout l'espace qui sépare ces deux grandes cités s'en ira dans la mer." Archives du Séminaire de Québec, carton Polygraphie 38, 8, p. 3.
53. da Cunha, *Rebellion*, 135, quotes these lines from one of the notebooks found after the rebellion in Canudos.
54. Cf. D. Morton, *The Queen v. Louis Riel* (Toronto, 1974), 311 ff.
55. Quoted from T. Flanagan, *Louis "David" Riel*, 95.
56. PAM, Riel Family Papers MG 3 D 2, File 27, 229. The text has the title "Partie de Le Messinahican" (Cree for "book"). We suggest that Riel was considering his writings as a whole as a sort of Métis bible that would, just like the original, be a compilation of prose, poetry, prayers, psalms and prophecies. Cf. this passage from a document in which he rewrites parts of Genesis: "Dieu m'a révélé qu'au temps de l'arche, il n'y avait que trois continents... Sa puissance excita les vapeurs interieurs du globe; et ... le sol du 'Nouveau Monde' sortit de la profondeur des eaux..." AASB, T. 52982/3. It is typical of Riel's thinking that the fourth continent (mirroring the four corners of the earth in Revelation), the New World, was created last, thereby achieving special importance.
57. Quoted from Adas, Prophets, 101.
58. "Mon Dieu me ressuscitera le troisième jour" was Riel's conviction towards the end of his life. Glenbow-Alberta Institute (GAI), Dr. Augustus Jukes Papers, A/J93B.
59. Archives du Séminaire St. Sulpice de Montréal, Riel, 3. Riel's model is Jes. 2, 1–5.
60. According to Coté's statement, in 1886 Riel began most of his speeches in Batoche with such a formula: "S'il commençait à parler il disait presque toujours: l'esprit de Dieu m'a dit ... m'a fait savoir. "PAM, Riel Family. 108.
61. N. Frye, *The Great Code. The Bible and Literature* (Toronto, 1982), 179.
62. For example Zechariah 4 ff.
63. Cf. Matt. 17, 1–13.
64. Cf. Exodus 19.
65. Cf. Dan. 12: 45; Zeph. 3: 11; Zech. 8: 3; Joel 2: 1.

66. Cf. Mic. 4: 1.
67. Cf. P. Dinzelbacher, *Vision und Visionsliteratur in Mittelalter* (Stuttgart, 1981), 109 f.
68. Cf. Frye, *Code*, 160.
69. Cf. P. Dinzelbacher, *Vision*, 56.
70. T. Flanagan, *Diaries*, 144, wonders where the quotation is from. It seems very obvious though that it is Riel himself, a semi-transfigured Riel who now speaks.
71. The mountain in medieval visions often represented paradise. Cf. P. Dinzelbacher, *Vision*, 106.
72. Saya San's and Birsa's followers believed that their leaders could protect them from bullets and that talismans and sympathetic magic would make their final victory certain.
73. Cf. Adas, *Prophets*, 183 ff.
74. "Les gens ... le regardent comme un saint ou persecuté et nous comme les esclaves de l'ancienne Rome incapables de comprendre les grandes et infaillibles lumières de Son Esprit..." P.V. Vegreville to Supérieur-Général, May 13, 1885, AASB. Sergeant Brooks put the state of affairs in the following simple words: "There is no doubt that every one is hard up and they thought they must do something to draw their attention." Letter to Crozier, August 10, 1884, PAC, Justice, 521.
75. Flanagan, *Reconsidered*, 75.
76. Flanagan, *Louis "David" Riel*, 182 f.
77. Cf. Adas, *Prophets*, 123.
78. T. Flanagan, *Reconsidered*, 15.
79. Ibid., 53.
80. Cf. G.F.G. Stanley, *Louis Riel* (Toronto, 1963), 65 f.
81. André to Dewdney, July 21, 1884, ASHSB.
82. Cf. 17.
83. T. Flanagan, *Reconsidered*, 77.
84. Ibid., 71.
85. Cf. Adas, *Prophets*, 144 ff.
86. Cf. Stanley, *Riel*, 310.
87. PAM, Riel, 636, 25. Riel wrote that the police could only kill their bodies and explained: "nos consciences alarmées nous ont fait entendre une voix qui nous dit: La justice ordonne de prendre les armes." PAC, Justice, 134.
88. For the biblical foundation of the idea of holy war see Joshua, especially chapter 10.
89. Cf. Adas, *Prophets*, 130 ff.
90. Cf. G.F.G. Stanley, "Gabriel Dumont's Account of the North West Rebellion, 1885," *Canadian Historical Review* 30 (1949): 251.
91. Ibid., 257.
92. Wilson, *Noble Savages*, 48, points out that this sort of duality in leadership was common among North American Indian Movements (Pontiac, the Delaware prophet, Tecumseh, etc.).
93. Cf. Flanagan, *Louis "David" Riel*, 150.
94. All in all the Conselheiro rebels killed nearly 5,000 men and at one time wiped out a whole army unit.
95. G. Woodcock, *Gabriel Dumont. The Métis Chief and His Lost World* (Edmonton, 1975), 184 f.
96. Cf. the Land Claims Series in *The Globe and Mail*, March 5–11, 1983.
97. Adas, *Prophets*, 25.
98. Ibid., 180.

99. Cf. Frye, *Code*, 180.
100. S. Fuchs, *Rebellious Prophets: A Study of Messianic Movements in Indian Religions* (London, 1965), 34. The last sentence of the quotation also indicates the tendency to use the prophetic leaders to promote ideas which they in fact did not support at all or which were unknown at the time.
101. M. Atwood, *Survival: A Thematic Guide to Canadian Literature* (Toronto, 1972), 167.
102. Cf. D. Swainson, "Rieliana and the Structure of Canadian History," *Journal of Popular Culture* 14 (1980): 286–97.

Endnotes to Chapter 12

1. George F.G. Stanley (gen. ed.), *The Collected Writings of Louis Riel*, 5 vols. (Edmonton: University of Alberta Press, 1985). Other "fugitive" pieces of Riel's writings were published by Thomas Flanagan and Glen Campbell, "Updating The Collected Writings of Louis Riel," in Theodore Binnema, Gerhard J. Ens and R.C. Macleod (eds.), *From Rupert's Land to Canada: Essays in Honour of John E. Foster* (Edmonton: University of Alberta Press, 2001).
2. This research produced *Living with Strangers: The Nineteenth-Century Sioux in the Canadian-American Borderlands* (Lincoln: University of Nebraska Press, 2006).
3. National Archives and Records Administration (hereafter NARA), Records of the Adjutant General's Office, RG94, Letters Received by the Office of the Adjutant General (Main Series), file 4163 AGO 1876, "Sioux War Papers," microcopy M666, roll 287, frames 350–352, Black to Assistant Adjutant General, Department of Dakota, Ft Assiniboine, March 19, 1880 and enclosures: frames 355–358, Riel to Colonel [Black], Ft Assiniboine, March 16, 1880; frames 360–363, Riel to Black, Ft Assiniboine, March 18, 1880; and frames 365–370, Riel to Black, Ft Assiniboine, March 18, 1880. A draft of Riel's letter of March 16 is located in his papers at the Provincial Archives of Manitoba (hereafter PAM), Riel Papers, MG3 D1, no. 383, microfilm reel M162, and was published in Riel's Collected Writings, 218–19.
4. A fine account of Riel's years in the United States is found in Martha Harroun Foster, *We Know Who We Are: Métis Identity in a Montana Community* (Norman: University of Oklahoma Press, 2006).
5. See the second letter from Riel to Black dated March 18, 1880 above. See also NARA, Records of the United States Army Continental Commands, RG393, Department of Dakota, Letters Received 1880, box 36, no. 1880-3300, Black to Assistant Adjutant General, Department of Dakota, Ft Assiniboine, September 6, 1880, in which Black also summarized these events.
6. For a concise biography of L'Heureux, see Hugh Dempsey, "Jean-Baptiste L'Heureux," in *The Canadian Encyclopedia* (Toronto: McClelland and Stewart, 1999), 1,329.
7. National Archives of Canada (hereafter NAC), John A. Macdonald Papers, MG26 A, vol. 110, pp. 44894–44899, reel C-1525, L'Heureux to Macdonald, Ft Macleod, 1 November 1886. And see NAC, Records Relating to Indian Affairs, RG10, vol. 3771, file 34527, microfilm reel C-10135, L'Heureux to Dewdney, Ft. Walsh, September 29, 1880.
8. John Maclean, *Canadian Savage Folk: The Native Tribes of Canada* (Toronto: William Briggs, 1896), 380–81. Maclean did not provide a source, but had met Crowfoot and perhaps heard the story directly from him. An even more terse reference to Crowfoot's involvement in this affair appeared in "Points for Mr. Amyot," *Toronto Mail*, March 2, 1886, p. 4, c. 2.
9. See John Peter Turner, *The North-West Mounted Police, 1873–1893*, vol. 1 (Ottawa: Edmond Cloutier, 1950), 408–13; Paul F. Sharp, *Whoop-Up Country: The Canadian-*

American West, 1865–1885 (Minneapolis: University of Minnesota Press, 1955), 266; George F.G. Stanley, *Louis Riel* (Toronto: McGraw-Hill Ryerson, 1963), 242; Grant MacEwan, *Sitting Bull: The Years in Canada* (Edmonton: Hurtig, 1973), 146; Christopher C. Joyner, "The Hegira of Sitting Bull to Canada: Diplomatic Realpolitik, 1876–1881," *Journal of the West* 13, no. 2 (April 1974): 11; Tom Flanagan, *Louis "David" Riel: Prophet of the New World* (Halifax: Goodread Biographies, 1983 [1979]), 101–09; Joseph Manzione, *"I Am Looking to the North for My Life": Sitting Bull, 1876–1881* (Salt Lake City: University of Utah Press, 1991), 117–18; Maggie Siggins, *Riel: A Life of Revolution* (Toronto: Harper Collins, 1994), 285–87, 293–96; Beth LaDow, *The Medicine Line: Life and Death on a North American Borderland* (New York: Routledge, 2001), 68; Foster, *We Know Who We Are*, 93–95.

10. NAC, RG10, vol. 3652, file 8589, pt. 1, microfilm reel C-10114, Macleod to Dennis, Ft. Walsh, December 1, 1879.

11. Ibid., Crozier to Dennis, Ft. Walsh, February 22, 1880. See also NAC, Records of the Royal Canadian Mounted Police, RG18, B3, vol. 2233, folios 52d–54d, microfilm reel T-6573, frames 512–514, Crozier to Commissioner, Ft. Walsh, March 24, 1880 and ibid., folios 61–64, microfilm reel T-6573, frames 520–523, Crozier to Lt Governor, Ft. Walsh, March 29, 1880.

12. NAC, RG10, vol. 3691, file 13893, microfilm reel C-10121, Walsh to the Commissioner, Wood Mountain, May 19, 1880 and ibid., Walsh to the Minister of the Interior, Brockville, September 11, 1880.

13. PAM, MG3 D1, no. 565, microfilm reel M163, Louis Riel, "About the Titons," [Montana], [Oct.–Dec. 1879], and see the second letter from Riel to Black dated March 18, 1880 above.

14. NARA, RG393, "Special Files" of Headquarters, Division of the Missouri, microcopy M1495, roll 5, frame 559, Terry to Sheridan, telegram, St Paul, January 19, 1881.

15. See NARA, RG94, file 4163 AGO 1876, roll 288, frames 400–406, Allison to CO Ft Buford, Ft Buford, October 12, 1880 and RG393, Camp Poplar River, Letters Sent 1880–1886, pp. 14–15, Read to Crozier, Poplar River, November 9, 1880.

16. PAM, MG3 D1, no. 565, microfilm reel M163, Louis Riel, "About the Titons," [Montana], [Oct.–Dec. 1879].

17. See C. Frank Turner, "Custer and the Canadian Connections," *The Beaver* 307, no. 1 (Summer 1976): 10, and NAC, RG18, B3, vol. 2185, microfilm reel T-6269, Irvine to the Minister of the Interior, Ft. Walsh, 8 December 1880.

18. NAC, Records of the Department of Justice, RG13, Series B2, Records Relating to Louis Riel and the North West Uprising, vol. 805, pp. 459–460, microfilm reel C-1228, Riel to Isbister, Dumont, Ouellette, and Dumas, June 5, 1884.

19. An American priest, the Benedictine abbot Martin Marty, visited Sitting Bull's camp shortly after the latter's arrival in Canada in May 1877. A missionary on the Standing Rock Reservation, Marty was intent on convincing the Hunkpapa leader to return to the United States. Marty's reception, and that of his two mixed-blood guides, William Halsey, the interpreter from the Poplar River Agency, and John Howard, one of Colonel Nelson A. Miles's scouts, was cool. Sitting Bull suspected Marty of being a spy. Marty visited the Sioux camps in Canada for a second time in October 1879.

20. Riel discussed neither Marty's visit nor Sitting Bull being "falsely advised" in Canada in the draft of this letter located in the Manitoba Archives. The section of text from "they have prepared" to "he would not have been so obstinate" was added to the copy sent to Black. This addition is the only major difference between the two versions.

21. The Sicanjus, or Brulés, are one of the seven constituent groups which together make up the Lakota people.

22. The outbreak of mange, or some other equine illness, was noted on at least two Lakota winter counts. See the Jaw and Jaw Variant count for 1879–80 published in James H. Howard, "Dakota Winter Counts as a Source of Plains History," Smithsonian Institution, Bureau of American Ethnology, *Bulletin* 173, Anthropological Papers no. 61 (1960), 399 and an unattributed Hunkpapa count for 1880 published in Stanley Vestal, *New Sources of Indian History, 1850–1891: The Ghost Dance—The Prairie Sioux, A Miscellany* (Norman: University of Oklahoma Press, 1934), 351.

23. Known today as Frenchman River, this Milk River tributary was called Frenchman's Creek or White Mud River in the 19th century.

24. The Mud House was an abandoned trading post, built at a ford on Frenchman River close to the boundary and a favourite camping place of the Sioux.

Endnotes to Chapter 13

The maps for this chapter were redrafted, based on earlier samples, by Anne Krahnen, University of Regina, Department of Geography/HS Karlsruhe–University of Applied Sciences, Germany.

1. See among others, Captain Ernest Chambers, *The Royal Grenadiers. A Regimental History of the 10th Infantry Regiment of the Active Militia in Canada* (Toronto: E. L. Ruddy, 1904); Charles Boulton, *Reminiscences of the North-West Rebellion* (Toronto: Grip Printing, 1886); W.B. Cameron, *The War Trial of Big Bear (or Blood Red the Sun)* (Toronto: Ryerson, 1926); Joseph Kinsey Howard, *Strange Empire: Louis Riel and the Métis People* (New York: William Morrow, 1952); Desmond Morton, *The Last War Drum: The North-West Campaign of 1885* (Toronto: Hakkert, 1972); Desmond Morton and R.H. Roy (eds.), *Telegrams of the North-West Campaign of 1885* (Toronto: Champlain Society, 1972); C.P. Mulvaney, *The History of the North-West Rebellion of 1885* (Toronto: A.H. Harvey, 1885); G.H. Needler, *Suppression of Rebellion in the North-West Territories* (Toronto: University of Toronto Press, 1948); C.P. Stacey, "The North-West Campaign, 1885," *Canadian Army Journal* 8 (1954): 10–20; G.F.G. Stanley, *The Birth of Western Canada: A History of the Riel Rebellion* (Toronto: University of Toronto Press, 1936); G.F.G. Stanley, *Louis Riel* (Toronto: McGraw Hill, 1963); P.B. Waite, *Arduous Destiny 1874–1896* (Toronto: McClelland and Stewart, 1971). Although not all of these sources are quoted directly, they were consulted in both the writing of the text and in the preparation of the maps.

2. Canada. *Sessional Papers*, 1886, no. 5, "Report upon the Suppression of the Rebellion in the North-West Territories, and in Matters in Connection Therewith in 1885."

3. One of the earliest analytical pieces was an article by Colonel C.F. Hamilton, "The Canadian Militia: The Northwest Rebellion, 1885," in *Canadian Defence Quarterly* (January 1930): 220.

4. Stanley, *The Birth of Western Canada*; Morton, *Last War Drum*; and Morton, *Telegrams*.

5. Journal de l'abbé G. Cloutier, Archives Archiepiscopales de Saint-Boniface, 1886.

6. Major General Sir Garnet J. Wolseley, *The Soldier's Pocketbook for Field Services* (London: Macmillan and Co., 1869).

7. Captain C. E. Callwell, *Small Wars: Their Principle and Practise* (n.p., 1896).

8. The manoeuvres and positions on these maps are based on both documentary sources and on period maps. The period vegetation as it appears on these maps was based on R. Coutt's study "Batoche National Historic Site Period Landscape," MRS 404 (Parks Canada, 1980).

9. Waite, *Arduous Destiny*, 149.

10. For an interesting argument on this topic, see Richard Drinnon, *Facing West: The Metaphysics of Indian-Hating and Empire Building* (Toronto: New American Library, 1980).

11. P.G. Laurie was editor of the *Saskatchewan Herald* from its founding in 1878 until 1902.

12. The etiology of these fears that many whites had of the Indians is explored in the introduction of Drinnon's book and also in Roy Harvey Pearce, *Savagism and Civilization: A Study of the Indian and American Mind* (Baltimore: The John Hopkins Press, 1953) and, most recently, Frederick Turner, *Beyond Geography: The Western Spirit Against the Wilderness* (New York: Viking Press, 1980).

13. Callwell, *Small Wars*, chapter 2.

14. Morton, *Telegrams*.

15. See, for example, Robert Jefferson, "Fifty Years on the Saskatchewan," *Canadian North-West Historical Society Publications* 1, no. 5 (1929), especially Part III. In Part III Jefferson indicates that the dangers anticipated by those beseiged were exaggerated by them.

16. John Jennings, "The North-West Mounted Police and Indian Policy, 1874–96" (PhD dissertation, University of Toronto, 1980).

17. Derby Papers, April 28, 1885, Public Archives of Canada, microfilm A-32.

18. Public Archives of Canada, Minto Papers, Lansdowne to Melgund, April 30, 1885, microfilm A-129.

19. Minto Papers, Lansdowne to Melgund, April 30, 1885.

20. Mulvaney, *North-West Rebellion*, 193–94.

21. Morton, *Telegrams*, April 26, 210.

22. Morton, *Telegrams*, 216.

23. Boulton, *Reminiscences*, 252–53.

24. "Melgund Diary" in *Saskatchewan History* 23, no. 3, (Autumn 1969), 97.

25. Needler, *Suppression*, 44.

26. Ibid.

27. Mulvaney, *North-West Rebellion*, 194.

28. See "Melgund Diary," 91, and Mulvaney, *North-West Rebellion*, 198.

29. In discussing this matter with Jack Summers, he suggested that Middleton may have had more than his personal dislike of Denison in mind when he decided to leave the cavalry at Humboldt. Summers thought that the willful tendency of the calvary to confront every situation by head-on attack might have made them difficult to handle for what Middleton anticipated facing at Batoche.

30. The tactic to use the artillery to demoralize the enemy can be directly traced to Wolseley's recommendation in *The Soldier's Pocketbook* that "Its [the artillery's] moral effect is powerful; it frightens far more than it kills," 225.

31. Boulton, *Reminiscences*, 262.

32. Mulvaney, *North-West Rebellion*, 252.

33. Needler, *Suppression*, 44.

34. Minto Papers, May 9, 1885.

35. Boulton, *Reminiscences*, 260.

36. Mulvaney, *North-West Rebellion*, 199.

37. Needler, *Suppression*, 45.

38. Boulton, *Reminiscences*, 491.

39. Mulvaney, *North-West Rebellion*, 225.

40. Journal de l'abbé G. Cloutier, 5084–85.

41. Ibid., 5111.

42. Boulton, *Reminiscences*, 491.

43. Sessional Papers, 1886, no. 5, 41.

44. Mulvaney, *North-West Rebellion*, 231.

45. Saskatchewan Archives Board, A.S. Morton Manuscript Collection—W.B. Cameron Papers, C550/1/281.

46. Mulvaney, *North-West Rebellion*, 200.
47. Ibid., 199.
48. Journal de l'abbé G. Cloutier, 5085–86.
49. Ibid.
50. Needler, *Suppression*, 46.
51. Ibid.
52. Boulton, *Reminiscences*, 262–63.
53. Mulvaney, *North-West Rebellion*, 200.
54. Needler, *Suppression*, 46.
55. Ibid.
56. Boulton, *Reminiscences*, 262–63.
57. Needler, *Suppression*, 46.
58. Mulvaney, *North-West Rebellion*, 205.
59. Ibid., 200.
60. Journal de l'abbé G. Cloutier, 5123–24.
61. Chambers, *The Royal Grenadiers*, 62.
62. Ibid., 64, and also "Melgund Diary," 104–05.
63. Needler, *Suppression*, 46.
64. Mulvaney, *North-West Rebellion*, 206.
65. "Melgund Diary," 105.
66. Mulvaney, *North-West Rebellion*, 206–07.
67. Ibid.
68. "Melgund Diary," 103.
69. Callwell, *Small Wars*, 240.
70. Ibid., 244.
71. Ibid., 264.
72. Ibid.
73. Ibid., 246.
74. Needler, *Suppression*, 48.
75. Mulvaney, *North-West Rebellion*, 207.
76. Ibid.
77. Needler, *Suppression*, 48.
78. Mulvaney, *North-West Rebellion*, 208.
79. Journal de l'abbé G. Cloutier, 5125.
80. Mulvaney, *North-West Rebellion*, 202–04.
81. Journal de l'abbé G. Cloutier, 5089.
82. Ibid., 5088.
83. Ibid., 5095.
84. Ibid., 5113.
85. Ibid., 5111.
86. Needler, *Suppression*, 48 and also Journal de l'abbé G. Cloutier, 5092.
87. Mulvaney, *North-West Rebellion*, 210.
88. Boulton, *Reminiscences*, 270–71.
89. Canada, *Sessional Papers*, 1886, no. 5, 30.
90. Needler, *Suppression*, 80.
91. Boulton, *Reminiscences*, 272.
92. Needler, *Suppression*, 50.
93. Ibid.
94. Ibid.
95. Boulton, *Reminiscences*, 273.

96. Canada, *Sessional Papers*, 1886, no. 5, 31.
97. Needler, *Suppression*, 50.
98. Ibid., 50–51.
99. Callwell, *Small Wars*, 204–05.
100. Boulton, *Reminiscences*, 275.
101. Mulvaney, *North-West Rebellion*, 257.
102. Canada, *Sessional Papers*, 1886, no. 5, 31.
103. Boulton, *Reminiscences*, 277–78.
104. Needler, *Suppression*, 51.
105. Canada, *Sessional Papers*, 1886, no. 5, 31.
106. Mulvaney, *North-West Rebellion*, 257.
107. Morton, *Telegrams*.
108. Mulvaney, *North-West Rebellion*, 257.
109. Boulton, *Reminiscences*, 259.
110. Canada, *Sessional Papers*, 1886, no. 5, 33.
111. Mulvaney, *North-West Rebellion*, 221.
112. Ibid., 216.
113. Needler, *Suppression*, 52.
114. Ibid., 52–53.
115. Mulvaney, *North-West Rebellion*, 292.
116. Ibid., 292–93.
117. Journal de l'abbé G. Cloutier, 5120.
118. Ibid., 5111.
119. Ibid., 5114.
120. Ibid., 5106–109.
121. Ibid., 5097.
122. Mulvaney, *North-West Rebellion*, 275.
123. Needier, *Suppression*, 53.
124. "Melgund Diary," 314.

Endnotes to Chapter 14

1. Desmond Morton, "Reconfiguring Riel Does Not Change History," Ottawa *Citizen*, January 22, 1998.
2. Ibid.
3. W.L. Morton, "Sayer," *Dictionary of Canadian Biography* 7 (hereafter DCB): 776–77.
4. Kathryn M. Bindon, "Adam Thom," *DCB* 11: 874–76.
5. Abbé G. Dugan, *Histoire Véridique des Faits Qui Ont Préparé le Mouvement des Métis à la Rivière Rouge en 1869* (n.p.), 29; Alexander Begg, *The Creation of Manitoba* (Toronto: Hunter, 1871), 21.
6. Isaac Cowie, *The Company of Adventurers* (Toronto: W. Briggs, 1913), 381.
7. G.F.G. Stanley, *The Collected Writings of Louis Riel* 1 ((Edmonton: University of Alberta Press, 1985): 33–34, Riel to Schultz, Novmber 27, 1869.
8. W.L. Morton (ed.), *Alexander Begg's Red River Journal* (New York: Greenwood Press, 1969), 205-17, entries for December 4–December 7, 1869.
9. Morton, *Begg's Journal*, 256, entry for January 9, 1870.
10. Article by "R. McC," St. Paul *Daily Pioneer*, April 2, 1870.
11. Morton, *Begg's Journal*, 314, entry for February 17, 1870.
12. Colonel G.T. Denison, *The Struggle for Imperial Unity* (New York: Macmillan, 1909), 22–32.

13. W.L. Morton (ed.), *Manitoba: Birth of a Province* (Altona, MB: D.W. Friesen, 1965), 50, James W. Taylor to Hamilton Fish, April 19, 1870.
14. National Archives of Canada (NA), RG2, 1, Vol. 17, PC 708; Begg, *Creation of Manitoba*, 51–52.
15. NA, Macdonald Papers, Vol. 101, Minute of Council, February 11, 1870.
16. See, for example, Morton, *Begg's Journal*, 209–10, 515–19.
17. Canada, Sessional Papers, 1870 (12), Howe to Thibault, December 4, 1869.
18. Beckles Willson, *The Life of Lord Strathcona* (n.p.), 217; Provincial Archives of Manitoba, letter of Pierre Léveillée, *New Nation*, May 27, 1870.
19. Morton, *Manitoba: Birth of a Province*, Ritchot's Diary, April 27, 1870, p. 138.
20. Ibid., 97 (Northcote's Diary).
21. Manitoba Act, Section 30; see also Begg, *Creation of Manitoba*, 405.
22. Morton, *Manitoba: Birth of a Province*, 140 (Ritchot's Diary).
23. Supplement to the *Manitoban*, February 25, 1871.
24. *Manitoban*, March 11, 1871, from the *Telegraph* report of the February 20, 1871, debate in the House of Commons; see also Ottawa *Free Press*, February 20, 1871, Ottawa *Citizen*, February 21, 1871, *Globe*, February 21, 1871.
25. *Globe*, May 16, 1870; Colonel G.T. Denison, *Soldiering in Canada* (Toronto: G.N. Morag and Company, 1900), 179; Denison, *Struggle for Imperial Unity*, 43.
26. *Globe*, August 4, 1870. The constitution is in the Metropolitan Toronto Library, Denison Papers.
27. Canada. House of Commons, *Journals*, 1874, VIII, Appendix No. 6, "Report of the Select Committee," 71, 81.
28. It should be noted here that the diary for May 28 as printed in Morton, *Manitoba: Birth of a Province*, is defective, lacking six sentences. Compare with the version published in *Revue d'histoire de l'Amérique française* 17, no. 4 (March 1964): 560. The text of Cartier's letter is in "Report, of the Select Committee," 74, Cartier to Ritchot, May 23, 1870.
29. Morton, *Begg's Journal*, 375–77, entries for May 24, 26, 27, 30, 31, 1870.
30. Canada. Senate, *Debates*, May 23, 1870, p. 236.
31. Michael Bamholder (trans.), *Gabriel Dumont Speaks* (Vancouver: Talonbooks, 1993), 31; Morton, *Begg's Journal*, 374–75, entry for May 23, 1870.
32. Morton, *Begg's Journal*, 382; George Woodcock, *Gabriel Dumont* (Don Mills, ON: Fitzhenry & Whiteside, 1978), 81.
33. Morton, *Begg's Journal*, 385.
34. See "L'Amnistie" in *Le Métis*, February 28, 1874, reproduced from *Le Nouveau Monde*, February 4, 1874.
35. Morton, *Manitoba: Birth of a Province*, 139, Ritchot's Diary; ibid., 57, Taylor to Fish, May 2, 1870.
36. "Report of the Select Committee," 168–69, deposition of George Futvoye. The memorandum itself is on pages 171–78.
37. Ibid., 195–97.
38. Ibid., 169–70.
39. The term is Wolseley's: "Our mission is one of peace, and the sole object of the Expedition is to secure Her Majesty's Sovereign authority," Morton, *Begg's Journal*, 392. References to those taken prisoner are in several sources: *La Minerve*, September 9 and 10, 1870; NA, M. Bell Irvine, "Journal of the Red River Expedition," MG29, E5; NA, Lieutenant H.S.H. Riddell, *The Red River Expedition of 1870* (n.p.), 139–40.
40. Begg, *Creation of Manitoba*, 21; Alexander Begg, *Dot It Down: A Story of Life in the North-West* (Toronto: Hunter Rose, 1871), 282, 327.

41. The violence began when Schultz and his men put the *New Nation* press out of action on September 6, 1870, and continued all through the winter of 1870 and into the spring of 1871. References to the violence are numerous: C.S.P. 1871 (No. 20), Archibald to Howe, September 17, 1870; United States National Archives and Records Service (USNARS) microfilm T24 Roll 1, Taylor Papers, Taylor to Davis, January 6, 1871; *Le Nouveau Monde*, February 3, 1871; Cowie, *Company of Adventurers*, 429–30.

42. "Report of the Select Committee," 150–51, Archibald's deposition; ibid., 151–52, Archibald to Howe, January 20, 1872.

43. Preamble to the B.N.A Act of 1871.

44. British Parliamentary Debates, 3rd Series, Vol. 206, p. 1171.

45. "Report of the Select Committee," Archibald's deposition; ibid., 139–42, "Memorandum connected with Fenian Invasion of Manitoba in October, 1871."

46. Ibid., 140.

47. Ibid., 139.

48. A.H. de Trémaudan, "Louis Riel and the Fenian Raid of 1871," in *Canadian Historical Review* 4 (1923): 133–36; "Report of the Select Committee," 142, Archibald's deposition; ibid., 180, Girard's deposition.

49. USNARS, Taylor Papers, T24, Roll 1, clippings from *The Manitoba Liberal*, October 11, 1871.

50. Dominion Lands Act, Section 105, 35 Victoria Cap. XXIII.

51. Manitoba Act, section 30.

52. "Report of the Select Committee," 41–42, Taché's deposition.

Index